Not Saved

Peter Sloterdijk

Not Saved

Essays after Heidegger

Translated by Ian Alexander Moore
and Christopher Turner

polity

First published in German as *Nicht gerettet. Versuche nach Heidegger* © Suhrkamp Verlag, Frankfurt am Main, 2001

This English edition © Polity Press, 2017

Polity Press
65 Bridge Street
Cambridge CB2 1UR, UK

Polity Press
350 Main Street
Malden, MA 02148, USA

ISBN-13: 978-0-7456-9698-0
ISBN-13: 978-0-7456-9699-7 (pb)

A catalogue record for this book is available from the British Library.

Library of Congress Cataloging-in-Publication Data

Names: Sloterdijk, Peter, 1947- author.
Title: Not saved : essays after Heidegger / Peter Sloterdijk.
Description: Malden, MA : Polity, 2016. | Translation of: Nicht gerettet. |
    Includes bibliographical references.
Identifiers: LCCN 2016014002 (print) | LCCN 2016029542 (ebook) | ISBN
    9780745696980 (hardback) | ISBN 9780745696997 (pbk.) | ISBN 9780745697017
    (Mobi) | ISBN 9780745697024 (Epub)
Subjects: LCSH: Philosophy, German--20th century. | Philosophy, German--21st
    century. | Heidegger, Martin, 1889-1976--Influence.
Classification: LCC B3332.S252 E5 2016 (print) | LCC B3332.S252 (ebook) | DDC
    193--dc23
LC record available at https://lccn.loc.gov/2016014002

Typeset in 10.5 on 12 pt Times NR MT by
Servis Filmsetting Ltd, Stockport, Cheshire
Printed and bound in Great Britain by CPI Group (UK) Ltd, Croydon

For further information on Polity, visit our website:
politybooks.com

Contents

Contents

Translators' Introduction

The present text represents the first complete English translation of Peter Sloterdijk's 2001 *Nicht gerettet: Versuche nach Heidegger*. Alternate translations of two of Sloterdijk's essays or attempts (*Versuche*), namely, "Rules for the Human Park: A Response to Heidegger's 'Letter on 'Humanism''" and "'An Essential Tendency toward Nearness Lies In Dasein': Marginalia to Heidegger's Doctrine of Existential Place," can be found, respectively, under Peter Sloterdijk, "*Rules for the Human Zoo*: A Response to the *Letter on Humanism*," trans. Mary Varney Rorty, *Environment and Planning D: Society and Space* 27 (2009): 12–28, and Peter Sloterdijk, "'In Dasein There Lies an Essential Tendency towards Closeness': Heidegger's Doctrine of Existential Place," in Sloterdijk, *Bubbles: Spheres*, vol. 1: *Microspherology*, trans. Wieland Hoban (Los Angeles: Semiotext(e), 2011), 333–342, 648–649. Other than using language consistent with other chapters in the volume, our new translation of "'In Dasein There Lies an Essential Tendency towards Closeness'" does not substantially improve upon Hoban's able rendering in *Spheres*. Our new translation of "Rules for the Human Park," however, rectifies numerous errors and omissions in the previous English version. We have opted in favor of "Rules for the Human *Park*," rather than "*Zoo*," because Sloterdijk means more by the German *Park* than simply the enclosure of animals. He speaks of city parks, national parks, state parks, political theme parks, and eco-parks. He also speaks, on occasion, of zoos and zoo-logical parks. We have therefore preserved the distinction between zoo and park throughout the volume.[1]

Brief selections from "Luhmann, Devil's Advocate: Of Original Sin, the Egotism of Systems, and the New Ironies" and "The

Domestication of Being: The Clarification of the Clearing" are also available, respectively, in alternate translation under Peter Sloterdijk, "The Devil's Advocate, between the Ethical and the Systemic," in *The Future of Values: 21st-Century Talks*, ed. Jérôme Bindé, trans. John Corbett (New York/Berghahn/Paris: UNESCO, 2004), 34–40, and Peter Sloterdijk, "Anthropo-Technology," ed. Nathan Gardels, *New Perspectives Quarterly* 17, no. 3 (Summer 2000): 17–20; the latter was republished in *New Perspectives Quarterly* 21, no. 4 (November 2004): 40–44, and *New Perspectives Quarterly* 31, no. 1 (January 2014): 12–19. "The Time of the Crime of the Monstrous: On the Philosophical Justification of the Artificial" was originally translated by Wieland Hoban and first appeared in *Sloterdijk Now*, ed. Stuart Elden (Cambridge: Polity, 2012), 164–181, 201–202. We have modified Hoban's translation slightly for inclusion in this volume.

The most challenging aspect of translating Sloterdijk's book has been the Heideggerian terminology he frequently employs and creatively appropriates. *Sein* has been rendered as Being (with a capital 'B'), in order to distinguish it from the present participle and from the latter's nominalized form, *das Seiende* or *ein Seiendes*, which appear respectively as 'beings' or 'a being' (with a lowercase 'b'). We have translated the German *Seyn*, an archaic spelling of *Sein*, with the archaic English 'beyng.' When appropriate, the term *Wesen* also appears as 'being,' such as in the terms *Menschenwesen* ('human being') and *Lebewesen* ('living being'). *Dasein*, Heidegger's term for the human being, or that being whose Being is an issue for it, has been left untranslated and unitalicized, except where Sloterdijk employs it in its more common sense of 'existence.'

The distinction Heidegger makes between *existenzial* (to refer to ontological structures of Dasein and the theoretical understanding of them) and *existenziell* (to refer to particular ways in which Dasein carries out its existence) has also been preserved by the terms 'existential' and 'existentiell.' *Ereignis* has been translated as 'event,' except where Sloterdijk uses it in a more Heideggerian vein, in which case it has been rendered as 'appropriative event' to highlight the valence of bringing something into its own (*eigen*) or what is proper to it. Heidegger's *Lichtung* (and its cognates) appears throughout as

---

[1] Cf. the discussion in Peter Sloterdijk, with Hans-Jürgen Heinrichs, *Neither Sun nor Death*, trans. Steve Corcoran (Los Angeles: Semiotext(e), 2011), 59. Cf. also the French translation, which uses *parc* and not *zoo*: "Règles pour le parc humaine," in *La domestication de l'être: Pour un éclaircissement de la clairière*, trans. Olivier Mannoni (Paris: Éditions Milles et une nuits, 2000).

'clearing' (and its cognates). *Gelassenheit* appears as 'releasement' or, in its adjectival form, as 'serenely released.'

We have translated *ungeheuer* as either 'monstrous' or 'immense,' or used a hendiadys when Sloterdijk seems to intend both senses. The adjective *monströs* always appears as 'monstrous.' Depending on context, we have rendered the term *technisch* sometimes as 'technical,' and sometimes (as with *technologisch*) as 'technological.' *Technik*, for its part, appears as 'technology,' 'technique,' or 'technics,' as in the term 'anthropotechnics.' The reader should bear in mind that it has a much broader sense than the modern apparatuses developed from scientific knowledge. 'Science,' for its part, translates the German *Wissenschaft*, which refers to any domain of systematic research, including the humanities.

Unless otherwise indicated, bracketed text in the body and endnotes of the translation is our own.

We have occasionally used different translations of the same text, such as with Heidegger's *Being and Time*, depending on which version we thought best captured the particular context under discussion.

Finally, we would like to express our gratitude to Henry Dicks, who kindly read through the manuscript and offered countless suggestions for improvement.

Preface

Essays after Heidegger—the subtitle of this collection of lectures and essays—simply means that the author, through no fault of his own, finds himself in a time after the thinker, such that he can take up the man and the work historically and compare them with other eminent figures of the twentieth century's intellectual history, of which the essays reprinted here on Luhmann and the older Critical Theory furnish examples. Somewhat less trivially, the subtitle wishes to indicate that not everything which concerns Heidegger's work belongs to the past; rather, it is always still possible, advisable, fruitful, and perhaps scandalous to pursue Heidegger's indications and follow up on some of his suggestions. This circumstance can be most readily observed in the "Human Park" speech and even more so in "The Domestication of Being," which completes it. Lastly, the formulation *Essays after Heidegger* means that a theoretical terrain is opened up after Heidegger that one only encounters when—thinking with Heidegger against Heidegger, to cite a turn of phrase of an erstwhile reader of Heidegger, as well known as it is inconsequential—one has freed oneself from the master's hypnosis, so as to arrive, not least thanks to his strengths, at a position that, according to everything that we know of him, would have displeased him. This stance, both near and distant, is most readily expressed in the introductory piece "The Plunge and the Turn," which essays an intimate portrait of the thinker and at the same time, as from a great distance, sketches him into a tableau of Old European intellectual culture. We need not comment on the title itself. The god who could still save us is taking his time.

If anything estimable has resulted from the fact that Heidegger is becoming infamous on account of books that have exposed and incriminated him, such as Victor Farías's *Heidegger and Nazism*, then perhaps it is because the question concerning the possibilities of drawing on a blameworthy thinker was thereby radicalized. More than is customary, they compel later authors to give an account of the conditions of didactic relations between the philosophical generations of the twentieth century. By their one-sidedness they testify to the fact that in the ongoing "Age of Suspicion" the relations of power between distrust and trust are still out of balance. Whoever wants to draw on Heidegger today must pass through a flaming wall of suspicions without being certain in advance that the discoveries on the other side of the fire are worth the cost.

The present speeches and essays are on the lookout for the place where the bond of common learning can perhaps be rejoined, beyond accusation and apology. This would be nowhere more helpful than in the 'social philosophy' of the present moment, which only tentatively emerges from the shadows of extremism. One has still not paid sufficient attention to the extent to which the terror of grand politics has stamped the intellectual physiognomy of the past century. We are still waiting for a suitable presentation of its reflection in the terror-mimetic constructs of grand and critical theory. In a few passages in the present book, I allude to what such a presentation would have to achieve;[1] beyond this, I attempt to conceptualize which efforts are needed to free thought from its fixations on standards from the "age of extremes." Heidegger's accomplishment—and because of it the indispensability of his voice in the conversation of the present age with the future—in my opinion consists in the fact that, under the title of the question of Being, he worked for his entire life on a logic of commitment that, even before the division of ontology and ethics, remained on the trail of the antagonism between liberating and compulsory tendencies in the Dasein of those who die and those who are born. Heidegger's investigations thus belong to the ascendance of a problem that is the most serious thing to be thought today, that is, they belong to the development of a theory of participatory relations that is combined with a critique of emergency reasoning [*Ernstfall-Vernunft*].[2]

The essays in this volume are collected renunciations of exhaustive detail. They present findings from the 1990s, with the exception of the text "What Is Solidarity with Metaphysics at the Moment of Its Fall?" whose oldest parts can be traced back to a lecture held in Rotterdam in 1989 on the occasion of the twentieth anniversary of Adorno's death. They originated between 1993 ("*Alētheia* or the Fuse of Truth") and 2000 ("The Domestication of Being"), and were as a rule contributions to conferences and symposia. Hence all of them are elliptical, if one defines the ellipsis as the art form of precipitousness. Only the third text, for substantive reasons, comes a little closer to the conventional ideal of exhaustive detail. More recent additions have been included in footnotes and as additions to the texts. In addition to the speech "Rules for the Human Park," which achieved a distorted renown by being taken out of context, a few other texts from this collection have been published here and there, among other places in a French anthology that contained older versions of the speeches "The Plunge and the Turn," "Wounded by Machines," "The Time of the Crime of the Monstrous," and the Cioran essay.[3] I would like to mention that the two introductory pieces, the one on Heidegger's "Thinking in Motion" (1996) and the other on Luhmann ("Devil's Advocate," 1999), had their baptismal debut at the Freiburg City Theater. They trace back to invitations from the Institut für soziale Gegenwartsfragen [The Institute for Contemporary Social Questions], which during the second half of the 1990s conducted a series of matinees in collaboration with the Städtische Bühnen Freiburg [Urban Stages of Freiburg] and what was then Südwestfunk [Southwest Radio] under the title "Denker auf der Bühne" [Thinkers on the Stage]. For these impetuses and for including me in such stimulating contexts I am grateful to the organizers in Freiburg, especially Christian Matthiessen. As a token of this I have retained certain rhetorical figures in both texts, including the address "ladies and gentlemen."

Only in reading the texts can one learn about their internal coherence. I would like to note that I find satisfaction in being able to present together what belongs together. The speech "Rules for the Human Park," which for extrinsic reasons I have reprinted nearly unchanged (with minor improvements of a stylistic nature), benefits from this in particular. It now appears, as planned, alongside its neighboring essays "*Alētheia* or the Fuse of Truth" and above all "Wounded by Machines." The note "The Time of the Crime of the Monstrous" also belongs in their vicinity. The micro-historical critique of humanism in the human park speech is now to be considered together with the macro-historical definition of humanity in the "Wounded" essay. The remarks on 'anthropotechnics' are recontextualized with references to Western culture's calendar of truth and the continuum of the phantasms of a technological imitation of nature. The anthropological and techno-philosophical implications of the human park speech are developed more broadly in the central essay of this volume, "The Domestication of Being: The Clarification of the Clearing," which was initially written for an international colloquium on questions of biotechnology that took place at the Centre Georges Pompidou in Paris in March 2000.[4] The concluding section of this essay, "The Operable Human Being," was delivered as a lecture and discussed separately in various forums, such as at Harvard University's Center for European Studies in Cambridge, at a conference on questions of the biotechnological formation of the human being at UCLA and the Goethe Institute in Los Angeles in May 2000, at the Philosophical Seminar of the Universidad Autonoma in Madrid in October 2000, and at a forum organized by the newspaper *Le Monde* concerning technophobic and technophilic tendencies of modern society in Le Mans in November of the same year, as well as a meeting of the working group *Wissenschaft und Verantwortung* [Science and Responsibility], held by the Carl Friedrich von Weizsäcker-Gesellschaft in Munich. On the whole, "The Domestication of Being" sums up a series of lectures and seminars from past years that were devoted to historical anthropology, paleo-psychology, media theory, and the philosophy of cybernetics.

In the third section of the lecture "On Critical and Exaggerated Theory" there is a reference to the hyperbolic dynamic of philosophical texts, which can perhaps be read *pro domo*. If, following the rhetorical tradition, one understands hyperbole as a "proper exaggeration of the truth,"[5] what then is philosophy other than the search for the proportion between that which is exaggerated and that which is not exaggerated that would be convincing for the present day?

1

THE PLUNGE AND THE TURN

Speech on Heidegger's Thinking in Motion

1. Prelude in the Theater

Ladies and gentlemen, a few years ago, while walking around the campus of Bard College, one of the academic institutions in the state of New York favored by students from the upper-middle classes, which is situated a hundred miles north of New York City on the eastern bank of the Hudson River, I discovered—almost accidentally—the resting place of Hannah Arendt, that admirable and provocative philosopher, whose early love for Martin Heidegger is today not only a secret that has been disclosed, but was also able to be portrayed as a chapter of recent intellectual history—lately in Rüdiger Safranski's rightly much-praised biography of Heidegger. Hannah Arendt's grave is distinguished by its unusual simplicity— if one may speak in such contradictory terms: a stone slab on the flat earth with her name and the dates of her birth and death. One step to the side is the gravestone of her husband, the philosopher Heinrich Blücher, just as simple, taken back to the trinity: name, dates, stone. What touched me about Hannah Arendt's gravesite was the extraordinariness of its location. I do not mean the inconspicuousness of the place, nor the dignified lack of fuss that these two stones on the earth evinced. What astonished me was the fact that I found myself obviously at a campus cemetery at which the earlier presidents of the college and a number of professors, who no doubt had felt especially connected to the college, were laid to rest. A small island of the dead in the midst of the college grounds, a *locus amoenus*, planted with conifers and evergreen bushes, a meditative enclave, hardly a hundred steps from the library.

Apart from that, the small cemetery was an almost unmarked

space, without surrounding walls, as if, for the inhabitants of this region, there were no reason to distinguish the living and the dead in such a way as to necessitate a wall that would divide them. Thus a cemetery of professors—I must admit that a certain amazement overcame me at this sight, an amazement that in retrospect I would like to call Old European and that was perhaps equally both disconcerting and exhilarating. At the time I was in the process of beginning to contemplate whether I should take up the expected call for a professorship in Germany. Here in America it was now discreetly shown to me how far one can go as a professor. Up to that point it had not been clear that a session of the faculty senate could last an eternity—assuming that one had been a member of American academia during one's life. What European professor would today be laid to rest at a university's own cemetery? What university in the Old World possesses so much *esprit de corps* and community spirit that it would be embodied as a virtual community of dead and living teachers, as was so clearly revealed by the small campus cemetery on the Hudson River? In today's Europe, who would be so identified with his teaching position that he would take up the call beyond the end and wish to be interred among only colleagues and schoolmasters?

In light of Hannah Arendt's grave, a few aspects of American spatial planning have become somewhat more understandable to me. I have learned to observe at least three boundaries more attentively than before, boundaries that in the United States were sometimes drawn differently than in the Old World: the boundary between the city and the countryside; the boundary between the university and the city; finally, the boundary between the cemetery and the world of the living. It became clear to me that the philosopher, in allowing herself to be laid to rest next to her husband, a charismatic teacher who had belonged to the college for decades, had not chosen to be buried in a village, as did her former teacher and lover in Marburg, Martin Heidegger, when he decided on the cemetery in Messkirch as his last resting place. According to statistical criteria, there is no more remote province than Annandale-on-Hudson; one can scarcely imagine a place where the village, the first thesis, as it were, of humanity vis-à-vis nature, contrasts with the countryside so tentatively and almost helplessly as it does here. And yet the campus cemetery is not a village cemetery. The campus is the university abstracted from the urban body; the university, for its part, embodies in an ideal form the place where cities are most of all urban.

Campus, academy, university, college: these are the names of institutions or spaces that testify to the irruption of the world that has been extended by theory into cities. They indicate where plain human settlements were used for great purposes. Where universities and academies are established, provincial towns change into cosmopolitan cities. The United States of America, the hyperbolic European colony, has even managed to disconnect the logical heart of the city from the urban body and to isolate it under the name 'campus,' field of studies—not seldom like a backdrop in a countryside in which professors emerge as the first human beings.

I would thus like to say that Hannah Arendt's grave, in a manner different from that of Martin Heidegger's, in spatio-logical terms, lies in the midst of the cosmopolitan city, in the center of that academic space in which Western cities could become cosmopolitan cities and native sons could become world citizens, so long as they did not misuse universities as extensions of provincial life. Viewed in this light, the emigrant Hannah Arendt never left European soil behind; when in the 1930s she immigrated first to France and then to the United States, she simply relocated from a tainted province to a more open zone—from a Europe in the hands of the Nazis to a metropolis that was manifestly called New York but whose latent name could be nothing other than Athens. Athens was the real country to which Hannah Arendt immigrated, on the one hand because the first academic city symbolizes the reformatting of thought in the transition from the village to the city, on the other hand because the Greek right to hospitality kept the necessary resources available for Jewish and other exiles. Thus it comes about that the philosopher lies interred in one of the noblest cemeteries on earth, on the fringes of the campus that signifies the world, in a corner that we may not even call a village, in a hamlet that, because it is a part of Athens, nevertheless bears in itself the *universitas.*

Ladies and gentlemen, I would not have permitted myself to reminisce on Hannah Arendt's transatlantic last resting place in this typifying manner if I had not intended to characterize Martin Heidegger's place in the history of ideas and problems in the century that is now coming to a close by way of contrast to this choice of place. I would not have ventured this suggestion were I not of the opinion that Heidegger's position becomes immediately and vividly discernable when we think of the imaginary line that leads from the grave on the American campus to the grave at the Messkirch cemetery. I do not hesitate to claim that Heidegger's burial arrangements also testify to something that is philosophically significant. If the master from Germany did not choose any other site for his last resting place than the rural town's church cemetery, whose native he wished to remain—under a gravestone adorned not by a cross, but rather by a small star—then there is a piece of information here that is ignored only by one who preemptively refuses to believe the lessons that lie in that decision. One must explicitly note, as though it were a proposition, that Professor Heidegger's grave is not found on a campus but rather in a rural cemetery, not in a university town but rather tucked away in a little town with a pious name, not in the vicinity of lecture halls and libraries where the philosopher had been at work but rather not far from the houses and fields of his childhood, as though the tenured professor at the illustrious Albert-Ludwigs-Universität refused moving to the urban world even *in extremis*.

In what follows, I sketch a philosophical physiognomy of Heidegger, the thinker of motion, which takes its point of departure from this discovery: the thinker, whom many, without doubt rightly, consider to be one of the movers of philosophy at the end of this twentieth century, is someone who in terms of his personal dynamic refuses to move, who can only be at home in the vicinity of his original landscapes, and who even as a professor never actually relocated to the city where he held his chair.

It is not hard to see the contradiction to which this diagnosis would like to call attention. For if Western philosophy, as was sometimes claimed, actually emerged from the urban spirit, if it was an eruption of the city into a world-function and an irruption of great world-dimensions into the local soul, then what are we to make of the theoretical temperament of a man who never concealed his aversion for the city and his stubborn attachment to the spirits of the rural world? From where does this odd professor speak when from his chair in Freiburg he claims to inquire beyond the history and fate of Western metaphysics? What province does Heidegger mean when he takes it to be a relevant philosophical act that he of all people remains there instead of following the call to the big city? Is there a provincial truth of which the cosmopolitan city knows nothing? Is there a truth of the field path and the cabin that would be able to undermine the university, together with its refined language and globally influential discourses?

I will not attempt to answer these questions here. Only this seems certain to me: Heidegger was not a thinker on the stage, at least not if one proceeds from the everyday understanding of this formulation.[1] He is not a thinker on the stage in a twofold sense: on the one hand, because the theater and the stage are at home in the religion of the city and in urban culture, thus in the political formation that, although a professor, Heidegger obstinately opposed like a visitor from the country—at best like an ambassador from a region without cities or from a community of shared problems that is grounded not in space but rather in time; on the other hand, because every stage, metaphorical and real, implies a central position, an exposure to the front-and-center of visibility. However, that is a position that Heidegger, even at the height of his fame, could never have seriously sought, according to his whole mental disposition, because his place, inside and outwardly, remained that of someone on the margins and a collaborator. He does not think on the stage but rather in the background, at best on the side stage, or in a Catholic context, not before the high altar but rather in the sacristy. Because of influences that are older than his thought, he came to the conviction that what is visible and prominent, what is right in the middle, lives from the inconspicuous preparation of assistants backstage and in the wings. He too is such an assistant, and that is what he wants to be: a pioneer, a second, someone who blends into a greater event—in no case, or at least only momentarily and awkwardly, is he the hero standing center stage. Heidegger is never actually a protagonist who exposes himself in exemplary battles to the heroic risk of being seen on all sides. Moments of apparent deep emotion cannot change anything in this regard. A hidden power was at work in him, which was neither exhibited nor explained, let alone admitted or apologized for. When distressed or embarrassed, he tended to fall silent, and no god gave him the words to say how he suffered.

It seems important to me, in everything having to do with Heidegger's spiritual physiognomy, to take into consideration his father's occupation as a sexton. If, in his biographical studies, Hugo Ott has plausibly argued that much in Heidegger's thought is only understandable as a metastasis of southwestern German Old Catholicism circa 1900, then we should add that it was not so much a priestly Catholicism, thus a Catholicism of the high altar and the nave, that formed Heidegger's disposition; it was rather a Catholicism of the side aisle, a Catholicism of the sexton and altar boy, a religiosity of the quiet assistant on the periphery, desperate for acceptance.

One could only in a very precarious sense characterize Heidegger as a thinker on the stage, by imputing to him the dream of an impending state of exception that would convey him to his destiny. One might perhaps do that if one lends credence to the suspicion that the sexton's son was incapable of doing anything other than day-dreaming that, one day—through a wondrous, deeply grounded reversal—his diligent father would be transformed into an acting priest, so that, on a fateful day not far off, all power would issue from the sacristy. One would have to further assume that the fantasy must have arisen in the son that he himself had been called to take up the heritage of an official sexton. Only in this sense can Heidegger's hazy political philosophy—above all his gauche agitation in the eleventh month of his rectorship from 1933 to 1934 and his ministrations for the fateful

chancellor in far-off Berlin—be interpreted as thinking in the form
of a High Mass on a phantasmal stage. Here, as sexton in charge, he
would have thus become a liturgical revolutionary, who administers
to an unredeemed people an astoundingly ancient sacrament—
non-Catholic hosts and Presocratic wine. In this heterodox rite,
that which was previously inconspicuous would be brought forward
triumphantly, what was an accessory would become the main thing,
the courtyard would be transformed into the central structure, the
sacristy would become the lecture hall, and the lecture hall would
become the logical Chancellery of the Reich. To make such a dream
seem plausible only one additional assumption is necessary, which,
so I believe, has quite a bit going for it. This can be obtained by
interpreting the Catholic Mass in terms of theater studies. In these
terms, the Mass and High Mass are mystery plays of a Catholic
kind in typological proximity to, and with a historical line of succession from, the Athenian Dionysia. If this is granted, then the
Mass would appear to be tragedy returned to the rite once again, the
de-dramatized goat-song, static and without the aspect of expression, as unsuitable for upswell as it is for subsiding. In light of this
analogy it becomes conceivable why the mass could never have
developed into a Catholic religion of the theater: Catholicism recoils
from the introduction of the second actor into the Mass. It never
found the power to repeat Aeschylus's bold innovation, after which
the dramatic genius of the Greek playwrights, who were at that time
called *theologoi*, was first able to break ground. The goat-song, in
Catholic terms, had to remain hierarchical and centered on priests.
It could not renounce the monarchy of the first actor in the Mass.
No second individual separated itself from the chorus. It is thus
obvious why Catholicism neglected to transition from the drama
of the Mass to a theatrical culture of the cathedral, perhaps to the
detriment of European civilization as a whole. Now if it is true that
Heidegger half-consciously and subconsciously arranged to take
over the sanctuary from the position of the sacristy, in order to set a
monstrous sexton alongside the undermined priest, a thinking sexton
who at the same time held the rectorship of a mobilized university,
then, seen from a distance, this would correspond—yet only on the
stage of the dream—to an Aeschylean reform of Catholicism and
the introduction of a second actor into the Mass. Thus it remains
the case: Heidegger is no thinker on the stage.

   That is not a surprising statement, but rather boils down to the
well-established observation that European philosophers, even
twentieth-century ones—insofar as they stand within an academic
succession—as a rule presuppose philosophy's break with the
theater that was carried out by Plato. None are thinkers on the stage

and all are satisfied not to be, because they have been able to inherit from Plato the calm conviction that God stands in a relation of privilege to thinkers in the Academy or the Peripatos and no longer reveals the truth to imaginative theater persons who are full of lies.

How it could come about that European philosophers were able to understand themselves *ex officio* as thinkers on a non-stage, and that they were able to do so for more than two thousand years, merits a short explanation. I want to suggest one such explanation by recalling the fateful Athenian years of 387–386 BC, in which two initially inconspicuous events occurred in the city, which was grievously scarred by war, pestilence, and civil war; they both had world-historical consequences, and both were intimately connected with each other—events, incidentally, that to my knowledge have nowhere been considered in terms of their connection. The first is well known, because it belongs to Plato's *vita* and directly concerns the prehistory of the ancient Academy. The second is almost unknown and concerns the moment when the theater became historical—if one can speak in such terms.

In the year 387, Plato returned to Athens from his trip to southern Italy, where he had sought contact with the Pythagoreans. It is the trip that is also known as the first Sicilian one and that brought the philosopher, who was at that time forty years old, into the acquaintance of the King of Syracuse, Dionysius I, an acquaintance that resulted in the philosopher supposedly later displaying a nervous reservation about everything that reminded him of this name. Back from Syracuse, Plato bought a piece of land in Athens, as far as we know, on the edge of the city, which was dedicated to the demigod Akademos, in order to open a new kind of school on it. Legend and reality may coincide in the fact that this undertaking was immediately an extraordinary success. Even if, based on their own experience, folks today will scarcely believe it, the first of the academies was a place where the word 'school' must have been tantamount to enchantment through instruction. Only thus can one understand why Plato's garden developed into a magnet for gifted young people who dreamed on the one hand of transfiguring knowledge and on the other of public careers, mainly youth from Athens's middle and upper classes, not a few with homoerotic tendencies, as it corresponded to the didactic concept of the institution. For the moment, I do not want to say any more about this school's success than that it is supposed to have been forcibly closed down, after nearly a thousand years, by a Christian emperor from Constantinople—only to be reanimated after an interruption of another thousand years in the Florentine Renaissance. Incidentally, one may draw from these dates the conclusion that in

ѵ.   Europe the idea of a community of thinkers is considerably older
than the Christian church, which wants to be a community of saints,
or at least of the faithful, and is much older than the modern state,
which presents itself as a community of beneficiaries of bourgeois
legal relations. The only social formation of the European tradition
that could make the ancient precedence of the academy a matter
of controversy—and in certain respects even the claim to priority regarding questions of the public use of reason—is that of the
gathering of people for debate in Athens, which perhaps represents
the oldest attempt to give collective intelligence a political form.
Accordingly, the quarrel between school wisdom and popular intelligence has also been institutionalized since Plato.

The second event occurred a few months after Plato's acquisition
of the academic garden—it belongs to the secret dates of European
culture. One has to suppose that long debates had preceded it,
debates which could not possibly have remained hidden from
someone as interested in literature and almost desperate in regard
to politics as Plato, although these discussions in large part may
have been played out among a group of elite Athenians consisting
of the so-called *chorēgoi*, rich citizens who were responsible for the
financing of the 'goat-song,' the tragic festival in honor of the god.
In the year 386, almost the same time as Plato's installation of his
logical-erotic school, these *chorēgoi*, the sponsors of the Athenian
theater, made the decision, to the acclaim of the citizenry, to allow
the restaging of pieces in the future that had been particularly successful at earlier festivals for Dionysus.

It is almost impossible for contemporary human beings to appreciate the consequences of this decision, precisely because no modern
reader or author can be transported back to a time in which the
rule obtained that each piece, the most poetically perfect as well
as the most cathartically effective, was only allowed to be played
a single time. Recalling this prescription suffices to indicate that
Old European dramatic poetry did not begin under the auspices of
autonomous art and literature, but rather as a practice of the political cult and as a civic-religious community effort. When, in the year
386, the Athenian citizenry decided to allow the restaging of pieces
across the board—certainly also under the impression that the
standard of pieces produced in the cult suddenly began to decline
after the heroic age of Sophocles, Aeschylus, and Euripides—they
were acting as cultural revolutionaries in the genuine sense of the
word, though with hardly any knowledge of what they were doing.
Athenian citizens set an ambivalence into the world that has inhered
ever since in all courtly, later bourgeois, and ultimately museumized
and mass-mediatized cultic and aesthetic practices: namely, that

what was religion becomes an aesthetic phenomenon, while art
presses ahead to supersede religion. To supersede religion, however,
means to parody it, that is to say: to undercut its seriousness or
its irreplaceability. The right to restage ancient pieces of the cult
brings in its wake something that today might be called a revolution of the media landscape; and, so that we rightly understand,
the media at that time were always and above all religious, or, put
better, religio-political and group-forming media. In them lay the
power to attune and stamp human beings in such a way that they
could become halfway consonant participants resonating within
their social ensemble. Through what is designated in Europe by
the Roman-tinged term religion, all ancient societies regulated their
tonal synthesis, one could even say their mytho-musical integration
and their moral balance. With the decision of 386, the Athenian cultural politicians ran the risk of altering the tunings in their city in an
uncertain and potentially dangerous way.

It seems that Plato was the first one to grasp the significance of
this intervention and to react against it with precise insight into
the new conditions of cultural formation [*Bildungsbedingungen*];
he thereby became the first conservative. He immediately braced
himself for the danger of a nihilistic-aesthetic education from the
semi-religious, mythico-veristic repertory theater. The *Republic* is
the great testament to Plato's resistance to the divergence of the
polis into deregulated educational relations. What, to the present
day, we call philosophy, is directly and indirectly a consequence of
Plato's novel media offensive. It signifies the invention of the school
from out of the spirit of resistance to the unbounded theater. And
one readily understands, precisely as an admirer of Greek stage-
craft, what the philosopher had to do, if one submits oneself to the
wonderful effort of again working through the greatest of the classical pieces that have been handed down,[2] above all in view of their
theological messages and their possible influences on those youth
who at the time of the intact tragic cult were *eo ipso* excluded from
the one-off stagings and who, according to the new circumstances,
would now sooner or later obtain access to the pieces.

One probably does not say too much if one notes that even
today's reader of tragedies finds himself in a landscape of metaphysical horror populated by questionable gods. Whoever looks
at the piece *Ajax* by Sophocles gets to know a goddess, Athena,
who with impenetrable malice taunts the deluded warrior and deri-
sively, willfully drives him to his doom. Whoever devotes himself to
Aeschylus's *Eumenides* encounters a god, Apollo, who had incited
Orestes to matricide in order to subsequently demand, like a scru-
pulous defense lawyer, acquittal for his client. Whoever studies

Euripides' *Bacchae* witnesses the manifestation of a Dionysus who
finds satisfaction in bloody vengeance and thinks it right to evince
his divinity by having one who denies it torn to pieces by a pack of
women in estrus, until at the end a mother carries the bloody head
of her own son across the stage like some mad proof of the god's
existence. Such images may have struck a public of adult specta-
tors like numinous flashes of lightning during the time of one-off
stagings, provoking a shudder and lamentation, *phobos* and *eleos*,
as a reminder of the superiority of the divine over the human and
as a warning to mortals of their dispensation under an incommensurable power. But who would keep the corrupting influences of
such repeatedly performed representations of divine violence under
control? Who was supposed to compensate for the damages to the
body politic when dismay and spiritual devastation escalated on
account of the theater's compromising of the gods?

Plato appears to have been the first who attempted to envision
the political-pedagogical seriousness of the new situation, even in
its far-reaching consequences. Just as society today has reason to be
worried about the plague of information that is disseminated by the
mass media in the form of endlessly repeatable images of violence
and solicitations of prostitution, so Plato saw a great danger for the
body politic in the emergence of the all-too-human, indeed, bes-
tially engaged gods in the media of his time. His battle against the
poets, the theater-theologians, was actually a politico-theological
safeguard for the city under threat, aiming to offset the blasphe-
mous laying bare of the divine in the newly established theater with
repeat performances.[3] At that time, so one can surmise, the epochal
idea of a philosophical school opened up before him, a school that

offered itself to the god as a new medium through which the god, as
it suited him, could become manifest in his restored perfection, as
unconditioned truth and goodness, with conscious disregard of the
gruesome interventions of the poets' gods in the human world. The
task for Plato is thus to shed light on revelation, and this is entrusted
to philosophy for the future. Among the Pythagoreans, the pious
logicians, Plato had just experienced that the philosophical sect of
truth-seekers wished, in substance, to find itself on the right path
but settled into injustice because the form of their doctrines was split
off from common life. On the trip home Plato had a momentous
thought: where there was a sect, a school should be. Truth finds its
way back to the city through the school—hardly different than the
Trojan Horse, but manned with subversive interrogators of customary life. In the name of truth the sect of teachers makes a bid at
power.

Philosophy as school-power, however, is above all one thing: a

new medium—more precisely: a new medium of theophany. Plato
instantly brought to prominence the acute danger of the collective
neglect of the affects that a mere education by myth and drama
evoked. As a new medium philosophy is an emphatic non-theater,
its program is the non-portrayal and the non-laying-bare of the
god on the stage; its ambition is to provide the god with a purified,
internalized, and logicized channel for more subtle epiphanies. That
is the reason why, as was just said, philosophers—all the way to
Heidegger—are for the most part and as a matter of course thinkers
on the non-stage. For they are, as long as they are good for anything
in their field, admittedly and happily academic. If someone should
ask what a happy academy might be, then the answer is: nothing
other than a school that is animated by the conviction that it is
the preferred space for the manifestation of the god, the improved
temple, the illuminated oracle, the theater overcome, the *mysterium*
rendered precise. In this sense, the oldest academy is completely
happy. It is assured of its new theophanic mandate, as though it were
an evangelical secret. It would proclaim it loudly, were it not evident
that strong words obstruct subtle manifestation—that is why from
Plato's day, at the latest, onward, the god learns to keep silent and
to hardly ever manifest himself, except in an intimate presence that
dazzles without speaking.[4] His true name is evidence. Hence, the
rumor of an unwritten doctrine in Plato is consistent; it involves
the discrete theophanic competence of the academic pursuit: Plato's
garden is full of gods. To those who are fortunate, the god allows
himself to be shown in the resonance of an exact thought.

That all has a clear point: after 386 philosophy surpasses tragedy
as the medium of divine manifestation. This is the intellectual-
historical sense of original academicism. As powerfully as Attic
tragedy may have treated of gods and heroes, over the long term
it will still be philosophy that keeps open the theophanic space at
the heights of the civilizing process. It is likely that what one calls
the history of religion and intellectual history is for long stretches
identical with the shifts of theophanic space in cultures. This space
had its most ancient focus in oracles and trance-cults,[5] before it
gained among the Greeks, as well, the Dionysian theater, and later
occupied the academy as we have characterized it here. Its legacy
was appropriated by the Christian church and melded with the
mystery-theology of the sacrificed God-Man, from which a melancholy hybrid, Christian Platonism, is supposed to have arisen, which
proved its viability all the way up to German idealism.

The process of shifting the theophanic realm is not concluded
with the transition to Christianity. If one looks back into European
intellectual history since the late Middle Ages, it is hard to escape

the impression that, beginning with the thirteenth century, it continually increases in momentum after the mystical, the evangelical,
and the early Protestant movements had begun to bring the language games and cultic practices of a god breaking through from
within to the urban masses. New spaces are progressively opened up
for receiving new manifestations of the Absolute in the European
civilizing process all the way into the twentieth century. Such spaces
were established in the innermost depths of individuals and in
shrines for works of art. They were frequented by political secret
societies and neo-religious sects, and placed on the fringes of the
affluent world; one wished to discover them in trash, in misfortune,
in excrement. But one can interpret this movement as broadly as one
wishes: to speak of thinkers on the stage would only first be meaningful when it could be shown that the theater had been instituted
with a new theophanic function. However, that is a demand that,
with the exception of Richard Wagner, does not seem to me to be
met anywhere in our time.

I must admit that, after everything I have suggested here, I can
only honor my responsibility for the formulation 'thinker on the
stage' if I make clear that it was reserved for Friedrich Nietzsche.[6]
I see in him an erratic figure who emerged as a theologian of an
undetected god. Nietzsche had reason, if not a factually correct then
at least a psychological one, to pose as the belated medium of the
divine life that goes by the name of Dionysus, because he combined
in himself the Dionysian extremes: existence under continuous
torture and the overcoming of torture in the euphoric states of art
and thought. For him and, as far as I can see, only for him, is the
formulation of thinker on the stage appropriate, and even for him
it should not be taken literally, since it is not a matter of imputing
to him a direct relation to the theater, but rather of characterizing
an existentiell tension and its 'world of expression.' Even Nietzsche
is not a thinker on the stage, but rather a thinker who is a stage.
He has the experience that a god who is not one, the fragmented
Dionysus, manifests himself in him as a clairvoyant, frenzied life
raging against itself. Nietzsche was a theater for powers that battled
within him and whose struggle is supposed to have made away
with the unity of his person. Now one may think what one will of
Heidegger's fundamental attunement; one may highly esteem his
share of the manic resources of philosophy and not underestimate
his familiarity with depressive phases—still, in his whole bearing he
lived far removed from Nietzsche's cycles of torture, secure as he
was in a disciplined and grim normality. Hence for the last time, and
set against the backdrop of the case of Nietzsche: Heidegger is not a
thinker on the stage.

2. The Plunge

Now, in order to segue from this negative result to a positive definition, I would like to suggest a formulation that summarizes, in a compact expression, Heidegger's spiritual physiognomy and his philosophical project: Heidegger is the thinker in motion. His original thought or virtual action [*Tathandlung*], as it were, is the leap or letting-himself-go into a disposedness [*Befindlichkeit*] in which he finds [*findet*] nothing more in himself and 'under his feet' than movement. In his case, kinetics precedes logic, or, if one will allow a paradoxical turn of phrase: motion is his foundation. The impulse of his discourse is to express movement—or rather, to 'follow' actual and unavoidable movement with the motion of discourse. Thus, like no philosopher before him, he deserves to be characterized by this unfamiliar and not fully clarified formulation: the thinker in motion.

What that means and where it leads I explain in what follows, at least suggestively. I forgo supplying another commentary on Heidegger's mythos of his 'path of thought' and limit myself to a structural observation of the form of his thought. Thanks to the concentration on the architectonic or formal side of Heidegger's thought, it can be shown that his professed path of thought is itself only the incessantly repeated and modified elaboration of a schema of motion that remains the same. From this perspective, the motions of thought of the master from Germany can be characterized as a primordial complying that comports itself by 'corresponding' to a threefold ontological movement. If I see things correctly, and if I may avail myself of these extreme and almost lyrical abstractions, in Heidegger's thinking and in general there are three universal and fundamental motions, three kinetic features of Being that are operative at all times in human existence, yet in each case differently according to cultural and epochal nuances. I here call these features, first, the *plunge*, second, the *experience*, and third, the *reversal*. Their permeation of or incursion into existence happens 'always already,' in each case and everywhere, without it being the case that anyone, including the classical hermeneuticists of fate, had ever observed this in a sufficiently clear light—unless we say that it was precisely Heidegger who began to do so.[7] It was this thinker who like no other before him laid emphasis on the fact that Dasein is always already 'set' in motion and pervaded by motion and cannot be secured against pervasive movement by anything. Its movement is the ground of its historicity and its relation to the open. Varying the famous formulation of the lecture *What Is Metaphysics?* from 1929, one could say: Dasein means being held into the incursion of motion.

It now thus appears as though Heidegger expressly turned to this sweeping contingency [*Zufall*] and developed a form of philosophical discourse that corresponds to Dasein in the grip of contingent incursion [*zufälligen Überfalls*]—a discourse on the plunge, a tale in the fall [*Fall*]. Whoever attempts to think in motion must show what it means to provide an example of the fall. Thus thinking becomes the serious case [*Ernstfall*] of movement.[8] Now, the one thinking must resolutely and calmly project himself in his discourses in his own person—since he no longer imitates an unmoved mover. Philosophy is no longer possible without speaking of oneself. Heidegger chooses this gesture with exemplary resolve, like an ontological gym teacher who provides guidance to his subjects who are stuck in their principles and worldviews by giving them exercises to be able to consciously abide in movement.

All discourse that develops along these lines emanates from a kinetic cogito: I exist, therefore a movement precedes me. I do not stand firm, for I am 'thrown.' It is given to me to think, to the extent that and for as long as I correspond to the incursion of movement. I am the *Fall*, because a movement—a history, an interconnected fabric of contingency and necessity—has carried me along and brought me here, into this situation, this insecurity. Thinking then means: developing a reflection within the incursion. Discourse is the gathering of the fall. In speaking in a thoroughly interrogatory way we retrieve [*wiederholen*] the contingent movement that has borne us to this place. That is not all: through the retrieval we deepen the contingent fall so much that it begins to verge on a necessity, perhaps even a 'truth.' Thus does retrieval become the mother of reflection; reflection responds to the unavoidable, the irreversible, the singular event. If I think and think again the fall that I am, I can no longer give myself over to theoretical illusion: the old dream of a distance without cost is shattered; the autistic phantasm of a contemplation that commits the contemplator to nothing has come apart. I have convinced myself that I am entirely permeated by movement, that I am included in the primal features of motion. I can no longer act as though I had not fallen into this, my situation. We no longer begin with stationary appearance, with the idea, with things, with the subject, with the system, with consciousness, with the facts, with what is objective, with timeless values. We can only begin with essential movement in ourselves, with our temporality, our temporariness, our situatedness and relatedness. Thus everything for us starts with 'Dasein,' which is interpreted as Being-in-the-world, and this is correct so long as we read this formulation as follows: to have reached, through the incursion of movement into us, the 'place' at which we most often disperse and only in exceptional moments gather ourselves together. Philosophy is a discussion of our situation.

In the trinity just indicated, the first feature of movement—Being-in-the-fall or plunging¹—precedes the other two features, experience² and reversal or turning³ in order as in fact. If, for a time, Heidegger made much ado about his decision to again use the Greek name for human beings, i.e., mortals, from a post-Christian position, this was a consequence overtly drawn from his analysis of the first mode of movement as falling or plunging. Whoever speaks in the early twentieth century with a fundamental conceptual emphasis on mortals must for better or worse mean those who fall, and that pertains both to the fallen and to the fallible.⁹ It is no accident that not only Protestant theologians recognized in *Being and Time* the formalization of their enactment of faith; also some who belonged to the generation of those who fought on the front were able to be of the opinion that they encountered here for the first time a language that was at the level of the monstrosities that they had experienced. Readers of *Being and Time* know that, instead of 'fallenness' [*Gefallenheit*] or 'plungedness' [*Gestürztheit*], Heidegger uses the expressions 'entanglement' [*Verfallenheit*] and 'thrownness' [*Geworfenheit*] for the mode of movement discussed here—turns of phrase that keep the ex- and anti-Catholic Heidegger at a distance from Roman dogma and bring him close to an obscure Gnostic approach.¹⁰ As one occasionally observes again since then, it is above all casts of mind who are critical of the world and apocalyptically disposed that interpret their sojourn in earthly gloom with this feeling of plunging; only he who shares in this perception can know what thrownness means in its obscure limit value. The expression belongs to the series of 'real-philosophical' concepts with which some thinkers, in the reflective aftermath of the French Revolution, sought anew and in their own way to make sure of what would henceforth be called the firm ground of facts. That is no longer the soil upon which from time immemorial the 'human being' moves and stands but rather that upon which he has plunged after his upsurge as a subject: in this quality, as the limit of the plunge, the harshness of the factical as it is experienced in modernity brings to mind the resigned agents of praxis. The naked 'that' is only informative for failed idealists and constructivists after the retreat from exaggeration: the world is everything that, after excursions into illusion, stands out [*auffällt*] as being the case [*der Fall*]. Yet human beings for the most part do not sense their fall, since according to Heidegger they hardly ever experience anything other than existence in the mode of everyday entanglement:

This 'movement' of Dasein in its own Being, we call its '*plunge*.' Dasein plunges out of itself into itself, into the groundlessness and nullity of inauthentic everydayness. . . . At the same time, turbulence makes manifest that the thrownness . . . has the character of throwing and of movement . . . . Falling is conceived ontologically as a kind of motion.[11]

When the philosopher uses the expression 'thrownness' [*Geworfenheit*] for the first mode of movement, it speaks for this turn of phrase that one can compose active forms from it: throw [*Wurf*] and projection [*Entwurf*]—and this inversion is what interests this young serious thinker. The active concepts lend themselves to a heroic modification of the ur-passive structure of falling. With them the supposition can be expressed that, under conditions that are still to be explained, a fall could come to be taken on from one already suffered, a projected fall, indeed an existentiell commando operation, as it were, in which the one thrown appropriates his fate for himself. This suffices to motivate the preference for 'thrownness' over the potentially synonymous, though more strongly Christian and angelically laden word 'fallenness.' For the Heidegger of *Being and Time*, the taking on of a fall by the one falling occurs as a result of a macabre meditation of a monk-soldier, as it were, in which the one thrown into the world lets himself 'fall all the way through' to his own anticipated death. Like the logos, death, as my most personal possibility, possesses a gathering power. From the prospect of his own nihilation the meditator returns to his present as though from a baptism by fire. Only now can he 'take' himself 'on,' trembling in the certainty of being not a natural outgrowth, but rather a projection.[12]

This change of expression affords us the opportunity to mention that even in the overarching kinetic primal features of Being as Dasein—in the plunge into what is factically dispersed, in the experience [*Erfahrung*] in the context, in the reversal from what one has experienced [*Verfahrenheit*]—a difference emerges that opens up a relation to truth and authenticity. It makes all the difference in the world—at least that is Heidegger's initial wager—as to whether Dasein resumes its fall in an uncollected fashion and thereby gets entangled in its dispersal into Being-in-any-old-way, like a sleeping passenger who without waking up dozes through the trip from the entry point into the world until the final station, or whether Dasein becomes intimately aware of its plummet, lets itself be penetrated by the simultaneous awareness of its groundlessness and determination, and ultimately makes from the plummet it has suffered a plummet that it has taken on, indeed even perhaps a throw of its

own, makes from the fall a project, makes from being the subject of
an incursion the decided correspondence to something that has been
fated. Let us hold fast to the fact that for the Heidegger of *Being and
Time* this taking up of the self is to be understood above all as "resoluteness" or "letting oneself be summoned out of one's lostness in
the 'they'"[13]: "*this reticent self-projection upon one's ownmost Being-
guilty, in which one is ready for anxiety*—we call *'resoluteness.'*"[14] At
this time, resoluteness appears to be the remedy for succumbing to
the contingent.

To renew again and again the distinction between a banal lostness
and projecting oneself in resoluteness: that belongs, to begin with, to
the ethical task of existence in the midst of prevailing arbitrariness.
Because the demand to distinguish is raised so explicitly, it is appropriate to observe that Heidegger's transformation of metaphysics
into onto-kinetics—the illumination of movements that touch on
the sense of Being—cannot possibly lead to an indiscriminate capit-
ulation to everything that is historiographically in progress.[15] In
movement brought to reflection there emerges a primary difference
that is on a par with the cardinal difference of bivalent thinking in
the logical field, that of truth and falsity, and with the cardinal difference of bivalent judging in the moral field, that of good and bad:
there is a false movement and its counterpart, the true movement.
Thus philosophical kinetics opens up a third dimension of difference that is to be addressed even before the logical difference of
the Being-true-or-false of statements and the ethical difference of
the Being-good-or-bad of activities. Even movement demands its
own power of differentiation or 'judgment [*Urteils*],'[16] a power
of changing direction, if one may put it in such terms, that manifests itself in turning toward and away from objects, persons, and
programs, in engagements and disengagements, in correspondences
or lapses.[17] There is dispersal into the inauthentic and into what
dissembles—notably in the unbearable lightness of Being—and also
the gathering into the authentic and unavoidable—indicated by the
unalleviated 'weight of the world.' There is (in its tendency) a false
letting-oneself-be-taken-along by hustle and bustle and reaction,
and there is (in its tendency) a true participation in being drawn to
the 'work' [*Werk*] and responsibility that shapes and makes whole.

Both 'tendencies' or traits must be understood as equally powerful
modes of movement; nevertheless, the primordiality of being drawn
to dispersal in that which is false is, in Heidegger's presentation,
given such a significant status that the counter-pull of gathering in
that which is true is glossed over by him, as a rule. We even have
to acknowledge that 'false motion,' the initial plunging or the dispersing thrownness, is the more comprehensive magnitude because

it comes about "proximally and for the most part"—Heidegger's warning formulation—simply from the continuation of the primordial ac-cident [*Zu-fall*]. To let the initial fall simply fall further—from contingency to contingency: that leads to the ultimate entanglement, and this is precisely the normal case [*Normalfall*] that, according to Heidegger, simply leads to that which is false, to indecision, to inauthenticity, to being driven by public and anonymous forces. The inclination to remain within the obscured hustle and bustle is the origin of the pull toward inauthenticity. Conversely, true or gathering movement can only emerge as a precarious countermovement from out of false movement. Or, to change the image: true movement occurs as though a parachute opened in the initial fall—a jolt then runs through the Dasein of the one who is plummeting. As he became aware of his 'situation' in the plunge he would give another meaning to the rest of his fall's distance, by making into a resolute project or into an opening up to that which is possible and essential something which would otherwise remain a trivial drifting about in the contingent that is determined in some fashion or other.

Incidentally, it is never really clear in the early Heidegger whether Dasein can actually attain in its 'ownmost' resolution for itself the capacity to choose a recognizably different direction, or whether that which is here called a project or a resolution is not merely an internalized falling and a somewhat more conscious continuation of lines already drawn. Indeed, in one passage that has not escaped attentive readers, Heidegger speaks of the fact that authentic existence is merely a "modified way in which [falling] everydayness is seized upon."[18] If that is apposite, then the existentially interpreted difference between false and true movement, plunge and project, can certainly be formally applied, yet it remains a difference that one can never actually 'carry out,' at least not in a way that can be verified, and concerning which no one in the falling world can judge according to identifiable criteria, let alone have at one's disposal. "Ontically, we have not decided whether man is 'drunk with sin.' . . ."[19]

Furthermore, it ought to be noted that this first determination of Dasein as a plunge or a plummeting movement covers vertical distance, indeed in a noteworthy inversion of the customary direction of metaphysical traffic, from the top down in the plummet, in the descent, in coming down. In this extraordinary sense, Heidegger is a theoretician of the descent: for him the human being is a being that initially and necessarily comes down to itself and lands beside itself. In the case of the human being, 'to descend from' also already means 'to fall away from.' He typically falls so far that he is dispersed at rock bottom, down among things, routines, and mechanisms, among minerals and the living dead—in Surrealism one would have even said: among the citizens. The baseline, down to which entanglement sinks, is called everydayness, or in a more acute expression: "uninhibited 'hustle and bustle,'"[20] which means the same thing as "our everyday preoccupations."[21] In the hustle and bustle 'the human being' misses himself from the beginning, because he understands his own mode of Being from the things and procedures into which he has plunged and in which he has become entangled. In the light of things and routines the human being appears before himself as something present at hand and carried away like everything else. In this primordial fallacy the 'tempting' essence of Dasein as such is borne out: finite, conditioned existing clings to something about which it can be concerned and in which it can become entangled. Entanglement levels the difference between the mode of Being of existence and that of what is present at hand. It is the initial tendency of the human being to conceive of himself as human material and a piece of the environment. In view of this flight into undifferentiation that has always already begun, anarchistic letting-oneself-go and submissive functioning are the same thing. Before Heidegger, only Johann Gottlieb Fichte formulated a similarly conceived circumstance with comparable radicality when he wrote in a polemical appendix to his *Foundations of the Entire Science of Knowledge* (§4):

> The majority of men could sooner be brought to believe themselves a piece of lava in the moon than to take themselves for a *self*.[22]

The early Heidegger would have agreed with this, under the condition that two modifications be made to Fichte's thesis: on the one hand, the observation that this entanglement in things and procedures is the spontaneous result of ordinary Dasein; for, something smacking of lava adheres to everything that is 'thrown.' Because our existence has always begun from an unfamiliar side, in a certain sense it continually comes too late; it encounters that which is present at hand and must grapple everywhere with what is earlier and unfamiliar. Even if a good god had made us in his image we would not be spared from having to experience that the lava was there before us and that the difference between the moon and the human world is not always easy to pin down. On the other hand, Heidegger would agree, but on condition that we talk not about a self, but rather about the being that is existing and held out into the open, an ontological ecstase-being that we usually call the human being without thinking twice.

With this, I have nothing more to say about the mode of falling

for the moment. According to Heidegger, the turnaround or reversal must now at once be added to the analytic of movements;
from the first, one would now have to transition, immediately and
without detours, to the third motion. For the great onto-kineticist, in the case of two possibilities only one will follow: either the
unturned plunge all the way up to the ultimate entanglement—or,
alternatively, the turn within the plummet. All thought for him,
whether he presents it as resolute [*entschlossenes*] thought in the
early work or as serenely released [*gelassenes*] thought in the late
work, comes down to showing beyond this how the danger of entanglement is also already able to engender a turn to "one's ownmost
possibility"—the contemporary surrogate for classical necessity.
The turning to that which is existence's own and ownmost has the
character of an ontological conversion: resurrection from inauthenticity, being born again in angst and trembling. Hence Heidegger's
continual concern for an introduction to essential thinking by pro-
paedeutic ecstases. Hence also the propensity for a certain monastic
seriousness, as though thinking were the highest *askēsis* when it
lets itself "be claimed" only by Being itself. In any case, it is not
an *opus dei* that the thinker aligns himself with, but rather an *opus
entis*. Hence, in particular, "the peculiar desire for hardship and
difficulty!" or for that "compelling compulsion" which Hugo von
Hofmannsthal, a distant relative in the spirit of striving for the
serious case [*Ernstfall*] that necessitates authenticity, discussed in his
1927 Munich speech *Das Schrifttum als geistiger Raum der Nation*
[Literature as the Spiritual Space of the Nation]. Without the total
convulsion of the one thinking there is no prospect of radically
seizing hold of oneself—or, said in view of Heidegger's errant year,
there is no decided self-inclusion within supposedly gripping fate.
Without the decided devotion to reversal there is no share in the
works of authenticity. Thus one could modify an English dictum
and say: 'Man's calamities are Being's opportunity.'[23]

3. Experience

In this sense, Heidegger is a neo-theologian, and theologians who
speak of new gods, whether they are gods who are concealed or who
have turned away, are inevitably in a hurry with their message. One
recognizes old theologians by the fact that they have time and that
the god no longer urges them on. Heidegger is in a hurry to come
from the predominant, false, dispersing motion to the true, gathering one. For more than a half a century the thinker meditated on the
fundamental movements of Dasein and remained true to his kinetic

apriori in this whole time of storm and calm after the storm. With ever new attempts, in modified attunements, with altered conceptual postulations, he repeats the question: how does Dasein, from its initial plunge among things, come to decided selfhood, from shallow thrownness to a deepening retrieval, from contingency's non-essence to that which is unavoidable, from the miscarriage into dispersal to being born again in one's ownmost gatheredness, from the provisional beginning to another beginning? Whoever gages a reference to Heidegger's modernity in all this could be assured of it by the fact that, according to him, what is decisive and fateful can also and above all manifest itself as a foundering that is taken up.

That these figures of speech have something that moves in them and are not without enchantment even in their bald abstractness is not hard to see. I will take up Heidegger's talk about the plunge and the turn once more by setting its profile against the background of analogous figures of speech in Plato and Augustine. Nevertheless, in the double-figure of fall and reversal—or of thrownness and seizing hold of oneself—one thing becomes immediately clear: Heidegger is obviously not very interested in the fact that between the potentially symmetrical features of Being, that is to say, 'falling into the world' (along with the dispersive tendency of entanglement) and 'reversal' (along with the power of gathering that makes one whole and authentic), there is a middle stage that eludes the symmetry of the way there and back again and is neither plunge nor reversal, neither a lapse of the self nor its embrace. Whoever does not allow himself to be misled by Heidegger's disinterest in that which is medial and horizontal must then insist on the fact that the fall of those who exist into the world does not happen only nor even primarily on a vertical scale; it does not only, and does not chiefly, have the features of a dramatic loss of self. Rather, most people rightly understand coming-to-the-world as an extension on a level plane.

We encounter the second movement, which normally appears so comprehensive that, in its everyday interpretation, most human beings since time immemorial have taken it to be the whole thing, as an entrance into worldly horizons. Reaching out into space belongs to Dasein from the start, whether literally, as with biological growth, or metaphorically, as with involvement in a cultural production of worlds. If one wished to speak in Heideggerian terms of this subject matter, which is rather foreign to Heidegger, then one would have to say that existing means 'always already' being taken in by a pull to enter into the world, insofar as it is a house, and by a pull to exit into the world, insofar as it always also signifies that which extends further—beyond the domesticity at the beginning. Dasein in the second mode of movement has the character of relocation and exodus, of colonization and settlement, of curriculum and a course to more distant goals. The comprehensive concept for all the modes of this movement is expressed by the German word *Erfahrung* [experience], whether this be understood colloquially as being conversant with things that have been seen from many sides, or interpreted philosophically as the result of overcoming naivety, of sacrificing an initial judgment, or of revolutionizing a thesis. The most salient feature of the motion of experience is that it is constituted in a cumulative fashion. In it one thing comes to another and forms a 'context [*Zusammenhang*].' One can read off from it that even the horizontal scale possesses gathering power. Contexts, thus understood, are horizontal structures, insofar as experiences form nets, series, vicinities. Whoever continues in an experience that has begun relies on lateral movement, on variants and plurals. Along these lines, human beings acquire world experience and, insofar as they are not closed off in anxious dispositions and hardened in the feral virtuality of psychosis, are able to get settled in the world-house shared with others: this is a feature for which the Greeks possessed the word *oikeiōsis*, which means *Einhausung* [housing] in Swabian German, a word which, not for nothing, was quite pleasing to the world-househusband Hegel.

Heidegger wants to know little about this feature, however, since the normalizing, civilizing, perhaps even promiscuous dimension of this concept does not fit in with his interpretation of Being, which is concentrated on revolution and is calibrated to what is immense [*Ungeheueren*] and serious. Not for nothing did he still lecture in his late work on homelessness [*Heimatlosigkeit*] as a 'world-fate' and affirm abiding in the uncanny [*Unheimlichen*] as the human being's fundamental truth in the modern world. He addresses his audience as though they could at any moment be struck by the vertical blow of the immense. Even his late praise of dwelling intends a form of traffic with the uncanny that has been transformed into something peaceful. It is obvious that this had to lead to a contraction of the image of Dasein's movement in the horizontal dimension. For the philosophical-kinetic guiding concept for the entrance of Dasein into the fullness of that which is experienceable cannot be formulated if one only sticks to the aspect of the plunge or of thrownness. It would be more fittingly defined as coming-to-the-world—an expression that is suited to form the cipher of movement for the not falsely solidified human being from the perspective of a permanent birth, and birth is always already a synthesis of vertical plunge and horizontal entry. 'Mortals' are to be characterized more fittingly as those-who-come-to-the-world; in view of the technological, criminal, creative, and tragic potential of this eccentric species, we could also say that they are those-who-go-far [*die Weit-Gehenden*]. Experience, which is persistently augmented, progressively integrates the contingent and singular into that which forms a context. It is the embedding power par excellence. The more that the thinking of experience is conscious of its own power, the more decisively it holds the vertical at bay with the horizontal.

Two aspects are of interest in the formulation 'coming-to-the world': on the one hand, it accommodates the horizontal movement of existence with an expression that indicates both the fall and the exodus. On the other hand, with this formulation Heidegger's resistance to every sort of anthropology can be marked off and dealt with from the heart of the matter. With the help of this formulation, we can, without fear, abbreviate the human fact—the discovery that human beings stand 'in the clearing'—and define those who exist as beings who relocate, who do not escape their own respective extension. These beings, which foundered as animals and from the beginning were culturally and technologically conditioned, live as coming to the world, are world-forming and 'historical,' because they follow a pull into that which is further, a pull which, for its part, stems from far away, from a naturally and technologically historical distance, which they themselves cannot understand without further ado and perhaps not at all.[24] As soon as human beings enter into the history of states and advanced technology they discover within themselves that they are creatures who, aside from domestic and tangible concerns, are sympathetically drawn in by great, elevated, and distant matters. Even when they want to remain modestly within their own affairs, that which is great and without measure gives them no peace. When it comes to human beings, they are condemned to becoming masters and to suffering from their rise to power. Power is not something that only befalls its subjects and victims; it strikes its agents just as much and puts them in situations in which capability means suffering. When human beings reach this point they begin to feel the pull of needing to transcend their suffering from power. That can initially be observed in the case of the Egyptians, the Babylonians, and the Persians, in which here the Greeks, there the Jews, slaved away with their intelligence that was critical of empires. Subsequently, this holds even more for the Romans and their successors, the Byzantines, the Europeans, the Russians, and Americans, who acted according to the imperial script. To the degree that it becomes apparent that something in the human being accommodates itself to these impositions of that which is great, elevated, and distant, during the times of cities and empires they end up in a kind of growth whose dimension bears a name among us as respectable as it is uncanny: spirit. That means the complex unity from out of which power is engendered, maintained, and increased, and also from out of which it is reconsidered and tempered. Thus, when human beings become decisively greater, they grow in regards to 'spirit.' By complying with the demands of growth, they become grown-ups, as we rightly and yet for the most part cluelessly say. At issue here is the connection between relocating and adulthood. Historical coming-to-the-world cannot be carried out without relocation and departure. Hence relocation to a greater dimension that is compelled or fated [*geschickte*] by history [*Geschichte*] must trigger a crisis in the human being's essential nature. It assumes the form of a permanent crisis, which for two and a half thousand years has been called *education*. It is a crisis of reform in the human being's essential nature. For this, the Greeks introduced the expression *paideia*, which literally signifies an art with respect to children, a word which has to be construed as an alarm. It signals that from now on we must do something with our children that was not yet recognized in simpler times. We had to realize that, under present conditions, our offspring would no longer adjust to the state of the world if we merely let them grow up alongside ordinary adults and put our trust in unspecified imitation. The young do not reach the standard if they are not formed in their formative years by a master or educator qualified for just such a thing.

Only in this context can one assess what the discovery of education means for European civilization.[25] The expression testifies to the chronic conflict between human beings of an advanced culture over the goals and methods of their formation. In an extended world, in empires and city governments the moment had to arrive when the meaning of becoming an adult became controversial. Now, the adulthood of the ruler means something different than the adulthood of the servant, the adulthood of the priest something different than the adulthood of the warrior, the adulthood of the statesman something different than the adulthood of the private citizen. Obviously, the adulthood of the Athenians has a different character than the adulthood of the Spartans, that of the Greeks a different tendency than that of the Persians. Beyond all these differences, the adulthood of the philosopher wants to achieve different results than the adulthood of the 'many.' Philosophy, as Plato designed and institutionalized it, is nothing other than seizing the opportunity to put oneself at the head of the revolutionized situation of education. If philosophy could become a form of life *sui generis* this is only because it very ambitiously promoted the *askēsis* of becoming an adult. In the strife between the few and the many, which is still today for the most part merely misunderstood as a result of an elitist pretension, the downhill gradient between the educated and the non-educated is concealed—a tension that permeates the era of regional advanced cultures and opens up a cleft everywhere between 'those who know' and 'those who do not,' which is emphasized, bridged, and occluded at the same time by the formal relations between master and pupil. To be sure, in present times, this tension changes its forms of appearance and multiplies its fronts; it proceeds under cover of egalitarian conventions, and is whitewashed into the equal communication of citizens with experts; it is translated into the peaceful coexistence of those competent in one thing and those competent in another. Yet there can be no talk anywhere of its resolution.

Early on, one could recognize a dark side to the pedagogical revolution: after the threshold from which education becomes a theme and is contested as a procedural control of the path to adulthood is crossed, thus in early advanced cultures, the expressions 'plebs,' 'rabble,' 'simple folk', and 'proletariat' take on their sense, because these expressions characterize human groups that, on the basis of their ad hoc irremediable, miserable conditions, can often just barely become adult enough to procreate in their hopelessness. Whereas those who are well off and ambitious want to make their children adults precisely through the education which is now possible and for which the latest technicians of culture are ready at hand.

Philosophy, as the centerpiece of the educational procedure, advances the excess of becoming an adult. Yet because it proceeds in an essentially exaggerated manner, it opens up the possibility for education to veer into a return to childishness at the level of the concept: such is the danger of all schooling when it is hived off and made independent. Nevertheless, philosophy, as long as it avoids scholastic aberration, makes it possible to take on an elevated charge of authority because it takes its suggestive power from its claim to stand at the peak of the pyramid of adulthood and to give the most knowing directions from there (a position that was contested for the first time in the twentieth century by psychoanalysis and systems theory). For this reason, philosophical pedagogy, following Plato's trail, could demand for itself the privilege to educate not merely the youth but also the educators—in moments of its greatest self-confidence it goes so far as to wish to empower the powerless and to hold a mirror before the powerful. Plato educated Aristotle; Aristotle educated Alexander, whom Plutarch still reckons among the philosophers and reclaims for the school.[26] Thanks to philosophy, education becomes a delirium with institutional status. It experiments with the question of whether the most serious philosopher might not be the one who has been the most successful in the endeavor to become the best-educated individual of his culture.

What would the description of the complete philosopher look like? What would the ascetic of comprehensive *paideia* have to achieve, according to this view? How far does this leader of children and conqueror of childhood go? By what means does he offset his own childish dispositions with a method of procedure that is directed against his very self? How does he translate the dream of complete and conscious life into a versatile praxis of speaking and teaching? In any case, he would have had to have demanded of himself that he climb the steepest ladders and travel the longest paths. He would have undertaken the most comprehensive journeys in both the physical and the moral realms. He would have been to the ends of the earth, dwelled among gods and stones, would have investigated the *minima* and the *maxima*, interrogated the dead and the living, pursued all the thoughts essential in his time to the extreme and in detail, distilled what is knowable and what is not knowable in himself. He would have watched and learned the effects of enchanters and the arts of technicians, been intoxicated and sobered in encounters with uncommon human beings. In his expeditions he would have become master of his art and master of himself, and with his mastery would ultimately have overcome even temptation. And he would now be here among us again, in the city, which would only now become completely city-like through his instruction. The philosopher would have returned because he would have wished to explain, in the most open place in the world, in the academy, both himself and his connection with the world of experience, with *physis*, and with what lies beyond it. And he would remain here in order to offer himself as an example of being well educated, of its radiance and its limits. When the philosopher opens his school he calls on those who are uneducated not to remain where and in such a state as they are; it is his mission to show citizens and youth the way out of their caves: to become aware of their family prejudices, their tribal neuroses, the cages of their opinions. He may already presume a 'cultural-political' situation in which numerous individuals discover their interest in keeping a distance from the delusions of an identity bound to a place. However, in order for the philosopher to be able to reach out from the city into the periphery and to the heavens, one would need to presuppose that he had grown up entirely in the space of the city. His exodus from the city into the cosmic can only be played out on urban soil. The deterritorialization of the spirit depends on a territory upon which citizens pursue their interests, have their opinions, argue over what is just, and already even pull back from business pursuits. Whoever wants to set out for that which is beyond the city must first have been entirely urban.

With this fanciful sketch, ladies and gentlemen, with this almost ridiculous curriculum of the philosopher educated to the end, I have outlined what Heidegger, the Freiburg professor of philosophy and educator/inspirer of a generation of young thinkers and scholars, *never* did nor ever attempted. At no time did he reach the dimension of the city, neither in his disposition nor in his discourse. His entire life long he remained somewhere outside the gates, among the inconspicuous and uncanny things of ancient nature, among trees, grass, subterranean tubers, the belfries of small churches. His 'clearing' is a forest metaphor, not a reference to the market, to the bourgeois space for debate. And because he never made it to the city and the city center, to the agora, to the forum—because of this, that which extends beyond the city, that is to say of state politics, contemporary cosmopolitanism, and intercontinental traffic, remained even more foreign to him. What oceangoing ships, what capital and media are—means of extension, means of crossing over, means of relocating, onto-kinetic transporters, literally: that which carries one over and out into the horizontally open—he in no way understood or esteemed. He did not gaze out a window onto the Atlantic ocean, as contemporary Europeans are obliged to; he did not make good on the discovery of America in his thinking; he saw nothing fateful and worthy of repeating, nothing to be interpreted ever anew in Magellan's trip around the globe. In short, he was not a man of exodus, above all not a thinker of globalization, and even the path from the village to the neighboring city where his university was located was something he never traversed with his whole heart. He became a master without journeyman years. The paths into the wide world that are formative for modernity are unpleasant and suspicious to him; at bottom he considers them to be but continuations of the plunge in the horizontal. He ultimately believed that he had dealt with them by chalking them up to bad en-framing [*Ge-Stell*]. For an acquaintance who was about to take a trip overseas he wrote down Lao Tzu's dictum: "He who does not leave his home knows the world." That is not without cleverness, insofar as it seeks to make a sovereign comportment out of an inhibition.

Whoever has breathed city air and felt the connection between the spirit and the polis will not let himself be deceived: in Heidegger there is something that did not relocate, that turned away from the world, that harbored a rage for remaining where it was. One can enumerate what his old *Da* [here/there] consists in: the silhouettes of the village and the alleys of the small town, meadows, forests, hills and chapels, classrooms, school hallways, book spines, the banners of the Kirchweih, and bells tolling in the evening. He grew up in a Catholic, agrarian tribal culture; he remained bound to it up to and including the days of his fame, even when he presented himself as the raging anti-Catholic and donned the professor's cap. In any case, what counts philosophically is not the rooted bond to the original Allemannic scene; what counts philosophically is accommodating oneself to it ostentatiously and letting the primordial region prevail through one with flamboyant calm. Dwelling within this becomes a theorem for the thinker to put into practice. His reflectiveness endeavors to reformat the world spirit into a Greek-Swabian local spirit made monstrous. The village funeral is Heidegger's existential; it is always already there in him like the goal of his finitude that he recognized early on. He wants the region to guard him like a goddess who bears those devoted to her in her bosom. Occasionally he commits to writing, especially in his late work, sentences that sound as though he wanted to found a religion of his first countryside. Thus does remaining become a deed, an expression of the resoluteness to turn away from dispersing forces. In keys both jarring and soft he professes his wish to endure within the natal space. His remaining appears to him to be an achievement of Being, which brings forth and yet retains those whom it wants to have near. He would ultimately like to become, in his own person, a bell in the tower of the first region, summoning the gathering. And since a bell cannot ring itself, it seems Being itself will have to pull the cord. In this enfolding into his provenance, the distinction between true and false movement again asserts itself—in an unavoidably ambiguous, disputable, and controversial way. Heidegger ultimately attributes all real expeditions into extended space to a false going-out that is governed by the dynamic of dispersal, while the truly spacious pull into that which is more encompassing would have to come from Being itself. The best chance for encountering it, so he believes, lies in a patient disposition that is at home in the ancient land, with birch trees and bees nearby, the works of Aristotle and the sayings of the Presocratics within reach. When he teaches the leap into the open, he means an open that is right here. He behaves as though he had to wander around ever more deeply in the region where he was born. What he calls dwelling involves an unending practice of thinking of oneself as belonging to a place that is not indifferent. He meditates on his own countryside as the epicenter of a task to be performed and as the domain of an obligation.

And thus, as we anticipated above, he becomes someone who refuses to relocate, who intellectually elevates rustic reserve above urban unrest. He even goes so far as to refuse the horizon, because this still smacks too much of spaces that open up behind it and bears witness to a subjectivity that, certain of its accomplishments, impertinently peers out into them. Corresponding to this is his rejection of every bad public sphere [Öffentlichkeit]—and the thinker hardly recognizes a good one, certainly not a political one with many debating voices. The thirty-two parties of the Weimar Republic's parliamentary system are in any case not highly esteemed by him, for whom they are only organs of collective confusion and circulators of idle chatter. He may at best allow the publications of Being in the artwork to serve as positions that mark the public [*öffentlichen*] space, indeed perhaps first genuinely open it up [*eröffnen*]. Dasein, according to Heidegger's unswerving intuition, has nothing but dispersal to look for in horizons and public spheres. Without having been there, he lectures to students and friends: "Big-city life only serves to create a sense of excitement and animation: the outward appearance of alertness. Even the best intentions are stifled by sensation and show."[27] In cities, Heidegger expects to find human beings who have run away from necessity, are too free, and have been let loose into arbitrariness, who do not know what they want and should do, and hence for the most part settle for the first available option. In urban forms of life he senses the irony that is more suspicious and hateful to him than any other kind, perhaps because it also presents a temptation to the phenomenologist himself—it is the temptation of the distance that the philosopher demands by his own example, insofar as he takes an analytical holiday from life: the temptation to float freely and detach oneself from the Dasein that is anchored in a situation. In irony, subjectivism asserts itself, a subjectivism which is only familiar with contingent, gratuitous devotion to things and persons, together with the correspondingly arbitrary aversion to them. The city engenders forms of life in which everything "washes together into the uniformly distanceless,"[28] into a gathering within the false. The metropolis houses the ironic masses of underwhelmed human beings, who are hooked on opportunities to be overwhelmed because they have no idea of what a work is and what being carried away by that which is unavoidable makes possible. That the majority in cities are also not merely dispersed, but have duties and must face emergencies [*Ernstfällen*] both privately and publicly—the philosopher of gathering will know nothing of this. For this reason he remains in the province where he wants to belong, where he celebrates the fact that he has stuck to the matter of native-uncanny Being [*heimatlich-unheimlichen Seins*].

In this respect, Heidegger, the one who remains there, is a thinker in inhibited, restricted, reserved motion. That is the reason why one can learn nothing from him about the movement of existence in world-opening relocations and departures, or rather can only learn something about this *ex negativo*. The thinker in motion, strangely enough, hardly has a word to say about that which is binding in research, travel, and experimentation, about making friends, undertaking business ventures, working something out, about reformatting and translating, about connecting texts and traditions, or forming alliances and teams. With this attitude, he is only one among many critics of modernity who let an inexperienced and hostile silence be heard when it comes to speaking about our best powers: about bricolage, intersection, collation, compromise,[29] the whole spectrum of operations that constitute organized knowledge as a profession and community building as a social plastic art. Heidegger's depth is without breadth. Lateral movement interests him as little as advancing on a level surface. He has no theory of research and no positive idea of the encyclopedia. One is able to hear his stunning variations on the philosophical Axis Powers, namely, Greece and Germany, yet no word on other fatherlands of reason, and only a little on other primordial regions of reflection. All of these sources of multiplicity disturb his adherence to essentialization, gathering, and being taken. For him, experience as such is already too covered with ontological dust, with contingency that cannot be taken up.[30] Whoever seeks experience is seen by the thinker as already pulled into the undertow that draws one into that which is arbitrary. But to the extent that Heidegger presents himself as indifferent to horizontal movement he squanders the chance to say something fitting about a motif that urgently concerns him from out of the matter of thinking. Hence as an onto-kineticist he has only done half the work. Certainly, he spoke monotonously, like no other, of going on the path and of leaping into the open, yet that always holds only for the place among beings where his birth had thrown him. His 'paths' are supposed to lead nowhere else than where existence already is in each case. When Heidegger uses the metaphor of the path, even this is to undermine the sense for directions that point elsewhere. He leaves aside the pull of historical departure into the expanse and into what is farther yet, as though it were something that does not concern him. To the end he limits himself to interpreting the ethos of moved Dasein as a 'sojourn' in an assigned location within the world. He takes the homeland to already be so deep that a single lifetime is not enough to reach it. Hölderlin's words, that spirit loves a colony, and his other statement, that yearning always seeks the unbound[31]—remain dead letters for the man from Messkirch. Sometimes he deigns to insinuate that love is a kind of being enamored which draws human beings into the expanse, indeed uncovers for them beings as a whole in a certain attunement. But he does not encounter real strangers, empirically distant others, by an extraversion of his own. He finds human beings in an almost exclusively indirect way via the equipment that points to them and to which they belong. In order to have an experience with them others must have already moved toward him. When Buddhism, in the form of Japanese visitors, comes to his house he offers it the right of hospitality. On the other hand, the love of space as decisive movement, the trip as a proper accomplishment of life, which heads out and meets up with strangers as other, the main journey outward, the exodus to a (better) land, even ? different becoming an adult on other continents—none of that is Heidegger's thing. Whoever would like to portray this as an advantage could point to the fact that such thinking cannot be bent on conquest and proselytization because it is constituted in an anti-expansive fashion, corresponding to its reflective and gathering pull. It would be, according to its nature, a thinking for a post-proselytizing, post-scientistic, post-universalistic, post-voluntarist epoch. But there is no such epoch.

We understand that, for Heidegger the thinker, the dimension of the city remains inaccessible, because he lacks a theory of experience or of horizontal movement. Hence, he also cannot have a theory of knowledge or of the sciences. The verb 'thinking' is reserved for the reflection attained in plummeting and its reversal. Hence the dictum: "Science does not think"—and how could it, since it moves entirely within the horizontal? To be sure, for him, the sciences do take part in entanglement in a certain way, insofar as one can go astray precisely in experience and in abstraction, but how this would lead to a turn or a decided turning against their own operation must remain unclear for the time being. The direct opposition of science and reflection initially affords no help to the sciences. Heidegger mistrusts experience as the lure of the arbitrary, which permeates the sciences just as it governs the cities and directs the masses. Since he cannot move to the city, he at no point in time achieves the urban idea of the political, because for him the political mainly belongs to experience and its 'non-essence [*Unwesen*].' For him, the factors of political life—competition as the encounter of free rivals, the society of friends, the play of polyphonic opinions at the market and in the public assembly[32]—remain alien from the ground up.

These findings draw narrow limits on all attempts to read a 'political philosophy' into Heidegger's work. When Heidegger becomes political, he does so in an unpolitical, a pre- and extra-urban way. The word that seizes hold of him is extra-parliamentary and supra-parliamentary. In his appearance the disposition of an aristocracy of the knowing, which is of Platonic provenance, is mingled with the pride of the older German professoriate in its extraterritoriality vis-à-vis princely power and popular opinion. The only access to the political realm that is opened up to Heidegger is through the state of exception in which, so he believes, the declaration of a common state of emergency would bring an end to private, corporative, and party-political talking past one another. The only political gesture that Heidegger has at his disposal is that of coming-forward-of-one's-own-accord in the moment of danger. Here a positive en-framing is articulated that is oriented to the works assigned by 'fate.' In this respect he indeed remains committed not to the ideas but to the emotions of 1914 when, like millions of others who were carried away at the same time, he had come forward of his own accord. Under the influence of this model of experience, the thinker, in March 1933, can remark to a female friend that he senses "an unusual gathering power" in contemporaneous political events, however much may be obscure in them as well. He believes that obligatory communal works result from the fated emergency as though of their own accord because it is the emergency that gathers the many and dictates what they are to do. The proper emergency is the true dictatress, however much her dictates ask to be carefully interpreted. Only he who has been dictated to from the highest pole—and for whom the highest resources for understanding are granted from the hermeneutic pole—can be called to become the leader [*Führer*] of emergency-altering [*notwendenden*]³³ works, for his own land, for Europe, and for the whole world that has been riven by gigantomachies.

That there could be a task here for philosophers, if indeed the role of a national security advisor of Being is to be assigned—who could blame a member of the profession for this idea? But Heidegger fails to see that, to the leader of the Germans who were brought into line under *Gleichschaltung*, things were not dictated in the way that the philosopher had anticipated. At no point in time does he grasp that the fascist politicians only 'serve' as a container for collective infatuations and as canvases for self-fabricated projections onto them—yet as long as the thinker himself is acutely endangered by self-infatuations and projections he cannot recognize the bloated character of the 'movement.' The difference between the state of exception and infatuation remains unclear to him for a while. Thus it was able to happen to the philosopher that when he wanted to be summoned by the German and European emergency it was only infatuation that had called him. In any case, from 1934 on it is evident to him that the supposed 'people's community' is philosophically useless and must be replaced by another guarantor of commitment, a community of the artwork, let us say, or a gathering of recipients of signs from concealment that has emerged into unconcealment. The essay on the artwork is the testament to this change. Still, Heidegger's 'politics,' both earlier and later, continue to have either a supra-political or a sub-political quality. Whoever seeks a theory of the political in Heidegger will find a poetics of the state of emergency.[34]

I am not saying that these moments of narrowness and failed attempts would have been completely incomprehensible. In all of their circuitousness, not getting the matter at hand, and ineptitude, they pretty much reflect the ordinary fate of German professors in the first half of the twentieth century. This becomes extraordinary by the fact that it belongs at the same time to the endgames of heroism, whose passing takes shape in as convoluted a fashion as did that of the classical metaphysics of ancient Europe. Heidegger's lapses would be fatal for philosophy under the assumption that one could not find what is missing and what corrects for this elaborated elsewhere. The gap would be disastrous if (among a number of others whose strengths lay where Heidegger's gaps yawned) Ernst Bloch had not existed, Heidegger's contemporary from the decade of Expressionism and his genuine antipode in philosophical matters. With as much conceptual intensity as sensitivity to image and sound, Bloch developed a philosophy of experience and departure that Heidegger neither wanted nor was capable of. Bloch also develops a political ontology of the state of emergency, which admittedly is a permanent one in class societies and gives rise to a continual influx of emergency-altering phantasms into cultural and political happenings. In response to the pressure of the emergency, he expects that it might be transformed into a propulsive moment in the history of the species by means of the power of dreams and judgment belonging to collective dissatisfaction. High politics is here interpreted as the setting-into-work of anticipations of a better life. Bloch's work was set on interpreting the existence of human beings in their essential history, the time of exodus, entirely from the second mode of movement, from the impulse forward that is nourished by dissatisfaction and opulence—all the way to the entry of the entire species into its planetary commune at the promised end time that was the goal all along, a commune which he wanted to recognize as the first true community. Bloch's strength as an ontologist of movement lay in the fact that he merged experience with the turn or revolution— differently from Heidegger, who was only able to think the plunge together with the turn or the counterturn. Here as there, philosophical thinking is calibrated by that which is most extreme and most serious. Hence it is typical for Heidegger to lament the emergency of the lack of emergency, the meaning of which amounts to: those who plunge for the most part have not been shaken enough to be blessed with an actual alteration of emergency [Not-Wende]; while for Bloch it remains characteristic that he points to the emergency of false alterations of emergency that lead more often to a right turn than to a left turn. The errancies of those who go astray on such levels quickly become extreme. Those to whom Heidegger's grotesque overinterpretations of National Socialist pseudo-communitarianism appear reprehensible will be just as little prepared to endorse Bloch's somnambulantly perverse *ubi Lenin ibi patria*.[35] When Heidegger and Bloch once met as older men at a podium the two metapoliticians could almost only speak of minor issues. The poets of the extreme were both too shy to come to an understanding on their division of labor.

4. The Turn

Ladies and gentlemen, I am now coming to the conclusion and thus, if one may believe the title of this lecture, to the main point. I want to say a few words about the third mode of existence assailed by movement, that is, about reversal, the turn, revolution. Only in regard to this motif can we finally explain what it is that the synchronous perspective makes visible in the Heideggerian structure of movement. Here again we encounter—as in the case of his analysis of the fall and the plunge—a Heidegger at a singular height. Here, he is the thinker who had no interlocutor among his contemporaries in the twentieth century. When the middle Heidegger begins to think the movement of Dasein within the reversal or the turn, he enters into a dialogue with his only two equals in the Western tradition: he finds himself, beyond modernity and the Middle Ages, alone with Plato and alone with Augustine. Only with them could he come to his principal issue, to the question concerning the third of the essential features of Dasein's motion; only with them is there to be talk of movement as countermovement and gathering back in that which is authentic in the manner in which this theme must be talked about— cautiously, rigorously, perseveringly, and with the awareness that here we are dealing with what is most extreme.

Indeed, only in conversation with Plato can the question of the turn to truth be retrieved, a question that the founder of the Academy had laid out in his teaching; and only in conversation with Augustine can it be clarified in the manner of a retrieval why our heart must be restless until it should find rest in the great Other. Plato, Augustine, and Heidegger are the only thinkers who, with a fundamental conceptual seriousness, have accounted for the fact that 'revolution' takes place in Being itself. The connection between Being and revolution is such a deep one for all of them that it is almost impossible to say what truth is without having to first say what revolution, reversal, and conversion are. Neither in Plato, nor in Augustine, nor in Heidegger can there be talk of a turning in truth or a turning toward truth without an upheaval of the total sense of Being.

Thus the observation is justified that for these thinkers the sense of Being cannot be expressed without regard for a 'counter-turning' or 'revolutionary' movement. Plato, like Augustine and Heidegger, proceeds from the fact that human beings 'initially and for the most part' live away from the truth and are caught up in an immemorial drift into error and endarkenment. In their eyes, erring is the most primordial possibility of Dasein, and not only in the sense that human beings can be 'doxically' on the false path in regard to this or that issue and of most things understand nothing, but also in such a way that they find themselves altogether in a false position and to a certain degree stand with their backs to authentic reality and truth. When Heidegger notes that "the human being is the *away* [*das* Weg]"[36] or that "Dasein . . . in falling, 'lives' *away from itself*"[37] (in the language of the early work: existence that is falling prey already has of its own accord the character of an evasion and a "flight"),[38] he ought to know that, over the graves that separate the moderns from the ancients, he has the two old masters at his side. For them erring is the first movement—above, we character-ized this primordial pull into that which is false as falling or as the plunge into dispersal. Human beings could correct their divagating propulsion in the stream of untruth only through an integral turn in the drift, a change of direction in the pull of their Dasein as a whole. Only after such a fundamentally precipitous reversal would they be in the position to turn to the source of truth again, living against the life they had lived to that point and thinking upstream. When one philosophizes in this way, knowledge is first and foremost a matter of revolution—it depends on a crisis of movement that is as difficult as it is important for salvation. In this crisis it is decided whether human beings will continually drift further away or whether they will find their way 'back' to the true relation.

Plato's revolution means a reversal of the soul or guiding it to turn around—in Greek, *periagōgē*. It implies nothing less than the total reversal of the direction of life's journey. Whoever recalls Plato's allegory of the cave knows what that means. There we are asked to imagine what would happen if the slaves in the cave who are physically bound and beguiled by the appearances projected on the wall, everyday human beings in the agora, and users of media who are dependent upon rumor were unchained, turned around, and led out to the cave's exit. If this were the first time they made their way to the exit, they would for better or worse note there the mechanism for the production of appearances and thus suddenly realize that they had fallen for mere projections. What has our life been to this point?—a blundering about in sensuous delusions, an illustrated illusion, a binge-watching of videos that signify the world. How is that possible? It is possible and does not cease to be the most powerful possibility of all because according to Plato all appearances in the world, all images, sights, and sensuous things are produced by a mental projector, which casts ideas onto canvases of mobile matter, thus onto bodies. The world as a whole—this much becomes clear after the illuminating reversal—is a totalitarian simulation. Existence is the acquired incapacity for beholding the ideas. It banishes us to internment, half phantasmagoria and half detention camp. If one breaks free of the play of images and seeks a way out of the cave of projections into the open air, then near the exit one passes by an *eidos*-projector, at the sight of which we finally realize: so that's how appearances are made! The smaller source of light in the cave's interior, i.e., fire, is, along with the archetypical objects that pass by, responsible for the shadows that signify the world. But the fact that this fire itself is only light from the light that stems from the sun of the Good, this is something which one only gains an intimation of outside in the open air, when after stepping out from the cave's exit one becomes aware of the sun itself. We can say that the Platonic reversal is an event that is carried out in two stages. In the first step, it draws attention to the human intellect, which fabricates truths for everyday life (even the modern critique of knowledge retains this much from the Platonic break with naivety); from the second step on it points the way to the transcendent intellect, that which is radiantly true in itself, which inundates the finite intellect from above with a limitless shower of light (modern thought has for the most part let this portion of the idealist lesson fall to the wayside).

The allegory of the cave aims at liberation through a critique of knowledge. According to Plato, through the turn that leads out of the cave, one learns the truth about appearances and is radically turned around. Whoever undergoes this has the experience of how a revolutionary irony overcomes him. Then the knower almost automatically joins the ranks of an ironic world-revolution that we know under the stale name of idealism. If, following Plato, the philosopher also plays the pedagogue, then what he actually wants to be is a periagogue, someone who turns souls around. The ordinary guides for children, teachers and others who also take money bring young people where they for the most part want to go anyway, to career stages and the orator's rostrum. The one who philosophically turns children around directs them to a goal that they did not initially strive for, because on their own they could not have gained

an intimation of what is there for them to be achieved. He is a psy-
chagogue who leads his pupils to the love of 'truth.' He familiarizes
them with the light shows of the *a priori* by releasing in them an
insurmountable irony toward the entangled, stupefied, possessed
life that is supposedly one's own. He does all that by informing them
of the other side of the images, their eidetic mechanisms. Let us note
that Schopenhauer still evoked this radically ironic level when he
put on record that the doctrines of Plato, Shankara, and his own
philosophy at bottom said one and the same thing.

With regard to Heidegger, when he reads Plato's doctrine of truth
it is not with a free eye but rather with a Catholic lens that has
been monastically ground, an Augustinian lens. Plato's idealist-
revolutionary irony is completely lost in the gloom of Augustine's
theological interpretation of world history. Augustine, too, thinks
of the world as an errancy in which the truth that was lost early on
only again breaks through by means of a late, saving turnaround.
Since the Fall, thus almost from the beginning, human beings have
propagated in their bloody cities and empires like a phony but
relentless procession in space and time. Everything that procreates,
kills, and expands itself is a descendant of Adam and an heir of
Cain. Only in Orthodox Judaism does a glimmer of undistorted life
smolder among Abel's offspring. For Augustine, God's incarnation
in the midst of the flood of peoples and empires is the revolutionary
axis; only he gives, potentially, another direction to the compulsive
and murderous parade.

Naturally, the God-Man's revolution far exceeds the revolution
through theory, since a saving turnaround is not to be accomplished
by a mere critique of knowledge, with a merely philosophical ascent
to the highest principle, with a merely analytic peep behind the
apparatus of images or a merely ironic deification of the one who
knows. That at least is Augustine's belief; this gives him a feeling
of superiority over the most elevated passages of ancient wisdom.
He purports to know that his revolution, the Christian one, is the
true one because it is of greater scope than that of the philosophers.
His worldly point of departure is not, as with Plato, ignorance, but
rather despair. Because he is permeated by despair and because he
allows himself to be completely influenced by it, Augustine reaches
the conviction that human beings must be not enlightened but rather
redeemed. Redemption is the gambit of a deeper revolution. Viewed
from this perspective, the virtues of the ancients are in fact merely
glittering vices, as theological jargon puts it, and their knowledge is
only an elegantly concealed ignorance. Incidentally, it would be rash
to believe that the surpassing of philosophy by 'true religion' has
become irrelevant in the post-Christian situation. In the twentieth

century, especially in the Jewish renaissance, 'true religion' answered back with the claim to once more surpass the philosophical mythos of truth with the ethical mythos of communication or justice.

Augustine thinks of world history as a process of double turns that is to be portrayed in terms of the conceptual pair, conversion and perversion. Perversion signifies the initial turning away from the loving devotion of all life to its divine origin, a turning away that carries out the earliest revolt, thus the turning from the center and the orientation to an epicenter that, after the contortion, has been warped toward itself. How does this happen? Satan, the radiant angel, gazes into the mirror and considers himself to be objectively, overwhelmingly beautiful—and why not, since nothing in him is to be found other than what shares in the best? Yet, in his turning out well, he wants to acquire a piece of private property. He would like to take his image into possession like a bit of start-up capital in order to emerge magnificently as his own master. Consequently, he will seal himself up within himself and begin anew on his own, without God. By sealing himself up he turns his back on the origin, on the common ground of the Being and happiness of all creatures. From then on he lives in despair, which is expressed as the wish to radiate in and of himself. This turning away from what is better is the Devil's motion; it provides the archetype of contrived, false countermovement as the self-privileging of a creature that once belonged together with its Other, with its origin. Egotism begins with self-warping, and with inherited egotism begins the history of perdition.[39] Thenceforth, all human beings strive after untruth, as though by nature.

According to Augustine, world history is what results from all local movements of the Devil, or the self-regard of individuals who imitate the First Egotist. Whoever has been seized by the initial misdirected movement, i.e., according to the opinion of the Church Fathers, naturally begotten humanity as a whole, remains by virtue of the original perversion caught up in an overpowering motion away from God. That brings about a fundamental relationship that goes by the name of *peccatum originale*, or the first secession or turning away from the initial, common good. Sin is not only a moral affair but also and just as much a kinetic one. It carries out the 'away from the good!' and initiates the malign turning toward the divided self.

It is decisive for Augustine that this secession can no longer be overcome by the fallen human being through his own power. The separation from God is an act whose result, i.e., separateness, turns into a fixation for human beings. Whatever they subsequently undertake, whether it be intended for better or worse, always drives them further away. Even if they clearly were to feel that they were on the false path they would no longer know how to find the right one on their own—or if they did find it they would still not know how to proceed upon it. They never again emerge 'of their own volition' from the tendency toward separation. Being drawn into perversion, self-concern, and the fury of obstinacy are stronger than every remorse, every homesickness, even in human beings with the best of intentions. Humanity before Christ thus drifts ever deeper into a hopeless situation. It is forcibly pulled into the maelstrom of sexuality and into the conduct of violent peoples. That would continue until the end of the political and sexual cataract, until the last act of procreation, until the last corrupt birth, until the last war between states, if the abandoned God had not resolved to do what was necessary for the repatriation of his creatures who had turned away from him.

For Augustine, 'true religion' emerges from God's intervention into the perverted course of the world. In this way, and only in this way, does a reversal, a conversion, *metanoia* become possible. God himself is the subject of the countermovement, for if human beings could convert to the faith that emerges as true 'after Christ,' this is not because they would have changed on their own but rather because God would have helped provide for their conversion from out of their perversion. If human beings succeed in finding their way back to the belief in the God of truth, the success of this capacity for belief—and theologians following in Augustine's footsteps to the present day assure us of this—is in no way the personal contribution of the subject willing to believe, but rather an effect of God, who allows belief in him.

Here the fundamental term of Augustinian theology, i.e., grace, becomes operative. Grace is the emanation of a divine subjectivity that supersedes or mediates human will by giving it what it cannot achieve on its own. It allows what human capacity and human will cannot make happen. It triggers the countermovement that could never again have come about in the tendency of the first movement as such.

The concept (or the model) of grace returns in Heidegger—transformed into the kinetic schema of releasement [*Gelassenheit*]. As little as grace can be compelled by the mere demand for it, so little is it within the discretionary power of the human being to will to make himself serenely released. Nonetheless, grace cannot be granted without an appropriate human effort in regard to it, and release-ment is unattainable without an intense loosening of the subject. Heidegger devotes an abundance of monotonous thoughts to it that revolve around the motif of the 'transition' to another attitude. Thus not only does grace return in Heidegger—the theocentric figure of movement does, too: 'God lets conversion happen' is rewritten as the centerpiece of the Heideggerian doctrine of the turn. Only the turn turns; the countermovement has its pivot in Being. It is only the availability of being taken along by the countermovement that has been granted that allows the human being to reach his 'ownmost possibility': to reach resolve, being seized in a valid way, the gathering, the revolution, the work, authentic poetry, the primordial intimacy of strife, 'the counter-resonance in Beyng [*Seyn*],' to reach ultimately even sparing protection [*Schonung*], 'the mirror-play of the fourfold' and 'authentic way-making movement [*Be-wëgung*].'[40] The names for the motifs of turning things around are so numerous because to the end Heidegger considers ever-new interpretations of the movement that offsets the plummet. He remains perpetually searching for something that would be deeper, more comprehensive, and more appropriate for Being than any revolution that is understood profanely. The motif of counter-turning, as we have seen, is already formally in play from the time the young Heidegger pressed for becoming authentic [*Vereigentlichung*]. It is realized in a politically somnambulant way as long as the thinker believes that he can insert into the 'national revolution' his own prompting to be carried along by an affirmable world-fate. It increases in volume and radicality when the thinker, disappointed by the National Socialist movement, begins to teach that it is no longer a matter of issuing new directives, predictably in vain, to a 'deadlocked human drive,' but rather that what counts is to prepare an integral "*dislodging* of the human"[41]—whereby for a while the gesture of the 'leap' was supposed to indicate how releasing oneself to being carried along could be effected by an occurrence of turning. The meditation on the counter-turn achieves its most clarified form in the late work, when existence is supposed to will nothing other than its serenely released deliverance [*gelassene Übereignung*] to the 'appropriative event [*Ereignis*].' The expression 'releasement' now stands for a guided and affiliated freedom that escapes arbitrariness. It would be that freedom that does not remain ironically underwhelmed and hollowly self-referential alongside or above everything, but rather that lets that which is encompassing and binding tell it what is to be done. Hence it can now be maintained that authentic thinking is on the "way into the 'underway.'"[42] Heidegger sometimes speaks as though, in his own case, the "actual proper movement on the way" turned out successfully for him.[43] At this stage philosophy as such is overcome as well—insofar as it still remains caught up in the business of the will to provide foundations. The turn to kinetics as 'first theory'—which is latent in the thinker's work from the beginning—

is explicitly carried out. It points out or declares how the human being, together with everything that is present in him, belongs to a game that gives and takes, disperses and gathers together, clears and conceals. (Levinas will later present an ethically emphatic version of this belonging [*Angehören*] that parades above all a 'hearkening [*Zugehörigkeit*]' to the plea of the Other in need.) If the mythos of Heidegger's 'path of thought,' which was cultivated by Heidegger himself and repeated by exegetes and philologists, still gives some insight into his work process, then it is in the progressive abandonment of the will as an agent of reversal—beginning with the heroic apprehension of the self that was demanded at the outset, mediated by the 'leap' into 'belonging to [*Zugehörigkeit*] the appropriative event,' intensified by the will to non-willing, and ending with the inclusion in the play of the 'fourfold,' which turns this way and that according to its own laws, and with the gathering power of the 'region.' Where, initially, it appeared that reversal could be compelled by a decisive application of oneself [*Selbstverwendung*] for revolutionary authenticity, later it is emphasized with increasing insistence that the human being as an agent of the reversal is never under consideration. For, if the agent were at the helm, then irony would remain in power as the actual mistress, who haphazardly turns to the tasks she has 'set' for herself, only to turn away from them just as haphazardly. In the end, even in Heidegger, as with the African church father, human obstinacy and the will are supposed to relax and adjust themselves to a letting be that has been allowed by Being [*ein vom Sein zugelassenes Lassen*]. Heidegger's pastoral has its place here: in order to become the shepherd of Being the human being must guard against his own non-releasement [*Ungelassenheit*]. Only after overcoming self-assertiveness can he correspond to Being, which gives itself over to his protection. The saving power—if indeed it does save—occurs in an essentially tardy manner even for the philosopher, such that one day he will look back at his decisionistic years like Augustine at his youth before conversion—was all this not just a *praeparatio philosophica* decreed long ago? As Augustine at the turning point of his life's story recognizes the epochal transition from paganism to Christianity, so Heidegger sees in his own 'path of thought' that is pregnant with error and yet still chosen the hinge for the turn from the epoch of the forgetting of Being to preparing for a renewed recollection of Being. What was the story of a life becomes transposed, here as there, into a salvation-historical or onto-historical wide photo shot, to the discomfort of those for whom such elevations of self-modesty appear to be presumptuous. In any case, Augustine is at an advantage over Heidegger in the fact that he carried out retractions of his writings *coram Deo et publico*, while Heidegger tended to rewrite rather than to reexamine his ambiguities. Nevertheless, after everything that has been traversed, that which is one's 'own' can only be attained by the one who knows how to wait until it is 'fatefully sent.' Only what is more primordial than the human being, thus the certainty which has ultimately been filtered out, may bring about the countermovement to the fateful drift in human constructs.

Heidegger's late style leaves no doubt that he regarded himself as the favorite of the reversal sent by Being. Even when he stubbornly presents himself as an assistant and as someone who merely prepares the way, his language betrays him as someone who discovered and was discovered *in propria persona*. The sojourn in a chosen preserve has come into being from out of thrown Being-in-the-world. And so, as Augustine had already answered the Christian question in such a way that something like a homeland was possible even in the midst of the human being's homelessness in the world, insofar as he summoned a monastic community on the fringes of the Roman Empire to life—a monastic community which still exists today—so too does the late Heidegger as a wanderer and a meditator found a reflective habitus that determines the rules of the order of the so-called 'fourfold,' rules of an order that is oriented to a carefully protected nature, an order that reclaims the 'region' for its saved-saving [*geheilt-heilenden*] sojourn within it. If it were up to the founder, even things and the gods would have to keep to the law of this strict idyll. Here a tendency toward pure ministering can be fulfilled. In the meditative preserve, human beings voluntarily behave as weakly as they did before the introduction of advanced technology. The second impotence, so its representatives believe, complies with the new turn toward Beyng. Now it can be understood why it is still ultimately Catholic theologians who find a formalization of their mode of belief in Heidegger's late writings.

5. The Twist

The modern world considers what concerns the human being's voluntarily accomplished reversal to be its most powerful word for movement: revolution. But Heidegger, who reads Plato's doctrine of truth with the eyes of Augustine in his theology of conversion, meanwhile knows (though, as I said, not from the start, but only after his own failed attempt to be a partisan of the supposedly fateful national revolution and its 'labor,' its 'work') how things stand with the subjective, agitated revolutions compelled by the will. His own errant devotion to a false emissary opened his eyes to the ontological quality of total revolutions in practice: however they proceed, they always end up in the most recent chapter of the drift toward perversion. In contrast, according to a later insight, salvation—or its preparation—can only lie in letting-be and waiting, along with letting sentences that have been fatefully sent resound. "We never come to thoughts. They come to us."[44]

For secular ears, that is difficult to hear. And yet, in the Augustinian interpretations of human hustle and bustle in the worldly community, an experience resonates that can also get under the skin of twentieth-century activists who have become reflective. In this epoch that has unprecedented faith in agents the question was indeed always formulated anew: who or what is the true subject of the emergency-altering revolution? All answers ended up doubling the problems for which they arose as solutions. Is it the working masses, is it the party? Is it the people, is it the race? Is it intellectuals, is it the marginalized? Is it women, is it the Green Party? Whatever was suggested and orchestrated, it was always the old Adam, the human being in the familiar drift, the human being who knows nothing new, who comes forth and exposes himself in his upheavals. We have seen the underside of the revolutionaries. Ambivalence has swallowed everything and spat it back up again.

Since 1945, the axiom of the so-called postmodern situation has exposed for anyone who wished to know: that nothing actually begins and that nothing actually ends. We are finished with nothing, we bring nothing new into existence. There is no *ancien régime* and no New Society. There is neither a true origin nor an authentic retrieval. All the way to the end there are no cuts; nowhere do radical discontinuities emerge. What remains are approaches, mixtures, transitions, shifts, reflections, series, drifts. As far as the eye can see, similarity rules the scene. What used to be called the *juste milieu* has now become the *juste mélange*. The center relies on unlimited combination. Of course, other differences emerge that are big enough to battle for the better state of affairs, differences such as that between open societies and tyrannies, between just and unjust distributions of goods and opportunities, between free expression and being compelled to lie, between art and deterioration—without these differences there would no longer be goals orienting our action at all. But, in the future, where should a more encompassing, 'fundamental' turn, a difference about the whole, come from? Who would form the subject or emissary of a turn that would be more than a private conversion, a localized counter-steering or a collective evasion? What could again reverse the prevailing sense of Being, which amounts above all to the distortion and ultimate consumption of everything? The answer that Augustine had to give is

obvious: the decisive turn was God's revolution and this took place
for all time. Whoever participated in it would be sheltered, to the
extent possible, from the prevailing meaninglessness. But what if
this turn from above did not help the world in its profane plunge? If
even the turn devours its children? If Rome's perspective, to put it
harshly, was clerical fascism? If Geneva's perspective was puritanical paranoia? If Wittenberg's perspective was the helpless private
religion that still cowers under the worst authority? Admittedly,
Augustine would have pointed out that the upheaval of the world's
course by the incarnation of the Son of God only provisionally had
a mundane sense. Indeed, he would have revealed in his inmost
circle that in God's revolution at best only a few chosen individual
souls are saved from the depraved multitude, while the world and its
corrupt human cargo are on the whole something that is not to be
retained even by the creator.

However, when modern thinkers of upheaval, whether therapists of alienation, world-revolutionaries, mythologists of Being,
or Critical Theorists, spoke of countermovement and otherness
they did not think of chosen individuals who would be spared
from universal entanglement and blindness. They were concerned
with a kind of movement that would come to the aid of human
world-productions as a whole in their vile course. They intended a
countermovement that would remove the destructive pull from the
current drift. Here the question must have impressed itself upon
them of whether the world's process in general can be controlled
by activity.[45] Insofar as they more or less unconditionally affirmed
this, the ideologists of praxis authorized leading roles for themselves
in the activist century's theater of revolution. The catastrophic
results of these authorizations are presently being drawn up. Yet
although the disillusionment regarding high-strung concepts of
action is well advanced, most of those who are not resigned today
still agree in conceiving the survival of the world as something that
depends on 'true' countermovements.

The world deserves a turn—who can give it one? The course of
the world needs profound corrections—from where can they come?
Before making any effort to give a concrete answer, whoever has
learned to mistrust the conceptual figures of total politics will pose a
counter-question: what kind of turn are we talking about here? What
does the expression 'true movement' imply? How is this demand for
total upheaval justified? Isn't it time to put these fatal singulars out
to pasture? Where the saving power comes to the fore doesn't the
danger increase, too? Don't we have to beware every expertocracy
of salvation above all else? The rightness of these objections ought
not to be contested, and yet: they cannot permanently mask the

lack of response. On the whole, they only increase the ambivalence. In the twilight where indifference encounters polysemy any distinction between true and false movements seems to have vanished. We participate in mass sports but have no idea of the movement that would aid the world as such. There are extreme athletes but no longer any credible revolutionaries. The intelligentsia of the late twentieth century must have seen that revolution was no longer the right name for the true countermovement. The list of disappointments is so long because being tempted by total politics bore many names: it was not the revolution of councils, it was not the conservative revolution, it was not the national revolution, it is certainly not the permanent revolution of the process of capital. The Green Party difference seems to have been leveled before it could even have a chance to be a turning force. Whatever was undertaken in the gestures of total politics was always just false and more than false. That which discrete politics was capable of remained at best ambiguous and polysemous. What names, then, could still today, after everything, bear an integral turn or the sum of individual corrections that would restore to the world's course a certain orientation to 'truth' (be it only in the minimal sense of delayed self-destruction)?

Heidegger's late disclosure, that only a god can save us, only makes clear once again that for him the human being as the subject of the turn does not come in for further questioning. But perhaps a crypto-Catholic and final metaphysician cannot speak otherwise. For minds of such provenance, everything right up to the very end hinges on what is entirely other and one, that is, the last great singular. But where should someone who does not accept Heidegger's answer seek the pivot for a possible turn of the world's course in realms that can be experienced in praxis? How should we think of a cooperation with something that could still be of help?

Ladies and gentlemen, now coming definitively to the end, I would like to indicate at least an indirect answer to these questions. To this end it is necessary to recall an adventure of movement that I believe was the most momentous one to occur in the history of Europe's intellectual endeavors. When, led by Portuguese sailors, the Europeans began to look out toward the Atlantic in the fifteenth century and began to think beyond it to a virtually different coast of the ocean, the seemingly insurmountable problem arose for them that one could indeed allow oneself to be carried away from Europe's western coast by familiar winds to the open sea, but then, by any human reckoning, there would no longer be a way to turn back to home port. Faced with this difficulty a thought occurred to the Portuguese *marinheiros*, to the ship captains in the time of Henry the Navigator, a thought of which one says too little if one calls it a

bold idea. Observed from a historical distance, it is the most unsettling thought of modernity, the most propulsive idea outside of the
religious domain, the most ingenious and dangerous notion ever
conceived by modern Europeans. The Portuguese sailors became
engaged, in a metaphorical and real sense, to the prevailing winds.
They devoted themselves—first in thoughts, then in actual ships—to
the breezes that continually blow out from Europe's western coast
to the ocean. With them they transgressed the limit beyond which
there can no longer be any reasonable hope for a return and let
themselves be borne into the open by trade winds in an uncondi-
tional commitment of their ships and their life.

In the midst of maneuvering, the sailors were seized by the insight
into the movement of the winds over the north Atlantic. They began
to understand, at first intuitively but later in an experienced, practical
manner and later still in a theoretical sense, that the Euro-American
winds form a system. Over the north Atlantic there revolves, mostly
in a clockwise direction, a whirling of air masses that produces
in more southern latitudes a relatively constant current from the
northeast and elicits in more northern latitudes a continuous, often
stormy western current. The European television viewer today sees
this structure in their so-called weather reports on almost a daily
basis from the perspective of satellites, without suspecting that they
have the climatic-political secret of globalization before their eyes.
In order for the wind to air their sails, the *marinheiros* of the fifteenth
century had to plummet into the invisible whirling vortex [*Wirbel*]
and expose themselves to its motion, come what may. "At the same
time, turbulence [*Wirbel*] makes manifest that the thrownness . . .
has the character of throwing and of movement."[46] It was their
idea, which gradually became clear, to drift out to sea for as long
as it took until, vertiginously far afloat after a tenaciously adhered
to western course before the northeastern trade wind, they pushed
forward into the western wind zones of the Atlantic, from which the
wind's propulsion would allow them to return home again.

This bold maneuver, which was soon so common that hardly
anyone noticed it except for captains, received a sonorous name
from the Portuguese sailors: *volta do mar*, the sea's about-face. It
is the turn on the high seas, so to speak. One can say of this turn
that, through it, the practical potential of Heidegger's philosophy of
movement was realized on board a ship. Complying with the wind
and being exposed to the play of its laws were responsible for the
fact that, from journeys into the open sea, the whole model of the
journey there and back again was able to come about.[47] Without
the sea's about-face America would not have been discovered by
Europeans; without it and its inverse application for the Southern

Ocean there would have been no European navigation of the world and thus no globalization of world commerce from European centers, no immigration of Europeans to the two Americas, no colonization of Australia, no Spaniards in the Philippines and Mexico, no Portuguese in Goa, no Dutch in Sumatra, no English in Africa and India. Without it there would have been no British Empire and no Anglophone commonwealth on every continent, also no United States of America. In short, without the maneuver of the sea's about-face there would not be a modern Europe and a New World as they have appeared over the last half millennium.

Far be it from me to glorify the expired Eurocentric era. Remembering that a nautical figure of speech, which inspired sailors and made philosophers wonder, lies at the center of terrestrial globalization, in which the earth was elaborated as a geological monad, belongs to a full critique of this epoch. The *volta do mar* embodies the main features of Dasein in motion—letting oneself fall into the initial tendency, egress into the expanse, the deliberate turn that brings back. It appears to respond from a distance to the doctrine of the resolute non-sailor Heidegger that the turning point lies concealed at the heart of danger.

Ladies and gentlemen, I would not have recalled this history of seafarers if I did not believe that a metaphorical clue to the current world crisis is contained in it. There is today once more a neo-Portuguese intelligentsia among us that thinks out beyond to other seas to be sailed on, which are again to all appearances impossible to traverse. While the majority of human beings today in the earth's zones of affluence worry about things that correspond to the issues of a society that has remained quasi-medieval—about continual economic growth and the permanent position of businesses that are blind to consequences, about vested rights to thoughtlessly destroy and customary rights to plunder nature—the contemporary Portuguese are already occupied with a new about-face of the sea. Here it can only be a matter of a turn into which the tried and tested heritage of revolutions hitherto attempted and foundered flows—a turn of technology against technology (if you will allow the fatal singulars once more), a turn of capital against capital, a turning of war against war, an overhaul of the sciences by the sciences, a turn of the media against themselves. The turning movements achieve a complexity that goes beyond mere 'upheaval.' Inversions super-sede the revolutions that are seen to be impossible and unfruitful. Twists take the place of reversals; with them a new dimension of kinetic intelligence becomes visible. Through the concept of the *twist* [Verwindung],[48] which was introduced late and remained obscure, Heidegger gave an indication of a fourth kind of movement that goes beyond the play of the first three. Only with it could kinetic thinking be adequate to the demands of complexity.

One will say that this is all too difficult for human beings. It is characteristic of *marinheiros* that they do not believe in talk of tasks that are too difficult. In their experience tasks are not given if solutions are not provided by the state of things. The ocean only became a problem through its answer, the sea-faring ship. The sailors of the future will navigate in contexts in which there can no longer be revolutions of the old style, but rather instances of unscrewing oneself from ossified and distorted structures and ways of running counter to deaf and fatal routines—movements of turning by which the sense of active, conscious, shared life in the multifariously mobilized world is necessarily changed.

Regarding Heidegger, he behaved in his province as though from there he could resist the course of the world in a manner that was at once collected and outlandish, a course which was leading ever deeper into an epochal winter. Wasn't his village a secret outpost of the *civitas Dei*? And isn't this the reason why his grave could not be located on a campus or in a city? This grave belongs to the counter-world, the nonconformist, questioning church that is concealed in the shadows of the visible, pontificating one. One could believe that Augustine of Thagaste and Heidegger of Messkirch lie at rest next to each other in a kind of counterbracing conjunction. From where they are, it is possible for one to try, in a manner that is as serenely released as is possible for intelligences who see what is immense, to wait as the unconverted world is instructed in its progressive self-annihilation. Heidegger's statement that the earth, seen in terms of the history of Being, is the "errant star" also seems to be spoken from this reserve. It is the star that is missing the turn. In another passage, from Heidegger's 1947 collection of sayings, *Aus der Erfahrung des Denkens* [From the Experience of Thinking], one finds the obscure line: "To head toward a star—this only."[49] Perhaps these two statements give us the code word for a maneuver yet to be attempted: follow the star, reach the earth.

2

LUHMANN, DEVIL'S ADVOCATE

Of Original Sin, the Egotism of Systems, and the New Ironies

Among the features of modern theorizations in the human and social sciences, there is one that stands out ever more noticeably: the increasing demands on the contemporaneity of their audience. Thus in the humanities, since at least the end of the Second World War, it is not merely a matter of etiquette but rather of substantive content that their representatives are compelled to note that they have made their way through the Freudian corpus. The title of a book by Jean-Bertrand Pontalis, *Après Freud* (1965), signals in a characteristic way this habit of theory's self-dating according to its position after a master. Giorgio Colli formally took the same line in his study, *Dopo Nietzsche* (1968). A series of authors from the nineteenth and twentieth centuries have likewise functioned as thresholds who imposed an obligation on those coming later to proceed from the level they had marked out: Marx, Darwin, Saussure, Heidegger, Lévi-Strauss, Adorno, Chomsky, Foucault, Girard, and others. The problem that arises in every list of this sort can easily be explained: the obligation to be connected to contemporaneous and advancing generations will be a precarious matter, and the history of the human and social sciences, with their pursuit's increasing progress, always also presents a history of refusals to be connected and a history of theoretical choices that are politically, institutionally, or personally motivated.

In the following, I would like to bring together a few arguments to show that Niklas Luhmann's work embodies a real and radical propagation of the patrimony belonging to modern theoretical culture. Luhmann is thus—however his objections against the idea of authorship may have sounded—an author in the precise sense of the word, because he made his name as a propagator of the existing stock of art achieved before him. For that reason, the expression 'after Luhmann' does not signify one of the customary dismissals of past positions in the name of a mere passage of time, but rather—of this I am certain—an authentic liminal formula. After Luhmann—that is the name for a break, an *epochē*, in the traditional sense of the word, which indicates both the caesura and also the time following it. Whoever lives after a propagator must, as a descendant, achieve something more. In the future, in order to reach the pinnacle of art, one will have to note the Luhmannian lesson. Likewise, in order to mention the magnitude of the thresholds—in whose authority in philosophical matters I believe—it will be necessary in pertinent theoretical ventures to testify that one thinks after Heidegger, after Martin Buber, after Gotthard Günther, and after Gilles Deleuze—where the first of these names stands for a movement that during this century arrived at the question of Being, the second for the opening-up of philosophical thought to the existence of the other, the third for the irruption of cybernetic logic and polyvalence into the stagnant stock of Old European bivalent reason, and the fourth for philosophy's breakthrough into the horizon of the virtual, concomitantly with the transition to the constellation of brain-and-world.

I have just now used the expression 'Luhmannian lesson,' without failing to recognize that I have thereby taken on a debt which the following reflections will hardly be able to pay. In a work of the scope treated here, it is clear from the outset that even a patient recipient can only comment on more or less private excerpts from a universe of discourse that is hardly straightforward. Only recourse to an analogy is left to us here, an analogy that I hope honors Luhmann without sickening his readers, namely the reference to the phenomenon of learning language: it is a truism that, while acquiring language, no two children in a given population are confronted with exactly the same sentence tokens, because every natural language is employed by its users in a manner that is tinged by incalculable variegation and idiolect, and additionally not seldom in an erroneous manner. Yet almost all children abstract the grammar of their native language from the most diverse collections of sentence patterns in a more or less precise way, so that they can someday approach one another as linguistic adults, at least in their milieu or their social class. Things are quite similar in the Luhmann archipelago, where on the basis of non-identical multitudes of readings one sometimes finds a kind of Luhmann grammar, on the basis of which one can communicate, albeit in a half-consonant manner, with other tourists in Luhmannland—and even a few actual inhabitants, should one encounter them.

In recognition of these difficulties and drawing on the cited grounds for hermeneutic optimism I would like to offer a few remarks for the record concerning what, in my eyes, constitutes the Luhmann event in the field of the social and human sciences and why the formulation 'after Luhmann' designates a standard, and not merely a contingent time frame after the death of a scholar.

1. Circumstance of Accusation

I thus speak of Luhmann as a devil's advocate—a formulation that allows one to surmise that I intend to map the Luhmannian impulse within the perspective of the history of morality and metaphysics, more precisely within a history of theologically determined constructions of the world-picture that was indeed interrupted by the beginning of modernity, yet has by no means reached its end. The sense of these constructions was—as remains to be shown—to hinder the reduction of worldly evil to the sphere of divine first causes by means of an overinterpretation of human freedom and the concomitant moral overburdening of the human being.

The expression 'devil's advocate,' as is well known, stems from the vocabulary of the Roman Catholic Curia, or, more precisely: it emerges from its popularization. The *advocatus diaboli* is a figure that has been translated into popular language and that derives from the Vatican's process of canonization or beatification before the Congregation of Rites. Its model is the so-called *promotor fidei*, whose task it was to put to a stern test the arguments of parties who pleaded for the canonization of someone who had passed away—a function whose ironic aspect was perceived more keenly by those in the streets and plazas of Rome who were not theologically educated than by the parties to the process, who remained caught up in the seriousness of the procedure. With the same irony, those who were on the outside labeled the role of the proponent *advocatus dei*. If one adds what is well known about popular opinion's views of lawyers, then one also knows what is necessary about the connotations of these characterizations. In any case, it is evident that the Devil must have an interest in hindering new entrants to the *communio sanctorum* in every single case—since from the adversary's perspective there is already today too great a crowd of those to whose corruption he can no longer contribute. For him each new entrant to the cloud of witnesses formed above his head is not only a nuisance, but also a compelling occasion for attempts at subversion. It is the Devil who, always with good reason, wants to prove that potential saints were not real saints—an interest that is not lacking in irony, since the agent of Hell ultimately always plays the game of the other side with his negations and subversions. He is condemned to this office, as long as he respects the prohibition on conducting the process as such *ad absurdam*—in which case the real saints would disappear with the ostensible ones. One may here perhaps draw the conclusion that the Devil is ultimately no less pious than the priest who plays his role in the process. The irony of this controversial opinion lies in the fact that the above-mentioned 'defender of the faith,' who adopts the role of a contestant, must be an especially adept theologian, since only then does the procedure for the discovery of holy or blessed dignity in a proposed candidate lead to a valid result of canonization—an early and typical kind of test, by the way, for what in later times would be known as the 'unforced force of the better argument,' though one here recognizes more clearly than in modern versions of the problem that the argument which contributes more effectively to the confirmation of the desired consensus will each time be held to be better. Here, too, consensus is always already a sacred consensus and rests on the merciful influx of a higher rationality into the terrestrial procedure. That one behaves as though one heard the arguments of the other side equally and as though consensus were the result of a procedure that reliably leads to the truth always belongs to this perspective. The piety in the procedure that is here manifested betrays the faith in processes as mechanisms of selection without fault or reproach. In them the logos itself makes the selection—and it cannot even do otherwise, because the only option still open for it is to become a process, since the option of becoming a human being has been exhausted. The faithful parties' process that is disputed in a bipolar manner before the court is a case into which the Holy Spirit, liquefied in such a manner, cannot go. He deigns on every occasion to waft within the outcome of a process, just as though he no longer bloweth where he listeth but rather where the procedure lets him.[1] For that reason, were we Catholic faithful, we might take delight in the certainty of never getting involved with the unworthy when we drew on the intercession, in our favor, of canonized saints near to God. Indeed, the procedural filter guarantees that no false saints appear in the ranks of the *communio sanctorum* that are officially listed and thus spares us diabolic simulacra, in the same way that in communications according to the Habermasian rules one may take delight in the certainty that, after the final cut, there can no longer be any dissenting theoretician, any pluralist, any constructivist, and above all any artist present in the circle of those communicating in a truly rational manner.[2]

Apart from that, there can be no doubt that the figure of the devil's advocate at the beginning of modernity was freed from Roman formalities and quite simply transformed into an emblem of useful negativity. As the *advocatus diaboli* ultimately had only one task in the process of canonization, allowing the positive affirmation in the final judgment to emerge all the more brilliantly, so the modern negative version had to prove to be a part of that power—fully employed in Germany until just recently—which continually wills evil and continually accomplishes good. This logic illuminated a contemporary German Franciscan priest to such a degree that during the Sacred Congregation of Rites of the Holy See in 1960 he requested a beatification procedure for Judas Iscariot—without whose faithful betrayal the Passion would never have occurred. We do not know how this request turned out. This proposal could have succeeded in Rome only if Hegel, Schelling, or Solovyov had been chosen to be official philosophers of the Vatican and thereby become the modern seconds of Aquinas—yet, as we know, the Holy See opted in favor of Husserl.

It requires no great effort to render plausible the reason why, in what follows, I abstract the model of the devil's advocate from its historical sources, in order to redefine it for a role within a field of problems that is described in a historically and objectively different way. It is here a matter of the opposite of procedures of canonization—namely, far-reaching procedures for accusing the race of Adam altogether—procedures in which the members of the problematic species were, from time immemorial, pressed into the position of being overcharged defendants. The trial that is at issue in the history of Christian-Western ideas, and in whose phase of revision I see Luhmann appearing as an associate defense lawyer, is nothing else than what the human being and his transcendental corrupter, the Devil, were brought to by Pauline and above all Augustinian Christianity, insofar as they described the race of mortals as creatures who were under the bondage of *peccatum originale* (or original sin) from an early moment in their history. I must emphasize that it is above all the adjective that counts in this term. For the observation that human beings are fallible creatures or that they, if you like, bear within themselves a disposition for sin and for occasional and rebellious deviation from ethical norms, a disposition for *hybris*, as the Greeks put it—this observation would be all too conventional if, on account of the addition of the adjective *originale*, it were not also maintained that a load was built into human fallibility from the beginning—thus a metaphysical legacy that would burden the *conditio humana*. From Augustinian times Christian anthropology has been characterized by a grave tendency toward hyper-culpabilization—one has long been able to state this calmly without being accused of views hostile to religion or neo-pagan slackening—moments of neurotic apologetics aside. If, along with all the well-known reasons for the modern shift away from the Old European tradition, another one is to be provided, one less noted yet very compelling, then it would undoubtedly lie in the circumstance that what has called itself the Enlightenment since the eighteenth century has carried out a permanent referendum on the de-culpabilization of the human being—or at the very least has initiated something like a petition spanning generations, which seeks a new vote on the fundamental guilt of the human being, a petition that in the interim we are able to regard as the moral-critical library of modernity, with contributions that stretch from Montaigne to Cioran and from Bacon to Luhmann. It should be noted *en passant* that it is Odo Marquard who has formulated the logic of this petition.[3]

In the fundamental discursive order of Old Europe—I note that 'Old Europe' was an expression casually coined by Nietzsche, before it was a key term of Luhmann's[4]—it is thus not so much the Devil who must allow himself legal counsel in the procedures, but rather the human being who needs counsel in view of the immense burdens of guilt that have been loaded down on him by his Christian accusers between Paul and Augustine all the way to Pascal, Dostoyevsky, and more recently by Levinas. For, as the European history of ideas and religious worship shows, the human race, after being driven out of paradise and after the God-Man's crucifixion, finds itself in a double bind: to begin with, that of being caught forever with the children of Adam in the first rebellion against the commandment, and then that of having participated with the Romans and other imperial and powerful human beings in the death of God. Both suffice to bring the culpabilized race into deficit, in terms of the economy of salvation, and, to be sure, to such an enormous extent and with such a hopeless overdraft of all accounts that, without action to reduce the debt by the crediting agency, the human being will never again get out of the metaphysical debt trap. The productive power of human morality could never be enough, on this interpretation, to manage the debts of the race in the afterlife. For that reason only a transcendent advocate for the human being is in a position to satisfy the highest creditor. In the New Testament, Christ is consistently characterized as *paraklētos*, a term that is sometimes translated as 'comforter' but more correctly as advocate or intercessor, yet apart from that, as is well known, one finds it used mostly for the Holy Spirit. It is obvious why this *advocatus hominis* must be God himself—because only a transcendent advocate can settle a transcendent debt, just as it is clear that he must at the same time be a human being, because human beings can only plausibly be represented in whatever court by someone who belongs to their race. The procedure is not without risk for the client: an immense debt to the advocate, because of his representation, can easily come about from the immense debt owed to God.

The construction of the procedural mechanism, the way in which human beings *toto genere* are to be brought into the red, deserves and needs to be looked into anew. It is developed—this can be shown relatively easily—from an almost inevitable side effect of the impulse for rationalization, which was carried out in the ecumenical forms of ancient life and thought by Hellenistic philosophy. This achieved a relatively stable compromise between cosmological idealism and anthropological skepticism in the era of the Stoics and the pragmatic doctrines of happiness—and thus a situation that already clearly looms in the standard Aristotelian distinction between the sublunary places affected by death and lack and the ethereal realms of superlunary perfection. The moral difference between what is above and what is below remained suspended in a quasi-physical distinction between the perfect motions of the heavenly spheres, which are stable in their circular motion, and the imperfect motions of the zones near to the earth, where only finite, fatigable, straight, and crooked lines are possible. Evil, as though it were an exhausted good, was also planted into these zones as the natural endowment of finitude. In this way, ancient philosophy succeeded in concealing the paradox of a nature contrary to nature within the concept of nature. —

To be sure, Christian theology could draw on these solutions, yet it could not stop there. It is what, with metaphysical acuity, construed evil as something more than anti-natural, namely, as anti-divine. It careened into this lane by joining the question of the origin of the turn *contra Deum* with the question of the human being's chances for salvation. In so doing, the human being veered close to the molten core of a possible original evil, and did so for reasons that were almost mandatorily imposed on the basis of the architectonics of a metaphysical-theological discursivity in the space of early Catholicism. The hyper-culpabilization of the human, which was concentrated in the concept of original sin, is a product of the increasing employment of arguments in favor of (human) freedom to explain the motivation for evil in a universe entirely created by God. When historians of dogma explain that the theological crisis worsened when the question *unde malum?*[5] became more acute as a consequence of Gnostic provocation, they also already indirectly confirm the significance of free will in the introduction and imputation of evil. Since, with regard to evil, the customary monotheistic reduction to the first cause is of course forbidden—since the latter is kept free of all responsibility for what is bad, failed, and evil by an unwavering partiality for good—the search for a non-basic secondary source imposes itself. Evil must be grounded epigenetically, so that the inference from it back to the good origin remains impossible. However, as long as the *omne-ens-est-bonum*-principle[6] holds valid, everything not-good remains in limbo in a twofold sense: genealogically, because one does not know from which bad parents one is supposed to descend, and ontologically, because, as a being that does not actually exist, it is expatriated in some sense from the range of real and valid beings. It can thus only be motivated privatively and by the will.

In this situation, human freedom must serve as a reserve *origo* from which everything that is not onto-theoretically safe flows. This orientation is almost self-evident in a state of the world that, according to the rules of Old European rationality, requires a principle-based, monarchical interpretation—thus in view of a world in which and above which there can be no God against God and there ought to be no origin beside the origin. If it must remain taboo to trace negativity in the world back to the divine first cause, should the whole cultural discourse and logical hygiene of biblical-Hellenistic language games not be endangered, then, when such negativity becomes obvious, there accrues to the human being as the creature gifted with freedom a literally superhuman, Atlantean task: he is called on to bear the guilt of an entire world of pain. Human freedom exonerates God from the impertinence of acknowledging a second principle alongside himself as the origin of that which is not intended by him. Thus the Old European tradition characterized itself with good reason as 'humanist,' because it had to locate in and only in the human being the possibility to accord with God and nature just as much as the temptation not to accord with them. Just as the Greeks had employed nature as a generic term and hiding spot for what is contrary to nature, so the Christians now used the human being as a generic term and hiding spot for what is inhuman, which is synonymous with what is contrary to God. The human being becomes important because exorbitant and frustrated expectations of order require clarification. For an aeon he appears to be a creature that can miss his appointment with God, which, so one hears, constitutes his humanity.

It is easier to understand the fact that, above all, problems with the hygiene of the world-picture were supposed to be solved by freeing the good, original cause of everything from authorship of evil when we recall the general provocation of dualism in late antiquity and the 'foul' discourse of Gnosticism in particular: Gnosticism famously and overtly reckons with a confusion at the level of first causes, indeed even with a failure of the creator God, of the stupid demiurge, as though willing and power were not unified up above either. In view of the theoretical architecture of orthodox Old European theology and anthropodicy it can be said that the free human being is constructed and put front and center in

order to disburden God of his position, insofar as the free human
being must remain on hand as a reserve-culprit and ersatz-principle
for all human and cosmic evil. This leads to an overburdening of
the essentially free human being by his systemically conditioned
hyper-competence for evil. Because the human being now appears
so deeply and quasi-fundamentally sunk in his corrupted state, anything less than an action just as deeply undertaken will not suffice
for raising him up again—Christian soteriology is the discursive and
cultic trace of this. In its elaborateness one can read off the radicality of the preceding maneuver of rendering culpable. For it is not
only the case that whoever thinks greatly must err greatly; it is also
the case that whoever has been greatly burdened must be greatly
disburdened.

We should add to this the observation that modernization, in terms
of the economy of the world-picture, can only consist in reducing the
need for disburdenment by lightening the load—an operation that
could have counted on Luhmann's approval, although he himself
would have hardly taken part in discussions of such metaphysical stuffiness. Furthermore, it would have been typical for him to
explain the trajectory of evil less from the impulse to explain, which
proceeds from the *unde malum* question, than from the paradox of
the assertion of unity. Without doubt, he would have emphasized
that, in order to take up the standpoint from which the unity of the
difference between creator and creature can be asserted, the Devil
must exist, for better or worse. For—except for theologians—who
if not the Devil can look on from outside at the unity of what is distinguished in that way? From this perspective, the diabolic nature of
that which is diabolic is to be interpreted not so much in voluntaris-
tic terms as in terms of topology and the theory of difference, since
its source is to be sought in the externality of observation as such.
If the Devil still wants to mark out a difference for himself in relation to the unsurpassably good One and his world in general, then
nothing else remains for him than to take up the standpoint of evil.[7]

Having come this far in the development of the problem, it is
useful to recall the formulations with which Augustine interpreted
and established for centuries the condition of fallen humanity.[8] We
find in them the first approaches to a problematic that will press
for a new answer only at the peak of modernity with the renewed
emergence of the question as to whether the self-regard of human
beings and systems is good or evil. Augustine recognized the strategic
significance of the concept of sin for stabilizing the Catholic universe
against ancient Skepticism and hence undertook with great ingenuity an ontological deduction of that which does not stem from God
and leads away from him. In fact, within the world of creation that

is distinguished as a whole by the fact that it has turned out well, it is no easy task to trace the starting point for radical deviations. Nevertheless, it is obvious that the nerve of separation must be found in the human being; it is just as evident that this will now no longer be accomplished with the repetition of the cultically employed term 'sin' for the explanation of issues that stand in question. Rather, it is a matter of conceiving the conditions for the possibility of resistance to divine law and to lay bare in this possibility the metaphysical foundations of sinful dissidence. Here, the Augustinian analysis comes close to modern expressions—we leave aside whether it does so in appearance or in substance—for it brings about a sort of profound diagnosis of the structures of corrupt human subjectivity and *eo ipso* formulations that can be heard up to today in the corroborative iterations of the philosophers of dialogue, whether of Protestant, Catholic, Jewish, or psychoanalytic provenance, as well as in those of the founding discourses of an anthropological psychiatry. Since the form of fallen human subjectivity is prefigured in the Satanic one, it suffices for everything else to begin with the Arch-denier and to observe him in his secession from the divine whole. Here the metaphysical deduction of externality is achieved.

We will be dealing with a bit of mythology in which the screenplay for the history of this world begins with its prelude in the beyond. The Augustinian Satan, who represents something like an allegory of negation on a level below the principal, does not resort—this much is certain—to any external motive for his revolt against the origin. He finds everything that is necessary for sedition in himself—to put it more precisely, in his capacity for freedom, his most important endowment. By virtue of this, he can, parodying divine creation *ex nihilo*, generate his 'no' from the abyss of an unmotivated act of the will. Thus one may not ask why and from where he has acquired his evil will. He wills as he will and nothing more. The will or, to put it in modern terms, the desire of the dissident orients itself to itself and not to the Big Other whom it has before itself ontologically and morally—he thus prefers himself instead of his creator, who is presented to him as both an invisible origin and a visible opposite. Thus he begins with himself in a free, uncompelled way that is therefore only attributable to him, now and forever. And it is just this—beginning with himself, although there had been another, older, more dignified beginning to respect—which is, according to the insight or viewpoint of Augustine and all conservatives since, the beginning of sin. Sinning is an operation in which originality and negativity are entwined. Ultimately, to sin is always to begin with the false—even where it seems only to be a continuation. It bears the character of a schismatic 'fact/act [*Tathandlung*].'

In Augustine's description sin achieves an operational precision of such elevated intensity that it accordingly appears as something which every mortal can spontaneously repeat if he had not already discovered it himself. Only now, after the onto-theological guidelines for precisely turning away from God have been specified, can it actually be shown to what degree human beings have been occupied with repeating Satan's operation all along. For, precisely insofar as Satan does what he does, namely, turns away from the Big Other and orients himself to himself with original pseudo-originality, he establishes the pattern for everything that will be castigated in Europe for millennia as bad self-regard and conceived as an irresistible temptation for mortals, even more, as their inborn flaw.

Augustine emphasizes that one may not presume any external necessitations, and certainly not any rivaling principle, behind Satanic self-preference: the Devil is no vassal of an evil, second god. Furthermore, he may not invoke the defense that, in order to become autistic, he must have had a deficient mother. The Devil needn't have had a bad childhood to be disposed in an abysmally bad way. For him, it is a matter of revolt in itself: he wants to turn away or unscrew himself from his face-to-face with the Almighty One as such. Only from unmotivated freedom does he carry out his turn against everything that represents order and divine precept. He realizes himself as the owner [*Eigner*] of his obstinacy [*Eigensinn*].[9] By means of this action, evil is substantialized in the direction of dissident wills. What begins Platonically as mere *malum privativum* becomes, in Christian terms, concentrated in the Devil's ego into a malign private sphere of self-authorized and irremediable intensity. The evil one draws his own circle around the Second; his circle stands for systemic closure.[10] Thus the Devil, lord of this world, becomes lord of self-regard.

From a later, perhaps more impartial point of view, the additional fact that a premise is concealed in this description imposes itself, a premise that if made explicit would have had to have destroyed the whole arrangement: namely, the disastrous paradox that the endowment of freedom remains bound up with a strict expectation of integration and subordination, so that the human being, like his mythical protector, Satan, could only have used his freedom without culpability if he had decided not to use it. To use freedom means, conversely, to automatically become implicated in uprising and to decide on one's own existentiell liberation, one could even say on distance and resistance. To exist means to be held into non-communion. The symbiosis with God must be broken, so that existence is realized as external or as thrust out. According to this analysis, which is full of assumptions, from this uprising

there emerges the distance that first enables external observation of
the unity between creator and creature. This observation remains
an external or diabolical one because the Devil rejects the idea of
asking to be allowed to be the third in the league of two. Thus,
insofar as it introduces externality, the principle of distance would
be the authentic dimension of the Devil.

Distance thus becomes the problem child of classical metaphysics. No theory of alienation to this point could relinquish the motif
of the guilt of distance in relation to a supposed primal proximity. However, when thought in these terms, the simple fact is
disregarded that for the most part otherness neither arises through a
dramatic division nor is solidified in the latter's traumatic engrams.
Otherness is the naturally occurring and blameless point of departure between groups and individuals—who were never anywhere
united—contingently encountering each other. Only the metaphysical prejudice for unity compels one to think otherness as alienation
and thus to deprive multiplicity of its ontological dignity together
with its practical innocence.

For the turning inward of the creature that frees itself from the
innate or at least enjoined devotion to the Big Other, Augustine
introduces a technical term that is equally revealing in kinetic and
moral terms—that of the *incurvatio in se ipsum* or curving inward
into oneself which exists everywhere human beings fail to live up to
the norm of extraversion or turning toward the object and put themselves before their relations with others. Until the present day, the
Old European specialists in imputing guilt recognized their clients
in this flawed stance, even long after they had transitioned from
reproaching sins to critiquing narcissism. What does the modern
theory of pathological narcissism offer other than a new psychological description of an irrevocably, theologically coded situation?
Curving inward into oneself, interpreted in Augustinian terms, for
its part has a twofold significance: it indicates not only the current
operation of sinning, which could be characterized today as breaking off communication with a counterpart who seeks conversation
or is pleading for something; it also refers to the habitualized result
of such turning away, a stubborn false position of the moral sense,
which no longer can be compensated for by the subject itself, even
if its intentions are good. If Augustine, as a phenomenologist of
the curving inward of the self, delivers a dark diagnosis of the post-
lapsarian *conditio humana*, and if his assessment of the human being
and his prospects for salvation turns out to be almost fatal, then it is
because he interprets the fall as a torsion, being fallen as being distorted, and the latter as an internally irreversible flawed stance. After
the *lapsus*, mortals, as imitators of Adam and of Satan, are fixed

in their orthopedic catastrophe; they are no longer free to uncurl themselves and by their own powers to restore the broken contact with the good whole and its personal principle, the snubbed God. They are incontrovertibly perverted or rolled up into themselves and are consequently entirely dependent on the responsiveness of the other side. This responsiveness has been represented for an aeon under the title of grace. The term gives an indication of the process of—as one says—straightening out the curve-inward that can only be carried out by another. It characterizes the corrective to a hyper-culpabilization that had to make from the gift [*Gabe*] of freedom the poison [*Gift*] of guilt. Admittedly, it is obvious that detoxification by means of grace above all calls to mind intoxication by means of the *mea maxima culpa*.

2. Fundamental Innocentism

According to a not very well known *bon mot* of Ernst Bloch, the process of the Enlightenment is characterized by a symptomatic asymmetry: while it was for a long time *bon ton* for the cultured to profess a methodical and perhaps even an existentiell atheism, the corresponding a-Satanism remained remarkably underdeveloped. The reason for this is only seemingly to be found in the fact that among moderns, in any case, no one believes any longer in the Adversary. In truth, the Enlightenment universalizes the category of the adversarial to such a degree that its religious provenance was able to be occluded and reshaped by a worldly occupation of the evil functional position. The reason or context for this can be explained in simple terms: the process that presents itself as the Enlightenment cannot be maintained if it cannot produce an explanation, which is to be brought continually *à jour*, of its non-success due to counter-enlightenment forces of resistance. The 'Enlightenment' is condemned to continually reflecting on its preliminary status and incompletion, a dilemma that it only avoids by making reference to the fact that it is a project, on the one hand, and to the persistent non-cooperation of powerful obstructers, on the other hand. What religious metaphysics had interpreted with the help of a systematic overburdening of the human being's sinful freedom—the enigma of persistent evil in a fundamentally good world—is transformed in modernity, determined as it is by the philosophy of the subject, into the question of why the human praxis of freedom, which had since come to power and was almost universally approved of, still had not brought about a sufficiently good world. The Enlightenment is the progressive interpretation of this problem. Obviously, the meaning of freedom must be interpreted in a radically different way: while in its medieval *dispositif* it represents the capacity for sin and the possibility of its imputation to the sinner, in modernity it signifies the competence to project, establish, and universalize morally satisfying world-relations. When these are not found, one must identify culprits for their non-existence. Consequently, in the modern approach, the culpabilistic matrix continues to remain in use, which is obviously more powerful than the difference between medieval and modern metaphysics. In the meantime, new entities and novel candidates come into play for the position of First Evil, upon which is distributed the still imposing burden of the world's evil: the bourgeois system of private property, class rule, the process of capital, the logic of identity, the abstraction of exchange, the death drive, the perverse rebellion of the subject against the symbolic order, the objectivist subjectivism of modernity, logocentrism, the refusal to admit the primacy of the Other, the colonization of the lifeworld through systems of power and wealth, and a number of others as well.

All of these forms of evil draw their power from their adversarial quality, with which they pervert what humans could, would, or should make better. The *peccatum originale* is transformed into the *obstaculum originale*—into a primordial nuisance, an obscene indolence, an unbearable hindrance and a perverse self-insistence of unacceptable conditions. The removal of these resistances now shifts to the center of the Enlightenment interpretation of the world in a manner that is as essential as the redemption of the first sin for the Christian *ratio* was indispensible. In modernity, not only does the statement that he who thinks greatly must err greatly hold true; it is even more true that he who sees himself greatly hindered has a great deal of clearing away to do. As soon as clearing away and upheavals on a grand scale were put on the historical agenda, theories and praxes of what one called revolutions (in the non-astronomical sense of the word) emerged, that is to say, projects of movement emerged that structurally signify nothing other than attempts to eliminate obstacles standing in the way of the development of a subjectivity striving for complete power. Such endeavors present themselves as the activism of the Good. What is modern about fantasies of elimination of this sort is the fact that they are no longer aware of the premodern dampening of violence by grace. Marx formulated early on the maxim of a new kind of intensified, radical-humanistically motivated critique of elimination: "Its object is its enemy, which it wishes not to refute but to destroy."[11] One can champion the view that Luhmann's work on the whole represents a therapeutic confession against the temptation of intellectuals by the violence that clears away. He gave the most laconic of his responses in a press conference: "It's not a matter of simply eliminating the other half and putting oneself in its place."[12]

The position of advocacy in the process of modernity must therefore be interpreted in entirely different terms than in the Catholic procedure of canonization. Under present conditions, the *advocatus dei* is on the side of the subject still hindered in its development, while the *advocatus diaboli* represents the party of hindrances that are exposed to the danger of being cleared away by the agents of a more expansive subjectivity. During the heyday of Enlightenment journalism this seems to result in a sufficiently clear scenario that points to progress on the side of God and reaction on the side of the Devil. In fact, numerous progressive intellectuals in modernizing societies understand themselves to be paracletic functionaries, insofar as they, through their agitating and acting as representatives, embrace the office of speaking on behalf of groups not yet sufficiently liberated for self-representation. In contrast, speakers from the so-called reaction plead for established interests, which they maintain are more closely interwoven with the regulatory tasks of the whole than the progressivist frivolity is able to grasp. Looking ahead to a possible emergency, conservatives even attribute katechontic functions to themselves by claiming that they have the duty to intervene, as inhibitors of the worst. In the other camp, it is striking that progressive or paracletic intellectuals prefer to read the writings of their conservative or reactionary opponents and take their critique of these writings to be the beginning of all critique. In so doing, they suggest that the elimination of mental hindrances forms their point of departure for the elimination of real hindrances. Critique becomes a euphemism for exterministic reading. Hence during the heyday of critical philosophy the conviction was able to flourish that the theory which detected other theories' contribution to securing the so-called established order [*das Bestehende*] was itself the most important part of praxis.

As you can see, the form of thought that lies at the basis of these schematizations is characterized by features of culpabilism and proceduralism in modern scenarios of conflict as well, although the roles are arranged differently than in the medieval procedural order. In particular, it is still interested in a stark conception of freedom— but now under the triumphant title of the subject. The position of the agent who bears high or the highest imputations of guilt remains in question. The delivery of exaggerated accusations on account of the neglected or hindered improvement of the world corresponds to the exaggeration of subjectivity. Hence it is understandable why the intellectuals engaged in such processes take up not only forms of rhetoric and routines of Old European legal disputes but also just as much the habit of priestly mediation and even more the concern for protecting against heresies. Despite Hegel's remark, applauded far and wide, that philosophy has to guard against wishing to be edifying, the intellectual culture of the Enlightenment is constituted in a crypto-pastoral and paracletic manner, as much as it tries on ever new disguises for its theological designs. In accordance with the respective circumstances of the time, this can be reformulated in neo-Marxist or pragmatic terms, social-liberal or humanitarian terms, in neo-Aristotelian terms or in terms of discourse ethics. Walter Benjamin deserves credit for his achievement of articulating the modern compulsion to camouflage pastoral interests in the expressive image of the chess-playing dwarf under the game table of human history.

I would now like to show, or at least to indicate, how Niklas Luhmann's intervention into these scenarios brings about a radically transformed awareness. It need not be kept secret that Luhmann's point of departure, biographically and pre-theoretically, is probably to be sought on the side whose guiding interest I just now deemed to be the defense of hindrances against their eliminators. Luhmann begins as an ordinary conservative only to become in time what an Italian column called an avant-garde conservative—one could even say to become a representative of a genre of thinkers who have devoted themselves to the art of not being priests, with consequences that have yet to be recognized. Intellectuals who were close to Luhmann have noted in this respect that in methodological terms he had long since surpassed, from the left, the classical left. Precisely because Luhmann remained existentielly an outsider to the rebellious or revolutionary impulse; because, on a fundamental level, it was foreign to him to want to clear away the obstacles opposing the expansive claims of an ascending group subjectivity; because, with an inexplicable modesty with regard to himself and his surroundings, he could find nothing that under all circumstances should be thrown into upheaval and cleared away—because of these things, he was disposed to disengage himself from all positively or hypocritically paracletic roles. Thus he is perhaps the only actual a-Satanist of this century because he does not clash with any sector or, as he would put it, any subsystem of the social multiverse as such, but is prepared to give each realm its due without being beset by any fantasies of elimination.

The consequences of this approach are extraordinarily far-reaching. This can be grasped most clearly in the key distinction that Luhmann characteristically chooses: that between system and environment, a distinction that even indicates a relation in which no side is suited for elimination. In this first distinction a Being-related-to-each-other of poles is also expressed, which one cannot do justice to by the reflexes to clear away a supposedly adversarial part. But even the concept of system, for its part, already bears the traces of a counter-paracletic irony, since whoever dares to emerge after 1960 in German contexts as a systems theorist must grapple with a semantics according to which systems were the epitome of hindrances that needed to be removed—from the Weimar Republic on, in which the abolition of the 'system' was held, in the jargon of both the right and the left, to be a condition for salvation, all the way to the 1970s and 1980s of the Federal Republic, in which the terminology of the Frankfurt School and neo-Marxism in all its varieties evoked more or less discreet fantasies of elimination in relation to that which one wanted to blame on the capitalist system, the logic of exchange, non-ideal speech situations, and similar crystallizations of the adversarial. Paracletic exterminationism comes to the fore most clearly in the radical wing of the student movement, which wrestled with the phantom of armed resistance. Motifs of resistance are also structurally present in the theoretical design of the Habermasian theory of communication, insofar as it distinguished between the 'lifeworld' and the 'systems' that besieged it almost as between salvation [*Heil*] through what is one's own and perdition [*Unheil*] through what is foreign.[13]

Faced with these terms of reference, in which an occulted doctrine of the adversarial had academically established itself under the self-aggrandizing title of critique, and indeed, tellingly, not in theological departments but rather in sociological ones, Luhmann had to carry out his primary intuition in protracted processes: that, in order to actually investigate systems, one must tolerate them being allowed to appear as what they are, without reproaching them for being a certain way or functioning in a certain manner and without holding it against them that they are not what they cannot be. It is in this sense that I characterize Luhmann as an *advocatus diaboli* of a quality that has yet to be acknowledged. The point of his advocacy of the systemic lies in the fact that he de-Satanizes the realm of what pertains to the system as such and steers clear of paracletic impatience that would like to eliminate what cannot be immediately classified under the desire of the subject and can also not be so easily and indirectly classified under the long march to the rational domination of the world by supposedly higher-level subjectivities. At the same time, I do not wish to say that Luhmann's approach was entirely unprecedented, since, for instance, in the early Plessner, when he emphasized the "limits of community," or in Gehlen, when he treated of the "birth of freedom from out of alienation,"[14] analogous movements of thought emerged that were critical of subjectivity—incidentally, with a similar irony regarding the needs of politicizing immediacy and with a comparable attentiveness to the systemic proper sense of great social structures. But never before has the methodical atheism of the modern sciences been complemented by such a thoroughgoing methodical a-Satanism. It is almost a new tone in the social sciences when one does not begin with a *peccatum originale*, with a First Crime, or with an initial plummet into alienation. Something of this resonates in the title of an essay by Luhmann on the transformation of juridical and historico-philosophical interpretations of the origin of private property between the sixteenth and eighteenth centuries: "Am Anfang war kein Unrecht" [In the Beginning There Was No Injustice]. If one bears in mind how cautiously Luhmann was accustomed to formulate the titles of his books and essays, then one can legitimately suspect that in the title of this specific investigation of the semantics of justice a hint of confession probably also comes into play. Even more, in the second primary thought of Luhmann's, the theorem of the differentiation of subsystems, the author's concern for the defense of theory against the infringements of *ressentiment* is noticeable. Considering the century-long history of sociological theories, he had in view the risks that emerge from economistically totalizing descriptions of the relations between social partial-systems. The theorem of differentiation also serves as a hygienic measure that is supposed to protect from renewed, wild applications of the schema of base and superstructure.[15]

The methodical presumption of innocence in relation to systems in their environments can only be sustained if the analyst maintains a specific kind of abstinence—I would like to characterize it here as a systems-theoretical releasement [*Gelassenheit*], at the risk of being tempted to speak Luhmann's name in the same breath as those of Meister Eckhart and Heidegger. At first sight, that would be an incongruity, not to say a far-fetched association. Nonetheless, one could object that one of the sources of Luhmannian releasement is in no way worlds apart from those of the Heideggerian version. Both are characterized by their connections to Husserlian motifs and by their respectively maverick strategies of pushing away from these motifs. When, on occasion, the thesis was to be heard that Luhmann was not 'really' a sociologist, but rather a philosopher behind the mask of the social scientist, that statement was true to the extent that Luhmann repeated, by his own means, the theoretically ascetic founding figure of phenomenology: the bracketing of the vital intentions and existentiell positions of the theoretician, in order that "the world and all I know about it shall become a mere 'phenomenon.'"[16] One could even say that he discovered anew the *epochē* in relation to another host of phenomena. If in the case of the first host of phenomena it is a matter of the conscious life of a 'subject' that investigates its activity of representation as though it were not its own, then in the case of the second host of phenomena it is a matter of the life of the system in general, which is treated with a neutral attitude, as though the agent of the system-analysis were not himself at issue. To this belongs the presumption of innocence in the face of systems as such, which first makes it possible to study them without zealotry. Yet as the theorist has to opt out and cannot advance with his expectations of meaning as the measure of all systemic things, so should it be conceded in view of these matters that there is nothing in them that calls in advance for a rejection of a region of Being without hope of salvation. Whoever is ready to agree that there are systems and that, if there are, their *proprium* must be to function as they do within their internal spaces that are constituted differently in each case, he would perhaps also be inclined to admit that the intentions of systems are not evil from the very beginning.

In this doubly 'epochal' maneuver of un-evilizing, we must now target the hotspot more precisely—I mean the question of self-regard, of which we know from the indications given above that it was of crucial significance for the metaphysical procedure of rendering the human being and his terrestrial *civitas* evil. I must here content myself with the suggestion that the verdict concerning human self-regard is a constant of moral-critical discourse in Europe from late antiquity to the present, and here one should assume a continuum of anti-narcissism options, however riven and twisted this continuum may be. There is nothing surprising about this observation for the Christian tradition, but it achieves a non-trivial and conspicuous profile in modern movements of thought, in which the prohibition against narcissism is maintained in a paradoxical proximity with a culture of explicit emphasis on subjectivity. This is the case not least in German idealism, which managed the feat of squeezing beings as a whole through the needle's eye of reflexive and pre-reflexive sub-jectivity and yet furthermore of serving as a warning against human hubris, as though German Idealism had not itself stoked such hubris. That even Pascal called the ego a hateful word may have been moti-vated by his closeness to neo-Augustinian conventions. But what is to be said concerning the anti-egoism of the idealists, who pummel the empirical ego in order to be able to exalt the transcendental or absolute ego? I recall Fichte's excommunication of what he called the self that is animated by its own self instead of God, a self of which he believed to know that it continually "desires, that . . . there should be revealed . . . on all sides . . . only the image of his own worthlessness."[17] I refer to Hegel's invectives, hardly still able to be cited, against the ironic state of mind (to which Ernst Behler has most recently called attention and contextually situated)[18] and his raving against everything that he dismissed as empty subjectivity or frivolousness. I refer lastly to Schelling's abyssal considerations in his treatise on freedom, in which the relation between egoism and malice is emphasized. That Heidegger also argues in the tradition of an anti-narcissism or 'anti-humanism' that is coded in Augustinian terms and moreover molded in a crypto-Catholic anti-modernism does not need to be explained again. Incidentally, even Lacan, who attacks the fiction of the strong ego, and Derrida, who would like to dissolve the illusion or deceptive echo of self-presence, continue the practices of the Old European critique of supposedly unholy self-regard.[19]

In view of this sustained series of rebukes of overvalued and harmful human self-referentiality, the devil's share, even in modern times, clearly seems to be allotted to the side of the subject. An a-Satanism of a second type must now deploy its resources against this distribution of the devil's share and provide proof that the much-reviled self-regard of the subject or of other poor devils is not disposed in such an evil manner. One may claim that it is at precisely this point that Luhmann's typical abstinence from moralizing conceptual formations exhibits its best effects. In Luhmann's sober exposition and new description of the whole field of the relational bearing of systems between self-reference and reference to what is alien, he effects an exhilarating de-escalation with regard to everything that has to do with the culpabilization of the human being. The irony of the procedure consists in emancipating human beings from the ways in which they have, for the sake of an architectonic world-picture, been overburdened as subjects who are supposedly excessively turned in on themselves; and it consists in allowing them to participate in the quasi-innocence of naturally occurring, systemically conditioned self-referentiality, which we know only presents a necessary and inevitable offshoot of a universal relation of reference, which cannot do otherwise than continually oscillate between the pole of the self and the pole of what is alien—and this with a primacy of the internal that is necessary for the system. In this regard, Luhmann, to his and the reader's advantage, is a student of Husserl in the best sense, from whom he takes up the sovereign precision of the analysis of intentionality without adopting the overexertions that follow from Husserl's program for a subjectivity that does it all.

The dismantling of the overburdening of the subject has also at the same time an epistemological and moral-theoretical implication, because now self-referentiality—conceived as a universal aspect of the system—must neither be ascribed exclusively to human subjectivity nor be encumbered *a priori* with a suspicion of narcissism. Husserl's analysis of intentionality, which is oriented by a spontaneous bipolarity of acts of consciousness between the noetic and noematic poles, and Luhmann's analysis of referentiality, carried out in parallel fashion, which makes the successful pendular movement between endo- and exo-reference as such into the condition for the existence of systems, agree in restoring to self-referentiality in general its due share in what one could call, with Nietzsche, the innocence of becoming—in the present context it is better to say the innocence of functioning.

The mention of Nietzsche evokes a broad horizon of theories that, since the seventeenth century, have endeavored to naturalize the human being by articulating an unburdening of the theoretically and morally engendered excessive demands of the human position— beginning with Spinoza's discreet mockery of the Christian moral philosophers, who seek the causes of human weakness not in the universal power of nature, but rather "attribute human infirmities and fickleness . . . to some mysterious flaw in the nature of man, which accordingly they bemoan, deride, despise, or, as usually happens, abuse: he, who succeeds in hitting off the weakness of the human mind more eloquently or more acutely than his fellows, is looked upon as a seer."[20] Coming at the problem from a different angle, the English philosophies of moral sense[21] find a perspective of disburdening by deducing from the human being's natural sociability that he can be free of excessive tension, as he should be, because he is oriented by nature in such a way that obligation and inclination converge in him, to be sure only approximately, but still on the whole to a sufficient degree. A further front of disburdening is opened up by the French moralists and the eighteenth century's psychology of motivation. Here—beyond the universal disposition to reason for self-preservation—a naturalized self-love as a universal drive is attributed to the human being, and in no way is it stipulated that this self-love is predisposed to evil in every respect from the beginning.

The most important motif of disburdenment is taken up by Luhmann from modern biology and metabiology, in which it is shown that self-regard is not something that came into play after the emergence of ego-consciousness—as if it were a parasitical addition to an organismic Being that, beforehand, was oriented in a manner free of reflection, as if it were an unjustified indulgent introversion that distanced itself from an older selfless norm. Rather, self-relations already emerge at the first stage of life, insofar as the latter must be described as the epitome of self-created codes of procedure. The self of the autopoiesis of living, systemic unities reflects the goods of successful creation rather than narcissistic revolt—for organisms are constituted as embodiments of intelligence, in which the double movement of self-relation and relation to what is alien can be observed from the outset. In higher organisms self-relation can even take on the form of lived self-experience and symbolically mediated self-consciousness. Yet, although organisms present materializations of their design of intelligence and success and accordingly are meant to permanently sample and readjust their own conditions, they are never oriented in such a way as to completely reflect or represent themselves in themselves. To put it in different terms, they are not meant to have within themselves the truth concerning themselves. This fact can be most readily explained by looking at the most sophisticated example: there is no human brain, and for fundamental reasons there can be no human brain, which could know completely how it itself functions, let alone one that, in its ongoing operation, could have before it a complete representation of its historical and structural conditions for operation—in the sense of a mind that has here and now come to itself in total transparency. Because the autopoiesis of the system, which precedes consciousness and is turned away from it, has an insurmountable lead on its self-representations in consciousness, it is evident that self-relations always have a certain functional sense—and this with all normality and long before all problems of malign self-emphasis. In this respect, there exists neither a subject that is transparent to itself all the way to its foundation nor a free ego predisposed to revolt and to evil self-indulgence that could function as the central point of a culpable refusal of communion with all other organisms or co-subjects. But without doubt there exist forms of autopoiesis that are badly directed or unsuccessful, which—if one wishes to remedy them—must be studied with a therapeutic outlook. Here the example of the brain is unquestionably apt; as long as arguments count for something it would have to impress even those who do not so easily escape from the phantasm of the linguistically mediated, integral self-reflection of society in society or from the higher level subjectivities in their history.

Luhmann is thus a devil's advocate in the paradoxical sense that he puts the diabolical nature of that which is potentially diabolical as such into question. If what is 'subjective' does not mean what is arbitrary, then the arbitrariness of the subject is not that which is evil per se. "In reality there is no arbitrariness that, as it were, attaches to the subject."[22] Luhmann defends the self-relationality of systems insofar as he does not emphasize in them a culpable curving inward of the self and an immoral turning away from the other, but rather calmly devotes himself to verifying that in any case it is impossible for systems to proceed otherwise than in primarily self-referential terms. Consequently, he takes himself to be the advocate of a naturalized or, better, systemically neutralized self-referentiality, which for him simply represents a phase in a permanent oscillation—a fact that he described as 'bi-stable oscillation' in a lecture that is philosophical in the most advanced sense of the word, namely, his Vienna lecture from May 1995 on Husserl's Vienna lecture from May 1935, "Philosophy and the Crisis of European Man." The point of this conception consists in the fact that it displaces philosophy's customary mode of proceeding from a principle—whether it is called God or the subject or the process of reaching an agreement—by a pendular movement, supported by memory, in a psychical system— Luhmann calls it the bi-stable vacillation between internal and external reference—in which the problem of an 'original sin' simply does not arise. By means of its own procedure, the oscillation, which makes continuity possible, ensures that the system escapes both dangers that would threaten it in the case of a unipolar orientation. A correctly functioning reference-oscillator, let us say a consciousness of human quality, neither entirely loses itself to the world as the reference pole for that which is alien, nor entirely becomes submerged in itself as the reference pole for the self. Rather, by virtue of a permanent self-adjustment it shrinks from both positivism and autism, and indeed precisely when it was supposed to have drawn all too near to one of the poles because of an internal imbalance of its learning process.

It thus remains to be observed that turning toward the pole of the world is only conceivable as the system's own accomplishment. It is typical for freely oscillating intelligences that they learn from their extremist episodes. When fixed positivists who lose themselves in the pole of the world, or autistics who have closed themselves up in the pole of the self, or even paranoiacs who are one-sidedly motivated by a bad other that is too close, become prominent, we need no longer search for the trace of sin; rather, we must ponder strategies for reincorporating them into the community of bipolarity.

I would here like to allow myself the remark that Luhmann's use of 'bi-stable vacillation,' with all its technical coldness, bears a certain pathos, which we can understand when we become aware of the fact that it formally converges with Heidegger's explanations of the difference between metaphysically interpreted movement in rest and post-metaphysically rethought rest in movement—and furthermore, that here, in the most discreet way, a Buddhist feature, as it were, is imprinted upon the premises of systems-theoretical reason. It is manifest that in Bielefeld, as in Kyoto and Todtnauberg, salvation no longer lies in assuring one's own safety in the face of movement by retreating to an ultimate foundation. If Heidegger claims for his thought which is twisting free from [*verwindend*] metaphysics to know the answer to the question Plato posed in the *Sophist*—the question of how Being or the whole can be simultaneously at rest and in movement—insofar as he brings the word of releasement into play once again—an expression that characterizes a form of abdication from absolute knowledge—then Luhmann has steered releasement even further out of the zone of pathos insofar as he emphasizes the discovery that in any case there is nothing left for a consciousness other than to proceed from every one of its internally attained states.

At the beginning I used the somewhat awkward expression 'Luhmann's lesson' and at the same time warned of possible implications of this turn of phrase. In the meantime, it appears that at least a fragment or layer of meaning of that which was intended might have become a little clearer. Luhmann, as a resolutely modern a-Satanic devil's advocate, is the defense attorney for a social normality that is more complex than ever before described—a normality concerning which it is now recognized from the start that it is characterized by a high complexity and entanglement of all systems in immanently unavoidable paradoxes. Luhmannian normality is the normality of the immense, which is given a shape—or rather, numerous local shapes—in the self-ordering of that which is alive.

Were I thus to provide a comprehensive expression for Luhmann's lesson, I would suggest that his contribution to the culture of theory in the future be characterized as a fundamental innocentism—a hybrid phrase that contains a juridical and a philosophical part. Innocentism signifies a basic attitude that can be encountered among good advocates and therapists, which is marked by the presumption of innocence vis-à-vis subjects and systems of whatever kind. This presumption is supported by the realization that systems and other suspicious entities ordinarily have nothing better to do than to function in the way that they function, including the possible functional variants, and that the burden of proof for the thesis that they could and should function otherwise than they do lies with the accuser—an imposition that does not enjoy universal acclaim—because all forms of critical theory proceed from the precedence of accusation and expect the accused conditions to justify themselves before their accusers. This procedure, which one can call Jacobian or fundamentalist, is at the same time also hypocritical, because it is guided by the conviction that the condition described as a deplorable state of affairs would never be in the position to carry out its own apology.

Luhmann's fundamental innocentism removes the assumptions from this arrangement by situating his analytic procedures in a scenario that is interpreted completely differently. It operates in a space in which serenely released [*gelassene*] fluctuations between distance and participation are possible and in which it may be assumed that critics also participate in that in which they participate and that they do not *not* participate in that in which they still participate, although they imagine certain retreats and reserves of purity. Thus the hypocrisy of the critic's consciousness, supposedly engaged only for the good, is described as what it is: as a coincidence of hypocrisy and utopia in the literal sense of the word, which means play-acting on a stage that is located in a non-place and which nevertheless draws attention because of its capacity to fascinate with aggressive speech acts. For, because critical theories have accusations, alarm, and the gesture of excommunication at their disposal, they continually allude to the emergency that demands the moral obliteration of the opponent. "He who does not rejoice in such teachings / does not deserve to be a man."[23]

Innocentism is not qualified as 'fundamental' in order to add fundamentalist features to systems theory, but rather in order to indicate that as soon as it operates on equal footing with traditional paracletic philosophies and theologies it has no other option than to begin at just as deep a level as fundamental culpabilism, in which the Old European tradition of overburdening the human being manifests itself, along with its late ignitions in existential ontology, in Critical Theory, and, if I am not completely mistaken, even in a branch of dialogue theories that have lately taken up a noteworthy part of the discursive energies ranging from social philosophy and pastoral theology to ethics.

While fundamental culpabilism achieves its success through the allure of evil, which it emphasizes in a manner as critical as it is hypocritical, fundamental innocentism works with the discretion of non-evil. It is concerned with proving that human self-regard is too weak of an address to which to deliver the whole dossier of accusations against the world's deplorable states of affairs.

According to Luhmann, there is indeed extensive scope for contingency in the structure of systems, but nowhere can there be talk of so much freedom that so much criminal liability and justification to bring charges could follow from it. It is Luhmann's great strategic theoretical intuition to restore the metaphysically overextended motif of freedom in the structure of systems of action along with their ethical foundations to a standard that disposes one to rationally withdraw from the disposition to accuse.

This objection was able, in the long run, to bring about an important change of emphasis in the moral-critical economy of modern societies, because the Old European practice of understanding evil as a synthesis of the egotistic malice of agents and the adversarial malice of states of affairs was thereby replaced by a discrete investigation of what Florian Rötzer has called, with a felicitous expression, systemic evil.[24] This evil characterizes total situations of miserogenous complexity, in which the intentions of personal systems—even when they possessed so-called criminal energy—came into play more as marginal effects or, in police terms, as the causality of the little fish. In systemic terms, human beings are not only overburdened, but also and above all overrated when one wants to see the origin of all evil in their capacity for deviating from communion with the prevailing One and in their capacity for contravening its laws. Under the conditions of the Old European architectonic picture of the world, this overburdening and this overrating are pretty much unavoidable, as was suggested—a discovery concerning which one would know the particulars in an authoritative sense only if a Pelagian Europe had emerged alongside the Augustinian one through a schism in late antiquity, such that one would have been able to observe a culture of original sin in direct comparison to a culture of discrete distribution of guilt and innocence—the split between Rome and Byzantium/Moscow was in this regard an unproductive experiment. Such internally impossible comparisons can today be substituted only indirectly by contrasting Christian/post-Christian cultures and cultures outside Christianity. Where something of this sort was sought, for instance by comparatists of religion, who brought Europe face to face with Hindu Indians or with Buddhists from the Far East, results emerged that did not yield the better part to European culture in each case and in each respect.

The only experimental arrangement in which the contrast between a rather Augustinian and a rather Pelagian evolution can at least be indirectly observed is found in recent times, thanks to the US secession from Europe. While in the Old World, at the end of the twentieth century, in particular because of the experience of totalitarianism, a general cultural climate co-determined by skepticism and normative pluralism has played itself out, the United States, although it possesses noteworthy enclaves of freedom, has retained a climate that in broad strata is stamped by puritanical premises, in which culpabilistic, victimological, and inquisitorial mechanisms are intertwined in pre-Enlightenment naivety and psychological refinement. It cannot be an accident that the penal system of the United States is the most intensively and extensively comprehensive one in the world, and that in proportion to the size of the population almost ten times as many delinquents are jailed in American prisons as in European ones, a difference that is trending upward.

Yet, independently of external comparisons, a culture of complexity, as it is today beginning to free itself from its old Western premises, must develop from out of itself the resources to dissolve the hyper-culpabilistic, hypocritical-paracletic disposition. It can only adhere to the latter where the polemogenic effects of moralism and the sterility of the desire to critically elevate oneself over persons and issues have not yet been sufficiently seen through.

3. Irony-Theoretical Addendum

Having referred to excerpts from the work of the sociologist, which I attempted to explicate for my own domestic use under the title of the Luhmannian lesson, I would again like to reformulate what has been said up to this point and to extend it in the direction of consequences that are relevant for a diagnosis of the times, and ultimately in the direction of ethical or therapeutic consequences. The key word for this operation is already at our disposal—I am talking about a culture of complexity, and I would now add that for a society characterized by it a corresponding ethics of complexity must also be developed, thus an ethics that will no longer be determined by the *furor metaphysicus*, which always seeks the "absolute in history." An ethics of this type keeps its distance from the moralism of the need to accuse, which in better cases occurs as a critique that delights in accusation and that has been tamed by a culture of constructive contention, but in worse cases occurs as a helpless dream to eliminate and in the worst case occurs as applied extermi-nationism. As soon as the overdue redetermination of fundamental attitudes is embodied in individuals and reflected in their arguments, it will become generally evident that there exists a virtually almost necessary convergence between the approach of an innocentism regarding systems and an ethical comportment regarding complexity. In this situation, the intuition that Luhmann formulated early on, which is critical of moralism and according to which so-called critique must inevitably have a polemogenic and miserogenic effect because of its opaque, Old European premises, will cease to be only a piece of evidence for minorities and lead to more extensive recognition as a plausible interpretation of the basic moral relations in a differentiated society.

Regarding individuals in the modern European space of thought and behavior, with their clearer intuitions they will adapt themselves to a neo-Pelagian point of departure, in which it is no longer a matter of overculpabilizing individuals and circumstances *a priori*, without it therefore being the case that a Rousseauian regression of great scope would have to be feared. With their darker intuitions they will rather present themselves as citizens of catastrophes, surveying great risks and total disasters, which are not to be ascribed to the malicious deeds of culprits. This fluctuation between a neo-Pelagianism in regard to the human being and a reckoning with systemically conditioned catastrophes, which can be attributed to their perpetrators all the less the more globally they occur, today already characterizes the scene in the subcultures of a more sophisticated contemporaneity.

It seems impossible to remember such a state of affairs without addressing its irony. A 'state of the world [*Weltzustand*]' such as this, to use Hegel's term, in which the risks increase while the imputability of guilt and responsibility is on the decline, simply calls for a Luhmannian description—indeed, the state of affairs calls for an advocate who does not accuse or defend it so much as show why the days of such a condition are numbered for both defender and accuser. We saw at the beginning that an ancient correspondence exists between the speech of advocates and ironic speech. Now we find the opportunity to note that this is not only the case for the *advocatus diaboli* in the Roman procedure before the Congregation of Rites, but from the moment when Greek rhetoricians, comedic poets, and philosophers began to concern themselves with the dramatically tense relation between the way speech is conducted and the discovery of truth. Among the early manifestations of ironic consciousness the Socratic version has become the most consequential, of which one gains the impression from Plato's prose that it was a rhetorical tactic in seemingly modest disguise with which the superior inquirer, Socrates, brought to expression his amazement at the purported knowledge of his opponents. Irony would accordingly be a language of modesty, in the face of which immodesty regularly makes a fool of itself. From here the path leads through the Aristotelian distinction between understatement and exaggeration, *eirōneia* and *alazoneia*, to the school doctrines of the ancient rhetoricians, which, with a success that reached all the way to the eighteenth century, defined irony as a figure of speech with which a speaker, in the mode of playful dissimulation, propounds the opposite of what he means—a technique without which no advocate could make an effective plea nor could any Enlightenment author manage an elegant polemic.

Faced with this state of things, irony functions over the course of an age as the silent partner of philosophy, one among the many figures of *ars oratoria*, which subordinates itself to philosophical speech's mission to find truth; and it does so whether it subordinates itself more or less deferentially, as in the individual cases of Erasmus, Shakespeare, Rabelais, and Grimmelshausen, or whether it subordinates itself in a refractory manner, in order to occasionally withdraw from that mission with radical-poetic obstinacy. It is no accident that movement only enters back into irony when, with the transcendental turn to German Idealism, philosophy itself occurs under new auspices. Because of the elevated operation of reflection after Kant and Fichte, a form of irony raised to a higher power emerges in contemporaneous poetic theories, which was designed, received, and defended under the title of Romantic irony—an irony in which the art of intending something otherwise than it appears, or even more the art of removing the base of that which appears—reaches a new height. Irony raised to a higher power anticipates a state of consciousness that we associate today with the term 'constructivism.' It accentuates the sovereignty of the positing and canceling subject that is conscious of its hovering between productivity and destructivity, a stance characterized in part by enjoyment and in part by depression. *Naturally*—as one would like to say using the word of the great Austrian ironist, Thomas Bernhard—no longer is it so much rhetoricians and lawyers who use this type of irony as it is above all modern artists. In contrast, it will inevitably be the defenders of the substantial and the institutional, of the serious, the difficult, and the unavoidable, who push away from this form of mindset that is suspected of being merely artistic. The collision between Hegel and Schlegel is, in the history of ideas, a trace of this animosity. In it is articulated the political realists' mistrust in a subjectivity that is supposedly all too captivated by its own ability to operate, which took itself and its hovering between its own constructions for that which is highest and imagined that it saw as beneath itself everything fixed, everything that is accepted as valid, everything ordered and real. Under Romantic irony, it is no longer only the *urbana dissimulatio* that is to be understood, which seemed to be indispensable to the stylists between Cicero and Voltaire, but the capacity to posit and to revoke, with which a creative subjectivity imparts to and removes from its creatures the foundations of their existence. Modernized irony is distinguished, above all, by the fact that it frees the subject's turning away from its momentary engagements as a legitimate mode of playing with things and persons. This is shown not only in the brilliant tension that becomes unfaithful to its former products, because it is bent on outdoing every formed construct by means of a creative process that must move on; infidelity vis-à-vis the object soon takes on vulgar features. The irony of the producer, pendulating between creative work, reformulation, and destructuring, is generalized into an irony of consumers, as soon as everyone feels the freedom to draw to themselves disposable persons, texts, and objects of all kinds for a short time and then cast them off. A consumer is whoever maintains an association with the given that is no longer characterized by belief in its lasting value. The most ironic consumer is the collector, in whom casting off coincides with preserving. Here, infidelity functions as ownership. Among the general public, the standpoint of the irony of the end consumer is used for objects of the designed environment; in relation to discourse it appears as deconstruction.

If I may allow myself to suggest that we situate Niklas Luhmann within the history of irony, this can only happen with reference to the fact that in his work the advent of a third type of irony is indicated, which I will call cybernetic irony. Cybernetic irony presupposes the Romantic kind, as the latter had presupposed Socratic irony for its premise. But it prepares a subversive fate for the subject of Romantic irony, for the subject hovering between its posits and their cancellation, insofar as it asks of this subject that it understand itself as an epiphenomenon in a system of systems that is much too complex and tenacious to be posited or canceled by a subject. This does not imply a return to an objectivism of order or to a second humility, which one observed in the nineteenth-century post-Romantic realists and in other retreats from hybrid ultra-aesthetic or ultra-Protestant attitudes. As Romantic irony undermined the appearance of objectivity by making the constructed given appear and disappear, so does cybernetic irony cut the ground from under the appearance of subjectivity by dissolving the ego and then letting it return. Romantic irony is not thereby discounted, but rather elevated, since even the subject that has returned can again carry out operations that, as before, seem to demonstrate his sovereignty—only now the subject's position is itself ironized, because the subject that has disappeared and returned remains characterized by the memory of its flickering. The subject of cybernetic irony knows, to be sure, that it constantly misunderstands itself—indeed, it finds the evidence of its compulsion to misunderstand itself, such as in the theory of the blind spot, so convincing that it would be ready to drop misunderstanding altogether if only it were in its power to do so. But it now makes the discovery that instead of getting away from itself or losing itself, it only falls back into itself all the more again and again, and this is precisely what makes material available to it for a new position of irony, which results from the quandary of being a subject that doubts its ability to be a subject, even more: of being a subject discredited as a subject. Thus a good part of that which until now has been described under the title of humor is shifted to the side of irony, for if classical humor implies a good-natured condescension of the higher self to the quotidian one, then cybernetic irony generates a veering of knowledge from the canceled self to the recurring self-effect. The subject will thus appear to be something between a local hero and a local loser.[25] It must take itself up and thus show a strength that it does not, according to everything that it knows of itself, have. It is condemned to hold out, although its reserves are used up.

Doing theory at the third stage of irony must advance a propensity toward disengagement from fixed viewpoints, because systemic thinking prompts of its own accord a comparative study of illusions. It deals with convictions as though with individualized versions of software. It is hardly necessary to say that such a stance can be generalized, can have a civilizing effect, since it inevitably tempers fanaticism and reinforces politeness. It stimulates a form of communication among thespian-citizens, who would encounter one another on the basis of a well-distributed self-distance because each would have begun to conceive of himself as an end consumer of vital illusions and pragmatic arrangements. It is precisely this that is refused by the intellectuals who reclaim for themselves a higher seriousness, because they behave as proponents of a reality of the first degree, of an immediate need or of an untempered fury.

The potential of the third kind of irony to shape behavior has a bearing not only on civil forms of communication between tranquilly enlightened [abgeklärt aufgeklärten] actors of modern social systems, but just as much on their logical forms of communication and the philosophical superstructures of such forms. Only at the level of the third kind of irony can the civilizing effect of both preceding versions be appropriately conceived, because it becomes possible to more generally formulate why the older kinds of irony had already been essentially more than merely rhetorical transformations of a semantic stock. Rather, they—like all modalizations of expressions by humorous, grotesque, and hyperbolic strategies of discourse—mark an indispensable contribution at the linguistic level of coding to modulating the risks of fundamentalism, which are inherent to every bivalent logic. Without irony and its checkered cognates, without the 'perhaps' and the 'who knows?,' without the subversive smile and the laughter that overturns, without the *Je ne sais quoi* and the *Presque rien*, without the interplay of the seriousness of reproduction and the parody of presentation, in short without that additional civilizing valence which in everything that is well said goes beyond that which is expressed, the universe of metaphysical productions of the world would, to a still greater degree, remain a hell stoked by dogmatisms and structured by binarisms, which in any case the universe has basically been. The ironic code anticipated polyvalence from the beginning of the era in which bivalence appeared to forever determine the fate of thought. It presented itself as that third which could not be given on the level of propositional logic.[26]

We can at least briefly indicate now why the alliances between the good and the serious, on the one hand, and the evil and the non-serious, on the other hand, had to turn out to be so inseparable in descriptions of the world that stood under the law of binary metaphysics. Because such projects of ordering always had to do with emphasizing the good as the real, which was to be represented only as what is substantial, valid above reflection, momentous, deeply grounded and continually existing, the volatile, groundless, evil side was always reserved for that which is non-serious. Indeed, even what could not be decided to be good or evil tended to fall to evil because it indicated a third thing that allowed evil a greater share of the real than the partisans of the good were able to tolerate.

Yet, from the standpoint of the third kind of irony—if this still pertains to the taking up of a standpoint—an advocate of evil comes into play, who sees through all such occurrences of imputing evil as an emanation of bivalent logics. In so doing, he does not operate with a private reservoir of sovereign derision but rather with a precise attentiveness to the positional differences between subjectivities—for which Heinz von Foerster, with his discussions of first- and second-order cybernetics, has established the formal presuppositions. Their point consists in the fact that subjects observe other subjects in their subjective Being—a stance that is suspected to be evil per se by decided ethicists. Intensifications of irony are the unavoidable result of widened observation. They foster the methodically controlled taking up of positions in the face of which the tradition could only secure itself with liberal applications of holy water. Because precisely the third kind of irony takes real differences and distances between persons or personal systems more seriously than the most serious doctrines of communion and communication would heretofore like to allow, it is able to formulate with uncustomary radicality the external observation of persons by persons. This irony is cybernetic, because it is involved with the finitude of subjectivities that are viewed 'externally' in the second instance of observation, without it being the case that the observer becomes laden with guilt because of the externality of his vantage point. Observation does not serve to reinforce the stance of wanton presumption in the second observer but rather to attenuate it through the awareness of the insurmountable reality of also being an observer that is forever an observable observer. If Sartre, with regard to the infernal dynamic of the objective interchange of perspectives, allowed one of his dramatic figures to say, 'Hell is other people,' then Luhmann turns the heat of the observer's hell down to room temperature and recommends this as the office climate for post-humanist conviviality. Human subjectivities here are no longer, as in Hegel, absorbed by an absolute and cannibalistic spirit. I have characterized this elsewhere as the immunity-of-nobody.[27] Rather, they are located in discrete observations, without ever entirely becoming enclosed and established. The irony of this kind of irony consists in never bringing all sides of the foreign subject before oneself at the same time, never surpassing it and never expropriating it. It is essentially self-ironic, because it always also concedes the partiality of its own perspective in its relation to the other.

Cybernetic irony points toward the effects of immersion. Subjects are swallowed up in these effects as soon as they want to be or must be themselves without reserve. Immersions are always introduced when individuals or groups engage without reservation in encompassing situations—for instance when a battle breaks out, in a rampage, in a love affair, but also in the passage through an installation, or more generally in that which fundamental ontologists have called Being-in-the-world—a situation for which there is no alternative for human beings in their lifetime, according to the official interpretation.[28] The possibility of the third kind of irony stands and falls with the ironizability of immersions. Their hitherto most powerful philosophical anticipation is found in Heidegger's chapter on 'the They' [*Man-Kapitel*] in *Being and Time*, insofar as existing in the mode of falling prey to the shared world [*Mitwelt*] is interpreted there as immersion in a vulgarity that seemingly has no alternative and yet—ecstatically from the inside, as it were—can be radically turned against itself. In the passage through the total installation of Dasein a Heideggerian is still somehow capable of more resolute and distinguished conduct than the indecisive visitors en masse—at least, this is what he expects of himself. Still more ironic is the discretion with which Luhmann attempts to show that an individual can in any case never actually entirely immerse itself in its environment or its other and be swallowed up in it—unless it were to use the environment like a drug or a cyberspace from which there is no turning back. This amounts to a new systems-theoretical formulation of insights that Sartre noted concerning *mauvaise foi*.

I maintain that the ironization of immersion constitutes a new criterion of civilization. The civilizing function of science fiction[29] and related varieties of speculative technology can be determined from this angle. What has been called cyberspace is the technical production of immersions in view of their exchangeability. It shows the aesthetic flipside of fundamental ontology. One enters, body and soul, so to speak, a space of which one possesses two opposed ontological conceptions: on the one hand, that it is irreal or virtual because we do not look on as visitors, that it forms no part of the public continuum; on the other hand, that we inhabit it as a real space so long as we are visiting it and do not emphasize its virtuality. Past humanity experienced this difference through the alternation between the waking world and the world of dreams, of which the one was described as true and universal while the other was described as untrue and private. Christianity anticipated the irony of immersion with its belief that the human being who reemerges from baptismal water is no longer the same as the person who was submerged in it. The world today collectivizes and technologizes both awakening from dreams and baptismatic irony together, insofar as it offers cinematic variants of and cyber-alternatives to beings as a whole in the waking realm. In this sense cyberspace is the most important irony-generator of our epoch. No wonder that it is populated by androids, whose presence makes it impossible to determine on the basis of external observation whether they are genuine human beings or replicas. The art world today wishes to infect the real world with this problem of distinguishing. It triggers a race between humans and machines in the portrayal of subjectivity. In cyberspace, Being-in-the-world is elevated to a stage of technical simulatability: a consciousness from then on appears to be something that can be surrounded by an integral fake, which presents the functional equivalent of reality or the 'world.'

This concept is what the Wachowski brothers transformed into a vision of neuro-cybernetic total simulation under the name of *The Matrix*. Certainly, the world of the Matrix is constructed in a tepid, metaphysically conservative, and thus extremely paranoid fashion, because it is still concerned with the difference between the true world (which is obviously frightening) and the world of appearance (which is constructed upon pleasant illusions), yet the cinematic moving back-and-forth between both sides elicits a subversive leveling effect—because the film, ironically enough, cannot but provide the exact same visibility to both states. The directors of *The Matrix* are on top of the problem insofar as they shot both sides in color and have avoided the temptation to simulate an ontological difference by alternating between black-and-white film and filming in color. In this way, a *tertium* is to be recognized between Being-in-reality and Being-in-the-Matrix, i.e., Being-in-the-film, which is both and at the same time neither. The premonitions of a polyvalent ontology now leap from the hermetic discourses of Nietzsche,

Heidegger, Sartre, and Günther into the outlook of mass culture. The world of the Matrix continues the discussion of the problem, heralded since *The Birth of Tragedy Out of the Spirit of Music*, of whether philosophical redemption from appearance should not be superseded by a redemption through appearance—an alternative to which, upon leaving the movie theater, a further option is fortunately added: redemption from apparent redemption.

Systems theory, for its part, speaks a language in which it becomes increasingly less important as to whether it treats of persons or of higher mechanisms. As cyber-theory it is the organon of a polyvalent ontology that has pulled away from the Old European distinction of Being—which is—from nothingness—which is not—in order to establish higher complexities.

4. Therapy-Theoretical Postscript

In Musil's *The Man without Qualities* one finds this sentence: "If mankind could dream as a whole, that dream would be Moosbrugger."[30] The proper name refers to a figure from the universe of the novel, a mentally disturbed journeyman carpenter and murderer of prostitutes, who fascinates the Kakanian intelligentsia with his Jesuanic charisma. The murderer Moosbrugger is enveloped by the empathy of the well-educated and of advocates who are certain that nothing more can be done for their client. Musil's intuition allows the age of bivalent reason to be summarized and jumbled up in an autistic individual who marks the limits of inclusion by love, insofar as he killed women who, by their manner of being, caused "so much trouble"[31] for him, but even more in the procedure of justice that had to hand down an inadequate public verdict on the solitary act of the confused man. Musil's arrangement exposes paranoia as the truth about truth at a time when getting serious about it still seemed to help.

It would be nice for a moment to take the liberty of formulating a variation on Musil's hypothesis: If the modern world could be thought as a whole, Luhmann would have to emerge, provided that his version of systems theory articulates the auto-therapeutic corollary of modernity, i.e., withdrawing oneself from the compulsory constructions of reason-paranoia and its totalizations in high politics and large-scale consensus. In the course of our reflections, we have already spoken about the most important agents of Luhmann-therapy against the monomaniacal risks and side effects of Old European forms of thought: the repetition of the phenomenological *epochē* in relation to systemic magnitudes; the supplementation of methodical atheism with methodical a-Satanism; the deployment of elevated ironies against the elevated pretensions of totalizing subjectivity; laying bare the polemogenic character of supposedly critical theories and good morals; and the replacement of established descriptive routines by new, incongruous approaches. The most significant feature in this program, nevertheless, is the bracketing of that which was traditionally understood under the term 'normality'—and even more the suspension of the belief in reality as such. Only at this point can we understand what is implied in the demand assumed by Husserl: that in the future reason must provide itself with a fundamentally self-critical constitution. To this end, Luhmann notes:

> Reason is self-critical not because of its European heritage but only if and insofar as it can exchange its own belief in reality and thus insofar as it does not begin to believe in itself. The tests of its validity are found in therapy, which attempts to attain less painful solutions and itself maintains a disengagement in matters of reality. They are also found in claims to communication, in claims to a subtler language . . . that functions even under polycontextural conditions. Self-critical reason is ironic reason.[32]

To describe the belief in reality as an interchangeable magnitude: it seems to me that with this turn of phrase Luhmann has accomplished the most explicit approximation to the concept of the third kind of irony as the form of dealing with dissolvable immersions. It is surely no accident that this turn of phrase occurs in the context of therapeutic reflections on foundations. Luhmann, in agreement with the principles of radical constructivism, here says that therapeutic practice may no longer be understood as the successful adjustment of the subject to a supposedly objective reality, but rather as the exchange of an unlivable construction of reality for something less unbearable. In this arrangement irony does not at all appear to be the subject's setting itself above virtue and reality, but rather irony itself becomes a virtue and modifies the real, insofar as it cancels the mechanisms that produce the effect of reality, of being locked into an immanence of misery and a totality of struggle. This effect was elsewhere traced back to a "deficit of self-relativization" in rigid formations of the subject.[33]

Against the backdrop of these remarks it becomes clear why Luhmann's lesson is not to be separated from Luhmann's *askēsis*. If, with a lifelong practice of observing and redescribing social phenomena, he provided proof that modernity is able to create its own peculiar style of the *vita contemplativa*, then the virtue of its contemplation seems to consist in its being able to serve as a general background of contra-immersions. This is indeed a genuinely philosophical effect. To it can be joined the insight according to which even the most encompassing of Old European immersions—our supposedly immemorial and unrevisable immersion in a construction of reality construed in terms of bivalence—is tendentially dissolvable by the praxis of an ironic interchange of immersion. In this affair, Luhmann has chosen a decidedly different path from that of Derrida, who commends himself as a paradoxical therapist by conducting, from a fundamentally neo-skeptical attitude, an endless war of attrition against the fictions that result from bivalent reason—obviously with the conviction that it is always better to dissolve convictions based on worldviews than to validate them—or, to speak in terms of psychological critique: that manias are always more dangerous than depressions, for which reason, depression and paralysis represent a legitimate result of philosophical efforts, while this is almost never true of their opposite. That is something which remains to be examined. According to Luhmann, it would seem that a kind of thinking which goes beyond pathological hues is rather to be sought in the interplay of immersion and emersion, in other words: in the interchange of reality. For the goal of this practice Luhmann, in another passage, has used the expression "becoming-self-disinterested" and adds that a "painful sacrifice"[34] will occasionally be necessary for this.

I permit myself to remark that one can only speak in such a manner if one has a greater evil in view. I would suspect that here it is a matter of nothing less than the potential for paranoia that is inherent in all first-order descriptions of the world and the violence that is contained and sparked by it. Wherever human beings begin to inhabit their world-pictures without distance and to experience their classifications of beings as a whole as an arena of real struggles, they become susceptible to the temptation to fight to the bitter end for their constructs of identity and to kill for their fictions. Here the polemological costs of identity in general come into view. In an especially acute way, Luhmann takes into account the conflictual effects that emerged from the diabolicization of the monetary economy in socialist traditions. He opposes the latter with the insight that "money staves off violence for the realm that it can order—and to this extent a functioning economy always also serves to relieve politics. Money is the triumph of scarcity over violence."[35] Luhmann does not fail to recognize that money, where it is present, establishes connections that justify its accolades as a medium of symbolic universalization, yet in the case of lack brings about divisions that allow it to appear as a medium of diabolical generalization. With these turns of phrase Luhmann confronts the Marxist tradition—at a distance that already observes the catastrophe of Marxism as a peak form of culpabilizing, paracletic, and aggressive-naive social theory. It seems we are perceiving a recurrence of forms of sapiential thought at the height of modernity when we witness how emphatically and at the same time cautiously Luhmann indicates that no inclusion happens without exclusion and no system avoids the embarrassment of paying for the benefits of one of its achievements with disadvantages in other places. Yet is there not a transition from operative to contemplative theory here—and does this not rather represent a case of philosophical reflection that Heidegger calls for in view of the technological world as only one form of self-reflection in sociological discourse that has become complex?

In essence, one can hardly object to Luhmann's argument: concerning the entanglements between violence and worldview—or to use one of Peter Fuchs's expressions: concerning the "noxious lack of ambiguity in the world"[36]—the burned children of the twentieth century are more in the know on an existentiell level than every previous generation, even if they are still in a bad way when it comes to the theoretical refinishing of this complex. In our time, where unambiguous worldviews and their inherent practical counterpart—unambiguous fantasies of elimination—came to power the consequences were disastrous, not least for the practitioners of naive belief in one's own construct. The only literary genre that registers the serious consequences [Ernstfälle] of naivety is hence the black book—for which, in any case, the black exhibition stands aside. Only in media of this type can one show what the ruling sub-complexity brings about. But did we ever leave behind the era of the black book? One can hardly doubt that we have only just reached the coastlines of the logical New World, of the continent of Post-Paranoia, of polyvalence and of the mental dampening of violence and do not yet know what awaits us in the interior. Furthermore, it becomes clear that the suppression of *ressentiment* as an impetus of judgments and theoretical formations is a much more tedious business than readers of Nietzsche to this point have suspected. The overcoming of *ressentiment* is a cultural project that, in its logical and psychological scope, demands hardly less effort than the Buddhist Dharma, the greatest effort at mental hygiene ever yet attempted. It is no accident that in view of this state of things the first results of landing on the new coast—to which belong the theory of second-order observation, the autopoiesis theorem, and the doctrine of systemic paradoxes—are defended with a certain colonizer-pathos by the otherwise so pathos-less Luhmann. The pathos of the systems theoretician is repetition.

Having said this, we can now explain without forced antithetics why there must be paths of thought that follow non-Luhmannian priorities—in my view, especially when we are dealing with the question of how human beings participate with one another and in surreal or symbolic or imaginary spaces that are interactively instituted. That there is a deficit in Luhmann's thinking when it comes to the philosophy of language is clear to any attentive reader;[37] that the social-naturalistic or systems-naturalistic options of this approach have not yet passed their probationary exam in real political crises also gives us something to think about for the future. And that, with his construct 'world-society' Luhmann has on his own behalf introduced an idealization into the world, will be clear to anyone who has chosen a more empirically determined approach to phenomena such as languages, cultures, peoples, and nations; thus it is no accident that, in the indices to Luhmann's main works, these entries are hardly or not at all to be found. But it appears less fruitful to me to insist that Luhmannian lessons yield less direct gains in relation to so-called vital or existentiell concerns and result in almost ruinous side effects for the needs of a life that would like to belong to a sufficiently good collective. In any case, thinking with Luhmann does not benefit the *libido d'appartenance*[38] (to take up one of Michel Serres's expressions). That systems theory is rather useless as a civil religion represents, to my eyes, one of its advantages. There has probably hardly ever been another form of theory that knew itself to be so explicitly dependent on the protective climate of its cultural niche—in this case the academic preserve—or one that would have had more to fear from what in other contexts is called the irruption of the real, whereby under the real one may always also understand the effects of violence that simplifies.

In my view, it is more important to show how existentialist motifs and anthropological themes are presented after they have passed through an alienation by means of systemic observations. There is every indication that anthropology can only again become a discipline or even a mode of thought that carries weight when it is reformulated into a second order anthropology—a thought that, to my knowledge, was first articulated by Dirk Baecker. As bizarre as it might sound, a second-order existentialism and—why not?—a second-order erotics could correspond to this upgraded theory of the human being. In turn, one could even see a second-order love of wisdom hinging on this. If Luhmann was actually the Hegel of the twentieth century, as is sometimes maintained, then that will prove to be well founded not least through the emergence of Young

Luhmannians who make their presence felt through a renewed existentialist deviation from systems thinking. Luhmann's ironic statement that to be a human, and even to want to be a human, is only possible in a dilettantish way is perhaps not the last word on this point.[39] Even if this were so, one would have to essay a discourse in defense of the dilettante. On no account can it be disputed that in the future the question of the human being will bring with it answers of an increasing theoretical oddness. I allow myself the remark that in my *Spheres*-project I have provided explanations that I believe at least tentatively illustrate what I claimed at the beginning: that doing theory in our time—regardless of whether it is inclined toward the scientistic or the literary pole—is a practice through which one professes a contemporaneity. Thinking after Luhmann—for me that means: reconceiving the venerable concepts of love, the soul, spirit [*Geist*], or to put it in terms that are a little more current, participation in the other and existence in bindingly common spaces of animation and motivation, in such a way that in their presentation itself the complications that are given with the current 'state of the world'—Hegel's word once again—become palpable.

3

THE DOMESTICATION OF BEING

The Clarification of the Clearing

1. Extreme Situations

The following reflections are best understood as a variation on Heidegger's statement that, as one cannot see the forest for the trees, *"ordinary understanding cannot see the world for beings."*[1] In its laconicism this statement not only expresses the notorious and not easily intelligible "ontological difference," but also recalls the civil war that has never died down since Plato's day between philosophy and 'ordinary' thought. The two levels of meaning in Heidegger's statement are obviously not to be dissociated. If philosophical reflection is only possible in its opposition to the everyday use of the understanding, then it is by its very nature compelled to wrest itself free from its handling of individual beings and to conceive of the world in its world-Being as such. If we do not see the world for beings this is because for the most part we do not look up from the given, the phenomena, toward their giver, Being. The philosophical turning of the intellect would accordingly not merely be linked to that which after Husserl is called "withdrawing" [*Zurücktreten*] or the *epochē*, the logical holiday from the routines of dealing with things, states of affairs, and ideas. It would moreover presuppose an ecstatic eye-opener that goes beyond individual givens to the appropriative event [*Ereignis*] of the gift of the world as a whole. Such a total regard for the appropriative event of opening cannot be learned according to discursive rules and can hardly be anchored in academic situations. By nature, it belongs to the realm of attunements rather than to that of statements, and hence is transmitted not so much by instruction as by retuning. The philosophical moment, like the musical one, is a tremor that

pervasively attunes those who have been touched by it. In actual
thinking a danger is thought.

Thinking that exposes itself to the Heideggerian lesson certainly
possesses the features of a study. Still more, it is a school of ecstase
in which a retuning from the average activity of the intelligence
to the philosophical state of exception would be carried out. The
fact that the scholastic is not actually compatible with the ecstatic
belongs to the bizarre premises of the instruction which Heidegger,
as the uncanniest of professors in his discipline, knew how to impart.
Not coincidentally, in his early phase, when he carried out his introduction to philosophy as an initiation into the putsch, he invoked
anxiety and boredom—the first, because it devulgarizes the ordinary
subject through the loss of the world, the second, because it achieves
a similar result through the loss of the self, and both together,
because they derail everyday Dasein and evoke an inclination in it
to meditate on the monstrous side of the fundamental situation, i.e.,
Being-in-the-world, as such. Thus the path to philosophical thinking leads only over that which the religious tradition called fear and
trembling or that which, in the political language of the twentieth
century, is called the state of exception. Philosophy, conceived of as
a meditation on the state of exception or wonder about the world, is
a counter-scholastic dimension. For the school embodies the interest
in normal states, and then becomes aligned precisely in an anti-
philosophical direction when it pursues philosophy as a discipline.
In its scholastic state philosophy feigns a normality that cannot
possibly belong to actual thinking. 'Thinking,' as Heidegger understands it, is not only an exercise of ecstase in the existentiell sense or
a reflection on 'Being'; above all it is brought about by an eruption,
which is always to be carried out anew, from the scholastic state that
it has in each case reached. The paradigm for this is the break with
the epitome of school philosophy, that is, Platonism, a break which
every modern generation of thinkers must make. Heidegger rightly
remarked that Platonic philosophy had already undertaken the task
of technically and scholastically organizing the forgetting of Being
when it went about establishing a theory industry. By erecting the
first school it saved philosophy, and with the same act betrayed it
or its concern—not only by restricting 'truth' to the beholding of
eidetic forms but also in its scholastic immobilization of the human
being's ecstatic relation to the openness of the world.

Here I do not wish to expose to closer scrutiny Heidegger's intention to see an element of errancy and the advent of nihilism at
work already in the Platonic institution of philosophy.[2] It suffices to
point to the fact that Heidegger radicalized the topos going back to
Plato and Aristotle according to which the origin of philosophy and

science lies in wonder—*thaumazein*—in a way that remains symptomatic for the metamorphosis of philosophical thinking in the early
decades of the twentieth century. Heidegger modernizes wonder,
turning it into horror and thus basing philosophy as a whole upon
a darker logical affect. He takes it beyond the rational wondering-
how or wondering-from-where, which is traditionally considered to
be the sister of curiosity and which is credited for being the first to
kindle inquiry into the reasons for wondrous appearances. Lying
concealed in the concept of wonder is European reason's 'destiny of
drive,' which reaches from the medieval devotion of the intellect to
the modern expulsion of wonder from knowledge[3]—until the twentieth century when wonder becomes terror-mimetic and transitions
to meditation on the monstrous. Heidegger emphasizes a radicalized
pre-rational wondering-that, which ignites in view of the non-datum
that is the world. Such wonder, beyond the question concerning the
reasons for what is discretely wondrous, bends over the abyss of 'the
wonder of all wonders,' *that* beings are.

For the historian of ideas it is obvious that the ontological intensification of wonder must have a connection to the catastrophic
distortions of life in the era of cosmopolitan civil war—it provides
the existentiell foundation for the breakthrough into modern revisions of the world-picture. If twentieth-century wonder changed
its colors to alienation and horror, this is because the convulsions
of the age have spread into the innermost recesses of philosophical
discourse—although it is not easy to describe how incidents within
the series of gruesome action can be transposed into incidents within
the series of rigorous discourse. Nevertheless, the detonations at the
Battle of the Marne and the Battle of Verdun continue to reverber--
ate in the statements of Marburg and Freiburg phenomenology; the
screams from the Gestapo's torture chambers penetrate existentialism's fundamental conceptions. The monstrosities of the politics of
human extermination in Germany, Russia, and Asia force many a
thinker after 1945 to question how, faced with the fact that one's
fellow human beings have been struck by or are threatened with
obliteration, the thinking of Being can be converted into a thinking
of responsibility.

It is Jean-Paul Sartre whom we have to thank for the clearest words
on the consciously adopted impregnation of contemporary thought
with the terror of situations. In his essay "What Is Literature?" from
1947, Sartre speaks for a whole generation of writers who labored
under the spell of terror when he notes: "It is neither our fault nor
our merit if we lived in a time when torture was a daily fact."[4] For
the generation of intellectuals of the resistance the task of creating
"a *literature of extreme situations*"[5] arose from the resonance with

nearby terror. This formulation sheds light on a basic feature of twentieth-century thought: not only does it interpret the horizon within which the sublation of the specific difference between philosophy and literature had to be carried out; it also motivates newer authors' break with the reconciliation in which bourgeois culture had bathed. With an unparalleled disdain expressionist authors from 1918 and existentialist authors from 1945 looked back on that "literature of middling circumstances" in which for them the essence of bourgeois existence was plainly manifested—as well as on the forms of expression of liberal indecision and of progressive compromise. They had promised their consumers a world in which the absolute remained suspended and in which one would never have to choose between good and evil.

The authors of "extreme situations" or of "great circumstances" could surely not have acted out their hatred for the bourgeoisie and its cultural appurtenances with such lack of restraint had aspects of the philosophical and literary praxis of the time not been prepared that waited for radicalization. Only in the confluence between immanent and external motifs could extremism become the intellectual style of an epoch. Only in a specific conjuncture was the radical mode and tone able to form a common matrix for excessive thought and revolutionary action.

This extended over almost the entirety of the twentieth century. Already in 1911, Georg Lukács had postulated redemption from mediocrity when he wrote: "When something has once become problematic . . . then salvation can only come from accentuating the problems to the maximum degree, from going radically to its root."[6] In 1933, Heidegger lectured that essential questioning means "not closing oneself off to the terror of the untamed [*Ungebändigten*] and to the confusion of darkness [*Dunkels*]."[7] It hardly needs to be said that it was Nietzsche who already in the 1880s had opened the auction of extremism: "The spell that fights on our behalf . . . is *the magic of the extreme*, the seduction that everything extreme exercises: we immoralists—we are the most extreme."[8] Let us hold fast to the claim that there were authors and artists from the time before and after 1917 who established the tone for what was to come. What from then on and in hindsight was called expressionism was the beginning of a long conjuncture of hyperbolic worlds of expression that were invoked to correspond to the monstrosities of the history that was transpiring. The radicalisms that emerged from 1945 onward under the titles of existentialism and Freudo-Marxism form only the next variations on the epochal configuration of radicalism and hypermorality—a connection that necessarily ran into hyperamoralisms. The conjuncture was operative up until the 1970s when it again allowed a neo-Marxism that was tolerant of terror to come on the scene with the addition of the 'subjective factor.'

This recollection of European philosophy's prelogical presuppositions in the first half of the twentieth century is of significance for understanding the current cultural dynamic and its mode of handling problems, because the epochal premises of thought at the end of the century have begun to change again. Under the buzzword 'postmodernity' a post-extremist state of consciousness has played itself out over the past two decades, in which a thinking of middling or, in the better way one now puts it, integrated circumstances is consciously called back. Internal and external motifs can also be distinguished in such thought: as regards the first, it is above all the balance between this century's left and right politics of terror that has elicited an abandonment of not only the means but also the ends and their justifications, especially the phantoms of the philosophy of history and related projections of an overextended, teleologically engaged actor-reason. The results of these post-radicalist, post-apocalyptic, neo-skeptical, neo-moralistic reflections flow into a social situation that has been permeated as it hardly ever was before by the myths and rituals of communication, of consumption, of willingness to perform, and of mobility—a new El Dorado of middling circumstances, the globalized *juste milieu*. In this neo-mediocre climate the willingness as well as capability to critically appropriate the heritage of the epoch of extremism deteriorates—today one must as a rule take the detour through biography if one would still like to promote the work of radicals who have been compromised or have been pensioned by the *Zeitgeist*. Rüdiger Safranski did this for Heidegger a few years ago with brilliant results and Bernard-Henri Lévy recently achieved a comparable reconstruction for Sartre.[9] One should also approve of the welcome reception these books found, because they came along at just the right time, in the final minutes, as it were, before the thread of recalling the adventure of intellectual existence from out of the spirit of extreme circumstances would have been entirely yanked out. What the twentieth century was will one day be known when a synopsis of its radicalisms can be written.[10] It would be, as a history of grand politics and its terror, also a history of the moral general staffs and cognitive missionary orders, in a word: the history of intellectuals—if we define the latter as groups who embody the spectrum of discursive positions toward the violence that is happening, from the activists' clamoring for violence through the expressivists' mimesis of violence to the pacifists' abstinence from violence.[11]

Eighty-five years after the storms of steel of the German-French fronts, sixty-five years after the peak of the Stalinist mass exterminations, fifty-five years after the liberation of Auschwitz, and just as long after the bombardments of Dresden, Hiroshima, and Nagasaki, the swinging back of the *Zeitgeist* to the preference for middling circumstances is to be understood as a tribute to normalization. In this regard, it has an unconditionally affirmative civilizing value. Furthermore, democracy *per se* presupposes the cultivation of middling circumstances. As is well known, spirit spits what is lukewarm out of its mouth; in contrast, pragmatism holds that the temperature of life is lukewarm.[12] Thus the impulse toward the middle, the cardinal symptom of the *fin de siècle*, does not have only political motives. It symbolizes the weariness of apocalypse felt by a society that has had to hear too much of revolutions and paradigm shifts. But above all it expresses the general pull toward the conversion of the drama of history into the insurance industry. Insurance policies anchor anti-extremism in the routines of the post-radical society. The insurance industry is humanism minus book culture. It brings into shape the insight that human beings as a rule do not wish to be revolutionized, but rather to be safeguarded. Whoever understands this will bank on the fact that in the future contra-innovative revolts from out of the spirit of the insurance claim are most probable of all.

As regards philosophical thought, which is called to radicality for internal reasons, this turnabout into the moderate also has, in addition to its great advantages, its problematic side—because it runs the risk of being all too contemporary. It increasingly accommodates itself to the new routines of the *juste milieu* and sinks into conventional academic autisms. This diagnosis applies all the more when the invigorated thinking of middling circumstances is no longer at eye level with the major events of the epoch and loses its correspondence with the enormities of the current process of civilization. More powerfully than ever, yet under changed forms, the present demands a thinking of extreme situations in a correctly understood sense, precisely because the paradigms of the trenches, torture, and the camps no longer have any currency for the Euro-American world. The extreme that gives pause today is hidden in the routines of the permanent revolution, of which we know that it belongs to the momentum of progressive societies animated by money, desire, and envy and will sooner or later provoke a renewed counterrevolution of the political against the primacy of the economic. The extreme becomes apparent, if one can still speak of appearance here, in the banalization of the monstrous, which converges with the trend toward the intellectual defense of middling circumstances. It has, today as always, its natural molecular presence in the lives of individuals who do not escape their intimate catastrophes, yet it is also present in the trends of the course of the world, which, if the great networks should ever be torn apart, will

reach heights from which any fall would prove fatal. What is monstrous today comes from the extreme middle. It has long presented
itself as a mere phase or a surging trend that the consultants say
must be rode since the illusions of central governance have burst
asunder. From the point of view of 'contemporary history,' for
decades after Hiroshima the monstrous manifested itself in a planetary game of omnicide, in which the nuclear powers had taken each
other as hostages. It reaches a new phase in the present through bio-
nuclear engineering—insofar as this produces a situation that, if it
goes off the rails, could degenerate into taking societies hostage by
their own advanced technologies.

In view of what has been said, Heidegger's recollection of ontological ecstase, of that reflection which sees, beyond individual beings,
the world-bestowing thunderbolt light up, suggests a currency that
does not expire with the conditions of its emergence. To be sure,
it arises from constellations of expressionist extremism in the first
half of the twentieth century, but it is not permanently bound to
them. Even the resonance between radicalism and presocraticism,
characteristic of the early Heidegger, does not exhaust the impulse
of his interpretation of Being and existence. Like many a first-rank
intellect who embraced the word in the Weimar Republic, he may
have been a deserter of modernity,[13] yet he was just as much its diag-
nostician, whose insights transcend personal, regional, and epochal
conditions. Hence he remains, I believe, for the foreseeable future,
the logical ally of those who revolt in thought against the trivializa-
tion of the monstrous.[14]

In what follows, I want to attempt to show that Heidegger's meditation on existential ecstase is also of significance for understanding
the present crisis in the biological self-definition of the human being—
that crisis in the modes of human access to the human being, for
which I introduced the term 'anthropotechnics' in my speech "Rules
for the Human Park."[15] Recently, in a wide-ranging debate, this
term was misunderstood as a synonym for the concept of a central-
egoistic, strategically planned human biopolitics and set off emotions
that would have been more suited to a religiously motivated battle
for the human being. However, the expression 'anthropotechnics,'
in the context of the work undertaken here, stands for a clearly outlined theorem of historical anthropology: according to this theorem
'the human being' is from the ground up a product and can only
be understood—within the limits of our knowledge to this point—
by analytically pursuing his methods and relations of production.
If according to Heidegger's tremendous definition technology is "a
mode of unconcealing," namely a bringing-forth and a making-lie-
before of beings by means of applications of tools of a logical and

material nature—then the question of which productions gave rise to the fact that is the human being takes on a significance that cannot be separated from the question of the 'truth' of this being. In fact, 'the human being,' both as a species-being and as a matrix of opportunities for individualization, is a magnitude that can never exist in mere nature and that was able to first form itself only under the retroactive effect of spontaneous proto-technologies and in 'living communities' with things and animals—in protracted processes of formation in which a para-natural tendency can be observed early on. Thus, the human condition is thoroughly a product and result— but a product of manufacturing that to this point has been seldom fittingly described as such, and a result of processes whose conditions and rules are too little known.

The moment has come to note that one can only maintain an alliance with Heidegger as the thinker of ek-stase and the clearing if one at the same time decides to bracket his hostile attitude with respect to all forms of empirical and philosophical anthropology and to put a new configuration between 'ontology' and anthropology to the test. It is now a matter of realizing that even the apparently irreducible fundamental situation of the human being, which is called Being-in-the-world and is characterized as existence or standing-out into the clearing of Being, represents the result of a production in the original sense of the word—a leading-out and uncovering of a being which before was rather shrouded and concealed, and in this sense 'inexistent,' a leading-out and uncovering of this being into an ecstatic exposure. One of the ventures of the following reflections is that they will give the expression 'ecstase-technology' an ontological sense. They wager that it is possible to read the ecstatic 'position of the human being in the world,' interpreted in Heideggerian terms, as a technogenic situation. We will skip over a few thresholds of problems and thus act as if we already had the conceptual means at our disposal to lecture on the history of hominization as a coherent narrative of the exodus from uncleared nature into the danger that is called the clearing. I am thus asking, thinking with Heidegger against Heidegger, how the human being has come to the clearing [*Lichtung*] or how the clearing has come to the human being. We should know how the flash of lightning [*Blitz*] was generated in whose light [*Licht*] the world, as world, was able to light up and be cleared [*sich . . . lichten*].

2. *Etsi homo non daretur*[16]

I would like to present the following reflections under the somewhat irregular generic term of a 'philosophical fantasy,' because they can be appropriately characterized by neither the ordinary title for reflective reason's acts of daring, i.e., speculation, nor by the formal reference to the subjective risk of thought, i.e., the essay. The designation 'philosophical fantasy' corresponds to a discourse in which the reconstruction of an evolutionary product of the type human-being-in-history is attempted. With the help of fantastical reconstructivism the two mistakes that are as a rule inherent to evolutionisms can be avoided: the spontaneous propensities to either always already presuppose the human being that is to be explained or to forget him in the zeal of explanation. 'Fantastical reconstruction' is distinguished by the fact that it never leaves behind the starting point in the clearing and at the present state of civilization. The dignity of the clearing shall be inviolable. Hence our investigation is anchored—if anchored is the correct expression—in that which Heidegger has called the wonder of wonders, in the awareness that beings are at all, whereby the meaning of 'are' here is tantamount to 'lying open' for human beings who reflect on the fact that they are 'in the world' or in the presence of 'Being' in a completely simple, unconditionally marvelous, exposed way. But our investigation refuses to stop with this discovery, and it denies that this represents a finding that cannot be surpassed and at the same time a presupposition that cannot be overtaken.

I do not want to withhold the fact that in my eyes the lesser evil would consist in persistently mediating on the clearing with Heidegger, without wishing to derive it technoanthropologically, while positivism is in fact a plague because it belittles 'the human being' with its determinations. If one actually had to choose between the piety of thought and the profanity of blind praxis, then the reflection that wants to be philosophical would have always already made its decision. Yet I am convinced that the alternative between meditation and positivism is incomplete; we are not committed to the choice between a pietism of uncanniness and a forgetting of the human being in the machinations of the everyday, strategic understanding dulled by its own instruments. In what follows I would like to sketch in outline how one ought to proceed if one wants to narrate the history of human genesis in a polyvalent style that is superior to primitive antitheses. It is not enough to let the apes climb down from the trees in order to then let the human being descend from the apes that have climbed down. Even recourse to the extinct pre-apes, although this is meaningful in paleontological terms, cannot improve the situation in regards to philosophy. Rather, the ontological version of the novel of descent must keep in view, at the same time as the pre-human's becoming human, the pre-world's becoming a world—a thought that is not thinkable as long as one is fixated on preconstructivist ideas of the One Being and the One Truth. What is decisive in this arrangement consists in the resolution to heed the fact that in no case may one presume 'the human being' in order to somehow find him once again in pre-human stages. Just as little may one assume an open and established world for the human being, as if one only had to wait until a pre-ape made the effort to arrive at it like a passenger at the central station of the clearing. The difficulty comes from beginning with an authentic—yet precisely a fantastically authentic—pre-humanity and pre-worldliness. With them we must begin—with the avowed goal of arriving at the result that exists in the form of developed *sapiens* cultures and of constituted, ecstatic, and world-forming *sapiens* subjectivities of a historical type. In doing so, at no point may we regard the human fact any less highly than Heidegger conceives it when he speaks of the clearing of Being. Whoever points to the clearing speaks of the coming to presence [*Vorstelligwerden*] of Being in a living being that resonates physically, neurologically, and technologically on such a high frequency that it can encounter 'the world' as world.

We thus intend to recapitulate Heidegger's ontological interpretation of existence in an onto-anthropology and to enter into the circle that in this case does not function as a hermeneutic circle but rather as an anthropotechnic one. Research on the human being and what makes him historically possible must run in a circle in such a way that our point of departure, our existential ecstase in our time or our belonging to the appropriative event—it must run in a circle in such a way that this openness concerns us, is attained again and at the same time never left behind, without it being the case that—as is customary among evolutionists—'the human being' is already presupposed and then speciously derived in evolutionary terms.[17] Aside from that it is obvious that here the theme 'human being' can no longer be treated in the style of naive humanist traditions, which, from time immemorial, only helped provide an academic cover for conservative common knowledge. The discourse on the human being in historical anthropology proceeds from the fact that the expression 'human being' does not designate any object concerning which one could formulate direct (edifying or lamenting) statements, but rather only presents a conceptual container that, to speak with Luhmann, holds 'vast complexities.'

Such an undertaking could not have begun at just any time; if it is now attempted it bears the signature of the moment. It reflects a sum of conditions that have accumulated since the 'revolutionary break in nineteenth century thought' and the entry into the supposedly 'post-metaphysical situation.' Behind it lies the turn toward 'human praxis' that remains characteristic for the Young

Hegelian or pragmatic approach. It knows that it is co-conditioned by the event that is marked by the name of Darwin; it presupposes the impulses of Nietzsche and of the psychoanalytic movements. It makes reference to the lessons of phenomenology and the philosophical extremisms of the early and mid-twentieth century. To a large extent, it draws on the breakthroughs of empirical anthropologies through which, in an odd synchronicity with Heidegger's existential analytic, from the 1920s onward the morphological and species-historical question concerning the human being was posed on entirely new bases—I am thinking above all of the work of Louis Bolk, Otto H. Schindewolf, Walter Garstang, and Paul Alsberg, which has been little heeded despite its paramount significance for understanding anthropogenesis. Our project further profits from the discoveries of paleontology, historical linguistics, narratology, structural anthropology, and behaviorism. However, the decisive premise of the following attempt consists in the supposition that the history of 'the human being' must be understood as the silent drama of its formations of space—which cannot succeed if the history of things, materials, and symbionts are not more closely consolidated with that of 'human facts' than was customary and possible in the traditional schools of cultural historiography.

One suspects why it was a risky proposition for philosophy to pose anew the question concerning the provenance and position of the human being against such backgrounds. To be sure, most of the theoretical approaches just cited offer the advantage of breaking the religious spell that until the threshold of the nineteenth century had hindered the development of an autonomous worldly investigation of the *conditio humana*. Even so, due to their dependence on the myth of Genesis, Europeans since time immemorial have unmistakably thought of the human being as a product or creaturely artifact. But as long as they allowed God to be taken as the answer that kept further questions about the whence and the how of creation at bay, they were not able to advance alternative, non-theological formulations concerning the production of the human being. Sacred explanations ceased to think further when they accepted a cause that according to its ontological status was set above the human being. Yet to explain from above means not to explain at all. The theological blockage no longer holds for more recent projects: they have taken the liberty of considering non-divine factors in human formation and of allowing *Homo sapiens* to arise from a matrix of exclusively worldly conditions. They still think of the human being as a product, but this time as a product of formative forces that according to their ontological status are situated beneath the outcome. Hence, for all their diversity, more recent theories have in common the characteristic that, corresponding to their 'post-metaphysical' and anti-theological basic feature, they think in descent and seek the human fact 'below'—in the realm of so-called hard facts and solid reasons. At least virtually, they belong to a form of thought to which the warning of Heidegger cited at the beginning speaks: that, as one cannot see the forest for the trees, ordinary understanding cannot see the world for beings. It could even turn out—and it happens constantly—that historical and empirical anthropology fails to see the human being in his ek-sisting, in his world-forming essence, for human and cultural facts. Such theories explain less than the human phenomenon, insofar as one understands the latter, with Heidegger, as that which towers up into the clearing of Being. Paleoanthropology is the most exacting and the most incomplete science, because in it the distance between the findings and their interpretation, between skeletal remains and ek-stase, is greatest. The approach to the human situation attempted here is rigorous and at the same time fantastical, insofar as it lets itself be guided by the motif that the clearing itself represents a result of history, indeed perhaps the appropriative event as such. Precisely for this reason it is not only 'to be remembered [anzudenken]' in a meditative way or to be exalted like an absolute discovery. It is impossible for the human being to step into a clearing that is merely waiting there for him, like someone hiking in the forest. Rather, precisely this: that something pre-human opens itself up toward the human; that something pre-worldly becomes world-forming; that something animalistic has outlived itself as an animal and is elevated from out of animality into existing with means; that something which actively feels, which is caught up in its environment, and which is expansive becomes ecstatic, sensitive to the totality and able to be affected by the question of truth—it is this which first yields the clearing itself. In this sense, the clearing and becoming human would be two expressions for the same thing. Insofar as the human becomes a human, Being establishes in him gathering points, clearings, focal points. Hence it is legitimate to also consider a history of the clearing 'from below,' without allowing oneself to be led astray by the contemptuous response of confirmed Heideggerians that something 'merely ontic' would thereby be misused to determine that which is ontological. And what if it came down to precisely this reversal, if contemplative philosophy is to regain the lost connection with cultural studies research?[18]

To start with, it makes sense to pay attention to the theological connotations of the expression 'becoming human.' The stakes of this onto-anthropological wager are hardly lower than those that were present when the mythos claimed that God created Adam in his own image, only then to add that he himself became man at a later point. The religious statements provide a concept that stands at the level of a task: 'the human being' must be thought in such elevated terms that anything less than the resonance with what the tradition called God is insufficient to state his condition. The accomplishment that had been attributed to a divine maker and protector is now to be taken over by a mechanism that makes an animal so de-animalized and monstrous that it becomes that which is ontically there [*Da-Seienden*] in the clearing. Heidegger at least indirectly conceded the legitimacy of such an approach when he wrote in his "Letter on 'Humanism'":

> Of all the beings that are, presumably the most difficult to think about are living beings, because on the one hand they are in a certain way most closely akin to us, and on the other they are at the same time separated from our ek-sistent essence by an abyss. However, it might also seem as though the essence of divinity is closer to us than what is so alien in other living beings, closer, namely, in an essential distance that, however distant, is nonetheless more familiar to our ek-sistent essence than is our scarcely conceivable, abysmal bodily kinship with the animal.[19]

Seen from this quite specific perspective, the human being is determined as a being that has burst out of the system of animal kinship, but in a manner that Heidegger does not encourage us to interrogate. By virtue of an impenetrable ontological alchemy the living beings who were our primate ancestors would have moved away from themselves and would have fit themselves into the system of kinship of ecstase beings, with the result that gods, if they existed, would be closer to us than our cousins, the animals, who are poor in world, without language, and ensnared in their environment. Rudolf Bilz expresses a similar state of affairs with somewhat less pathos when he remarks: "We are not animals, but reside, as it were, in an animal that lives in participation with those like itself and through sharing in objects."[20] What is animal is what moves within the ontological cage that moderns, after Jakob von Uexküll's ingenious coining of the term, call the *Umwelt* [environment], while it is proper to the essence of the human being to execute a breaking out of the environment and a breaking through into ontological cage-lessness, for which we never find a better characterization than the most trivial and deepest word of the human language, the expression 'world' [*Welt*]. Onto-anthropology asks about both at the same time: about human ecstase, which is called being-in-the-world, and about the status of the erstwhile animal that this becoming-ecstatic has befallen.

From what has been said until now one will recognize that the philosophical theory of the human fact can only make progress by an adequate interpretation of the ontological distinction between the environment [*Umwelt*] and the world [*Welt*]. In this pair of concepts the expression '*Umwelt*' seems by far to be the more plausible. Even if it is not older than twentieth-century theoretical biology it possesses the compactness of a universal concept that is able to interpret the aspects of world-openness in living systems retroactively and prospectively. The '*Um*' ['around'] in the concept '*Umwelt*' ['environment' or, literally, 'world around'] traces the ring within which biological systems are interactively engaged and stand 'open' to fellow beings [*Mitseiendes*]. The closure of these rings relativizes the world-openness of the living being to a section marked off from a broader totality. For this reason, '*Um*'-*Welt* has the ontological quality of a cage: the 'proper' environment of the living being is the open natural cage in which the animal's behavior is carried out as an undisturbed life-process. In the singular 'natural-philosophical' layout of his lectures on *The Fundamental Concepts of Metaphysics: World, Finitude, Solitude* from the winter of 1929–1930, Heidegger determined the position of the animal as a midpoint between worldlessness and world-formation and suggested for it the expression 'poor in world.' Within the ring of its environment, phenomena 'outside' are for the animal only ever laden with meaning in minuscule, often innate extracts. The 'world' remains kept on a short leash of biological relevance: as environment it is only ever the counterpart of a limited openness to it. Only one who had broken through this ring could be described as a being who has 'come to the world.' This is the distinguishing ontological mark of *Homo sapiens*. His as it were cageless relation to the world turns out to be ecstatic, because in him the bars of poverty and restraint that enclose the animal within limits are lacking. Radicalized openness is what first calls for the formation of world and self.[21] But this openness must be attributed to the human organism as its own accomplishment. A world-forming being of the human kind cannot possibly be thought along the lines of animal development because animals are at most born or 'hatched' but do not 'come to the world.' The site of the human being is displaced from the mere environment both inwardly and outwardly. In order to illuminate the spatial implications of the concept of world one would sooner have to survey metaphysical fields than physical ones. Nietzsche provides a clue for understanding the connection between world-formation and ecstase in a well-known aphorism, which can be read as a paragraph from an environmental science for gods:

> Around the hero everything turns into tragedy; around the demigod everything turns into a satyr play; and around God everything turns into—what? Perhaps "world"?[22]

If one applies this suggestion to Heidegger's doctrine of Being-in-the-world, then the suspicion arises that it remains stuck in traditional metaphysics to a much higher degree than it is itself aware of, insofar as it would merely rededicate the position formerly occupied by 'God': now it is the human being or Dasein of which it is said that everything around it becomes world. What is here characterized as world must be grasped as an environing world [Um-Welt] without boundaries. It forms a circum-stance [Um-Stand] in which what is striking is precisely that the stationary [stehende] and enclosed character is missing, because, and so long as, it forms a horizon in the face of that which is without boundaries. The situation of the human being 'in the world' befits existentiell seriousness because the question of truth is posed in it. Thus, just as for the animal in its environmental relations it is a matter of success in life, above all in the fields of nutrition, procreation, and its relation to predators, so for the human being in his relations to the world it is a matter of truth—as adequate correspondence to the conditions of existence for individuals and cultures.

Two aspects that stem from unmistakably speculative sources enter into Heidegger's concept of world: on the one hand, contemporary infinitism, according to which the world can only count as world insofar as it bears a relation to the infinite (changed here into the figure of the open); on the other hand, a theological residue that amounts to the claim that the human being is only a human being to the degree that he operates 'in a world-forming fashion' and lets himself be encompassed by the world—as though he were tasked with repeating poetically and technologically the six days' work of Genesis in a second cycle. Thus Heidegger was able to emphasize that the divine comes closer to the 'essence' [Wesen] or mode of Being of the human than to all other living beings [Lebe-Wesen]. One must understand this thesis a-theologically, since it does not aim at religiously enchanting the moderns once more. Rather, it implies that precisely the metaphysically disillusioned human being, for the first time in his recent history, is again able to ponder his own monstrousness in an adequate manner, as perhaps the Greeks were the last to do successfully when they described the world as a compromise reached after the battle of the Titans and Olympian gods. Heidegger thinks of the modern world as a post-Olympian order, in which gigantic impersonal powers vie for supremacy. The monstrous has taken the place of the divine. Hence the valid form of anthropodicy can no longer be an anthropo-theological one, but rather only an anthropo-monstrous one.[23] Around the human being, everything becomes world—yet not because the human being is a god empirically incognito, as ancient and modern idealists who personally stand ready for the airing of a secret suggest, but rather because his positionality is monstrous and because the human capacity for truth proves to be his most uncanny and dangerous endowment. The ontologically monstrous consists in the fact that, around a non-divine being, everything becomes world. Becoming world means being uncovered in a way that is relevant to truth. What Heidegger calls the clearing designates nothing other than this fundamental relation. The term 'clearing' is part of the logic and poetry of the monstrous. Through it philosophy assures itself of its possibility of being contemporary and its ability to converse with the times.

With what has been said to this point we have already gathered together a few elements of the current situation of onto-anthropology. That this perspective, this form of reflection, this combination of the resources of thought, in taking as its point of departure the possibilities of the human sciences conquered by the nineteenth century, could only now have been formed expresses the fact that part of the present human race, under the leadership of the Euro-American factions, has begun to conduct a trial against itself in which a new definition of the human is at stake. All thinking that takes part in this trial takes on the character of a plea in the dispute over the human being. The starkest lessons in the modern self-instruction of the human being proceed from two kinds of nuclear technology, by means of which one was able to break into the safe of nature's secrets in the twentieth century. The question inevitably surfaces for philosophical contemplation as to whether and how these technologies that open nature up 'belong together' with the essence of the human being. The epoch fades away in which human beings believed that they were capable of absenting themselves into an unimpeachability by the monstrous. Because they have become monstro-technicians they repeat with current means the position of the ancient theurgists or maker-gods. Even everyday consciousness perceives something of the uncanny and epochal character of the new technological possibilities that have come into existence. Collective memory correctly identified August 1945 with the two detonations of the atomic bomb over the Japanese cities as the date of the physical apocalypse and February 1997 with the publication

of the existence of the cloned sheep as the date of an incipient biological apocalypse. They are two key dates in the trial of the human
of technology against himself, two dates that attest to the fact that
the human being can less than ever before be understood from the
angle of the animal that he was or that he still sometimes pretends
to be. They testify to the fact that the human being—for the time
being, we are sticking with the suspicious singular—does not exist
under the sign of the divine but rather under the sign of the monstrous. With his advanced technology he conducts a demonstration
of the human that immediately transitions into a demonstration
of monstrosity. He is the subject of onto-anthropo-monstrology.
Unlike Heidegger, we take it to be possible to question back to the
ground of the human capacity for apocalypse. This cannot be found
in 'modernity' alone. We must conduct our inquiry into the human
in such a way that it becomes comprehensible how he emerged into
the clearing and how he became receptive to the 'truth' there. It is
the same clearing into which the first human gazed when he raised
his head, gaining an intimation of world, and in which the flashes
alighted on Hiroshima and Nagasaki. It is the same clearing in
which the human during pre-historic times ceased to be an animal in
its environment, and in which the bleating of man-made animals is
now to be heard. It is neither our fault nor our merit if we live in a
time in which the human apocalypse is a daily fact.

3. Thinking the Clearing, or: The Production of the World Is the Message

In order to understand better the provenance and the possibility of
what human beings as stewards of nuclear energy and as writers of
genetic code are doing today with noteworthy real and imaginary
repercussions on themselves, we once again begin with the basic
principle that 'the human being' is a product—of course, not a
completed one, but rather a product that is open to further elaboration. We add to this the fact that we do not know who or what his
producer is. This not-knowing ought to be adhered to, above all
against the temptation to disguise it by means of the two classical
pseudo-answers, one of which invokes 'God' while the other invokes
'the human being himself' as the producer. Both answers rest on the
same grammatical mirage, insofar as they both apply the schema of
the language game 'X engenders Y' and thereby presuppose the gradient in which the producer precedes his product. But to presuppose
this gradient already means to presuppose the human being and to
short-circuit the *explanandum* with the *explanans*. Thus the human

being could only engender the human being because he was already a human being before he became a human being; similarly, God will only make the human being because he already knows him before he has made him. Such instances of short-circuiting may be meaningful within narrow limits in the case of so-called autopoietic systems; with regard to the human fact, however, which is not a system but rather a historical event, they lead to a blockade against any attempt at a deeper investigation. In onto-anthropological analysis we must begin with an unequivocally pre-human situation in which the result is not already latently or explicitly anticipated. The human being does not hop out of the magician's hat in the way that the ape climbs down from the tree; he also does not emerge from the hand of a creator who surveys everything in advance with his foreknowledge. He is the product of a production that is not itself a human being and was not intentionally undertaken by human beings. The human being was not yet what he would become before he became it. Thus it is a matter of describing the anthropogenetic mechanism and making clear that it proceeds in an unequivocally pre-human and non-human manner, and that under no circumstances may it be confused with the effects of a producer-subject, neither a divine one nor a human one.[24]

Since the late eighteenth century it has become customary to invoke 'evolution' in regard to anonymous productions and to make it, like an allegorical subject, responsible for everything that cannot be traced back to the authorship of the human being. There is a certain wisdom in this linguistic convention, insofar as it contains a first allusion to an engineering without an engineer. In fact, it belongs to the elementary tasks of modern systems theories to think artificialities without recourse to an artist. Nevertheless, we should be attentive to the fact that there is a certain risk involved in using this term, namely, that one may be led astray by means of allegory, because all too easily one again thinks of evolution as a kind of divinity, which would have brought about its outcomes according to a master plan laid out in advance—according to a cunning of reason that produces mutations and selections. This warning becomes acute when it is a matter of contemplating an outcome such as the existential situation that is called the clearing, of which we said that it should be thought from below but respected in its height and breadth. Thus the task for thought is to observe a living being in its breakthrough out of the environment into world-ecstase and to retroactively bear witness to this event with the aid of fantastical reconstructivism.

Again we take the liberty of drawing from Heidegger, the opponent of all well-known forms of anthropology, to specify the key terms for this new configuration of anthropology and the thinking of Being. We find them once more—as in the speech "Rules for the Human Park"—in the "Letter on 'Humanism,'" in connection with statements and turns of phrase in which the role of language in the clearing of Being is discussed. Not for nothing are they the most famous and most obscure statements of an amply obscure text, statements whose obscure luminosity is for the most part perceived as ridiculousness and to whose extraordinariness the following circumstance also contributes: namely that Heidegger here for a moment debates with Sartre at a distance and in French. The decisive expressions are house, nearness, homeland, dwelling, sojourn, dimension, and [the French word] *plan*—which is left untranslated in the German text. I would like to take the liberty of citing at length and culling some passages:

> In its essence, language is not the utterance of an organism; nor is it the expression of a living being. . . . The human being is the shepherd of Being. . . . Being is the nearest. Yet the near remains farthest from the human being. . . .
> . . . The nearness occurs essentially as language itself. . . . But the human being is not only a living being who possesses language along with other capacities. Rather language is the house of Being in which the human being ek-sists by dwelling. . . . So the point is that in the determination of the humanity of the human being as ek-sistence what is essential is not the human being but Being—as the dimension of the ecstasis of ek-sistence. However, the dimension is not something spatial in the familiar sense. Rather, everything spatial and all time-space occur essentially in the dimensionality that Being itself is. . . .
> But does such thinking . . . still allow itself to be described as humanism? . . . Certainly not if humanism is existentialism and is represented by what Sartre expresses: *précisément nous sommes sur un plan où il y a seulement des hommes* [We are precisely in a situation{or on a level} where there are only human beings]. . . . This should say instead: *précisément nous sommes sur un plan où il y a principalement l'Être* [We are precisely in a situation{or on a level} where principally there is Being]. But where does *le plan* come from and what is it? *L'Être et le plan* are the same. . . . 'Ek-sistence' . . . is ek-static dwelling in the nearness of Being. . . . The homeland of this . . . dwelling is nearness to Being.[25]

I do not wish to linger on the assessment that these statements are virtually unparalleled in the philosophy of the last century for their abstractness and hermeticism. Nor do I wish to subject them to an exegesis which could at least show that they are quite rigorous in their logical structure, although at first they sound like sayings proclaimed from the tripod, which exude a malign ambiguity. For now, I would like to draw attention to the fact that we here encounter a Heidegger who no longer ponders so much the equation of Being and time, which had made him famous. Rather, the author of these passages is dealing with a different problem, which without any great effort of interpretation one can identify as that of Being and space. The metaphors and key terms of the text belong to an attempt to advance a non-trivial theory of space or dimension. Above all, the two logically and onto-topologically quite demanding turns of phrase—that everything spatial 'occurs' [*west*]²⁶ within the dimensional and that Being and *plan* are the same—point to an effort at a deepened understanding of that which first primordially 'makes space' for a space or that which first gives a dimension its extension. As obscure as these statements are, they appear to ask what it is that enables expansion and extension from one thing to another thing or into something else; they urge us toward an understanding of that upon which a spatial tension, a relation to that which is further, an ecstase into the open, just as much as a lodging and a deepened Being-at-home-with-oneself [*Bei-sich-Sein*] rest. The remaining terms of this discourse—if they are terms—house [*Haus*], homeland [*Heimat*], nearness, the nearest, dwelling, sojourn, allow us to recognize that human ek-sisting is thought under the auspices of spatiality rather than those of temporality, particularly if one respects Heidegger's etymological pathos, with which he wished to have ek-sistence and ek-stase understood as standing-out or being-held-out into a spatial and temporal-spatial 'dimension' or openness that is not further described.

We employ the metaphor of dwelling in the house of Being as a guideline for the anthropological movement of thought and thus ask how an entirely pre-human living being, a herd animal, which, seen from the paleontological perspective, must have lain somewhere in the spectrum of species between a post-ape and a pre-sapiens, can have started out on the path that led to the "house of Being." In large part the answer is already included in the metaphor as soon as one suspends its figurative meanings and imagines the genesis of the human being as an actual house affair, as a drama of domestication in the radical sense of the word. If one could formulate the theory of the house as the site of human genesis—or better: of housing [*Hausens*] as the engendering of this site—then one would also already possess a paleo-ontology—a doctrine of the Being of the most ancient conditions. It would immediately be the theory of the primal site. It would show how the 'sojourn' or the mode of being-in [*In-Seins*] at a specific site was able to become a motive and ground for the clearing of Being and thereby for the hominization of the pre-hominid. The expectations regarding the investigation of such a primordial bursting site are high, because it must correspond to the state of the art on both sides, the ontological as well as the anthropological. The analytic of the house before the house is the proving ground for the new constellation of 'Being and Space.'

The concept of space that comes into play here is obviously neither trivial nor that of physics or geometry, because, as Heidegger's obscure remark shows, it must be older than all ordinary dimensionality, older in particular than the trusty three-dimensionality by which geometry represents the relations of spatial measurement in a system of places. Like the Platonic *chōra*—to which Derrida has devoted a noteworthy commentary[27]—it must be a space that can provide a matrix for dimensions in general and to this extent be the "nurse of becoming," to recall Plato's metaphor for 'space' as the 'where' which harbors what is able to be. I have suggested the expression 'sphere' for this non-trivial space and attempted to show how in it the primordial stretching out of dimensionality is to be thought. Spheres can be described as places of inter-animal and interpersonal resonance, where the way in which living beings are together achieves a plastic power. This reaches a point where the form of coexistence physiologically changes the ones coexisting. This can be strikingly illustrated in the facialization of *Homo sapiens*: in spherical resonances, human faciality is released from the animal's snout.[28] These spherical localities, in the beginning mere inner spaces for groups of animals, are most readily comparable with greenhouses, in which living beings flourish under particular self-effected climatic conditions. In our case, the greenhouse effect extends to ontological consequences: one can plausibly show how a human Being-in-the-world was able to come about from an animal Being-in-the-greenhouse-environment.

With the concept of spheres a gap, hitherto unnoticed by and large, in the field of theories of space is mended, one which yawned between the concept of environment and the concept of world. If having-an-environment can be ontologically understood as being enclosed by a ring of relevant circumstances and co-conditions for organic life—above all by 'phenomena' with the sense of nourishment, copulation, and danger—and if Being-in-the-world, in contrast, is to be interpreted as an ecstatic towering up into that which is open and cleared, then one must assume that there is a mid-world-position or a between that is neither inclusion in the environmental cage nor the pure terror of being held out into the indeterminate. The transition from environment to world becomes apparent in spheres as between-worlds. Spheres have the status of an 'intermediate openness.' They are the membrane shells between inner and outer and thus media before all media. Without specifically grasping it, Heidegger points to this middle 'zone' with very noticeable emphasis when he introduces 'into the field' words such as nearness, homeland, dwelling, and house—expressions that present the values of acclimatization [*Anheimelungswerte*] on an ontological level. The spherical is the midpoint between dense animal enclosure and the light apocalypse of Being; it allows its inhabitants to be simultaneously localized in the dimension of nearness and in the monstrous immensity of world-openness and world-outwardness. It establishes the primordial spatial 'structure' of dwelling-relations. At the same time, spheres can function as interchangers between forms of animal-corporeal and human-symbolic coexistence, because they encompass physical points of contact, including metabolism and procreation, as well as distant intentions concerning that which cannot be touched, such as the horizon and stars.

How the archaic versions of spheres are formed and how hominization could occur in spherical 'houses' remains to be demonstrated. Now and for the time being I am again using the expression 'house' metaphorically, but with a view to the fact that pre-human beings are, in evolutionary terms, already on a path on which the construction of houses in the literal sense of the word will begin. In any case, this points to the fact that dwelling is older than the house and that en-housing [*Ge-Häuse*][29] is older than the human being.

If we insist on thinking the human being as a product and not presupposing him in any way, then we must take seriously the site of his production: those situations that in the genesis of the human being must have simultaneously been means of production and relations of production. The metaphor of the house has the advantage of representing a site whose distinguishing feature is to stabilize the gradient between the internal climate and the surrounding climate. It allows us to think of protective climates as technological products and of interior locations as institutions. Houses are isolated enclosures that provide their inhabitants with the advantage of securing themselves and reproducing in an internal space, by setting themselves off against a non-interior—for the moment we need not elaborate the difference between vertical isolation, the roof, and horizontal isolation, the wall. Archeological discoveries in the Olduvai Gorge indicate that for more than one and a half million years pre-human dwelling places of the *Homo habilis* grade were surrounded by palisades that kept the wind out. Thus the principle of a wall as a climatic manipulator would already be attested to in a period long before the formation of *Homo sapiens*. If we want to interpret the genesis of the human being and the clearing by proceeding from the 'house,' then there must already be something in the case of the still predominantly animal pre-sapiens that corresponds to a formation of the interior and to a house building before the invention of the house in the architectural sense of the word.[30] Let us therefore observe how animals that will have one day made the leap to becoming human designed the interior in which the leap occurred. Let us attempt to reconstruct how the greenhouse effect that made possible the flourishing of human ecstase was established.

For admission into the human-forming situation the interaction of four mechanisms is necessary, whose intertwinement led early on to bizarre circular causalities. In conformity with paleontological literature, we call these the mechanism of insulation; the mechanism of deactivation of the body [*Körperausschaltung*]; the mechanism of paedomorphism or neoteny, which is characterized by the progressive infantilization and retardation of bodily forms; and the mechanism of transference, which makes clear how the human being can be "on the way to language."[31] (I would like largely to leave aside here a fifth mechanism, that of cerebralization and neocorticalization, on the one hand because its consideration would necessitate a complexity that is no longer manageable for the current outline, and, on the other hand, because in a certain way it synthesizes the effects of the first four mechanisms in an organ developing specifically for this purpose.) Taken by themselves, none of these mechanisms could alone motivate hominization, let alone the emergence into the clearing, but in their synergy they operate like an elevator into human ecstase.

The oldest and least specific mechanism is what Hugh Miller has described as "insulation from selective pressure."[32] The insulation effect is the formal premise of all creation of inner space. Its beginnings reach far back into the history of gregarious animals, indeed back to the world of plants. It is essentially based on the circumstance that the rather marginal exemplars in biocenoses, with their physical sojourn on the peripheries of their own population, produce the effect of a living wall on the inner side of which a climatic advantage emerges for the individuals of the group that habitually keep to the center. Especially in the case of herd and horde animals, it is the mothers and their offspring who profit from this first grade greenhouse effect, insofar as they can move within a climate that is less threatened and presents fewer compulsions for adaptation. Where external selective pressure is diminished, criteria internal to the group take the lead in the allocation of prizes for inheritable characteristics. It is already recognizable at the primate level how 'climatic' advantages flow from the existence of groups into developments that result in the intensification of the relations between animal mothers and their offspring. One could go so far as to say that the most important result of insulation consists in the transformation of the offspring into the child. A mother-child-space as such thereby first genuinely develops, which facilitates refinements, foments participation, and is extended in time. The fact that already in the early anthropoids a trend in the direction of increased childhood was triggered allows one to recognize that it is the riskier form of life that has come out on top evolutionarily—something which would be impossible to comprehend without a solid increase in security in another regard. For all these phenomena the principle holds that the higher forms of gregarious life tend to play the role of 'environment' for themselves; they do not simply grow into an ecological niche but rather produce and organize the niche in which they will move. In this way a natural history of luxuriating forms begins.

The consequences of this extend incalculably far: they show that the laws of Darwinian selection pertaining to fitness are elastic magnitudes that can even be circumvented. A large part of typical human characteristics are formed—as if to fool the social Darwinists—in non-adaptive kinds of evolution that are immanent to groups: in fact, decidedly better conditions of security for the rearing of young prevail within insulated spaces. Evolutionary variations grow into extended spaces that allow for leeway and in which above all a higher standard of sensibility and communicability between the beneficiaries of the mother-child incubator is set. On the emerging human islands "the presence of children permeates human society as no other. . . . [C]hildren's needs have to be accommodated to many if not most adult activities."[33] There is much that speaks for the idea that children were the essential innovators of human cultural behavior. The motif of competition in expression—to which Rousseau devotes his attention in deriving art from jealously in imitation—was certainly introduced by them into culture.[34]

Yet on the paths of insulated evolution nothing more than an advanced apehood would have been able to emerge, such as what we see in the case of the current favorite animal of social psychologists, the bonobos, with their advanced group dynamics and their 'proto-lesbian' sexual life. In order to advance the movement toward bodily forms that are closer to the human and toward comportment that is connected to the clearing, a further mechanism must intervene, a mechanism of which one does not say too much if one remarks that its introduction first triggered anthropogonic drift, in the stricter sense. With it begins the history of *homo technologicus* as the history of an animal that takes things into its own hands—or better, into its paws that develop into hands through the taking of things (for we ought to presuppose the human hand as little as we do the human being). It was Paul Alsberg, with his book *Das Menschheitsrätsel* from 1922,[35] who laid the decisive cornerstone for a theory of human genesis. Alsberg recognized the key mechanism for anthropogenesis in that which he called the deactivation of the body. At issue here is a concept that apprehends the natural-historical possibility of cultural evolution at the critical point; with its aid we can show how the natural history of distancing oneself from natural environments can be thought: proceeding from spontaneous insulations that prefigure to a certain degree the protected spaces in nature against nature, a new dimension of nature-distancing is formed in the evolution toward the human being in the case of certain pre-hominids, along the lines of an at first contingent but then elaborated and chronic use of tools. The Alsberg theorem interprets the genesis of the human being as an effect of a hyper-insulation whose chief consequence consisted in emancipating the pre-human being in many though admittedly not all respects from directly organismic adaptation to the environment. With good reason, the event that is described as a deactivation of the body was characterized as "breaking out of the prison" of an environmental relation determined merely biologically.[36] This breaking out is achieved by the space-creating effect of certain pre-human actions: deactivation of the body depends on a certain activation of the hand [*Handeinschaltung*]. If there were thus something like a primal scene of the clearing from an evolutionary perspective, then without doubt it would consist in a sequence of activities [*Handlungssequenz*] in the course of which the pre-human being—supposedly an agile east African ape on the savannah with generalist features, more scavenger than hunter, far advanced in the tendency toward erect bipedalism, endowed with a robust foot for running on the ground and a paw that for the first time approximates to the human hand—grasps a stone, and does so from the beginning in accordance with aspects of 'handiness' [*Handlichkeit*], as though the interesting stones were formed *a priori* with two sides: with a grasping side for the paw and a contact side for the object so as to make use of the thing in its paw, which forces phenomena in the environment to yield, either by throwing into the distance or striking nearby. By means of this first work of the paws the ontological niche of the human being opens up in nature.

Consequently, the long formative phase of the human is a stone age in the non-museological sense of the word, or an age of hard resources. Here, one may underline Heidegger's observation that language is neither the utterance of an organism nor the expression of a living being. This is already the case *a fortiori* with the stone and every other hard material that is ready to hand for the earliest and simplest applications, particularly bones and branches. The stone does not express the human being; it gives him a chance to step into the clearing. The first resources already bring primitive truth-values in their train, namely successes and failures in their deployment. Hence they have a character that primordially makes space for the world and is *eo ipso* formative for the human being. In the stone the fundamental feature of the readiness-to-hand of equipment [*Zuhandenheit von Zeug*] in the lifeworld gains contour for the first time. But hard resources are more than equipment in the normal sense of the word. The pre-human being produces the first gaps and tears in the environmental ring by becoming the author of a distancing technique by means of striking outward and throwing projectiles, which has repercussions for his very self. The human being neither stems from the ape (*singe*) as overhasty vulgar Darwinians believe, nor from the sign (*signe*), as one finds in the language games of French surrealists, but rather comes from the stone or, in more general terms, from hard resources, provided we are in agreement with the view that it was the use of stones that opened up the horizon of prototechnics. As a primitive stone technologist, as a thrower, and as an operator of equipment with which to strike, the pre-sapiens becomes an apprentice of hard resources. Becoming human happens under the protection of lithotechnics. For the principle of technology comes into play for the first time with the use of stones for throwing, striking, and cutting: relieving the body of contact with presences in the environment. That allows the nascent human being to deactivate bodily contact and replace it with stone contact. While flight is a negative evasion in the face of unwelcome instances of bodily contact, stone technology effects a positive evasion that transitions into a capability. It preserves the dense relation to the object and provides the path to its mastery. Thing-mastery thus becomes advisable as an evolutionary alternative to the distance engendered by flight. Technology transforms stress into sovereignty. That holds for the proximate range that can be manipulated by blows and cuts, as it also does to an even higher degree for the relations of distance to objects that one can throw. The limits of my throws are the limits of my world. The gaze that follows a stone that has been thrown is the first form of theory. If the human being is the animal that has a project then this is because he is disposed to anticipate the results of throws by means of a competence that is acquired early on and that is organismically anchored. The feeling of consentaneity that comes with a successful throw, hitting a target, or an effective blow is the first stage of a post-animal truth-function. One must not allow the primitive nature of the first use of tools to seduce one into the opinion that their range would not yet have been great enough to burst the pre-human being out of his environment. It was sufficient to trigger the primary event of anthropogenesis: the first ontologically relevant production in the sense of manufacturing an effect in an observable space. In order to produce, and thus to be able to bring forth and effectuate, an agent must see in front of himself an opening—some kind of space of leeway or window—in which a transformation in the environment can be perceived as a successful work of his own doing. Precisely this opening is engendered by the technology of stone throwing and hitting, technologies that were soon complemented by those of stone splitting and cutting, which is based on striking stone against stone. The stone, as equipment discovered to throw and strike with, thus becomes equipment for cutting and thereby the first produced means of production. Some paleontologists would like to view the employment of the *second* stone as the genuine criterion for distinguishing what is essential in the human tool department from animal usage.[37] There is also the evidence for early preparations of wooden objects by means of stone. Other researchers see the criterion in the tending of fire, which for perhaps one and a half or two million but certainly for a million years, as the findings in the Escale Cave show, was in use by pre-human groups. Its power for forming niches and spheres and thus the means of emancipation for human groups from climatic and biogeographical backgrounds should never be underestimated.

Through the triad of throwing, striking, and cutting (supplemented by manual operations such as tying knots, scraping, polishing, piercing, etc.), a window is opened in which productions happen and products can appear: in this opening that which 'comes forth' *steps into appearance* [tritt . . . in Erscheinung] in an entirely new way. This coming forth from the results of one's own actions is of a fundamentally different quality than the becoming visible of beings in the plant's budding or in animal births. It is also fundamentally distinct from the 'occurrence' [*Eintreten*] of meteorological phenomena and from the 'appearance' [*Auftreten*] of wild animals or sicknesses. We are already dealing with an authentic bringing about of something by 'labor': in the case of success as in the case of failure the action (*factum*) and the observed and evaluated situation after the deed (*verum*) converge for the first time. The pre-human being as a thrower, striker, and one who cuts apart thus represents, if not the sole producer of, then at least someone who cooperates with the clearing. Only in the clearing—the realm of the observation of success—can truths and activities refer to each other and be on a par with each other. The activity intends success; the success refers to the activity that effected it. The clearing is a work of stones that become suitable for other stones, for nascent hands, and for things that are able to be worked on or struck. The successful blow is the prototype of the proposition. The throw that hits the mark is the first synthesis of subject (stone), copula (action), and object (animal or enemy). Cutting all the way through something prefigures the analytical judgment [*Urteil*].[38] Propositions are a mimesis of the throw, blow, and cut in the space of signification, where affirmations reenact successful throws, blows, and cuts, while negations are born of the observation of missed throws, unsuccessful blows, and failed cuts. The oldest stone artifacts are equipment for work and equipment for signification in one. From the beginning they speak of the power that follows from being-able-to-be-vis-à-vis. Therefore: whoever does not wish to speak of stones should say nothing of the human being.

The ontological result of these first instances of bringing forth is thus much more than an isolated product—it is the opening up of the space in which there can first be results: in this window onto the success of one's deeds, labor processes are carried out, throws are assessed, and results understood. The effects of blows, throws, and cuts establish the bond between success and truth, which in elevated cultural situations is, admittedly, stretched taught, though it can never be torn asunder. (For which reason the late Heidegger, in my opinion, no longer does justice to the clearing when he tends to align being a reflective human being entirely with the renunciation of the will and with a neo-humble insertion into the play of the 'fourfold.' The clearing is thereby thought too much from the perspective of a freewheeling Being-attentive that is elevated to the status of releasement [*Gelassenheit*]. The inceptual clearing, however, is already *in itself* the space of success in which technological approaches to things become observable: as a window onto observations of success it is initially thrust open solely by active interventions and an offensive creation of distance—before it invites aesthetic and meditative perspectives.) In this space the character of hitting the mark belonging to 'truths' and the character of fit belonging to operative syntheses coincide. In it the possibility of readiness-to-hand is achieved—the clearing in the hand, as it were. At the same time, the horizon emerges for the eye that accompanies the throw—the clearing is the expanding of the space of circumspection. In this sense one may say that the result of the Stone Age consisted in the conquest of that natural distance with which the environmental ring bursts in the direction of world-openness.

Heidegger is thus incorrect when he says that it was the Greeks who, with their expression *alētheia*, had first perceived and expressed the 'unconcealment' of phenomena as such. The ability of phenomena to lie open, phenomena that rise to the surface from a prior concealment and can fall back into it, already emerges from the nascent human being's oldest attention to the results of his operations of throwing, striking, and cutting. From these operations truth is read off *primordially* as accurateness: it manifests itself in a throw hitting the mark, in a grasp taking a fitting hold, in a cut passing through in the right place.[39] Only in contrast to the outcomes of his own doing and making does the gaze wander back to the horizon, which now becomes more than a background against which movements stand out. The horizon itself becomes thematic: as an unattainable ring around the whole it provides an ultimate context for everything that is present and appears. It is that which no throw reaches, that which no blow harms, that which no cut wounds. From here the classical concept of Being in early advanced cultures can be unfolded: it designates and encompasses the simultaneously open and concealed, partially attainable but ultimately unattainable substance[40] that is common to all things.

The difference between successful and unsuccessful activities becomes acute in the first openness: even more, from the earliest emergence of language on, even vocal gestures, shouts, and statements are sensitive to the difference between success and failure. The parallelism between materially successful actions and accurate utterances thickens. To the extent that it is a matter of the truth of self-knowledge and not one of strategic or evocative utterances, the evolutionary preference for truth over error and lies thereby makes itself known. Thus does truth enter into the 'statement' and into the picture. The success of hard resources—the resources of the throw, blow, and cut—is reproduced in soft resources, in saying and signifying. Seen from this perspective, language is nothing other than a medium for representing and presenting successes—hence a form that reproduces successes, on the one hand, while on the other hand it is itself the pure accomplishment of discursive success. With every success that is achieved, spoken, and retained in memory, with every word that hits its target, is striking, and is incisive, the pre-human being's distance from his 'environment' grows as he weaves it into the sphere of successfully said things. The pre-human-almost-human animal now becomes expansive and sensitive to distance: its ecstase begins, its space of leeway grows, its capacity for sheltering itself in technological accoutrement and memories of success—and then narratives—increases. In this sense all human beings do in fact strive 'by nature' for 'knowledge,' which is success.[41]

At this point, the all-decisive feedback between the pre-human beings' own cultural accomplishments and the channeling of the gene flow[42] in the direction of the human is played out. One might be tempted to summarize the entire process under the title 'Natural History of the Distancing from Nature' or even 'Natural History of Refinement'—the one thing that would speak against these formulations is the fact that the concept of natural history,[43] which is anchored in British Empiricism, always remained too bound up with the standards of a biology that was habitually blind to culture and technology.[44] In truth, in the case of these seemingly simple, highly explosive processes it is already a matter of nothing less than the clearing. The use of hard resources during the entire span of Paleolithic anthropogenesis engenders an evolutionarily singular situation in which pre-sapiens organisms are increasingly liberated from the pressure for mere bodily adaptation to the external environment. This does not mean that the unburdened species would remain physiologically in the condition in which it found itself at the onset of the body's deactivation. On the contrary, the bodies of pre-human beings now begin to luxuriate: they 'humanize' themselves to the degree that it becomes possible for them to cede hardness to the exterior and to drift inward in the direction of refinement, pampering, and variation. Let us note that the concept of deactivation of the body does not entail that there would no longer be any sort of selection or that adaptive mechanisms would be rendered inoperative. But selection becomes increasingly defined in terms of the greenhouse: it does not so much lead to adaptation to an environment that is exerting pressure, but rather rewards characteristics that facilitate the nascent sapiens' elevated distancing from the environment and thus further non-adaptation to it—for instance, the physical and mental qualities of the thrower, in which, alongside tool making,[45] a good part of hominids' primordial potential for distance must be conjectured.[46] In the greenhouse, tendencies toward fitness and pampering are intertwined and engender an animal orchid effect, as whose outcome the physiological-mental organization of *Homo sapiens* now stands before our very eyes.

At this point we can bring up the intervention of the third evolutionary mechanism. It is what elicits the most dramatic and mysterious effects of all the cited processes. They are at the same time effects from which the unique physiological, morphological, and psychological constitution of the sapiens-species can be read off most strikingly. It should have become clear from the description of the first two human-forming mechanisms that the situation of pre-human beings in their tool-dependent, autogenous greenhouses amounts to a reversal of the tendency of selection. In the greenhouse of the group it is not the most proficient at proving successful on the frontline of given environmental hardships who survives, but rather the most successful at utilizing the climate and exploiting the opportunities internal to the greenhouse. Human evolution is extensively carried out in a group milieu that displays the tendency to reward variations that are aesthetically advantageous and more cognitively capable. In addition, numerous genetic variations become selectively neutral. From now on the human being is on the way to beauty—beauty is conferred as the bioaesthetic prize for sightliness. The luxuriating of feminine forms and the clearing up of human faces testify to this effect in the most conspicuous way.[47] Moreover, it is above all the human brain that in this situation begins to luxuriate in an enigmatic way, insofar as it rushes ahead, as it were, in honing a potential for accomplishment that points quite far beyond the strain it is currently under.[48] All of these effects combine in an evolutionary drift whose results can be grasped in the bodily image of *Homo sapiens*, which was extremely improbable in biological terms. Sapiens-beings, as paleo-anatomical research has unmistakably shown, exhibit a set of features that can only be understood as retentions of juvenile, indeed even fetal, developmental traits into the stage of adulthood. It is the proprium of sapients that monstrous results of pampering were able to be stabilized in these sapients over the long term thanks to the privilege of the greenhouse: this goes as far as the retaining of intrauterine morphologies in the extra-uterine situation—as though this dissident animal could permit itself to escape the laws of maturation.

All of this points to the fact that the 'house of Being' in which the human being will be invited to dwell is attained not only and not even primarily by the clearing power of signs. Before language there are gestures of the hard type (technologies of throwing, striking, and cutting), which distance one from the environment, and which engender and secure human incubators. The specific site of the nascent human being thus functionally possesses the qualities of a technologically supplied external uterus in which those who have been born enjoy privileges of the unborn their whole life long. Thus do living beings who will one day be human beings reproduce initially and exclusively in a preserve that can most fittingly be characterized as an autogenous park. The preserve in which there are human beings is an effect of primitive technology. What Heidegger calls 'en-framing' [*Ge-stell*] and understands as a dire sending of Being is initially nothing other than the en-housing [*Ge-Häuse*] that accommodates human beings and by means of such accommodation imperceptibly fabricates them.[49] This prompts the unsettling conclusion that human beings are living beings that do not come to the world, but rather come into the greenhouse—admittedly, a greenhouse that signifies the world. (In any case, what the late Heidegger said about the 'region' [*Gegend*] and dwelling can be read as a rediscovery of primordial en-housing.)

The exploration and formulation of these contexts is connected with the name of the Amsterdam paleoanthropologist Louis Bolk, to whom the fetalization theorem later modified by Adolf Portman essentially traces back.[50] In essence it implies that a time revolution took place in the case of modern *Homo sapiens* whose consequences continue to keep us in suspense. In this turning point there is a risky acceleration of the period of birth and a much longer delay in becoming an adult—two processes that are guided by endocrinological-chronobiological mechanisms that in evolutionary terms were acquired late. In fact the preeminent feature of nascent sapiens groups is the unprecedented expansion of infantility: it is intensified by the introduction of retained fetal features into the adult phenotype. For this trend the luxuriating of cerebrality is jointly responsible, which can in part be explained by elevated evolutionary rewards for increases in intelligence (probably also by constant access to nourishment from animal protein). This leads to a dramatic increase in volume in the brain, to the more advanced development of the neocortex and to a risky intrauterine cranial growth, whose immediate side effect is the necessity for premature birth. Both tendencies, cerebralization and premature birth, depend on each other in a circularly causal way. They are also supported by the fact that the stabilized group greenhouse is over long spans of time able to guarantee the functions of an external uterus, indeed far beyond the period of postnatal symbiosis between the human mother and child, by means of which, as we know, the uterine deficit of the newborn is counterbalanced. According to psychobiological findings, the human child would need a gestation period of twenty-one months if it were to reach, within its mother's womb, the state of maturation for birth that primates have. However, it must be born no later than nine months in order to have a chance to pass through the maternal pelvic opening. (Thanks to depth-psychological explorations it is well known that even this tends to be too late for countless newborns, because the already very precarious dystocia experienced in complicated human births not only frequently leads to the death of the child, but also after problematic births can induce traumas of enormous scope; this is testified to not only by a series of sexual and religious perversions typical of traumatic births, but also by manifold distortions of the existentiell fundamental attunement into that of panic and catastrophe.) In the case of the modern human type one can proceed on the assumption that the traditional anthropogonic greenhouse already entirely takes on the characteristics of an incubator. The utero-mimetic qualities of human 'en-housing' subsequently reach all the way to adolescents and the adult members of groups and even unleash tendencies in them to delay mature forms.

In this way, existential time emerges within the 'dimension' of human space: it is first noticeable as the dimension of retentions, delays, and pamperings (they constitute the substance of prehistory as the time of hominization), later also as the dimension for anticipations, accelerations, and fortifications (they are the substance of history as the era of rival cultures and wars). The human time machine is subject to the principle of regressive revolution. The depth of regression indicates the need for progression.[51] The extent of refinement determines how much hardship must be directed outward. The achievement of the incubator in turn specifies how far refinement can go in its interior. The clock that tells the human being the hour that has struck for him is set in motion by the fact that the increasingly 'delaying,' juvenilizing sapiens-body is challenged by means of its intelligent potential to take care of its own cultural envelopment—not only its present, but also its future cultural envelopment. Precisely because humanly risky bodies were, on the basis of group-incubator technology that is stable and successful over the long term, able to afford taking features of their fetal and early childhood pasts along with them into the present, they had to learn to tend, in an increasingly explicit manner, their own incubators—to use another kind of terminology: their 'laws.' Pampering compels provision [*Vorsorge*], provision stabilizes pampering. What Heidegger calls care [*Sorge*] is the self-insurance of the context of pampering. This feedback becomes necessary because the improbability of the luxuriating condition unleashes a sense of danger. It becomes possible because the means for the defense of its pampering are given to the pampered animal that is the 'nascent human being,' along with its high-performance brain, its innate thrower-qualities and its quasi-universal hand. Having arisen from the process of pampering, these evolutionarily acquired endowments must serve further pampering. The future is initially nothing other than the dimension in which the improbability of an almost impossible condition, in biological terms, will be stabilized with technological cunning. In this sense, human beings are luxury conservatives *a priori*.

Only because the human being is condemned to provide for its luxury [*Luxusvorsorge*] can Being be understood as time. Heidegger comes very close to this insight with his theory about care in *Being and Time*; however, because of his anti-anthropological interests, he does not succeed in making clear that all care is initially care for en-housing (for which reason he will later separate large opaque intuitions of a highly advanced technological civilization that constitute en-framing from the simple form of en-housing and lament that the former are disastrously excessive). The care for en-housing and the care for self are not to be distinguished in the beginning. Because pre-human bodies become bodies of luxury—and all luxury begins with the license to be immature and with the retention and enjoyment of an infantile past—human beings must tend 'to themselves' and even more to their cultural incubator, their greenhouse of technology, art, and customs. They must become care-animals, which means living beings who take precautions for tomorrow and the day after tomorrow because they already live now (thanks to the opportunity for delay afforded by the incubator) more in the past and in the future than in the continual present of the animal, which on one level they can no longer be and which on another level they nonetheless forever remain. Thus the dichotomy in the human being's essence—striving for pampered carelessness and submission to the imperative of care—is insurmountable. The human being luxuriates ontologically because he physiologically luxuriates, and he luxuriates physiologically because he lives in a greenhouse that *must* be offensively stabilized. One day, these greenhouses of human groups will be called 'cultures'—which one could translate as systems of self-care, assuming that one understands the self of care not in a Foucauldian manner as the individual that labors on the work of art that is his life, but rather as the civilizing residential community of humans, devices, animals, spirits, and signs. Only an animal of luxury, a mature fetus, who hearkens at night in the steppe and gazes wide-eyed at the falling stars ends up in the dilemma of feeling obliged to assure his own future capacity for luxuriating. The time of deliberately securing luxury, and its drawn-out foundering, is history. History begins much earlier than its narrators to this point have believed.

To begin correctly, all anthropological thought must become a way of drawing nudes: a logical and historical meditation regarding the naked human body of both sexes.[52] Human physiology unequivocally shows on several points that are essential for humanity how that which is prenatal has been carried over into that which is postnatal and fixed in place. The female genitalia, whose subventral position in human women is only to be understood through the retention of where it is in the fetus, as exhibited by the unborn of female primates, belongs to the most spectacular phenomena to which Bolk refers—and Gehlen follows him here all the way to reproducing anatomical drawings. In this case, normalized premature birth to a certain degree overtakes the female genitalia, which no longer receives any later maturational imperatives to shift to the ancestral subcaudal position. Human *face-à-face* sexuality with its psychical and symbolic extension depends upon this fixation of the female sexual organ in the frontal fetal position. By means of it human childbirth becomes a literal bringing forth in distinction to the direction of mammalian birth. The formations of the viscerocranium, unmistakable human faciality in particular, can only be conceived if one meditates on the bio-aesthetic wonder of all wonders: that from out of the uterine past a smooth, worldless face—a front side that sees—emerges and stands before the open world. Experiences are inscribed into this fetal slate—but whatever it is that impresses itself, that which was a face can never again entirely revert to an animal snout. The clearing as face remains. Every face is a snout formation that has ceased to take place. In addition, the loss of fur and the unique evolution of human skin only make sense in light of the neoteny hypothesis, as forms of retardation, and as fetal formations that are set in place permanently. In the thin skin of *Homo sapiens* its existentiell program is expressed in an organ language—the clearing as epidermis.[53] Human eyes and ears are organs of the happening of the clearing because they function as biological institutions, as it were, which have taken control of the coming together of the perceptual world and the organism. The organs of the clearing testify to the transition of the biological into the metabiological.

Human intelligence's Being-at-the-home-in-the-world [*Bei-der-Welt-Sein*] is thus not to be thought of in some kind of spatial sense as Being-outside-itself or going beyond. The human being does not comport himself in the world like a bewildered tourist in a foreign land. Rather, human ecstase must be regarded as the self-accomplishment of the humanized organism, which has pre-formed in itself its Being-able-to-be-in-the-world and Being-able-to-be-at-home-with-things [*Bei-den-Sachen-Sein-Können*] and actualized its ecstase in each case according to what the circumstances offer. Human brains are the general organs of the clearing; in them is concentrated the epitome of possibilities for openness to that which is not-brain. The ability of sapient brains to learn amounts not only to a self-proof for organismic intelligence, but together with that to a proof, however indirect, for the reality of the external world. Its dramatically luxuriating development made the most perfect means available for the exodus of the human being from 'poverty.'[54] Through the embedding into the concert of brains like theirs, the exemplars of *Homo sapiens* first become world-capable in an endogenous way. What is crucial is that the largest part of human brain formation occurs in the extra-uterine situation. Through their readiness for late formations, waiting and being open for non-innate, situational, and 'historical' information definitively achieve the upper hand over that which is innate and brought along. The human brain retains continuums of the first world-embedding that are formative for trust just as much as it accumulates incisions, lesions, and losses of world that are formative for suspicion. Thus it becomes the workshop for the relation between *a priori* and *a posteriori*, that is to say, it becomes the organic condition for the possibility of experience.[55] It is the most elevated spawn of the incubator-situation and at the same time the organ of the ecstase that points beyond incubator-Dasein.

If we wish to explain, against this backdrop, how en-housing emerged as the 'house of Being' and how it was furnished and acclimatized, then we must emphasize that it represents above all a repetition of uterine achievements in a space that is publicly open, common, and 'objective.' En-housing is an open incubator. Only through the application of crude technological means for distancing one from the environment can it be produced and established in perpetuity. But only sophisticated technological means of a communicative and symbolic kind—media in the stricter sense—are fit to order and acclimatize the internal space thus produced. The incubator is the intelligent space that language and attention animate. Hence it follows that language is initially the second house of Being, a house within the dimension that promotes and demands houses, which here we are calling, with differing emphases, good en-framing, en-housing, the greenhouse, the incubator, the anthroposphere, and sometimes simply the sphere.

In view of these contexts one can maintain that all technology was originally—and for the longest time unconsciously—greenhouse technology and *ipso facto* indirect genetic technology. From the perspectives of evolutionary theory the pre-human, and even more the early human, praxis of distancing from the environment is always already a spontaneous genetic manipulation—a technology of housing the self [*Selbstbehausungstechnik*] with the side effect of becoming human. Its initial effect consists in the enabling of evolutionary plasticity for the inhabitants of the bizarre space that emerges to the degree that it is opened up and extended by a kind of ecstatic inhabitation. Because human beings exist only as creatures of dwelling, they are unstable, fleeting, by their nature as unfaithful as every animal before them. But they are for that reason by no means 'without essence.' They are essentially pampered and essentially disposed to defend their pampering with the most extreme commitment. Thus they take innate instances of stress programming with them into cultural situations. Indeed, it appears as though cultures to this point had only been routines for bridging between extreme stress that was cooperatively overcome (which is experienced in historical time as war) and the next apex of stress to recur with certainty (the anticipated war).[56]

When Merleau-Ponty says—"We must therefore avoid saying that our body is *in* space or *in* time. It *inhabits* space and time"[57]— what he means is that this dwelling cannot be an inert filling up of a volume given beforehand; inhabitation [*Einwohnen*] is what creates space in the first place and allows itself to be carried from a plastic drifting over to progressive 'habitability' [*Wohnlichkeit*]. It cultivates a being that is pampered [*verwöhntes*] by dwelling [*Wohnen*]. From this an abundance of regional biological differentiations result: from the fabulously hypertrophied *labiae minorae* of certain Khoisan women (macronympha) to the innate resistance to malaria among specific West African populations and the presence or absence of certain digestive enzymes among Europeans and East Asians, to mention but a few among thousands. Primordial dwelling has breeding effects on the dwellers insofar as it draws local gene flows[58] toward forms that are physiologically successful in the greenhouse, but also only possible in the local greenhouse. Thus from the beginning the human being is everywhere a hybrid, or to put it in the language of the nineteenth century: a Decadent—the product of an unconscious domestication, a state within a drift in which the features of the species begin to flow in a dramatic fashion. Insight into the workshop of evolution has been complicated by the fact that this widely unnoticed, pampering, progressive, refining fundamental tendency of human evolution in numerous cultures of the historical era was masked over by secondary inurements and masculine virtues of war all the way up to arbitrary brutalizations. One has allowed oneself to be overly influenced by violence and its internal and external precipitations. The time has come to see that, with regard to the human being, nothing is more successful than decadence.[59] In the intensified harboring of pre-human beings within self-incubating spaces we can see a paradoxical preparation for the world-openness of human beings. The pre-human being first had to be domestic before he could become ecstatic. In this respect, his dwelling and his ecstase signify the same thing; the spherical constitution of his sojourn 'in the world' makes it possible for him to exist 'out there on his own' [*bei sich draußen*]. With the emphasis on dwelling nothing is said about a primacy of autochthony [*Bodenständigkeit*] in the sense of territorialism; on the contrary, only because human beings have lived since time immemorial in (roaming or locally improvised) group-"houses" could they already in a relatively early phase build palisades against the wind and huts, and in a late phase of their history stationary houses, indeed even settle down long-term in celebrated lands and hallucinate land rights. The being that celebrates its land is the later manifestation, *The Nomos of the Earth* its latest delirium. One must detach the capacity for dwelling from an adherence to constructed houses and occupied-cultivated territories in order to conceive in a sufficiently radical way the primacy of the space-forming togetherness of human beings with human beings before the architectural construction of houses. No one has brought this to conceptual formulation in a greater way than Heinrich Heine, who characterized the Bible as the 'portable fatherland' of the Jews: a word which makes clear that the territory does not make the community, but rather the speaking and cooperating community is in itself already the site or symbolic incubator in which those living together cultivate their particular manner of being there [*dazusein*]. Consequently, the space-between-us is older than the land in which we live. The conversation that we are is more fundamental than the soil on which we stand.

Naturally, for the nascent human beings, certain side effects and personal risks in their evolution of luxury do not remain hidden: they see themselves compelled to put themselves in relation to their heightened physical and emotional vulnerability, to their motivational lability, to their endogenous unrest caused by unbound drive-surpluses, to their group-dynamic excitability, and all the way up to the unleashing of paranoid, orgiastic, and self-destructive violence. Thus do conventions become necessary for the reduction of the risks of coexistence belonging to living beings in the incubator. Arnold Gehlen in particular has drawn attention to these phenomena, to be sure in a quite tendentious manner, reaching back to Herder's only somewhat clear conception of the human being as a 'creature of lack' [*Mängelwesen*]. From insight into the labile and luxuriating constitution of *Homo sapiens* he drew the one-sided consequence that this species must continually feel the strong hand of stabilizing institutions. Heiner Mühlmann corrects this authoritarian-style theorem of the creature of lack in his essay *The Nature of Cultures* and shows that it is not so much the weaknesses and lacks that dictate the trajectory of the human *modus vivendi*, as it is the necessity to civilize the evolutionarily inherited stress programs and to tame their belligerent derivations.[60] With this, German philosophers' chatter that the essence of the human being is to have no essence collapses. Human cultures gravitate around the only all-too-essential connection between pampering and stress management.

In order to cope with the self-endangerments that increase for sapiens-beings from their unique biological position, they have produced an inventory of procedures for the formation of the self, which we discuss today under the general term 'culture'—an expression in which normative aspects converge with the invitation to bring in other possibilities for comparison.[61] To the culturally effective techniques for forming the human being belong symbolic institutions such as languages, origin narratives, rules regarding marriage, logics concerning kinship, educational techniques, the normalization of gender roles and age-based roles, not least preparations for war as well as the calendar and the division of labor—all those ways of ordering, techniques, rituals, and customs with which human groups have taken their symbolic and disciplinary formation 'into their own hands'—even more justifiably one could say: in whose hands they have first become human beings and members of a concrete culture. It is these ways of ordering and formative powers that characterize anthropotechnics in the proper sense of the word. Primary anthropotechnics compensate for and elaborate on human plasticity, which emerged from the de-definition [*Ent-Definition*] of the living being called 'the human' in greenhouse-evolution. Anthropotechnics is an appropriate name for this because it aims at shaping the human being directly through civilizing impressions. It encompasses what was both traditionally and in modern times described by expressions such as education [*Erziehung*], taming, disciplining, cultural formation [*Bildung*]. Yet it goes without saying that these procedures would have never sufficed to produce the human being as such: they presuppose an educable human essence but they do not engender it. The more primitive anthropogenetic technologies that triggered autodomestication must have predated them. We must repeat that these technologies engender the human being in only an indirect and completely unconscious way, insofar as they open up a space in which sapiens were able to be drawn into the genetic drift toward their anatomically and neurologically/cerebrally luxuriating forms together with their symbolic extensions.

If modern biotechnology should one day go so far as to conduct direct interventions into the genetic 'text' of individuals, then such augmentations will also be of an anthropotechnical nature—but in a new, more explicit sense. For the first time, secondary anthropotechnics permits the short-circuiting of hard and soft resources. (They are still hard resources, insofar as genetic technology presents a continuation of technologies for cutting, albeit subtler; and yet soft means, insofar as they remain conditioned by the symbolic operations of the sciences and embedded in social discourse.) Such interventions would only be justified if it could be demonstrated that they were insightful and foresighted updates of incubator-evolution on behalf of goals that are locally and possibly also universally recognizable. This would presuppose that both the research community and societies inquire into the evolutionary *and* cultural conditions of the exceptional being whose genetic information they intend to manipulate in individual cases. In particular, it is a matter of keeping away from extravagant ideas about optimization. What, in the American debates concerning genetic technology, one characterizes as enhancing the human[62] in relation to human potential, will, if it ever achieves practical application, in truth present not so much a betterment of human genetic inheritance as rather the active relinquishment of a part of the potential for morbidity that for a hundred thousand years has been carried along in the human gene pool. But whatever could be brought about by targeted interventions in the case of individuals, it would scarcely be of consequence compared to the already accomplished facts about the human genetic situation as a whole. On the one hand, this is characterized by the almost complete deactivation of natural selection; on the other hand by the trend toward the globalization of genes that over a long period of time will bring about the leveling of historical differences between peoples and races. In the long run[63] a post-racial situation will arise, governed by the evidence that the variation between individuals is always greater than that between ethnic groups.[64]

The stepping out of *Homo sapiens* into the 'open' thus does not mean a spatial state of affairs in the ordinary sense. It also testifies to more than the neurophysiological and anthropological findings that humans are beings with curiosity and a natural endowment for neophilia, stress-appetency, and readiness for expansion. What happens in the clearing goes far beyond the lifting of a living being out into a biologically disarmed, more pampered, more experimental mode of Being. It would hardly be significant if human beings turned toward the 'open' without a world arising from the side of things with which they exist to meet them. World-formation means the gathering of coexisting beings in something that encompasses them. In this light, Heidegger was right when he insisted on the fact that in the constellation of the human being and Being it above all comes down to the latter. Being is the world-giving authority [*Instanz*], and the human being is the recipient who, by receiving beings, becomes attentive to the sender, which however can never be present as a being. In this outline of the situation it becomes clear why one ought to hold fast to the ontological distinction of the human being. The affective and somatic refinement of the incipient human being enables him to 'take' notice, beyond the merely perceptual world and the environment, of the fact that from the side of the 'world' more is always to be expected than what has been shown in and by it to this point. With this experience the human being becomes sensitive to what Heidegger will call the ontological difference. Because of it the human being can be called world-forming, if to be world-forming means gathering and further writing the world-text. This implies that an environment can rise up as a world only to the degree that the entire circumstance makes its inexhaustible plenitude and its indecipherable ability to be otherwise palpably evident to the emergent human being. World is the circumstance in which human beings understand that something always 'approaches them' that extends beyond what is standing about, what is present, and what has been opened up. In the clearing it becomes manifest that not everything is manifest. The manifestation is never complete—and the suspicion against what is veiled and not appearing is in principle never to be put to rest.[65] The world attains contour as a composite of evidence and veiling. It is never merely the sum of all bodies or states of affairs ('everything that is the case'), but rather the horizon of horizons in which what is present in each instance is separated from what is concealed in each instance. Ever since there was organized research the question has been raised as to whether 'beings' as a whole can be shifted from being veiled to being opened up, all the way to the point of achieving the goal of virtual total unconcealment. The enlightenment is based on partisanship for total unveiling, while the thinking of Being remembers that every unconcealment remains bound up with a flipside of concealment. If one wished to follow Heidegger's recommendation, then it would be necessary to correspond to that which is still veiled—perhaps coming toward us, perhaps turned away from us forever—only with a stance of available releasement [Gelassenheit], a stance that was hardly ever given to empirical human beings in their historical existence. Either they have aggressively resisted the fact of veiling by means of enlightenment, i.e., techniques of unveiling, or they have subordinated themselves to it 'religiously,' if not in a manner hostile to knowledge, then in any case coweringly and without releasement. But 'to correspond' in an appropriate way to Being, as the differential between that which is manifest and that which is veiled, means to brace oneself for further disclosure or discovery—as well as for ever-new occasions to be suspicious—at the same time as the veiling once more of that which is presently manifest. That is also implied when one says in an everyday fashion that the future will bear it out or that time will pass something by. One then thinks of the difference between that which has been to this point and is today evident, and that which arrives later and will become clear after the fact—or that which today takes up the foreground and yet could one day be forgotten or vanish into the vault.

Human beings get pulled into the stream of time to the extent that they become open to gains in reality. If this increase in the real becomes too threatening to be lived through, then human beings attempt to block the new and to anchor themselves in the old, established, and ever same. Their most important instruments in resisting novelties are, first, custom as the quasi-natural form of the ritual and, after that, mythos—assuming that one defines this as the system that has been the most successful, in evolutionary terms, at dampening world-openness and that at the same time offers a norm of world-disclosure. It was Heidegger's intuition to see through the apotropaic character of even classical Greek metaphysics. In fact, metaphysics, like mythos before it, to which it remains functionally akin despite every divestiture, would like to minimize the risk of world-openness, yet with a new means: the reduction of fluctuating multiplicities to the so-called essence. This operation is supposed to bring the Becoming in Being to a standstill once and for all. The point of thinking with the concepts of essence and substance was to subordinate movement to rest and to tame the incalculable event-like character [*Ereignishaftigkeit*] of processes of life and history through repetition that is controlled by the archetype. Ever since, true philosophers have been the sophists of the eternal. Urged on by his insight, Heidegger sought to lay the ground for new paths, a more authentic constellation between 'thinking' and the 'appropriative event' [*Ereignis*], one which would no longer predominantly be characterized by warding off. What he designated as Being is the excess of that which can still come, can still be unveiled, and can still be said over and beyond that which has come, has been unveiled, and has been said. To correspond to that which has been unveiled and its non-unveiled excess: that means to think in a way that accords with Being [*seinsgemäße*]. In such thinking, that which already lay open is clarified. Thinking in this sense is always only the clarification of the clearing.[66]

In order to complete the schema of the anthropogonic process, the fourth mechanism still remains to be discussed, which we call transference.[67] With Alsberg, Bolk, Claessens, and others, we have interpreted becoming human as an effect of a hyper-insulation. Even highly insulated groups stand continually under external pressure; indeed, they construct for the sake of their internal refinement a precipitous connection with the outside and, when in crisis, come under increased tension. The incursions of the environment into the pre-human/human group-envelopments already reach a fatal climax early on. When among groups of sapiens the hunters again become the hunted; when natural catastrophes override insulated protection; when external forces, in animal and human form, break all the way through into the mother-child-space; when enemies lay waste to the storehouses, harm and carry off entire groups—then relations arise in which human beings pay the highest price for their biological refinement and their ontological ecstase. They suffer to the extreme when their generally stable internal space and the hyper-sensitive organization that befits it implode in the case of external attacks. Now they are, in multiple senses of the term, naked, aban-doned to devastations from without. All the more important for them becomes the capacity to draw on disruptions for a supply of memories and routines that permit a repetition, howsoever trans-formed, of earlier states of order and integrity. The horizon of a symbolic immunology and the psychosemantics of regeneration here come into view, without which the existence of *Homo sapiens* in the chronic suffering of its history is unthinkable.

The recourse to recollections of states from the time before catastrophes is the starting point for the emergence of reparative religions. Their core is constituted by ritual and psychical activities with which experiences of spatial integrity are transferred to states after the calamity. Hence many religious systems are familiar with the concept and the symbolic praxis of rebirth: with it the reconnec-tion of wounded life to the integrity of that which is unborn is most convincingly orchestrated. The demand for regenerative operations sets in when foreign human beings become the highest environmen-tal risk for human beings, thus in the imperial, political, and high cultural period of history, in which the domination of the human being by the human being became chronic torture for countless individuals and peoples. On this view, the historical era of states represents the continual emergency. Religions of salvation are the emergency laws for the perpetual violations of the human being by the human being. As soon as insulated hordes can no longer avoid each other but instead mutually and continuously pressure each other, co-opt each other, subjugate each other, and force each other into coexistence, the 'onto-historically' [*seinsgeschichtlich*] sig-nificant phase of the formation of peoples and their escalation into empires begins.

In these already completely human and historical processes the mechanism of transference ensures that qualities of the first space are carried over into external and extreme situations. Wherever new situations and emergency situations call for being understood and configured, human beings reach back for routines from older, rela-tively integral situations and insert them into the foreign space. Not coincidentally did the Romance and Germanic languages derive their concepts of custom [*Gewohnheit*] or habit from the sojourn in the primary space, i.e., from dwelling [*Wohnen*]: they interpret accus-toming oneself [*Sich-Gewöhnen*] to what is new as a transference of custom. The key to that which, in the case of human beings, one calls becoming an adult in a more than biological sense can be found in this occurrence. To becoming an adult there always belongs a certain settling in to what is not one's own—perhaps even a modest relinquishment of transference, without which no one would be able to encounter the new as new.[68] Adult relations between the sexes are characterized by the fact that at least one partner takes it upon him- or herself to relocate and partially relinquishes his or her privilege of immaturity. In terms of affective dynamics the rule is laid down that one can and should do nothing other than to search for the mother or sister and find a wife from elsewhere, or to beseech the father or brother and receive the foreigner. Endogamous desire must take exogamous paths. The Viennese psychoanalyst derived a comprehensive system of psychological concepts from the observation that the customs of the heart always undergo transference, although the subjects for the most part know nothing of 'whence it comes.' They treat their clients, in favorable cases, by establishing the uncustomary custom of recognizing miserogenous customs as such and replacing them with better ones.

When Heidegger characterized language as the 'house of Being' he laid the groundwork for insight into language as the universal organon of transference. By means of this, human beings navigate in spaces of resemblance. What is important about it is not only that it appropriates the world that is near, insofar as it assigns reliable names to things, persons, and qualities, and enmeshes them in histories, comparisons, and series. What is crucial is that it 'draws near to' the foreign and uncanny, in order to integrate it into an inhabitable, understandable sphere that can be lined with empathy. It makes human exposure to the open world livable, insofar as it translates ecstase into enstase. The 'tendency toward nearness' asserts itself in human language from the first word on; language is always already a poetizing that draws near [*Nähe-Dichtung*].[69] It assimilates the dissimilar to the similar—as becomes particularly clear in the case of the formation of metaphors. Conversely, one could also say that it carries enstase in the customary 'out' into ecstase in the uncustomary. Its essential achievement, as Heidegger observes, consists in the fact that it domesticates [*verhäuslicht*] beings as a whole—or should one say, 'consisted in?,' since one cannot mistake the fact that language in the technological world (where other techniques of drawing near have taken the lead) is increasingly overwhelmed by this task. The making of texts goes its way without metaphors and free of transference. Language is—or was—the universal medium of befriending the world to the extent that it is—or was—the agent of the transference of that which is domestic to that which is not domestic.

In his *Lectures on the History of Philosophy*, Hegel praised the

Greeks for the fact that it was they who domesticated the world for us Europeans who succeeded them: they interpreted the cosmos as the well-rounded house of beings.

> the common spirit of homeliness unites us. . . . Philosophy is being at home with self, just like the homeliness of the Greek; it is man's being at home in his mind, at home with himself.[70]

In the apostle Paul an anti-Greek fundamental attunement had already announced itself, when in the *Second Letter to the Corinthians* he defined the world as a place that remains inhospitable and uncannily un-home-like [*unheimlich*] to the end for human beings:

> For we know that if our earthly house of this tabernacle were dissolved, we have a building of God, an house not made with hands, eternal in the heavens. For in this we groan, earnestly desiring to be clothed upon with our house which is from heaven.[71]

The Graecophile Heidegger takes up the Hegelian motif of world-domesticity, but he transposes it from the idealist-Olympian mode into a pre-Olympian-Titanic one, by making clear that it is not the human being (and certainly not 'spirit') whose being-at-home-with-himself [*Bei-sich-sein*] or housing [*Einhausung*] in the world is at issue. Rather he asks how Being, whose clearing flashes through the human being, can at all be at home with itself. Or, to speak in the jargon of German sociology: how can the monstrous form a rational identity?

4. The Operable Human Being: Toward an Introduction of the Concept of Homeotechnics

It is neither our mistake nor our merit that we live at a time in which the apocalypse of the human being is something that happens every day. We do not need to be in the storm of steel, under torture, in an extermination camp, or to linger near such excesses in order to experience how the spirit of extreme situations erupts in the inmost recesses of the civilizing process. Eviction from the habituations of humanistic appearance is the logical main event of the present, which is not escaped by flight into goodwill. Its consequences reach further than the advocates of the status quo imagine: it shatters all illusions of being-at-home-with-oneself [*Bei-sich-Seins*]. It not only does away with humanism; it also subverts the entire relation that

Heidegger had addressed as the 'dwelling' of the human being in the world. Who couldn't have noticed that the 'house of Being' is disappearing under the scaffolding—and no one knows how it will appear after the renovation, since now even its foundations, the liaison of the culture of writing and the formative education of human beings [*Menschenbildung*], are being shaped anew. The distinctive feature of the current situation of the world, in terms of intellectual history and the history of technology, that most comes to mind is precisely the fact that technological culture yields a new aggregate state of language and writing that has little in common with their traditional interpretations by religion, metaphysics, and humanism. The old 'house of Being' has proven to be something in which a sojourn in the sense of dwelling or bringing-into-nearness from a distance is hardly still possible. The relationship between en-housing and en-framing is to be rethought from the ground up—yet certainly not like the relation between the lifeworld and the system. Speaking and writing in the era of digital codes and genetic transcriptions no longer have the sense of any kind of domestication. The written compositions of technology develop outside of the transference of that which is familiar to that which is unfamiliar and do not evoke any acclimatizations [*Anheimelungen*] or effects of befriending that which is external. On the contrary, they increase the scope of the external and that which can never be assimilated. The province of language shrinks, that of cleartext grows. Heidegger, in his "Letter on 'Humanism,'" expressed these relations in old-fashioned diction, but in a way that is still valid in terms of its substance, when he called homelessness the prominent ontological distinguishing feature of the contemporary *modus essendi* of the human being.

> Homelessness is coming to be the destiny of the world. Hence it is necessary to think that destiny in terms of the history of Being. . . . Technology is in its essence a destiny within the history of Being. . . . As a form of truth technology is grounded in the history of metaphysics.[72]

That there is a connection between truth and destiny which points beyond metaphysical recourse to the timeless belongs to the great intuitions of modern European thought since Hegel. They are prefigured in the schemata of the Christian theology of history. Hegel sums this up when he seeks to indicate a path for spirit that is modeled on the pattern of the sun's course between the Orient and the Occident. In Hegel, temporalized spirit appeared to have managed in the end to enter into a second timelessness that was supposed to ensue after its arrival in the occidental evening. The extreme situation of Hegelianism is the concluded self-apprehension of spirit, the extreme West its geopolitical symbol. Being-at-home-with-oneself would have attained its concluding form in it. Afterward there might still be for spirit but a few uninhabited provinces to round off on the fringes of the inhabited world. Essentially, this statement would already be valid: everything dwells—and where if not in the inevitable West-End of history? When Michel Houellebecq, at the end of his novel *The Elementary Particles*, has his hero, the depressed inventor of biological immortality, seek his death in the Irish Atlantic, at Europe's promontory, under a "soft, shifting light,"[73] this is initially simply a more or less adequate commentary on Hegel. After everything is accomplished one can sink into the ocean without regret. In this world-evening, 'errancy' [*Irre*] would have to come to an end.

Yet Heidegger, had he nurtured narrative intentions, would have had a late hero build his cabin in the hills in order to wait there and see how the story goes on. It was evident to him that errancy persists *en masse*. No total coming-to-oneself, neither of spirit nor of the human species, takes place; rather everything suggests that the disclosure and dissimulation of the human being by means of historical action and technology are in the process of entering into an era of even greater accomplishments and thicker veneers. In Heidegger's view, Hegel was right to provide truth with a history; but he was wrong to have it go from Ionia to Jena, just as he was wrong to represent it as a solar process between rising and setting. According to Heidegger, the history of truth, considered from the state of things in the year of 1946, is not any course of the sun, but rather the burning away of a conceptual fuse that winds from Athens to Hiroshima—and, as we can see, continuing into the laboratories of current genetic technology, and who knows where beyond. In this growth of technological knowledge and capacity the human being stands unveiled before himself as the most uncanny guest that ever emerged among his kind: as the maker of suns and the maker of life. He pushes himself into a position in which he must give an answer to the question of whether what he can and does do is actually he himself and whether he is at home with himself in this activity.[74]

Regarding technological advances, it cannot be denied that this history, insofar as it is a success story of capable knowledge and of knowledgeable capacity, must also be read as a history of truth and its ostensible mastery by human beings. At the same time it is evident that it cannot be more than a partial history of truth and its only ever fragmentary apprehension by human beings and organizations. When the atomic blast flashed over the desert of New Mexico there was no human coming-to-oneself at play. Oppenheimer had

just enough *chutzpa* to call the first nuclear test Trinity. When Dolly
bleats, spirit is not at home with itself as in its homeland—and if its
producers were thinking of their own, then they were doing so in the
form of patents.

NB   —   Now that history is making no arrangements to close the circle,
it remains, together with society that is animated by technology,
caught in a dynamic that Heidegger calls 'errancy.' Erring characterizes existence's historical form of movement, which is not 'at
home with itself' and which makes its way through what is not
its own—whether with the goal of finally coming home or in the
mode of an endless journey that never arrives. In directed errancy
as in undirected errancy dispersal and homelessness precede gathering and homecoming; misapprehensions in self-apprehension are
empirically the rule. Nevertheless: as long as errancy is presented
like an epochal doom the question will impose itself as to whether,
after the generally established subsidence or 'decay' [*Verwesung*] of
conventional metaphysical thought, there must not also be a profound transformation, a twisting out [*Verwindung*], as it were, of
errancy—which appears to be inextricably bound up with classical
metaphysics. The enormous growths in knowledge and capacity in
modern humanity force one to consider whether the diagnosis of
errancy can hold valid for modern humanity in the same way as
it did for times before the development of the modern potential.
Since a thinker such as Heidegger, after two and a half millennia
of European metaphysics and technology, still believes that he sees
reasons for interpreting the world's course as continuous errancy
ordained by destiny, one can surmise that perhaps here a habituated
optical illusion or, to put it in terms of the philosophical grammar
of Old Europe, a fallacy could be present—all the more in light
of the fact that Heidegger, after his unsuccessful experiment with
the 'national revolution' as a turn to that which is one's own and
authentic, no longer suggests how a return from errancy would need
to be rigorously thought. His recourse to the poetry of Being is, even
from a sympathetic point of view, at best a temporary solution.[75]

The suspicion that the theory of errancy, whether with or without
a goal, proceeds from a false account of the relation between the
human being and Being can be corroborated. Even Heidegger, as
much as his significance as a destructor of metaphysics is undeniable, remains partially caught up in a grammar that has for its
presupposition a simply untenable ontology and an inadequate
logic. We have Gotthard Günther to thank for demonstrating that,
in many respects, classical metaphysics, which rests on the connection between a univalent ontology (Being is, non-Being is not) and
a bivalent logic, needs revision. By means of classical metaphys-

ics, we cannot appropriately articulate either the basic views about the constitution of natural objects which are valid today or those about the mode of Being of cultural facts. Holding on to traditional conceptual classifications leads to the absolute inability to describe in an ontologically appropriate way 'cultural phenomena' such as tools, signs, artworks, laws, customs, books, machines, and all other artifices, because in constructs of this type the fundamental high-cultural classifications of soul and thing, mind and matter, subject and object, freedom and mechanism, must miss the mark: all cultural objects, according to their constitution, are indeed hybrids with a spiritual 'component' and a material 'component,' and every attempt within the framework of a bivalent logic and a univalent ontology to say what they 'really' are inevitably ends in hopeless reductions and destructive abridgments. If, in Platonic fashion, one accepts the ideas as what genuinely are, matter can form a kind of non-Being. If one substantializes matter, the ideas are brushed aside as not existing and epiphenomenal. These mistakes and abridgments are obviously not errors of judgment by persons, but rather point to the limits of a grammar. In this sense, they are errors as road maps for epochs. 'Errancy' on such a view is nothing other than the world-historical trace of the Platonic-Aristotelian (put in more general terms, of the high-cultural) program of becoming master over the entirety of beings by means of bivalence.

Now, with Hegel's work—as Günther suggestively demonstrates—for the first time a logical instrumentarium was created that allows one to determine the status of artifices: one can confer upon them the ontological title of 'objective spirit.' 'Objective' here means what is neither subjective nor absolute. Because of its predominantly intellectual- and cultural-theoretical orientation, this brilliant suggestion had to remain blocked during the nineteenth and most of the twentieth century, until finally cybernetics as the theory and praxis of intelligent machines and modern biology as the study of unities of system and environment compelled a new account of the 'artificial' as well as of the 'natural.' Under the pressure of new procedures the concept of 'objective spirit' was transformed into the principle of information. This functions as a third value between the pole of reflection and the pole of the thing, mind and matter, thoughts and states of affairs. Intelligent machines—like culturally created artifices on the whole—compel traditional thought on a wider front to recognize the fact that 'spirit' or reflection or thinking has undeniably entered into concrete states and persists in them in ways that can be recovered and further worked on. Machines and artifices can only be understood as really existing negations of states before the imprinting of the *in-formatio* in the bearer. They are storage sites for their histories of production or memories bound up in things. One can characterize them as materialized reflections or reflections that have become objective. In this, they indicate a kinship with persons, who in their degree of educational 'formation' ['*Bildung*'] likewise represent agencies and states of 'objective spirit.' In order to think this, we need a bi- or polyvalent ontology in connection with an at least trivalent logic, thus an instrumentarium by means of which we can articulate the fact that there are really existing affirmed negations and negated affirmations, or existing nothingness [*das seiende Nichts*] and the existent that is enriched by nothingness [*das nichtsangereicherte Seiende*]. The statement 'There is information' ultimately implies only this. Concerning its facilitation and consolidation there has been a clash of the titans of thought in the past century, in the denouement of which authors such as Günther, Adorno, Bloch, Deleuze, Derrida, and Luhmann (along with Klaus Heinrich, Michel Serres, Bruno Latour, Heinz von Foerster, and others) have intervened with notable consequences. They all labor to seize hold of the *tertium datur*.

Statements such as 'There are systems, there are memories, there are cultures, there is artificial intelligence'[76] depend on the statement 'There is information.' Also the statement 'There are genes' can only be understood as a product of the new situation—it indicates the leap of the principle of information into the sphere of nature. On the basis of these gains in concepts that are capable of seizing hold of reality, the interest in traditional figures of theory such as the subject-object relation fades. The constellation of ego and world has lost its sheen, to say nothing of the polarity of individual and society that has become completely lusterless. What is crucial is that with the idea of really existing memories and self-organizing systems the metaphysical distinction between nature and culture becomes untenable, because both sides of the difference only present regional states of information and its processing. One must brace oneself for the fact that understanding this insight will be especially difficult for intellectuals who have made their living on positioning culture against nature, and now suddenly find themselves in a reactive situation.

If one looks for deeper motivations for the 'errancy' of historical humanity, one of its causes can be discovered in the fact that on the whole the agents of the metaphysical age have obviously approached beings as a whole with an inadequate account. As we have seen, they divide beings into subjective and objective and set that which pertains to the soul, the ego, and the human off to one side and that which pertains to things, that which is mechanical, and that which is non-human off to the other. The practical application of this distinction is called domination. If a legitimate reason for mastery and for Being-Master over something can be demonstrated, then it will consist in the fact that according to this schema the soul claims an incontestable precedence over that which is non-psychical, that which pertains to things. In the course of the technological enlightenment—this occurs *de facto* through machine engineering and prosthetics—it turns out that this classification is untenable because, as Günther emphasizes, it attributes a profusion of properties and capacities to the subject and to the soul that in reality belong on the side of mechanism. At the same time, things or materials are denied an abundance of properties that they undeniably possess upon closer inspection. If these traditional mistakes on both sides are corrected, a radically new view of cultural and natural objects emerges. One begins to understand both that and how 'informed material' or advanced mechanism can yield para-subjective accomplishments—all the way to the appearance of an intelligence that plans, a capacity for dialogue, spontaneity, and flexibility. Conversely it becomes apparent that numerous manifestations of traditionally conceived instances of subjectivity and the soul only represent overinterpreted kinds of mechanism.

It is not an overstatement if one characterizes this revision of the false metaphysical classification of beings as the contemporary gigantomachy that reaches deeply into ingrained human self-relations. Very many view this revision suspiciously as an expropriation of the self and condemn it as technological devilry. The uncanniness of the process is not to be denied, precisely because it impresses by means of its results. The humanistically minded observer cannot withdraw his fascination because everything that happens on the technological front leads to consequences for human self-understanding. In the progress of technological evolution the citadel of subjectivity, that is to say, the thinking and experiencing ego, is impinged on, and to be sure not only by symbolic deconstructions that were, incidentally, anticipated in various ways in regional high cultures—one might think here of the mystical and yogic systems, of negative theology and Romantic irony—but also by material modifications, for instance, the alteration of mental states with the help of psychotropic substances (a procedure that for millennia has been common in drug cultures, and for decades in Western psychiatry). In addition, a time is foreseeable when the contents of ideas and experience will be induced by means of nootropic substances.

The most spectacular encroachment of the mechanistic into the subjective field that formerly appeared autonomous is ushered in with genetic technologies. They draw a broad span of corporeal preconditions for the self into the range of artificial manipulations.

Tied to this is the popular, more or less fantastical idea that one could 'make' entire human beings in the foreseeable future—in the course of which fantasies primitive biologisms vie with helpless humanisms and theologisms, without the proponents of such views demonstrating a trace of insight into the evolutionary conditions of anthropogenesis.[77] The basis for the anxiety-ridden incursion of technology into the imaginary field of the 'subject' or the 'person' is to be sought in the fact that even on the side of the so-called object, in the basic material structure of life, as is present in genes, hardly anything is encountered that is thing-like in the sense of the old substance ontology, but rather a form of informed and informing information that has been reduced to the material minimum—genes are, as bio-computer scientists [*Bio-Informatiker*] say, nothing other than 'commands' for the synthesis of protein molecules. (What they are 'in reality' cannot be further determined in a manner that is independent of the observer, since only in the interpreter's mode of access can it be decided whether he is dealing solely with biochemical causal mechanisms or with information bound to a material bearer.) It is clear that in these processes the traditionally interpreted personal subject no longer rediscovers anything to which it was accustomed— neither the side of the self, as it was presented in the moral traditions, nor the side of things, as one was familiar with them in dealing with them in the lifeworld and preparing them for scientific study. For this reason it appears to the subject that is bound to tradition as though it were confronted with an alarming case of anti-humanism: it seems to the subject as though in current biotechnology there were the sharpest opposition to the humanist and Olympian program of appropriating the world as a home for the human subject or the spirit/person and integrating its externality into the self. It now appears rather as though the self would be submerged without remainder into thingliness and externality and would be lost there.

It is almost unnecessary to say that this terrifying idea is only a hysterical illusion and as such represents a psychological side effect of the bivalent basic division of beings. The human being is not an authority [*Instanz*] that would have to, or that would be able to, choose between Being-entirely-at-home-with-itself and Being-entirely-outside-of-itself. He can decide just as little between total self-transparency and completely mistaking himself as between absolute gathering and utter dispersal. He is a regional possibility of clearing and a local energy for gathering. The human being is a gathering site for truth and power, but not a gatherer of everything: herein consists the concept of a post-metaphysical logos and poetizing [*Dichtung*] that one day will probably be understood as Heidegger's most momentous idea; he unleashes the transition to

the Deleuzian doctrine of multiplicities. It is this which the thinker
of 'Beyng' worked out in his protracted battle to resist Hegel's ideology of absolute spirit and its humanist iterations. In the "Letter on
'Humanism'" one reads:

> Thinking does not overcome metaphysics by climbing still
> higher, surmounting it, transcending it somehow or other;
> thinking overcomes metaphysics by climbing back down into
> the nearness of the nearest. . . . The descent leads to the poverty
> of the ek-sistence of *homo humanus*. . . . To think the truth of
> being at the same time means to think the humanity of *homo
> humanus*.[78]

The passage is noteworthy not only because it allows one to surmise
what one should think of Heidegger's denouncers, who can't indict
his supposed 'anti-humanism' enough. It provides a starting point
for understanding human existence as a noble flaw and a local
power of poetizing. Dasein is a passion in view of the monstrous and
immense. The poverty of ek-sistence is not the world-poverty of the
animal, but rather the sheer exposure to the incongruous. Here we
encounter a Heidegger who stands closer to Augustine and Pascal
than to Hegel and Husserl. By the way, one can also express these
matters in an almost Nietzschean language: one would then say that
the human being is a vector of forces or a bundle or an aleatoric
composition.[79]

The anti-technological hysteria that holds broad sections of the
Western world in its grip is a product of metaphysics' decay: it is
betrayed by the fact that it clings to false classifications of beings in
order to revolt against processes in which the overcoming of these
classifications has already been carried out. It is reactionary in the
essential sense of the word, because it expresses the *ressentiment* of
obsolete bivalence against a polyvalence that it does not understand.
That holds above all for the habits of the critique of power, which
are always still unconsciously motivated by metaphysics. Under the
old metaphysical schema the division of beings into subject and
object is mirrored in the descending grade between master and
slave and between worker and material. Within this disposition the
critique of power can only be articulated as the resistance of the
oppressed object-slave-material side to the subject-master-worker
side. But ever since the statement 'There is information,' alias 'There
are systems,' has been in power this opposition has lost its meaning
and develops more and more into a playground for pseudo-conflicts.
In fact, the hysteria amounts to searching for a master so as to be
able to rise up against him. One cannot rule out the possibility that

the effect, i.e., the master, has long been on the verge of dissolving and for the most part remains alive as a postulate of the slave fixated on rebellion—as a historicized Left and as a museum humanism. In contrast, a living leftist principle would have to prove itself anew by a creative dissidence, just as the thinking of *homo humanus* asserts itself in the poetic resistance to the metaphysical and technocratic reflexes of humanolatry.

As was indicated, to think *homo humanus* means to reveal the level at which the equation of being human and the clearing is valid. But the clearing, as we now know, is not to be thought without its technogenic provenance. The human being does not stand in the clearing with empty hands—not like some destitute alert shepherd with his flock, as Heidegger's pastoral metaphors suggest. The human being disposes over stones and the successors of stones, over tools and weapons. What he becomes is conditioned by that which is at hand for him. *Humanitas* depends on the state of technology. The more powerful the technologies become, the sooner human beings drop the tools that have grips and replace them with tools that have buttons. In the Second Machine Age the activity of handling recedes in favor of operations at the tips of one's fingers[80]—a process that radically transforms the understanding of the *vita activa*. Yet whether one contemplates the age of gripping or the age of pushing buttons, the incubators of human beings and of humanity are engendered by technologies of hard resources and acclimatized by technologies of soft resources. *Nous sommes sur un plan où il y a principalement la technique.*[81] If the human being 'is given' [*'es'* . . . *'gibt'*], then that is so only because a technology has brought him forth from out of pre-humanity. Technology is that which genuinely gives the human or the *plan* upon which the statement 'There are human beings' [*Es gibt Menschen*] can be true. Hence nothing alien is happening to human beings when they expose themselves to further production and manipulation. They do nothing perverse or contrary to their 'nature' when they alter themselves auto-technologically. Yet these interventions and aids would have to happen at such an elevated level of insight into the biological and cultural 'nature' of the human being for them to become effective as authentic and successful co-productions with his evolutionary potential.

Karl Rahner articulated this insight in Christian terms, when he emphasized that "the human being of contemporary autopraxis" avails himself of a freedom of "categorial self-manipulation" that originated in the Christian liberation from the numinous compulsion of nature. According to the testimony of the Jesuit Rahner it belongs to the ethos of the mature human being to be obliged to and to wish to shape himself in a self-manipulative fashion:

He must wish to be the operable human being even when the scope and the just mode of this self-manipulation are still largely obscure.... But it is true: the future of human self- – manipulation has already begun.[82]

One can express the same insight in the diction of a radicalized historical anthropology by interpreting the human situation through its emergence from out of an autoplastic development of luxury. Because of this development plasticity remains a fundamental reality and an unavoidable task. Yet one must guard against conceiving the anthropo-plastic operations that have recently become possible, from current organ transplants all the way to future gene therapy, still from the perspective of false classifications—as though, for instance, a subjectivist master still wished to enslave an objectivized material—or, even worse, to develop himself further into a super-master who tyrannizes subjugated material even more deeply. The schema of the master subject that wields power over a servile material possessed an undeniable plausibility in the era of classical metaphysics and its simple bivalent policies and technologies. For this era it tended to be true that the subjectivist master, when he used tools, enslaved objects and was seldom or never just to their own nature, especially when these 'instruments' were themselves human beings who should have been able to make a claim to subjectivity or freedom from masters. From this there arises an image of technology that is based on simple tools, classical machines, and traditional relations of domination between souls and materials: this complex remains determined by allotechnological means that serve to carry out violent and counter-natural incisions into that which is discovered and to employ materials for ends that are indifferent or alien to them. In the traditional concept of matter it is assumed that, on the basis of its resistant and minimal qualities, it will only be used heteronomously. The older technology shifts the world of things into a state of ontological slavery: to be sure, the intelligentsia has always risen against this when it was insightful enough to take the side of the otherness of objects that were only used and perverted for extrinsic ends. Yet hardly anything could be changed about the supremacy of domination. Where, nonetheless, an opposition to compulsory idealism is articulated, it speaks the language of an emancipatory 'materialism' that was pre-theoretically expressed in the spheres of ancient craftsmanship as the reminder that it is the wisdom of master craftsmen not to compel things. Among the master craftsmen of thought it was probably Spinoza who most lucidly pointed out how the joining of current power to the potential of things should be carried out without delusions of domination and artificial despotism: "If, for instance, I say that I can rightfully do what I will with this table, I do not certainly mean, that I have the right to make it eat grass."[83]

At the level of the statement 'There is information' the traditional image of technology as heteronomy and enslavement of materials and persons increasingly loses its plausibility. We become witnesses to the fact that with intelligent technologies a non-domineering form of operativity is emerging for which we propose the name 'homeotechnics.' By its nature, homeotechnics cannot desire anything wholly different than that which the 'things themselves' are or can become of their own accord. In complex thinking, 'materials' are conceptualized on the basis of their own proper sense [*Eigensinn*][84] and are factored into operations on the basis of their maximal suitability—they cease to be that which used to be traditionally characterized as 'raw material.' There is only raw material where domineering subjects in the traditional sense—here we would be better off saying: raw subjects—apply corresponding raw technologies to them. In contrast, because it has to do with really existing information, homeotechnics only progresses on the path of the non-violation of what is present. It apprehends intelligence intelligently and produces new states of intelligence. It can only be successful as non-ignorance vis-à-vis embodied information. Even where it is initially employed as egotistically and regionally as any conventional technology it must draw on co-intelligent, co-informative strategies. It has the character of cooperation rather than that of domination, even in the case of asymmetrical relations.

A few prominent natural scientists of the present day express similar ideas with the metaphor of a 'dialogue with nature.' This expression only makes sense if one also keeps in mind that it is supposed to supersede the standard idea of a war with nature. From the side of the human sciences Foucault has stipulated that as a bearer of a piece of knowledge one never escapes from the compulsion and the opportunity to be powerful—in this way he undoes the metaphysically and illusorily tied knots of the critique of power. A mode of thinking germinates here that is anticipated in modern philosophies of art, particularly in Adorno—even if still under a misleading title such as 'primacy of the object.' It now awaits its completion by the philosophy of technology and above all by social theory and its popularizers. For the future, to develop technologies means: to read the scores of embodied intelligences and to help provide for further performances of their 'own pieces.' The extreme situations of homeotechnics are the critical cases of co-intelligence.

Technology, Heidegger has taught, is a mode of revealing. It brings results to light that would not do so of their own accord in that particular way at that particular time. Hence one could even characterize it as a mode of accelerating success. History appears to be the temporal form in which human beings increasingly work with anticipations and bring themselves into situations in which they cannot wait for things to happen by themselves. From this results a characteristic correspondence between a technology of manufacturing and economic enterprises on the one hand, and between ethnotechnics and war on the other hand. For entrepreneurs and generals it is a matter of deciding on competitions with rivals and enemies that will lead to their own success and advantage. They are condemned to become intelligent earlier than others. But as a rule they only get to that degree of intelligence that corresponds to the current state of enlightened egotism. They cannot break free from the relation of raw subject and raw material.

As long as this is the case, homeotechnics—the acceleration of intelligence par excellence—is also affected by the problem of evil, although this is now portrayed not so much as the will to enslave things and human beings as the will to handicap the other in cognitive competition.[85] It is no casual observation that classical allotechnics was wed to suspicion as a way of thought and to cryptological rationality; its psychological sediment is consequently paranoia. Up to this point there is no technology that cannot be suspected of being a resource in the hands of an enemy. To be sure, the emergence of a post-paranoid culture of reason is on the agenda of very technologically and communicatively advanced civilizations, but is delayed by powerful forces of inertia from the era of bivalence and its habit of violating beings in general when it comes into contact with them.

One of the starkest contributions to the hypothesis that the mistrustful mood will remain in line with reality even in the future was made by the American Supreme Commanders in August 1945 when they did not refrain from immediately using the most extreme allotechnological weapon, the atomic bomb, against human beings. Thus they have provided an epochal argument for the suspicion that is characteristic of the moral state of modernity against the alliance of the highest technology and vulgar subjectivity. Because of Hiroshima and Nagasaki human beings around the world have another strong reason to believe in technologists' fundamental lack of restraint. In view of what has happened they feel they are justified in mistrusting potential Oppenheimers and Trumans of genetics. These proper names summarize the fact that for an entire age raw subjects and allotechnologies have fit each other like a hand on a grip.[86] From fear of this constellation, one dictates discourses which prophesy that genes, as the raw material of the biotech century,[87] will play the same role as coal did in the Industrial Revolution.[88] Such ways of speaking proceed on the assumption that relations between human beings as well as between humans and things would forever have to follow the historical pattern of bivalent domination or of the primitive subjective disposal over alienated materials.

We need to test the validity and appropriateness for the future of such deep-seated stances of fear. From the complexity of the things themselves the suspicion forces itself upon us that allotechnological habits will no longer be effective in the homeotechnological realm. The genetic scores do not work together with the violators for very long—as little as open markets comply with the whims of the dominant. One may even ask whether homeotechnological thought—announced up to now by titles such as ecology and complexity science—does not possess the potential to open up an ethics of relations that are free of enemies and domination. It virtually bears this tendency in itself, since it is arranged less for the reification of the other than for insight into the internal conditions of what coexists with it [des Mitseienden]. While in the allotechnological world domineering subjects are in command over raw materials, in the homeotechnological world it will hardly be possible for raw-masters to exercise power over the finest materials. The very condensed contexts of the interconnected world no longer favorably receive domineering inputs—here only that which also benefits countless others can successfully spread.

If these civilizing potentials were to be generalized, then the homeotechnological era would be distinguished by the fact that in it spaces of leeway for errancy become narrower while spaces of leeway for gratification and positive association grow. Advanced biotechnology and nootechnology groom a refined, cooperative subject who plays with himself, who is formed in association with complex texts and hyper-complex contexts. Here emerges the matrix of a humanism after humanism. Domination must tend in the direction of ceasing because, as crudeness, it makes itself impossible. In the interconnected, inter-intelligently condensed world masters and violators only still have chances for success that last little more than a moment, while cooperators, promoters, and enrichers—at least in their contexts—find more numerous, more adequate, more sustainable connections. After the abolition of slavery in the nineteenth century a more extensive dissolution of the remnants of domination looms for the twenty-first or twenty-second—no one will believe that this can happen without intense conflicts. One cannot rule out the possibility that reactionary domination will once again band together with the mass *ressentiments* of losers to form a new mode of fascism. The ingredients for this are above all present in the mass culture of the United States of America. But like their rise, the foundering of such reactions is foreseeable.

In a world in which the condensation of context [*Kontextverdichtung*] and determination of all relations by knowledge progresses, the principles of Platonic ontology often derided by critical intellectuals—all beings are good, evil is only the absence of the good—will be vindicated with a delayed significance. The change in meaning pertains to the transition from nature to technology. Where Plato has the good of (nature) in view, modern thought intends the *hardly* good of technology (or the good of method or the good of institutions). While the classical concept of nature traces the goodness of what is real to timeless archetypes of perfection, the artificial works of the modern world must prove their goodness by being tested over further generations of praxis. Here nothing is good that is not continually improved. To be means to be tested. Overwhelming evil or badness operates in a manner that delimits and eliminates itself; overwhelming good has virtues that extend and advance themselves.

The gravity of the bad experiences that human beings have had speaks against such a view of things. The pathogenic heritage of bivalence and strategic-polemological paranoia casts its shadow far into what is to come. The habits and pressures, which have developed over an era, to classify complex relations in a way that violates them are not resolved overnight; cultures in which suspicion and *ressentiment* are in power flourish intensely on a regional level. Egotistical constructions of identity contribute their part to blocking the generous potentials that can be released by the thought of polyvalence, multiplicities, and homeotechnics. As long as this holds valid, that which has been surpassed will remain more compatible than is fitting for it. Hence, raw subjects strive further for disposal over raw materials—although there can only still be both in reactionary positions. Reaction remains a world power. Must one emphasize that it is up to the creative intelligentsia to rebut the reaction?

Under such premises it is no accident that one often describes the current race for the genome and its economic exploitation as a cognitive war. In the worst and most conventional case it would again be nothing other than the exercise of power by raw human beings over raw materials—that is to say, protracted errancy and adherence to a false classification of beings. It is to be expected that this disposition will already disprove itself in the medium term by failures and increasing social incompatibility. As in all wars the strategic, egotistical, and raw use of intelligence reinforces dissimulation, one-sidedness, and the de-democratization of knowledge.

That allows for a revival of the suspicious disposition. Highly condensed contexts, as advanced cultures of technology express them, are nevertheless not continually operative on the basis of suspicion and dissimulation. The society of the future is condemned to have faith. Pascal's statement that the human being infinitely exceeds the human being tended to be true for the era of classical metaphysics. In that epoch nothing was as fierce as the feeling that the human being is not yet what he can become; the scales of his sublimation stand open toward the heights. In the current period, rather, it becomes evident that the human being undercuts the human being without end—and does so with a semblance of justification, as long as other undercutters make it necessary for him to enter into a competition for crude acts with them. Only a minority is aware of the fact that with postclassical technology—as with the authentic arts—the better competition has already begun.

When capital and empires grasp after information, the world's course increasingly changes into a kind of divine judgment that antagonistic intelligences pass on themselves. Not for the first time does it become evident to human beings that using their intelligence necessarily involves making decisions. In a key passage of the bivalent era one reads:

> I call heaven and earth to record this day against you, *that* I have set before you life and death, blessing and cursing: therefore choose life, that both thou and thy seed may live.[89]

How can we repeat the choice of life in an epoch in which the antithesis of life and death was 'deconstructed'? How should a blessing be thought that goes beyond the all-too-simplified opposition of curse and blessing? How would a new covenant be formulated in view of complexity? Is it a covenant with a transcendent pole? Is it an alliance between human beings who have grasped that in everything that concerns them, insight and blindness are interlaced? In questions such as these the recognition is also expressed that no ethics works successfully for modern thought, as long as its logic and its ontology remain unclear.

4

WHAT IS SOLIDARITY WITH METAPHYSICS AT THE MOMENT OF ITS FALL?

Note on Critical and Exaggerated Theory

Nous vivons sous le règne de l'hyperbole.[1]

F. Bruno

1. Informal Redemption

As we learn from Adorno, there is also an obsolescence of new philosophy. Its more significant works pass through an intermediate state after the death of their authors, a state in which they are neither up to date nor canonical, but rather float suspended in a ghostly disintegration. The motifs that were once linked with a proper name become separated from the bearer of that name. They become unmixed and pass through a stage that can be compared to composting. In this regard, arbitrary radicalizations of individual themes are just as typical as new combinations of separated elements with transformed emphases; others sink into the irrevocable past. Only in decay, so it seems, does the truth concerning the structure of a philosophical synthesis find its way into the light. This analysis by means of dismantling happens even when the philosophical text, such as the Adornian one, sought to escape such a fate through its antisystematic confessions. Decomposition is in store not only for systems in the genuine sense of the word, but also for informal thinking, which reflected its loose structure by arising not as a system, but rather as *écriture*.

Systems and *écritures* are synthetic efforts to work their way through something that is currently obscure. Yet it holds for symbolic syntheses as for consciousnesses in general: you never step twice into the same confusion. For every later consciousness, its predecessors' acts of processing chaos tend themselves to be potentiations of given confusions, and my further processing must respond ever anew to the preceding accomplishments as though they were part of the problem and not the solution. Whoever comes late in the history of ideas is irritated by growing obscurity.

This has consequences for the possibility of being a student. To be sure, as an adherent of a school I can seek shelter for a while in a teacher's way of thinking and borrow order from those who have thought before me. But when being a student comes to an end, the intellect, which is now alone and hardly protected, is confronted with the chaos exacerbated by the system of the teacher. In any case, a sufficiently restless ego never holds out for long in a system that provides shelter. From its own states it gathers that systems and written works are only possible as the homes of others. Only others can reside in their attempts at self-reassurance, while my unrest condemns me to the impossibility of having a system. This unrest grows with the advancement of the history of ideas while the quota of those who position themselves in the heart of unrest sinks. The free spirit is only another name for the affirmation of this unrest, which allows me to disregard my own needs for identity.

We must proceed from the fact that no two philosophical intellects, no two instances of unrest can be located at the same generative point of a formation of a system or of a contrivance of a written work. Therein lies a formal reason for why in modern times even great synthetic efforts are already condemned, in the medium term, to disintegration. In the mind of a creator of syntheses what are only more or less loose syntagmata for students and even more for free recipients may compellingly cohere. Not unjustly did Nietzsche remark that the most important function of a philosophical system consists in convincing its originator. One can check the correctness of this realization by surveying authors from the perspective of when and how often they repeat their fundamental theorems. What appears as a system is always also an autohypnosis. Communities of plausibility inevitably disperse in the drift of changing mentality, although the protective academic climate artificially postpones their expiration date. Only those syntheses that provide the impetus to a variety of deviations and fragmentations prove to be culturally successful. This took place after Hegel, it took place after Husserl, and it obviously took place after Heidegger, whose anarchitectures have provoked as many erosions as the most highly towering doctrinal system. To what extent does this hold for the work of Adorno and the legacy of the older Frankfurt School?

From the beginning it is to be expected that here things will take a different course. The dissolution of Adorno's synthesis does not

occur on account of the contradiction of those who come afterward, but rather on account of a kind of historical pressure drop.
It is the transformed intellectual circumstances that increasingly
detract from the plausibility of his work. If the Adornian Hegelian-
Nietzscheanism was already in its own time an idiosyncratic
construction and highly unlikely, then a quarter-century after its
author's death it appears to be completely unrepeatable. This takes
nothing of the sheen away from the work, but the idea that, proceeding from such an impulse, it could form a lasting school ever
more clearly turns out to be an illusion. Among the components in
which the once so suggestive synthesis of radical aesthetics, messianism, and sociology disintegrates, the theological motif takes on
a special, if not easy to determine, significance. What, in the integral form of the Adornian texts, was an undertone, hardly more
than an unvoiced reference to an implication and an inhibited
embarrassment, became an autonomous, an as it were stark theme
during the editing of the posthumous work. Whether one finds
it scandalous or not, one can now, indeed one must now, admit
that the older Critical Theory was always a cryptotheology—a
form of *Haskalah* or Jewish Enlightenment that affiliated itself
with Young Hegelian forms of critique and complaint in a manner
that was as effective as it was discreet. In the act of uttering this
insight the original *écriture* is broken open, its polyphony disas-
sembled into individual voices. Adorno's style of writing, which
purported to avoid referring to fundamental thoughts as modern
music avoids the tonal center, dissolves into distinct complexes,
and we are unexpectedly confronted with a set of problems whose
true locus seems to lie rather in the philosophy of religion than in
sociology. Here it becomes apparent that the older Critical Theory
arises from a messianism that abruptly transitions to epistemology.
It is a stage in the quarrel between Jerusalem and Athens insofar
as it orchestrates the entrance of the thought of redemption into
the question of knowledge. Under the code name of critique the
messianic impulse, which was already a latent impetus in Marxism,
begins to permeate the idea of the science of society and of nature
toto genere.

   We admit that Adorno would have considered the clamoring
speech of third parties regarding what is secretly theological in his
thought as an outrage. Without doubt, he would have found it
tactless to see his concealed theologoumena emphasized in isolation and thematized out of context. In his antisystem such a failure
of tact would have at the same time been a transgression against
the matter for thought, especially since he, both as an aesthetic
theoretician and as a philosophical author, did not recognize the

separation of style and truth. Had he not sought with every line of his work to demonstrate that there is not only beautiful art, but also beautiful science—here unmindful of Kant's warning and following Nietzsche's example?

In his beautiful melancholy science he overcame timidity in the face of explicitly theological discourse only in exceptional moments—in particular when he constructed an acoustic space in which a kind of messianic narrative voice could speak. Such formulations are directed to the ear of a public that has been keyed into the aesthetics of the formulation that goes out on a limb. The classic passage is found in the opening of Aphorism 153 of *Minima Moralia*, which reveals its program with the quasi-eschatological heading '*Finale*':

> The only philosophy which can be responsibly practised in face of despair is the attempt to contemplate all things as they would present themselves from the standpoint of redemption. Knowledge has no light but that shed on the world by redemption: all else . . . is mere technique. Perspectives must be fashioned that displace and estrange the world, reveal it to be, with its rifts and crevices, as indigent and distorted as it will appear one day in the messianic light.[2]

As dumbfounding as these statements are with their haughty lack of deductive reasoning, they are not equally overwhelming each time they are reread. There comes a moment in which the pathos of vulnerability has exhausted its appeal. From then on one reads the passage without quotation marks and virtual brackets, but also without psychoanalytic ulterior motives and above all without the intention to unmask. From this moment whispers of a prolonged crypto-messianism would be more embarrassing than a language that takes the liberty, and allows itself the weakness, to speak of a longing for the redemption from evil, even if one cannot blot out the motif as such, whether it appears deplorable or excessive.

Thus as soon as the older Critical Theory, in its disintegration, releases a theological fission product that until then had been bound up with social science and aesthetics, the opportunity presents itself for interested parties to account for the necessary and sufficient elements of critical theories. There are reasons to suspect that a theory can become 'critical' in the sense of the older Frankfurt School through a theological motif—or an equivalent for this. If that is the case then it is undeniably productive to develop such conditions as explicitly as possible.

As was indicated, one must prepare oneself for the fact that under the seemingly humble name 'critical,' the messianic finds its way into the social sciences.

If one attempts to determine the features of positive or traditional theory as they presented themselves to the most important thinker of the Frankfurt School, the kinship between the fundamental conceptions of Adorno and Heidegger that are critical of science and metaphysics comes into view for the observer. In fact, in his own way Adorno advanced a doctrine of en-framing [*das Ge-Stell*]—which in his work is called the existing [*das Bestehende*]—according to which there is a continually self-corroborating play of reciprocal fixations and distortions at work between a subject that is egoistically calloused and calculates everything, and an object-world that has been tailored to this subject. In Adorno's en-framing, traditional theories, which are allied with the serial methods of production of advanced capital and with the culture industry's coercions to imitate, always already order things so that they can be apprehended as objects of cognition and so that they can be brought into an authoritative identification. For positive theory the subjection of the individual to the leveling fixation and the incorporation of individual fixations in rigidly joined systems of declarative statements would always be characteristic. Its pattern is the monetary economy, which, with its invariable currency, presents in the leveling expressions of value the universe of things that have been made purchasable. However, as little as the price expresses the true nature of the object—its 'proper sense' [*Eigensinn*], its 'use value'—so little does the concept express the individual's non-identity, its 'singularity.'

In contrast, the theory that presents itself as critical wishes to undo existing identifications and liberate individual things from the grip of reason.[3] Such a theory already manifests its theological aspect in this feature: it is out to save individuals, whether as persons, natures, or artifacts, from fixation and classification in logical coercive orders. It figures as a 'micrological' undertaking, insofar as, for this theory, it is less a matter of the synopsis of the many in the great whole than it is a matter of the liberation of the individual and of that which is small from the compulsion of subsumption: "There is solidarity between such thinking and metaphysics at the moment of its fall."[4] In the concluding sentence of *Negative Dialectics* Adorno admits that Critical Theory is a code name for the work on the redemption of the individual from captivity in abstract systems of representations and ordinances. Hence the discourse of the theoretician, which calls things by their true names or summons them by their true anonyms, bears a hardly concealed mission of redemption. With this claim, critique presses forward into the distorted world as the *Tzadik* does into dark life.

The smallest intramundane traits would be of relevance to the absolute, for the micrological view cracks the shells of what . . . is helplessly isolated and explodes its identity.[5]

Messianic intelligence proceeds to where things and human beings are most hopeless, that is, to the market. It raises its objection where sciences appear most self-assured, in their positivist core that has pledged its allegiance to the power of the factual. Its liberating work can only make its presence felt, and even then only in an indirect way, to the degree that the critic has broken away from the will to power. Only as a non-master or as a friend of things is he in the position to crack the 'shells,' to break the 'spell' of identity and turn toward the lost and deformed individuals without reservation. His intelligence must have preserved the regard for what is irreplaceably singular just as much as it must have preserved the belief that even the corrupted, the hardened, the maimed can never fully be severed from a potentially successful ground. With noble sentimentality the Critical Theorist remains convinced that all beings are capable of happiness in their own way, perhaps even worthy of happiness, although they initially, for the most part and often forever, seek their salvation on hopeless paths. This belief is the righteousness of the righteous. Adorno's logical soteriology wants more than the traditional saving of the phenomena. It also reaches beyond Husserl's rallying cry to the things themselves. It acts as if it were ready to go to hell in order to lead the ineffable individual up into the light. Micrology is the watchword for the work of an intellect that does not consume its ability to move freely and its powers of perception in self-indulgence, but rather attempts to follow the maimed beings in their misfortunate complexity up to the point where the possibility of incorruption emerges in what is corrupt.

If this were the complete upshot of the soteriological features of the older Critical Theory, then things would be easy for the opponents of this thought. They could dismiss it by diagnosing it as a rationalization of a messianic phantasm, of the sort that was able to flourish in German Jewish intellectuals of the early twentieth century under various guises and in forms that are readily understandable biographically and in terms of the history of ideas—not least in authors who were no strangers to paracletic and eschatological interpretations of their personal mission. But Adorno makes it more difficult for his critics than they suspect even on this point. In truth, his discourse, even where he employs messianic timbres in "passages" that go out on a limb, operates throughout on the level of Young Hegelian atheism and the second soteriology inaugurated by Nietzsche's philosophy of art. In a way that is different from the first doctrine of redemption, which proceeds from an objective metaphysical asymmetry between the redeemer and those who are to be redeemed, the second, which is decidedly modern and steeped in psychology, makes the relation of redemption self-referential. It brings the redemption of the redeemer away from his mission to the order of the day—together with the emancipation of those interested in redemption from all conditions in which anything less than being saved by a transcendent helper would no longer be enough. The messianological aspects of Adorno's work have their place in this second soteriology. Because it is constituted in a self-reflexive fashion, it belongs to the gravity of his discourse of redemption that it must signify a 'redemption-as-if.'[6]

2. The Prison of the World and Soft Monsters

A primal scene from the text of the older Critical Theory stands out, which in important features resembles the Gnostic mythos: the condition of the individual in historical class societies, whether these are constituted in ancient or modern, bourgeois-democratic or totalitarian terms, is akin to an extramundane soul that has been thrown into the prison of the world and is so out of it that it no longer knows how to say who and where it really is. The only thing certain for this soul is that its place of sojourn fundamentally alienates it. This certainty is as stark as the evidence that the soul in world-exile feels condemned to long for something 'that would be otherwise.' But while the Gnosticism of late antiquity, by means of a grand narrative to answer the questions "who we were, and what we have become, where we were or where we were placed, whither we hasten, from what we are redeemed, what birth is and what rebirth,"[7] trusted itself to develop interpretations of the fall into misfortune and ascetic practices for returning home to euphoria, modern Paragnosticism is content to invoke ever anew the gloom of the world scene, while views of lost and hoped-for happiness are only allowed to be painted in black. They depict an image of grandiose austerity, "grey as after sunset and the end of the world,"[8] ruled by modern archons, by evil administrators of the lifeless world: abstraction of exchange, tyranny, bourgeois coldness.

Adorno's critical ontology describes the world's surface as a total trap. Over wide stretches his text reads like a set of instructions for interpreting Being-in-the-world as an absurd pre-trial detention. There seems to be a compulsion for repetition in his thought that, in the most varied social and historical conditions, stereotypically reformulates the dramatic schema of imprisonment and the dream of breaking out. The primal scene is so powerful that it penetrates all the way to the ultimate abstractions and tinges the usage of the logical categories. Identity is monotonously associated with shackles, difference with their loosening; Being with disconsolation, non-Being with hope; immanence with bedazzlement, transcendence with insight. Everything that forms a system, whether it is social or logical, evokes the phobia of the bad enclosure. Only the fissures and the weak points of the total fortress, to which one nevertheless gladly assigns the epithet 'impervious,' allow one to surmise a hardly accessible outside—just as the Alexandrian Gnostics considered the irritatingly blinking stars over the Nitrian Desert to be tiny holes in the vault of the cosmic prison wall through which the light of the world above broke into the Egyptian night. The odor of the concentration camps sticks to the concept of totality, while individuality has an aura of salvation hovering over it. Accordingly, what is actual is like an evil enchantment, whereas what is possible remains withdrawn like a promise that is too good to be kept. If the whole is the untrue, truth can only appear in the individual that somehow avoids equalization. This thought would happily admit to a pluralist ontology and set multiplicities free, were it not for that evil One that integrates everything into the compulsory context of the false whole.

With this apparatus the thinker whittles away the horizon of appearances. All logical operators in Adorno's discourse function as cast members in the ever-same scene. His textbook allows for the fact that misfortunate subjectivity must relentlessly seek its liberation from the prison of the world, but it remains so spiteful as to portray every apparently successful breakout as only relocation to another block. If sometimes the thesis, or the compliment, was to be heard that despite his anti-systematic avowals Adorno was at bottom a very systematic thinker, then this observation has its factual basis in the presence of this discursive mechanism in even the briefest of his statements. He deployed this mechanism with such redundancy that it was no longer possible to distinguish his conviction from his autohypnosis. A throng of imitators knew how to appreciate these propensities.

It is unnecessary to remark that such thought did not have to first wait for the fall of metaphysics in order to be in solidarity with it. It even remains metaphysically stamped to the last fiber, though with a negative sign and contemporary distance from the idealist tradition. In place of the official praise of Being, there is an all-encompassing reserve vis-à-vis the so-called existing, and in place of the traditional alliance of holism and optimism, there is a linking of individualism and skepticism that is simultaneously rebellious and epochally conforming. The theory is initially critical to the extent that it is engaged in an anti-positivist, anti-pragmatic manner and hence is always also a bit anti-American. It is critical in the strict sense of the word when it fundamentally places that which is unrealized over that which is realized. It has this feature in common with the dialectical theology of Karl Barth. Still more, it shares this feature with certain Gnostic systems in which the redeemer God may never be compromised by means of a realized creation. But in order to express something firm concerning the typological status of the older Critical Theory one should examine whether Gnostic systems, to which Adorno's project is formally akin, can be sufficiently characterized with the predicate 'metaphysical.'

Here is an opportunity to point out a fundamental, seldom heeded difference between Gnostic doctrines of liberation and metaphysical exegeses of Being. According to their dramaturgical and cognitive content, Gnosticisms of late antiquity of both the Marcionite and the Valentinian type are precisely not 'theories' that presuppose the individual's absorption in the complete whole, as is typical for metaphysics. Rather, they determine the world as the failed work of an unwise demiurge. Already they allow no doubt that the whole is the untrue. They have the characteristics of a first philosophy of the event, which adapts the drama of falling-into-the-world and becoming-free-of-the-world. Gnosticisms are thus not to be structurally traced back to the schema of First Philosophy. Their primary motif is not the venerable cantus firmus of Being that has persevered in the history of 'Western' thought from Parmenides to Hegel. Gnosticisms are First Dramaturgies that incessantly interpret a single fundamental event—the passing of the soul, which has been constituted above and outside this world, through the world, and the soul's fate in covering the stretch of errancy allotted to it. Not seldom does this happen under exuberantly allegorical forms that, although they are deployed in essentially therapeutic terms, occasionally also claim an apparent theoretical status.

The Gnostic position of Being-in-the-world is by no means primarily motivated—as the existentially motivated misunderstanding of the twentieth century would have it—by the feeling of alienation and nausea for Being. What Gnosticism designates in the original sense of the concept as such, whether dissident-Jewish, Marcionite, or Alexandrian, is a euphoria that distances one from everything, a euphoria whose extraordinariness puts the subject out beyond terrestrial gravity. Primary Gnosticism assails dim cosmic continuity, which is obviously inadequate for explaining the ecstasy of the soul. According to the testimony of late antique sources one does not become a Gnostic because of hostility toward the world and a misological reaction—in immanent terms, this would only testify to the imprisonment of the psychic in an affective life that has fallen prey to the world. The appeal to Gnosticism, rather, arises from incommensurable experiences of happiness, in comparison with which most profane situations seem unreal, insipid, and unacceptably crude.[9] If the individual affected by the state of exception is not good for any employment under the sun, it is not because he is dedicated to a Great Refusal, but rather because he has discovered the non-communicability of exhilaration. The pneumatic frequency may be contagious—capable of synthesis it is certainly not. It is at best communicable in small orders of the equally enraptured. Whether it is achieved through aesthetic experience, through erotic enchantment, through meditative techniques of the subject or through chemical substitutes for grace—as Aldous Huxley called psychedelic drugs—it continually leaves the ecstatic subject at a loss, unable to maintain the state of exception. In contrast, the subject must adjust itself to the rupture of its vital experience and its regression into the everyday—to its dismissal into a lifeless world of facts that, to those who suffer it, seems to be a dismal exile. There is nothing to be done with immense happiness—it is only accepted as a background of the world against which almost all figures from empirical life appear to be wayward. From then on it is only a question of metaphysical style and of historical convention whether the antithesis between the transfigured and the trivial state is coded in ontological, in religious, in psychological, or in aesthetic terms.

If one lifts one's eyes from these findings in order to survey the older Critical Theory, then it becomes immediately evident how sharply the dualism between the euphoric and the dysphoric mode is marked in it. Yet to its distinctive features belongs the fact that one may only speak about the dysphoric mode, while the euphoric mode presents a secret that is to be stringently guarded. What further distinguishes Critical Theory from its counterparts in late antiquity is its affinity to the modern 'state of the world' and to an understanding of Being that no longer needs or tolerates the opposition between the world and the world beyond. If, according to Adorno, the world is nevertheless not everything that is the case, then this is so from a neo-ontological ground: because even its 'unrealized possibilities' belong to his concept of the world. The world itself, and only it, is the site of euphorias in which, should it be possible, the total transfiguration of all things, their shining in the light of justice, comes to pass. Critique is already the anticipatory sheen of this light—hence a salvific undertaking. It is as such the fulfillment of the other. The Critical Theorist is not only an occult herald of the Messiah, but also the Messiah himself, veiled in the deepest incognito and come into the world with the mission to gauge it for its better possibilities. Because he cannot dare to confess himself to be the privileged memory of happiness and to this extent to be truth incarnate, the critical Messiah must choose—as the deliverer of the Gnostic vocation once did—the form of indirect communication and help the world to experience itself as untruth incarnate. This happens when he confronts it with its unbearability—without regard for the everyday needs for reconciliation and compromise: salvation comes from exaggeration. It is here that we should look for the reason as to why Critical Theory must develop into an aesthetic theory, or, to be more precise, into a theory that 'breaks out.' In Adorno's view it is above all in advanced works of art that the maimed world experiences the truth about itself, and this in two forms—as a reflection of its deformation and as a secret revelation of its missed capacity for success. The aesthetics of the ugly, which has been entrenched since the nineteenth century, swells into the aesthetics of the implacable. The most rigorous works are entrusted with the task to carry out the accelerated Judgment Day in the world. Here we see why an Aesthetic Theory that purports to be critical cannot proceed further than to a Gnosticism-as-if. It does not have to do with a redemption from the world, let alone an ascent to extra-cosmic sites, but rather with distinguishing the world from the world within the world. This operation—going beyond the actual in such a way that one does not, for all that, end up in an idealistic beyond—constitutes the nucleus of critique, which takes from neither objects nor subjects the fact that in their current being such-and-such they already are as they would appear in the ultimate light. Jacob Taubes has rightly explained this towering over the world within the world in such a way that it is possibly entirely different by comparing it with the poetics of surrealism as summarized in Louis Aragon's statement: *Seule signification du mot Au-delà, tu es dans la poésie.*[10]

> Poetry is the only beyond, not because it bridges "this world" [*Diesseits*] and the one "beyond" [*Jenseits*], Above and Below. It is the beyond itself. The word does not bear testimony, rather it is itself transcendence.[11]

Thus, to be sure, works of art, especially those that Adorno likes to call great, are *materialiter* and *mentaliter* entirely from this world and yet at the same time enclaves of otherness, which stand out from it like a counter-world. 'Other' is what is in the world as though it were not of the world.

According to these premises the older Critical Theory had to describe social reality as such—not only its reflections in mass culture—as a bad work of art whose waywardness reaches all the way down into the ultimate layers of Being, into maimed life. Critique of art is hence only possible as critique of the world and critique of the world is possible only as critique of art. In it questions of taste lead to decisions about the whole. The inexcusability of bad works of art is conceivable against this background: as falsifications of redemption they contribute to the perpetuation of hellish conditions. The sympathetic or resigned fellow players of the vile piece that was called late-capitalist or state-socialist reality all consequently had to be seen through as, to use Gnostic terminology, sarkics and psychics. They were to be exposed as world-agents who deceive their clients about what is best for them, about their feelings as to what is discordant. Thus the social psychology of Critical Theory is assigned the task of investigating the human being's psychical structures as inner outgrowths of the terrible whole. The analysis of the historically conditioned constitutions of the subject gives a scientific appearance to the pneumatic peering through of human darkness. Adorno's anti-humanism is grounded in the insight, or perhaps only in the assertion, that human beings, as they emerge from the mold of the status quo, can never embody the utopian potential that points beyond the given. In his eyes, they are the general doom once again, congealed into subjects. Even their most intimate wishes are trapped by the great machine, even their dreams are prefabricated by the rulers of this world, even their revolts feed back into the evil whole.

Because, according to the well-known dictum of Grabbe, only despair can still save us, messianic theory impresses upon its adepts the task of preventing small escapes. Horkheimer, in his programmatic essay, formally decreed the prohibition of a "personal peace treaty with an inhuman world."[12] Every wounded individual owes to the whole the contribution of his unreconciliation to the imaginary total revolution. From this comes Adorno's precious thesis: that there is no right life in the false one—a statement that became successful not least because of the fact that, owing to citations that were blind to context, it was elevated into the emblem for the negativism of the older Critical Theory.[13] He obviously uses for his spokesperson the exceptional position that alone provides the criterion for distinguishing the false and the correct. Whoever speaks of universal contexts of blindness must stand in the gaps that are free of blindness and from which the bad totality can be observed. The thesis that "the strength for breaking out of the immanent context"[14] emerges from dialectical thinking is a self-serving declaration. In truth, the pneumatic observer does not wish to be seen so as to not have to provide information about the nature of his exemption. In order to deflect from himself he calls compulsions gapless. Because the critic may never admit that he is one of the elect and can see and speak a truth that remains concealed to the non-elect, the crude, the deformed and the adjusted, he must seek to derive his claim to the superiority of his verdicts from their especially deep adequacy to the things themselves and their inner movement.

In view of such a high-strung claim the mistake that the authors of the older Critical Theory committed is striking, when, in order to formulate the totality of relations in so-called late capitalism in as conceptually true a manner as possible, they chose the expression *the existing* [das Bestehende]. They did this in sharp contradiction to insights of the Marxist tradition that since the *Communist Manifesto* have known that under the influence of the permanent revolution of capital "all that is solid melts into air." With their accusatorial and resigned talk of the 'existing' they set themselves against the evidence of their era, in which the tendency toward the mobilization and desubstantialization of all relations attained a historically new degree of visibility. It is impossible that the epochal tendency toward medialization, virtualization, and flexibilization of states in the world moved by money escaped the notice of the authors of the *Dialectic of Enlightenment*. It is obvious that Horkheimer and Adorno with the language game of the 'existing' spoke neither as sociologists nor as contemporaries. Under the appearance of social critique they incorporated forgotten practices of negative metaphysics as critique of the world. They followed the rules of Gnostic grammar, which allowed for the fact that it is the agitated soul that plunges into the unyielding world-dungeon and forgets itself in immanence: a primal scene of what is later called alienation.[15] What beings are for the ontologist the existing is for the Paragnostic. The later Horkheimer was without doubt more clearly aware of the conservative, defensive, and transcendent character of his criticism than Adorno, who, with his orientation to aesthetic modernism, was more disposed to maintain the progressive semblance. Horkheimer had the opportunity to explain to his younger friend: "The infinite . . . cannot be made into the existing, into 'society' at some point in time."[16] In the case of such preliminary decisions, the modern world, which nevertheless continually mobilized and irrealized itself, had to be described with metaphors of walls and storehouses [*Mauer- und Bestandsmetaphern*] from the old mythos of alienation. The Paragnostic language game prevailed at a moment in which it would have been more appropriate to say that it is the world that goes off the rails, while subjects insist on themselves and their own under the pretext of critique.

In the few decades that have passed since the crystallization of older Critical Theory and its dethronement by a younger version, which carried out a culturally Protestant adjustment, the basic description of reality has changed *toto genere* for the contemporary intelligentsia. Indicted reality, according to its basic feature, has factually and metaphorically ceased to resemble Max Weber's 'iron cage' or the world-dungeon of the dark Gnostics, without it being the case that it is somehow more homelike or more free of suffering. But the fragility of the so-called existing has been so dramatically demonstrated and at the same time in so many places that even its sworn enemies are compelled to ponder programs for its maintenance. Adorno's tenet: "The task of art today is to bring chaos into order"[17] meanwhile sounds like a chip that even in aesthetic subcultures loses its value. In order to speak of the evidence of the whole, we no longer choose images of the petrified, the congealed, the impervious. What now gives pause for thought are vague monsters. Social systems appear to be mellow giants who are tormented by problems of self-reference. We are dealing with chaotic, accelerated structures, with nets and foam, with turbulences and indeterminate drifts, with attempts at ordering that are dispersed by great centripetal forces and are displaced by immanent catastrophic risks in states of chronic self-irritation. These constructs are too intangible for one to lash out against them, and too complex to be guided by such a primitive movement as a 'revolution'—a kinetic metaphor, of which one eventually notes how much it remains bound to the era of simple ontologies of solid bodies. Now it is no longer Critical Theory that subversively jars an existence [*Bestand*] persisting in itself. Rather, a reality that is going off the rails reflects to existing theory its own insufficiency.

3. Hyperbolic Theory

As suggestive as the analogies between the older Critical Theory and the Gnostic tradition's world-critical projects of redemption and overcoming may also be, they do not get to the bottom of the filial relations between critical philosophy and Gnosticism, on the one hand, nor those between messianism and metaphysics, on the other. This becomes apparent as soon as one considers the origin of these styles of thought or species of discourse from a common rhetorical source. The reason for the familial similarities between Gnostic, critical, metaphysical, and messianic language games—to which one has to add their ultra-skeptical, deconstructivist versions—is to be sought in the fact that all of them make extensive use of the figure of exaggeration. Thus classical metaphysics hyperbolically elaborated the idea of reason coming to be in the world; Gnosticism relied on the hyperbole of the soul's kinship with extramundane goods; messianism's figure of exaggeration is waiting for justice; critical philosophy hybridizes these hyperboles by anonymously inheriting, combining, relativizing, and reversing them.

Quintilian, in his doctrine of tropes, defined hyperbole as a "proper straining of the truth" (*decens veri superiectio*)—and in so doing he led with the not very subtle example that a certain someone, when he vomited, filled his lap and the entire tribunal with the remnants of his meal.[18] From this point one could come to the opinion that exaggeration is to be reckoned as one of the oral functions; it adds an eruptive surplus value to running one's mouth in a typical way. But it belongs to the orator's art to heed proportion even in exaggeration: "Although every *hyperbole* involves the incredible, it must not go too far in this direction."[19] Whoever wants to exaggerate must know at what point he may go too far: *quo usque deceat extollere*. The delicate field of excesses can only be bounded by the sense of tact. One can recognize a successful exaggeration by the fact that it brings about smiles in urbane contexts, while producing embarrassment in the provinces. Quintilian furthermore accounts for the possibility that a certain factual correspondence may exist between an excessive object and hyperbolic discourse: "*Hyperbole* is, moreover, a virtue, when the subject on which we have to speak is abnormal [*naturalem modum excessit*]. For we are allowed to amplify, when the magnitude of the facts passes all words, and in such circumstances our language will be more effective if it goes beyond the truth than if it falls short of it [*melius ultra quam citra stat oratio*]."[20] The justification for exaggeration is its suitability [*Angemessenheit*] for that which is beyond measure [*das Maßlose*].

It seems worthy of note that Quintilian did not carry out the obvious transition from these reflections to a performative definition of philosophy—an omission that becomes understandable as soon as one recalls the rhetorician's attacks on the presumption of philosophers of his time in the proem of the *Institutio oratoria*:

But in our own day the name of philosopher has too often been the mask for the worst vices. For their attempt has not been to win the name of philosopher by virtue and the earnest search for wisdom [*virtute ac studiis*]; instead they have sought to disguise the depravity of their characters by the assumption of a stern [*tristitia*] and austere mien accompanied by the wearing of a garb differing from that of their fellow men. Now as a matter of fact we all of us frequently handle [*passim tractamus omnes*] those themes which philosophy claims for its own.[21]

In Quintilian's eyes, the philosophy of his time—between Nero and Domitian—sins because of its specialization in pretentious mournfulness. Its exaggerations, propounded with a serious face, are received by the public with just as serious a mien—like a sermon that leaves us in the dark as to whom it is addressed. The surest method for not being put out indeed consists in becoming a philosopher oneself and breaking with human notions and concerns in the manner of these odd lovers of wisdom. Yet because even simple fellow citizens, indeed even 'bad human beings,' in Quintilian's view can never cease speaking of the just, the fair, and the good, they never become entirely incompetent when it comes to those questions for which philosophers presume special competences. Were the *ars oratoria* practiced at the highest level of skill to which it ought to be by definition, then soon no one would be obliged to turn to philosophy any longer to receive information about the true and the virtuous. With an argument that can never be heeded enough, Quintilian reverses the relation tendentiously misrepresented by Plato between true thinkers and the sophists who give mere speeches, insofar as he points out that one can of course easily simulate being a philosopher, but could not possibly pretend to be a good speaker if one is not. Hence it becomes a matter of restoring to the true speaker—more precisely: to the rhetorically experienced *vir bonus*—his precedence vis-à-vis the philosopher—a suggestion that the guild has never followed, and the public only occasionally and half-heartedly.

In view of his harsh assessment of the early imperial pursuit of philosophy, it was not to be expected that Quintilian in his treatise on the trope of exaggeration would have wanted to have a closer look at the fabric of philosophical discourse, however much the turn of phrase of the "elegant straining of the truth" touches on the mystery of the philosophical text. The suggestion that hyperbole becomes virtue when the object itself exhibits a pull into what is beyond measure reads like a defense of philosophy with arguments drawn from rhetoric: whoever undertakes an apology of exaggeration also already justifies the disposition of the philosopher to treat of God, world, and knowledge with a chronic excess of universality, explicitness, and unpopularity. How else, other than exaggeratedly, should one speak when one *ex offico* has to do with material enormities and logical behemoths—with the foundations of the world and with prime matters, with the Titanic and the Olympian, with the Ouranian as the monstrously immense from above and the Chthonian as the monstrously immense from below? Even the seemingly most familiar magnitude among the objects of philosophical contemplation, that is, the human being, was already addressed by the Greek poets as a *deinon*, something violent, and as *deinotaton*, as the highest intensification of the 'perpetrator of violence [*Gewalt-Tätigen*]' and that which is non-ordinary. The excessiveness of objects condemns corresponding discourses to a suitable lack of proportion, with the result that the words chosen by philosophers are certified as philosophical precisely by what makes them suspicious to common sense. Nonetheless, philosophers make an impression because they know how to portray the monstrous immensities that do not depend on us as though they depended on the hyperboles with which they are captured in philosophical discourse. In this sense, philosophers as eccentric speakers, according to their disposition, would be the last magicians and the first radicals: since they are occupied with objects in which a suitable 'mode' cannot be determined, they follow their intuition that it is better to situate their discourses beyond (*ultra*) the probable than on this side of (*citra*) it. Before meta-physics stands ultra-rhetoric.

The Quintilian objections against the deviant disposition of philosophers may be substantiated already in the Stoic-Cynic phase of the Hellenistic and Roman pursuit of theory. It is not only with the beard and the cloak that the philosophical life contrasted with other ways of life. It was grounded as a whole in an existentialized hyperbole. The ancient concept of *conversio*, before it was Christianized, characterized the turn to philosophy as a form of life—whoever – accomplished it vowed to henceforth exaggerate with rational assumptions. The hyperbole of reason had the form of a wager in which life itself was at stake. Let us not forget that the decision for philosophy among the ancients was a commitment to an existence that practices, inquires, and renounces. It subjected its adepts to a harsh *askēsis*, which included daily self-examinations and sustained training in logical and ethical resilience. Occasionally it was also considered to be philosophical to sleep in one's own cloak on the floor and to make do without a pillow. With a light hand, Nietzsche sketched out an interpretation of this tendency to take serious measures with oneself: "Man takes a real delight in oppressing himself with excessive claims."[22] In this respect, the mode of Being of the philosophers is prefigured by that of the athletes, who had introduced bodily exaggeration into everyday Greek culture and that of the festivals. Through its contests doing-more-than-was-necessary on principle achieved a recognized status among the gestures of *andreia*. Athleticism is the cultural form of the too much. – As continual exaggerated performance it organizes the paradox in which one expects what is above average of men in the average life of cities—which is then celebrated as manliness. The projection of this toil-loving (philoponic) disposition into the ranks of intellectual endeavor engenders the wisdom-loving comportment—for which reason the origin of philosophy is *not*, as Plato and Aristotle suggested, wonder and its speech act, the question—even if Heidegger may make considerable fuss over this, as though it were a charism and not a sort of contest like any other. One can still perceive the athletic tone of the question and his effort to move up to the highest weight division in the declarations of the Freiburg rector from 1933, which sound like a trainer's speech before the final round: "For us, questioning means: exposing oneself to the sublimity of things and their laws. . . . We know: the courage to question, to experience the abysses of existence and to endure the abysses of existence, is in itself already a *higher* answer."[23]

Here the real beginning of philosophy is once more clear: it lies in the contest for taking the justification of opinions seriously and consequently in the sporting exaggeration of wonder. Its athletes act as if they wished to find each and every thing questionable and – demanding an investigation. From the competition of wonder is developed the exaggeration (*hyperbolē, superiectio*) of the question that since Socrates potentially meddles in each life and since Plato reformulates all assertions into problems. Thus with philosophers the first experts of 'thinking otherwise' step onto the stage; they drive to extremes the reduction of 'appearances' to so-called essential bases; they practice being reserved in the face of everyday opinions and their rhetorical props. Not for nothing have they learned, through their formal education in exaggerating justifications, how one disavows popular forms of knowing the score. As partisans of an exaggerated idea of the proof *more geometrico et arithmetico* they fall into a frenzy of contempt for ordinary knowledge. This is the case even though until now they have remained indebted to their contemporaries for the proof in which the advantages of their highly strung claims to proof consist—except for the satisfaction that an exaggerator draws from another's failure to meet his high standards. But that only implies that one must have experience in exaggeration oneself in order to be able to appreciate an exaggeration. In antiquity it sufficed to join in with established exaggerations. The modern call in philosophy to think for oneself, however, is an indirect challenge to develop an exaggeration of one's own.

Against this background the fate of a theory that steps on the stage as critical can be soberly assessed. According to what has been said a theory can only be critical when it is engaged in a manner that is critical of exaggerations and shines a light on the hyperbolic features of traditional theories—especially classical metaphysics' hyperboles of order that have become unpalatable. In the case of exaggerations, as a rule, laying them bare is already as such the cor-

rective. The critical effect results from the fact that the participant NB
in a habitualized game of exaggeration normally no longer notes its
excessiveness, for which reason only a disagreeable reflection can
show the true proportions and costs of a hyperbole. Because all
advanced cultures, particularly monotheistic ones, are organized
around hyperboles, from the eighteenth century onward—when one
began to comparatively observe religions and other exaggerations—
the analysis of hyperbole becomes the sharpest instrument of cultural
criticism.

The most powerful embodiments of critical theory in the nineteenth century, Marx and Nietzsche, when they were faced with
the logical and ethical traditions of Old Europe, dismantled the
entire framework of settled hyperboles and thus—in the tradition
of the moralists, yet with a more advanced theoretical approach—
created the discursive type of corrective observation: Marx wanted
this correction and cutting down to size to be seen as a production
of revolutionary knowledge, while Nietzsche took it to be the pre-
school for strong spirits. Both were linked with the Young Hegelian
deflating critique that demonstrates everywhere that what is supposedly divine and eternally fixed is actually only made by humans
and historically changeable. The genuinely hyperbolic activity of
the human being is here thought of as projecting, to be sure not
in the horizontal dealings between human beings and the like, but
rather in the vertical: exaggeration throws human concepts up to
the heavens and believes with 'hyperbolic naivety' that they could
be objectivized there.[24] What in Nietzsche is called the gay science is
in fact already radical critique of hyperbole. As Marx dissolved the
bourgeois exaggerations of the fairness of exchange and the idealist
hyperboles of order from above by contrasting them with factors
from the so-called base, so Nietzsche made the hyperboles of the
ethical world order, of the divine will, of purity, of holiness, of the
redeemer and of genius, indeed of the subject and of the agent in
general, burst asunder in a cheerful naturalist examination.

With this operation the ancient insight of rhetoricians and
poets was once more brought to bear, according to which ironic
understatement is the best way to cut exaggeration down to size.
Undoubtedly, Nietzsche's critique of hyperbole went much further
than the Marxist one, because it discovered for the first time the
hitherto most comprehensive exaggerating power as such for theory:
the vindictiveness of the 'disadvantaged.' Thus it called attention to
the connection between hyperbole and *ressentiment*, which is constitutive for the classical versions of metaphysics. Nietzsche was able
to show how here a non-Quintilian hyperbole emerged that does not
approximate an overlarge object, but rather stems from a limitless

need for self-aggrandizement and revenge. Proceeding from the insight that the governing Old European hyperboles of Platonic and Paulinian origin had been impelled by loser-*ressentiment*, he devoted himself to the attempt to found an emancipated hyperbolicism: instead of arising from the overcompensating denial of insults and defeats it would be based on a surplus of the capacity to posit and the power of assertion. Exaggeration set free was to become that of a playing child.

If critical theory is only possible as critique of hyperbole, which *eo ipso* subsumes the critique of myths and ideology, then the predicate 'critical' can only be reserved for a sustained skeptical theory. Skepticism is the habit of allowing that which is overdrawn in the customary realm to run aground and of always presenting final results as preliminary. In any case, skepticism for its part can become hyperbolic—then it steps onto the platform in a neo-pathetic fashion and is called deconstruction. In this posture the capacity for renouncing certain results becomes an exhibition of doubt.

If one proceeds on the basis of this definition of critique, then it is already recognizable at first glance that Adorno's work in its elementary gestures cannot be a critical theory, because it constantly casts out one exaggeration with another: the imperial one with the messianic one, the affirmative one with the negative one, the promotion of the identical with the counter-promotion of the other. As per its aesthetic disposition as well as its intellectual motifs, it is grounded in the "extremism between the world wars,"[25] hence in relation to the complex of wars of attrition and mass exterminations, which the thinkers and artists of the epoch presuppose as a specific background of exorbitance in order to correspond to it with a new array of hyperboles—mimetic of terror, mimetic of excess, mimetic of catastrophe, mimetic of chaos. In so doing, the anti-idealist disparagement practiced since the nineteenth century is popularized—which without doubt yielded productive effects for a time. Whoever had adapted himself to the Platonic hyperbole that all beings are good (one probably should not speak of belief when it comes to such figures of speech) is certainly not helped along by Adorno's modernist counter-exaggeration: 'The whole is the untrue'—yet exaggerating is explicitly presented as a philosophical performative.[26] Whoever has striven with existentiell seriousness to meet the demands of the great exaggeration in the ancient thesis that the wise are at home everywhere will find cold comfort in the modern contrasting hyperbole, that there is no right life in the wrong one— yet the alternative draws attention to the leeway in which one-sided positions are formed.[27] Accordingly, Critical Theory is at best half-critical: by offering its clients an exchange of exaggeration, it grants them an intermission between excesses. The interested party de facto jumps out of the idealist frying pan and into the criticist fire, because Critical Theory—like every disappointed idealism—indemnifies itself against the existing through escalation. The antithesis, that the whole is the false, attains its sharpness only from surpassing the already sufficiently exaggerated thesis. It perfectly illustrates the Quintilian rule that in the case of themes without true 'modes' it is better to speak *ultra* than to remain behind *citra*.

The strength of the older Critical Theory consisted in the fact that it did not deliver what its name promised. Even where it presented itself in ways that were critical of ideology, myths, and society it was still consistently out for an exchange of hyperboles. It remained in solidarity with metaphysics not only in the fact that in the end it reluctantly acknowledged its 'utopian contents'—as though critique and speculation, given the triumph of positivism, were condemned to join a melancholy popular front. It was rather an immediate resumption of the metaphysical mode of discourse according to the aspect of its 'ultra-ized' [*ultrierten*] constitution. It is the purest metaphysics in inverse form and Paragnosticism in 'social-philosophical' incognito. Here Adorno's Nietzscheanism comes into view, insofar as the author of *Zarathustra* like no thinker before him shed light on the indissoluble connection between destruction and creation. What is missing in Adorno is only the additional point that whoever wants to create new exaggerations in what is good and evil must also be able to be a destroyer of old hyperboles. Admittedly, the new hyperboles that are proposed in Adorno's 'melancholy science' are permeated by a resentful tone that stands in contrast to Nietzsche's affirmative ethos. It was Adorno's weakness to be mostly unable to keep his hyperboles of grievance separate from those of *ressentiment*.

Nonetheless, one may say that in Adorno's work the traces of a twilight of exaggeration are everywhere present. Perhaps the supposedly critical theory had to be realized as Aesthetic Theory because to its author it was at least indirectly clear that only works of art still endure as spaces for exaggeration, while everything that is merely discourse, theory, and complaint aspires to the cultural center, where what is wagered is taken back and what is acutely intensified is eroded. Indeed, perhaps culture is another word for the taming of hyperboles—an assessment that becomes convincing as soon as one explains art as the counterpart of culture and thinking as the antithesis of philosophy. From this perspective it can be said what professors of philosophy are: namely, epigones of eroded exaggerations—in the best case they act as curators in thought's cabinet of curiosities, where singular upsurges and classic instances of one-sidedness are inventoried. Derivative thought dismantles exaggerations and works to make their recurrence impossible. The Young Hegelians first demonstrated this in the nineteenth century, and their stragglers in the present, Habermas and Rorty, assume an exemplary position. They both formalized the pull to the center. These belated *Vormärz* authors accomplish their work of leveling with good reason, as long as hyperbole signifies oppression in league with power[28]—only the powerless exaggerations of art and of individualized thought that cannot be imitated may claim the undivided sympathy for their venture.

When critique has done its work only the work of art and its philosophical interpretation hold open a refuge for metaphysical inflations. Because Adorno virtually behaved like an apologist for hyperbole he was able to demand of the work of art what he no longer dared to ask for from the mediocritizing discourse of critique and *a fortiori* from the standardized philosophical discourse of modernity: that is, decisiveness in regards to acute intensification. "The extreme is demanded by artistic technology; it is not just the yearning of a rebellious attitude. The idea of a moderate modernism is self-contradictory."[29] The postulate of the thoroughly articulated character of works necessitates that "every specific form idea must be driven to its extreme."[30] This is also the case where philosophy, like an art *sui generis*, develops its conceptual labor all the way to the most extreme consequences. Quintilian, with his definition of hyperbole as the correspondence of discourse with a thing (*res*) beyond measure, had indicated the formal reason for this. Nietzsche provided the real reason when he recalled the magic of the extreme, which works 'for us,' the most extreme.[31] Adorno's aesthetics of truth takes up this motif: it demands as much 'implacability' from the work of art as is necessary for assuring the adequation of the successful work with an unsuccessful world. Hence the great value of the hypersensitivities of the artist as psychosomatic premises of irreconcilability.

That Adorno was also a deliberate apologist for hyperbole outside of the sphere of art is shown in his loathing for all forms of reformism and moderatism.[32] Because and as long as the world forms a context of the false, which at best is torn open on the fringes, the middle is not capable of truth on its own. Hence the smallest step toward human joy should not be allowed, because it—supposedly—only prolongs human suffering. The decision for intensification in advance is nowhere so clear as in one of Adorno's aphorisms, which found its way from *Minima Moralia* into the treasure chest of quotations belonging to those educated in psychology: "In psychoanalysis nothing is true except the exaggerations."[33] While hysteria disappears as a form of sickness in society, it lives on as a hermeneutical form of psychoanalytic discourse. If one transfers Adorno's statement to metaphysics, not only are the latter's elevated constitution and dynamic of exaggeration conceptualized; it also becomes evident that the overcoming of metaphysics is only to be found in its de-hysterization or cutting it down to an average size—for those who really want this.

These reflections have consequences for the epochal understanding of the present moment. What purports to be post-metaphysical thinking today must rather disclose whether it is a post-hyperbolic thinking—or not a new exaggeration in a post-metaphysical maternity dress. An advantage of the critique of hyperbole consists in the fact that it silences from the outset the question of whether exaggerations lead to something. In light of this it is senseless to want to know whether there is actually a beyond toward which the exaggeration [*Übertreibung*]—the propelling over [*Hinübertreibung*]—points. It is as vapid as it is futile to insist that an exaggeration undercuts itself should its 'totalizations' redound upon it—the 'performative self-contradiction,' may it rest in peace. Whoever has exaggerated or has thought for himself will know that the exaggeration suffices for itself. Its application to itself is the least of its worries. It is not interested in what comes after it—because *hyper* designates a centrifugal power in which it is impossible for one to turn back to oneself. All transcendences are immanent to exaggeration. Exaggerations for their part are legitimate, if they ever are at all, through their pointing to the excessive incongruity that gapes between signs and things—or that is testified to by the dawning of a world.[34] This is shown most clearly in theology, whose object, like that of ontology, because of its excessiveness demands discourse that goes all the way in its exaggerations, whether on the path of positive hyperbolics (*via eminentiae*) or on the path of negative hyperbolics (*via negationis*). Certain monastic theologians in late antiquity showed how discourse can rise from what is ineffable to elaborate litanies of silence before the height of the object. The traditional *topos* of unspeakability was propelled to the highest performances of refusal before the task of speaking of God. It is no wonder that Pseudo-Dionysius the Areopagite, the master of apophatic theology, knew how to make an excessive use of the prefix *hyper*—including turns of phrase such as that God is the 'hyper-unknowable' (*hyperagnōstos*) for the terrestrial intellect.

One can infer from the fortunes of theology in the present the decreased lifespan of the great systems of exaggeration. It is the weakness of contemporary theologians and churches in general to wish to provide their own shares in the premiums of the rationalized world's reason and normality, without considering that they only remain faithful to their immeasurable subject when they tend the sacred fire of exaggeration.[35] This sheds light on the older Critical Theory: insofar as it was theology it presented itself as minimalist and concealed its excess in social-scientific incognito; as aesthetics of hyperbole it maintained its position and did not concede anything to classical overreaches. Only in its second phase did critical theory curb its exuberance and do its part to reach the safe harbor of relatability. Perhaps this is what defines the student: that he becomes traitor to the master's exaggeration in order to please others. After this revision Critical Theory for the first time was entirely deserving of the name; only it merits noting that its significance escapes its users, so long as one does not explicitly say that critique in its precise sense means leveling, mediocritizing, translating back into the trivial. It responds to the transfiguration of the familiar with the familiarization of the transfigured. It practices the Young Hegelian reduction to the pragmatic level all the way to its banal end. Even hyperboles have their entropy—sooner or later they are overtaken by their improbability or deprived of their effect through repetition. Normalization is the incapacity to withstand an exaggeration. When hyperbole becomes feeble, consensus comes in and scatters the remainder.

After what has been said, it is evident that only the critique of hyperbole provides a clear view of the pretension of moderns to think from a basic post-metaphysical position. The meaning of the talk about solidarity with metaphysics at the moment of its fall can only be grasped inter-hyperbolically: because even the supreme hyperboles—and swarms of hyperboles of the kind found in high forms of religion and doctrines of Being—are exhaustible enterprises, the subsequent ones can empathize with the preceding ones and surmise in the latter their own fate—just as Alexander cried over the corpse of Darius and Scipio at the ruins of Carthage sank into meditation concerning the fate of Rome. As with European aristocracy, all exaggerations are remotely interrelated. And like the aristocracy, they do not think they are dying out even long after they have nothing more to say to the masses. There cannot be a post-metaphysical thought, but rather only a post-hyperbolic one. Post-hyperbolics from insight could be a stage of maturity; post-hyperbolics from weakness is a phase of the economy.

Within this perspective it is evident that a substantial post-metaphysics is impossible—there exist only intervals between waves of exaggeration and change of emphasis in regard to phenomena, from which new hyperboles take their starting point.[36] What emerges with the greatest fanfare as post-metaphysical is only boasting about the merit of having no merits of which one could boast. The predicate 'post-metaphysical' stands for theoretical products that want to score points through their accessibility to all; *nothing if not critical*,[37] they are jealously mindful of allowing no new hyperboles to arise. Nonetheless, understatement is neither entirely able to void the old hyperboles nor to prevent exaggerations when they are introduced.

Only in one point does the talk of the 'post-metaphysical' situation of thought have a basis in the matter at hand—i.e., a hold in transformed relations of exaggeration, as they are presented after Nietzsche's intervention. Nietzsche's significance for the history of metaphysics does not lie in his frequently noted and variously objected to 'inversion of Platonism.' It consists in the emancipation of exaggeration from the compulsion to justify, which for an age had tied the knot between metaphysics and *ressentiment*. Metaphysics justified its inflations by the solidity of the foundations upon which it wished to construct its propositional systems; it made the hyperbolic nature of its project invisible through its forced rationalism. In contrast, Nietzsche unleashed pure exaggeration that sent its arrows aloft without a hold in the putatively universal. The unleashed exaggeration unbinds the festive levity and auto-eulogistic power of language that had been tied up for all too long.[38]

> Truly it is a blessing and no blasphemy when I teach: "Over all things stands the sky accident, the sky innocence, the sky chance, the sky mischief."[39]

Even the hyperbolicist Heidegger had always wished to understand this only half-heartedly—in this he is closely related to Adorno: it does not escape him that the fundamental operation of metaphysics, the turning back to the deepest or most solid ground, must always be seen through as a machination of subjectivity that is marked by its striving for power and security. As a secret essentialist and open necessarian, as an apologist for necessity and the turning of need [*Not-Wendigkeit*] and for that which is hard, heavy, and fateful, Heidegger balked at taking over Nietzsche's emancipation of the contingent. To be sure, along with Nietzsche he destructures the fetish of the ground and shows how the latter changes from the ancients to the moderns: from the *hypokeimenon* of the Greeks over to the modern *subiectum* all the way to the modern will to power. But he completely misjudges the provocation that proceeds from Nietzsche's critique of hyperbole. According to this critique, the *hypokeimenon* is already to be understood as *hyperkeimenon*, the *subiectum* as *superiectum*, the will to power as waggish willfulness to exaggeration. That which apparently lies at the basis is in truth and from the beginning something that has been thrown up there. In exaggerations tendencies of mere taste and opportunities for one-sidedness are unfolded. The *sur* in Surrealism, the *meta* in metaphysics, the *trans* in transcendence are all derivatives of the *hyper* of hyperbole. There is no over [*Über*] that is not borrowed from the exaggeration [*Übertreibung*].

Emancipated critique of hyperbole will no longer operate disparagingly or deconstructively against constructs; without trying to deduce it, the emancipated critique of hyperbole takes upon itself the freedom to groundlessly applaud intensifications of life. It suffices that the 'sky mischief' extends over an exaggeration in order to do it justice. This takes nothing away from the civilizing power of skepticism. But in a different manner than criticism that remains interested in disparagements, skepticism fosters sympathies for exaggerations of all kinds, in the knowledge that it does not have to fall for them. The presupposition for this is created by the free spirit, who stands at a distance to seduction. Spirit has been free ever since it dissolved the metaphysical hyperbole par excellence, the logos-exaggeration:

> This freedom and cheerfulness of the sky I placed like an azure bell over all things when I taught that over them and through them no "eternal will"—wills. This mischief and this folly I placed in place of that will when I taught: "With all things one thing is impossible—rationality!" A bit of reason to be sure, a seed of wisdom sprinkled from star to star—this sourdough is mixed into all things. . . .
> A bit of wisdom is indeed possible.[40]

Nietzsche replaces the hyperbole of logos with the hyperbole of art, indeed with the free hyperbole, by virtue of which life and exaggeration are now equated. In order to find that plausible one must, with Nietzsche, maintain the unity of self-preservation and self-intensification. The critique of hyperbole brings critical theory to an end by establishing the precedence of exaggeration over its leveling. It was a ruse of aesthetic reason when Adorno's project presented itself under the name of critique. Its author long knew that works are only criticized by works. Against hyperboles only hyperboles help. Reality is the checks and balances of exaggerations. He who was aware of this may have had his reasons why year after year he unfailingly traveled to Sils-Maria to recover in Nietzsche's altitudes from misunderstandings in the Main River basin.

5

ALĒTHEIA OR THE FUSE
OF TRUTH

Toward the Concept of a History of Unconcealment

> When the human being flares up,
> Everything is given in an instant.
> *Maurice Merleau-Ponty*

If one wishes to interpret in a contemporary way the manner in which human beings find themselves in the world, then one can proceed from the principle that human beings are adventist creatures— beings to whom something comes and yet who are themselves the ones coming. This is an almost classical thought that nonetheless has by no means been thought through to the end. In its only partially clarified state it could happen that it succumbs to triviality without ever having achieved its mature form. Whatever its future development may be, its formulations to this point no longer satisfy the demand of contemporary thought.

In the Judeo-Christian tradition the fundamental human movement of coming-to-the-world was apprehended under the sign of createdness, which interpreted Being-in-the-coming as a trace of a divine making—from which it followed that human arriving must take second rank behind the ur-passive Being-inserted-into-the-world or Being-sent-into-the-world. In fact, the medieval Christian world is more interested in order and persistence than in the event and advent of the new. In contrast, both Christian and post-Christian modernity laid emphasis on the active and innovative moments in the human relation to the world. They shifted the accent from the human being's createdness to his own creative power—hence in the modern perspective coming-to-the-world signifies above all: to make the world, into which 'the human being' intends to come, according to one's own designs so as to bring it into a situation in which guiding images of a life worthy of human beings are universally realized. In the two most powerful anthropodicies of the Western tradition—in the Christian interpretation of the human being as a creature or vassal of God and in the modern Euro-American conception of the human being as a world-engineer and self-producer—stunted views of the fundamental human movement take shape. Both the passivism of classical metaphysics as well as the activism of the modern doctrines of self-activity are missing the medial nature of the being that is coming to the world. The adventist adventure has not yet found its proper self-description.

As a being that exists in coming, the human being is an animal that essentially comes from within. 'Within' here means: being a fetus, latency, concealment, the aquatic world, familiarity, being enwombed, domesticity, unconsciousness, what is unspoken. In view of these multiple senses of 'within,' coming-to-the-world must be understood in multiple ways: gynecologically as birth, psychologically as becoming an adult, anthropologically as elemental change, politically as entering into power struggles, poetologically [*poetologisch*] as literary production [*Dichtung*], ontologically as the opening up of worlds. Where human beings emerge they are not a biological species like all the rest that bustle about under the premade light [*Licht*] of the sun; rather it is the clearing [*Lichtung*] that occurs there, the clearing for whose inhabitants alone can it be the case that 'there is a world.' Thus advent and clearing radically belong together. The light over everything that is the case is not one given condition among others. The dawning of the world in an intelligible light is first made possible by an intelligence that goes to the world. Whether one conceives of this going-to as a 'plunge,' as a fall, as thrownness, as being borne along, as an exodus or as an eisodos, the advent of the human being is itself the 'opening up of one's eyes' toward Being—an opening for which beings are cleared [*sich lichtet*]. On this view, the advent of the human being as a whole—together with his epistemic-technological peak—can be understood as a lighting experiment [*Beleuchtungsexperiment*]. Human history is the time of the clearing; human time is the time of world-formative lightning [*Blitzes*], which we do not see as such because we, so long as we are in the world, are in the lightning.

It is also true that we continually have to do with what is illuminated and with light—in this context one could even say: with what is thought and with thinking—yet we seldom or never acknowledge the clearing itself. Nevertheless, for those who belong to our world circle there is a relatively simple way to draw attention to the clearing that is invisible as such. It suffices here to cast a glance at the present date and to alienate, with an unusual question, the information thereby attained. Supposing that, as placards and a glance at the calendar confirm, today we are writing on a certain day in the month of June in the year of 1993, then we need only ask of this 'at such and such a time': when do we really live, when we live in June 1993? I do not mean to suggest by this that an esoteric calendar lies concealed beneath the officially reformed Gregorian calendar, one which would reveal a different and true dating of the year of the world process to the few who have been initiated. Rather I would like to propose for consideration that our calendar displays almost everything that is to be known about it, as a formation of the clearing, in the form of an open secret—with the addition that what is decisive in its manifestness is concealed and that its secretlessness presents the most comprehensive diversion.

When we exist in June 1993, we do not know when we exist because we get no temporal feeling for the epochal from the perspective of everyday consciousness. We cannot read the face of our world clock, because we are caught up in a way of counting and dating that is blind to the event and have accustomed ourselves to abstract from the drama whose explication is our calendar. The reckoning of time *post Christum natum* initially presents only an analogy to the ancient Roman city calendar and imperial calendar that was established by popes of the fifth and sixth centuries and that counted *ab urbe condita*. Both Roman calendars (Romanization was chronopolitically carried through on a worldwide scale), like many other analogous calendars, express the conviction that there are events—here the founding of a city, there the birth of a child—which radically change the orientation of the world process.[1] The break, the distancing from history up to this point, in the Greek sense, the *epochē*, reaches so far that one must distinguish the years that follow from those that precede as two ages of the world or aeons separated by a rift. In this sense, our calendar conveys a statement about the epochal date of our Being-in-the-world: what befalls us happens to us within a spacious window in time that stands open from the founding of the city or since the birth of the Lord.

There cannot be a high culture without consciousness of the ages of the world, because high cultures as such are higher clocks or systems for counting time. The ancient world already formulated the conviction that the periods of the human world are not homogenous, but rather are separated by profound reversals in the modes of Being of things and the modes of existence of mortals. The most primordial doctrine of a turning of time or an epochal break appears in the quasi-universal proto-mythical difference between events that happened *in illo tempore*, back then in the fabled days of gods and heroes, and those that occur in the time afterward and ever since, in the time of humans. For the Greeks the primitive divorce between back then and afterward was, in the change from orality to literacy, further differentiated into the great narration of the ages of the world, according to which the world's course flows from an idealized beginning in the Golden Age that progressively runs down over a silver and a bronze age into the present time, which is an Iron Age populated by a hard race like ours.[2] Plato finally also gave the mythological awareness of the caesura between primeval times and the present time a philosophical and cosmological setting, when he presented his radical speculation on the Great Transformation, the *metabolē*, according to which every sequence of movement that in the era of Kronos ran its course counter-clockwise, as it were, from the end to the beginning, was converted in the era of Zeus to a clock-wise process from the beginning to the end. Thus the whole cosmos changed the direction of its circuit and course in the transition to the rule of the race of Olympian gods. The break in time, according to this figure of thought, marks at the same time a revolution in the mode of Being of things.

Against this background one may note that "great thought" always formally emerges as an exegesis of the differences of ages of the world: whether it is, as with Daniel and Augustine, a doctrine of the epochs in God's handling of the world, or, as with Hegel, a history of the stages of the self-penetration of spirit, or, as with Heidegger, an index of epochs of the unveiling and re-veiling of the truth, or even, as with Gotthard Günther—to mention the most discerning doctrine of the ages of the world known to this point—the gradual transition of logical projects and intellectual tasks that are posed to humanity, initially in the animistic era of univalence, and then in the local high-cultural era of bivalence and ultimately in the dawning world-cultural era of polyvalence.

In view of this state of affairs, one could say that the historical calendar invariably has the quality of marking out world reformations. In order to determine how the present time is to be positioned within world time they chronicle a great chain of events and states that preceded the current age of the world. Whoever lives now thus continually stands in the shadow of an inaugural event, from which the current numerical period received the imprint of its direction. Such numerical periods possess the form of calendars listing obligations to be performed. Measured against ancient mythical circumstances, we find reflected in them a novel awareness of the orientation of time and of the force that changes the sense of the world and that belongs to certain founding and inaugurating events.

In this occurrence the ancient natural powers of the mode of Being before calendars necessarily shift to the second level: the days, weeks, and months also additionally belong to the old gods (except for the Lord's day, *dies Domenica*, at least in the Romance languages), and through these communicate with old nature. The year that is counted, in contrast, belongs to the city, to the empire, the church, or the project of humanity. That is no different in this June of 1993, in which the month's name recalls the female ruler of the gods, Iuno Regina, who under the sign of summertime abundance may provide for the eternal or at least regular recurrence of marriages and harvests, while the year recalls the Christian world-project, which runs at an irreversible pace to meet a still veiled goal or end. In the relation between month and year the relation between nature and history as it is understood in high culture is reflected—like the relation between a stage and a play or between a racetrack and the race, as it were. The calendar of high culture cuts a temporal swath into ancient homogenous nature and creates within this a clearing in which the precedence of irreversible histories over the eternal recurrence of the same can become manifest.

Thus, when human beings in June 1993 contemplate 'man and nature' or 'nature in the mind,' they do so within this temporal swath and within the resulting history of the opposition between the time of humanity and the time of nature. To what is here called the time of humanity belong the propulsive powers of the political, technological, scientific, and religious worlds—the competitive race among states, the acceleration of the production of ideas, the impatience of missions, the global marketing of technological aids for living. In the historical-temporal swath an event-generator, as it were, appears to have been brought into position, from which what is revolutionary, surprising, and memorable bursts forth with increased frequency. That is to be understood not only in the sense that incidents between peoples and collisions of empires pose new noteworthy tasks for human memory (although it is true that only high cultures provide employment for chroniclers and historians), but also in the sense that activities which are proliferated on all sides—the Greeks used the word *polypragmasynē* for being an urban jack of all trades—bring a new didactic disposition onto the scene, which demands of human beings that they keep themselves at the ready for the proliferation of truths. An elevated place in the list of human virtues is now attributed to the striving for knowledge—and that means *eo ipso* for subjectively or objectively *new* knowledge.

Only in the midst of a world form already held in suspense by the influx of new truths could the sentence with which Aristotle begins Book Alpha of the *Metaphysics* appear: that all human beings by nature desire to know. In this latently polemical hyperbole Aristotle defends his conception of philosophy as research in contrast to the

Platonic definition of knowledge as recollection. At the same time
the task-like character of the philosophical and even more of the scientific search is emphasized. Where tasks for thought are conceived
of as 'problems' it is acknowledged that solutions are promised
only for later. What Heidegger in his explorations of the equation
of Being and time brought to light corresponds from the psycho-
historical perspective to the equation between time and desire and
from the dramaturgical perspective to the equation between the
time of the plot and the time of revelation. Schiller's words on the
Sophoclean tragedy *Oedipus Rex* as a 'tragic analysis' can within
certain limits be related to the time of investigation as a whole:
history, like research, is the occurrence in the course of which things
'come to light.'

Against the backdrop of these observations, it becomes understandable why one should entertain a correspondence, indeed even
an equivalence, between the theorem of the axial age brought into
the discussion by Jaspers and the Heideggerian concept of the
history of Being. For when Jaspers discusses various forms of the
image of the world and of the self that belong to 'axial' cultures
in China, India, Persia, Palestine, and Greece, he is talking about
something that Heidegger too envisages, particularly from the perspective of the Greek origins of thought, in his idea of the 'destinal
sending' [*Geschick*] of truth. In connection with both thinkers one
can recognize how the 'breakthroughs' they describe have brought
about a revolution in high cultures' economy of truth—a revolution
that presses for the radical subordination of ancient mythical and
everyday knowledge to new formulations that are more logically
and ethically sophisticated.

From the ideal-typical perspective, this is that singular moment
in the history of being in which, in Heidegger's words, 'the first
human being raises his head'; this is the genuine axis on which the
world-process separates into a before and an after. Here begins the
experience of thinking in the distinctively high cultural sense, which
grants to its bearers an intellectual [*geistige*] baptism, as it were, and
initiates them into another order of knowledge and into another
obligation of being claimed by truth. It thus becomes clear that the
Western world calendar with its division of time periods into that
of *ante* and that of *post Christum natum* does not present a singular
phenomenon of the periodization of the world, but is rather a particular monument of the general axial reversal. It articulates—in a
thoroughly typical and perhaps inevitable way—the ages of world
occurrence into those which did not yet know 'the new,' and those
to which what was hitherto veiled could be shown because the time
had come.

It belongs to the pathos of the Christian theology of the ages of the world that it tells of something new, something which shows what has been up until this point in a wholly different light. This way of treating temporality could never have taken shape and resonated if it had not corresponded to the temporal-logical demand of its epoch.[3] In the axial field the world form could recognize of its own accord a propensity for reform and broadly accommodate the talk of new truths and new times. What we are today accustomed to call antiquity is the first era that was cleft by a battle of the titans that could no longer be delayed, a battle between sticking with the old truths and unveiling new ones as well as their retention and transmission. Hence it knows itself to be fundamentally different from prehistoric times and earlier aeons. In the frontline attack by new truths, heterogeneous constructs of knowledge and types of discourse are allied with each other, such that it does not come as a surprise when here the early natural sciences, incipient ethnological and geographical knowledge, psychological introspection, imperial programs, religious promulgation, and maniacal mediumism communicate with each other in wild syntheses. Wherever a triumph of the new, which was still always presented as what is most ancient and eternal, came into view, a contest for a number of new truths broke out at the same time—as in the well-known quarrel of philosophical sects with each other and in the struggle rendered unforgettable by Plato between so-called true philosophers and their copies, the sophists.

That in the period of the axial age[4] a truth-historical upheaval was in the air in many ways and in many places, especially with the Greeks and by no means only in that Jewish prophetic subculture that led to actually existing messianism—any glance at the transmission of our antiquity persuades one of this. Ovid, in Book 15 of his *Metamorphoses*, depicted the emergence of the legendary Pythagoras in a way that would have to be characterized in every respect as evangelical, were this expression not an overly Christian one. It is not the case that Christianity possessed the sole authority for proclaiming the good news as the new truth. Rather, it belongs to the character of the new formulation of the economy of truth in high cultures that masterful intelligences emerge on all sides, who avail themselves of evangelical qualities and instances of quasi-divine witnessing in their statements. For instance, in Ovid's text, Pythagoras appears as an epitome of the wise master and revelator, who in the founding years of the breakthroughs of new truths shook up his fellow citizens with incredible sayings: "All that Nature has denied to man and human vision, he reviewed with eyes of his enlightened soul."[5] At the decisive passage of his speech, that is, at the transition between the proclamation of the universal prohibition on killing along with its implications for a vegetarian lifestyle and the doctrine of the migrations of the soul, whose death the ignorant wrongly fear, Ovid has his philosopher make a personal statement about the novelty of his doctrines:

> And, since a god impels me to speak out,
> I will obey the god who urges me,
> and will disclose to you the heavens above,
> and I will even reveal the oracles
> of the Divine Will. I will sing to you
> of things most wonderful, which never were
> investigated by the intellects
> of ancient times and things which have been long
> concealed from man.[6]

Obviously, Ovid already works with the paradigm of discourse of new truths and attributes the legitimacy of his philosopher to the fact that he has been sent by epistemically engaged gods. It is as though at that time the heavenly ones had made the decision to renounce the overly dense language of the oracle and reveal themselves to human beings under the forms of logical ideas and generally comprehensible moral instructions. From now on truth is that which comes to be articulated from out of what has long been unexplored and concealed (*diu latuere*) hitherto and is organized by a deictic, gathering, and demonstrative logos.

A new order of revelation thereby takes shape: a changed epiphanic regime steps into power, which through the imposition of new truths increasingly affects human beings. Precisely this thought was expressed by the Greek philosopher Xenophanes in a verse handed down by Stobaeus: "In the beginning the gods did not at all reveal all things clearly to mortals, but by searching they [gods or human beings] in the course of time find them out better."[7]

In view of these considerations I propose interpreting the temporal swath of the post-axial form of the world as an epoch of unveiling in the sense of the Xenophanic finding out 'in the course of time'—such that the Western calendar from the beginning onward reveals a dimension that is just as epistemo-epiphanic as it is soteriological. The Christian calendar, which recognizes the manifestation of God in his 'son' as the temporal axis, reshapes an aletheiological calendar that takes the incursion of new truths into genuine and really powerful thought as its point of departure—the time of salvation and the years of the Lord, which our official conventions of dating still cite, are also a cover for the time of research and the years of seizing power by verified knowledge. It is the age in which communities are put in suspense because of the influx of scientific, technological, and metaphysico-epiphanic formulations.

The majority of high cultures responded to this situation with priestly-expertocratic strategies; only in the Greek sophistic can one find approaches to a logical democracy and a forensic-exoteric mediation of research—reason enough for modernity to take up this pattern. When Heidegger stressed rendering the Greek expression *alētheia* with the German concept *Unverborgenheit* [unconcealment], he justifiably put the emphasis on the 'adventitious' character of the increases in truth in the human perspective and discourse—although he was suspicious of the enlightenment idea of a continual accumulation of knowledge. Heidegger also pushes back the meaning of unconcealment, supposedly understood in primordial Greek terms, primarily to the pre-scientific interpretation of the world. According to him, it is mainly the heroic endowment of the Greeks that grants them the chance to contemplate the play of disclosure and concealment without metaphysical tranquilizers, while the later emphasis on increases in knowledge and the assured disposal over it already betrays the fateful decadence of the understanding of truth, in Heidegger's view. Nevertheless, the philosopher for understandable reasons accentuates truth's sense of dis-closure, as the Greek word *a-lētheia* appears to express, insofar as one reads the *a-* as a privative. Truth is accordingly "gained," insofar as beings are robbed of their concealment or ineffability—precisely in this theft lies the "innermost confrontation of the essence of man with the whole of beings themselves."[8] The modes of the theft of concealment impart their extended history to truth itself. To a large extent, for our cultural sphere, it is coextensive with the history of technology and its socialization.[9]

Heidegger's aletheiology or doctrine of unconcealment ensures that all new truths must 'really' be read only as supplementary truths that can be added to the existing stock within an epochal framework. These epochal frameworks are for him great conjunctures, as it were, which delineate the sense of knowledge and truth with preparatory sketches that are different in each case. Accordingly, in the time before Plato, as we just heard, there was a primal conjuncture in which the essence of truth as dawning into the phenomenal day and as setting back again into pregnant concealment had been thought most purely: a state of affairs to which the correctly understood early Greek concept of *physis*, which has to be interpreted in terms of vegetal germination, would correspond. Then begins the Platonic-Aristotelian conjuncture, which is defined by thinking in terms of essence and substance and which we ordinarily call classical antiquity or the First Enlightenment; 'truth' now pre-dominantly means participation in that which exists always. The Christian-medieval conjuncture follows this with its swing back to an understanding of truth as revelation through grace, from which a prevailing interest in questions of salvation and a pervasive neutrali-zation of interest in the knowledge of nature had to result. Lastly, there is the modern conjuncture of the philosophy of the subject, which leads to the coldest night of the world dominated by the gigantomachies of wills to power. In its forlorn morning hours the first gray of a possible new epochal day at last becomes manifest, in which the sense of Being, truth, and knowledge once more would have changed in a post-modern, post-enframing, post-subjectivist, perhaps even neo-early-Greek way.

If one submits to closer examination Heidegger's great panorama of the quasi-anarchical sendings of the conjunctures of truth or of the inviolate twists and turns in the sense of Being, then it becomes evident that the series of five conjunctures (or better four and a half phases, insofar as the one introduced or waited for by Heidegger himself cannot yet be brought into sharp relief) actually only indi-cates a single authentic caesura—namely, the one at the threshold from early Greek to high Greek thought. From here on the condi-tions of the forgetting of Being or, as one could also say, of the misunderstanding of *physis* prevail: they provide the age-groupings of antiquity, the Middle Ages, and modernity, despite all of their profound differences, with their 'truth-historical' unity, which con-sists in the veiled identity of metaphysics and nihilism. Only thus can even Plato already be unmasked as an agent of the forgetting of Being and be ranged in a line that is able to anticipate the Cartesian program: to make the human being the *maître et possesseur de la nature*.[10] In the era of nihilism the fuse of truth burns all the way down to the epiphany of the great kaboom. The final annihilation would be the laying bare of the nothingness that everything that is becoming already 'really' is.

If one takes seriously the bold synopsis of antiquity, the Middle Ages, and modernity under the title of nihilism, then for Heidegger there are, according to this robust summary, fundamentally only two epochs of truth in history up to this point, the primordial one and the one in ruins. But after these two, as is common in great stories, there already looms the reference to the beginning of a third, in which the truth of the inception would be achieved again and—why not?—at a higher level (in this Heidegger's anti-Hegelianism is by no means unambiguous, since Heidegger too, like Hegel, would admit and claim that, on the whole, he knows more than Heraclitus). The *translatio philosophiae ad Germanos*[11] is one of the conditions for the recurrence of Greek truth thanks to the German contribution.

Heidegger, with this much-ridiculed narrative of the epochs and primary languages of truth, is nothing else than a classical story-teller and an exemplary therapist. Like all premodern storytellers he employs a triadic schema of an undisturbed primary state, a disturbed middle state, and a restored, or in the best case enriched, neo-primary state: inceptual understanding of Being, forgetting of Being, understanding of Being again. Heidegger's pre-Socraticism corresponds to the therapeutic disposition to return from the current crisis into the state before the disturbance and from there to move forward a second time into the present, this time as though past the disturbances of the middle state, even if the latter were two and a half millennia long. The procedure is grounded in the expectation, typical in therapy, of a new beginning: as personal histories do not necessarily have to founder, so too do civilizing processes not have to run off the rails once and for all as in the Euro-American case. As there are occasional new beginnings in the midst of biographies, so too for the culture of modernity as a whole a new, more suitable way of approaching things is, to be sure, improbable, but not unthink-able. The new beginning would be the god who saves us—not least from our false self-description as subjects and our fixation on the gadget-ontology of the technological world. Regenerative pre-Socraticism recommends a primary therapy of reason: getting past the rigid defenses with which metaphysical eidetic idealism wanted to undo the appropriative event. The therapeutic recommendation does not come without a threat: whoever does not want to feel the appropriative event gets to feel the enframing.

Since the axial revolution, Euro-American humanity, as we are able to conceive it according to this retrospective and only in it, sits on a truth-historical time bomb, which ticks down to the moment in which it is no longer single new truths alone that come to light, but the truth of the truth itself is also explosively unveiled. This is a state of affairs that the successes—I here use this expression in a deliberately uncritical manner—of modern natural science and its technology have demonstrated to such a degree that all pluralistic and relativisitic deviations are ultimately not in the position to do anything to adjust the ticking of the clockwork of knowledge.

The fuse-like character of the process of new truths can admit-tedly, as was emphasized, only occur to one from a late perspective, because only after the takeover of the nuclear fire and after the foray into the genetic fabric of the living does the European axial age's dawning of knowledge get set into relief as a 'prehistory' of these results. The recent and ongoing crisis of acquired knowledge forces us to go back and make conclusions about the history that prepared it. To keep with the image of the process of knowledge tapering off in the manner of a fuse to an 'explosion': here it is undoubtedly a matter of a detonation in two or three phases, at the beginning of which it is by no means foreseeable what the end will bring. Democritus and Leucippus are not the direct teachers of Niels Bohr and Max Planck, and yet they initiate the first phase of a procedure whose powerful cognitive influence reaches into the late Middle Ages. Then Galileo and his ilk, a new generation of physicists, appear on the scene, concerning whom Carl Friedrich von Weizsäcker could justifiably say that a straight line runs from them all the way to the atomic bomb. In this sense one may claim that the fuse of truth (in its slow burn) runs from Ionia to Los Alamos.

For the most recent section of this fuse cord of knowledge it is characteristic that new truths burst into the human world with the irresistibility of chain reactions. In the course of this irruption, they are typically only present to a few in their first manifestation, up to the extreme possibility that a single logician or a discoverer rushing ahead can end up being right in contrast to the rest of humanity, not, to be sure, because he would have a privileged access to truth or because he—as one occasionally says of Plato—would have aspired to logical monarchy, but rather because he takes the potentially universal approach somewhat earlier than others. Yet even if one accepts the image of the cognitive fuse cord for the history of physics from the Ionian dawning to the Manhattan Project, it remains completely unclear toward which explosion or implosion the history of human *reflection* [Besinnung] runs in the midst of this happening. Only this much appears to be clear: that it cannot be a matter of a mere repetition of the concept of *physis* as thought by the early Greeks.

For the moment, I do not want to continue to explain these references to the proper truth-historical sense of the world form that is contained in our calendar. In what follows, it may suffice to reroute the regard for the increase in legitimating truths to the side of the process having to do with the history of civilization. Here we will inquire into the cultural premises for the logical apprehension of power. One easily recognizes that with this turn the theorem of the cognitive will to power comes into play, and it is just as easily understood why this formulation plays the decisive role in almost all interpretations of the modern relation between the human being and nature. To the degree that late-modern humanity is seized by an uneasiness toward power, an inclination in its critical intelligentsia gains the upper hand to derive factual power from a will and in turn to think of the will as something that one can have or not have, affirm or deny. I must confess that I consider this custom to be a *Holzweg*, not in Heidegger's sense [as a timber track], but rather in the profane notion of a dead end, because, with a moralistic denial of the will, one underestimates the more fundamental compulsion to power and the authorization to will that is made possible by the history of truth. It seems more reasonable to me to start an inquiry into the cultural-historical sources of the will to power.

To that end, it is necessary to clarify certain features in the primary relation to nature of the gregarious being called *Homo sapiens*—features that do not tend to fit so neatly into the holistic image, which in earlier times was often invoked in order, in view of the evident dissonance between natural history and the industrialized human world, to recall the lost times of a more successful adaption or adjustment of *Homo sapiens* to a nature more to be revered than mastered. In truth, the history of our species from the beginning is only to be conceived as a secession from natural nature that is as slow as it is fundamental. The sphere of human existence from early on possesses a dynamic that stands apart, is singled out, and is based on unique developments.

Paleoanthropology can be characterized as nothing less than the science of the natural history of that which is counter-natural in the human being. It treats of the human being as the animal of distance that was able to shape itself into a luxury-member of natural biocenoses on the basis of a special evolution of distancing technologies. With such a definition one puts a stop to the holistic fairy tale which suggests that one ought to see in the human a being whose nature lies in giving itself over to a whole. The special history of early human times teaches us the opposite in all this: the human being is not the devoted animal that lets nature do everything for it and before it, but rather the genius of deviation that stabilizes itself in non-adaption in an amazing way. Human intelligence consists in the achievement of sustaining the improbability of its own form of life through supplemental constructs. In this regard one may say that the human being is the animal that does not give itself over; he is a being that for its non-devotion has paid the price of risky or, as one says nowadays: of creative developments. Because this is the case, within the paradoxical species the dream emerges of a state that we never were in—a nostalgia for the never-was, whose mythological name is paradise and whose quasi-scientific new formulation leads to idealized cosmologies or, better, cosmo-matriarchical holisms.

The objectivization of nature by modern natural sciences does not satisfy the conditions of ontological injustice—as a narrowly Catholic and eco-pietistic thought supposes—but rather is a consistent, however late, explication of dissident potentials with regard to nature, potentials with which the eccentric species was pregnant from the earliest days of its special development on. The natural history of the objectification of nature is the genuine affair of the human being—even the pre-Socratics are no exception to this. Its critical phase dawns in the time-bomb period of breakthroughs of knowledge in the form of new truths, which after the invention of inventing in modern engineering have dramatized our world-calendar and pull it for the time being into an ever more precipitous movement.

Whoever intends to describe this process not only as a history of loss and catastrophe—not only as that ominous spiritual decline of the earth, of which German philosophers of life told at the time of the First World War—cannot avoid the task of interpreting the history of the physical seizure of power as a history of anthropological self-experience—in the course of which different cultures form different groups of self-experience that until today have known little of each other. Only through the growing negativity of our relation to nature, through the increase of the possibilities for an annihilation of nature on the experimental line of Euro-America, could the eccentric species encircle itself and avow its essential negativity and distance. With regard to this tragic self-compulsion one could speak of a birth of the consciousness of the species from out of the spirit of the possibility to commit suicide. Only from the post-suicidal position that has been explicitly taken on, from the negation of self-negation, would nature come back from its materialist degradation and from annihilating objectification into a self that makes itself at home in 'physis' in a new way—neither in childish impotence nor with economistic hooliganism, but rather in a matured awareness of the possible co-productivity among pre-human, human, and post-human intelligences.

The innate negativity of the human position toward nature can only be turned into something positive when human beings themselves, to put it in figurative terms, have come sufficiently far to the 'other side' of nature—more precisely, to the other side of naturing. In fact, from the beginning a substantivist concept of nature results in error, because nature cannot be conceived through that which it 'is' or as what it presents, but rather only through that which it does or that whereby it eventuates. The deed of nature is naturing, and it must in truth be understood as the holder of a primordial monopoly on production. The human being, who changes to the other side, is *eo ipso* the negator of this monopoly and the providential rival of nature in questions of engendering, begetting, and producing. Where nature to this point possessed the sole competence for the engendering of organisms, in the course of European history a second mechanical engineering, a second organization, stepped into the light of day with the barely concealed tendency to realize an alternative configuration of reflection and matter.[12]

In the clarification of this rivalry, the *experimentum mundi* has its rational kernel in the new-truth phase of history 'after Christ.' The era that is marked by our form of calendar would come to its end if the human being's changing of sides were to successfully transition from birth and death as only results of nature to co-production of nature and man-made subjectivity. One would then no longer date only *post Christum natum*, but even more *post naturam imitatam*.[13] The metaphysical age of the world in which nature is overcome by faith—marked by the Christian key terms 'resurrection,' 'ascension,' 'new man'—would have transitioned to the age of the doubling of nature and the supplementation of nature by technology. Its main theme would be the self-observation of nature naturing itself by means of the human being—or if you like: an age of nature going to its own head begins.

This is not merely a fanciful speculation in the style of the late Romantic, idealist philosophy of nature, but rather an inherent, intimate driving force in the intervention of modern technological sciences in energy and computer science matrices of the physical process of the world itself. This can be learned from even a fleeting glance at the uncanny advances of modern know-how. Behind the historically relativized forms of the laborer, the craftsman, and the engineer of the first order the silhouette of the second engineer, the manufacturer of natures, stands out.

From the perspective of the history of ideas one can easily show that dreams of demiurges, phantasms of breaching the natural monopoly on producing, are much older than modern technology, even if it is indeed only quite recently that modern technology, as operative genetics, has attempted to seize hold of the mysteries of reproduction in plants, animals, and human beings. There is an ancient line from proto-technological visions that aim at emancipating the human being from the position of being passively produced, engendered, and born, in order to transfer him to the other side of creation, into the hearth of emergence, into the generative center of formations.

When it comes down to thinking nature in the precise sense, namely the power of birth, as a process with two sides, we find ourselves in a field where the generative process itself is in play. The raised human stake pertains to the changing of sides, which makes an engenderer from the engendered, a begetter from the begotten, a producer from the produced. For long stretches, the history of technology, together with its precursors, has been nothing else than an account of the attempts to turn the human head—or as one now should say more correctly, the masculine head and its prototypical workshops, the smith and the laboratory—into a uterus. Contexts of this kind are well documented, above all for the universe of the most ancient metallurgy. Historians of ideas have shown a continuity of conceptions that stretches for millennia, extending from ancient metallurgists up to the medieval and early modern alchemists, only to lead a noteworthy afterlife in messianic doctrines of production of the Marxist type as well as in techno-maniacal subcultures.

One knows that in certain civilizations of the Bronze and Iron Age, labor on the transformation of mineral ores was enveloped by a complex system of ritual and magical ideas, based on the stirring experiences of the power of human work and on the synergies of fire and knowledge. One suspected early on that something monstrous was underway in the smithies, which could no longer be interpreted on analogy to the quiet growth of plants in the fields. Ancient smithies were centers for demiurgic euphoria—enveloped by the ambivalent shudder that belongs to the sacred devil's work of transforming matter. Thus early texts testify to how, for the first metallurgists, it was a matter of reaching the other side of reproduction. The forges had the status of wombs and the metals the status of embryos that underwent a magically accelerated maturation in an artificial interior. What the mountain otherwise appeared to prepare in its womb over the course of millennia, i.e., the quiet carrying to full term of metal children, especially the incubation of gold, this took place, according to the traditional view, within a few weeks in the workshops of smiths and in the flasks of alchemists. If there were something like a precisely identifiable origin of the idea that natures can be shaped by human intervention, then it would certainly lie in the obstetric phantasms of early metallurgists and mineralogists, who understood themselves to be the midwives of mountain wombs and the consummators of the works of nature.

The decisive emphasis in these demiurgic practices, which wanted to bring new life from the workshops and spawn from the forges, continually fell on the aspect of time. The illuminated engineer is a catalyst for imaginary gestations, a manipulator of the tempo of naturing. On this view, even smiths and alchemists are initially not producers of nature; they are at best masters of another time, an accelerated time. They conceive of themselves as assistants and consummators, who apprehend the latent tendencies of mountains and earth-wombs, in order to advance them, true to their intentions, into procedures both sacred and dangerous—admittedly more quickly than the old nature, left to itself, would allow.[14]

As soon as the typically modern combination of knowledge and power emerges, human beings, that is, again, men above all, no longer content themselves with only being the stewards on the ship of evolution—they develop an ambition that has more in mind than bringing a cocktail every now and then to the Great Mother in her chair. The ambition is indeed initially expressed in symbols drawn from midwifery; yet at its core it no longer has to do with mere midwifery, but rather with a share in the power of creation as such. For whoever negates nature in order to create nature, it is a matter of the capacity for being a new beginning for beings. He strives for joint ownership of the competence for the original creation of life. From this alchemical hearth of attraction there still stem ultra-modern statements such as the one of Novalis: "We are called to form the earth." One has good reason to question whether the decisive phantasm of the Marxist movement had not for its part been a half-obstetric, half-demiurgic program. The basic term of magical modernity, 'revolution,' understood in its most sophisticated form, meant nothing other than to bring fortune-bestowing prodigies, which go by the name of productive powers, from the womb of the infernal mother bourgeoisie, a.k.a. relations of production, into the open, entirely in the sense of the motto of alchemists and engineers invoked by Ernst Bloch: "Every kernel intends wheat, every metal intends gold, every birth intends human beings."

One must guard against taking a sarcastic stand on such conceptions in view of the darkened ecological horizons. The failure of the council communist systems proves nothing about the overall prospects of the technological-magical project that is as old as high cultures and in some places even considerably older. For whether in Marxist coding or in a liberal-capitalist or neo-holistic key, the motif of the re-creation of the earth and the ambition to get behind the mechanism of nature and birth are even potent in a post-Marxist global situation, indeed more compelling than ever. Hence, this motif and this ambition possess so much propulsive power, not least because in them the two most powerful motivators of the human being in historical time, the religious expectation of salvation and protection and the economic hope for profit and prosperity, begin to merge. The connection of capitalism and Protestantism conjectured by Max Weber is solidified before our eyes into the alliance between biotechnology and the mentality of stock exchanges. The health-care industry and economic health will in the future be steered by a common center of illusion.

Nevertheless, it presently seems as though the demiurges playing with naturations are on the defensive as regards the ongoing ecological crisis. The human being today stands in the dock in his character of being a maker who is not convincing, and must listen to the pleadings of attorneys, who enumerate for him his hubris, his self-overestimation, his frivolous capability that cannot do enough, and his semi-criminal semi-competence in the technological seizure of power on the earth. Yet one ought not allow oneself to be deterred by moral-rhetorical conjunctures. The dream of arriving on the side of *natura naturans* through technical knowledge of creation will become more contagious than ever before under the pressure of ecological or demographical disasters that are imminent or have already begun. The accused will to power will be called into the next phase of the trial as an assistant in the emergency—even if he himself was not innocent in triggering the emergency. More than ever, technologically advanced humanity is condemned to 'alchemy.'

If the *experimentum mundi* is still to succeed, in however temporary and regional a manner, then it will only do so if our calendar once again is torn open in favor of a hitherto latent truth, whose manifestation will compel one to frame anew and to re-date all knowledge to this point. Heidegger, in his ominous interview with *Der Spiegel*, uttered the statement: "Only a god can save us." After everything that we know today, the word 'god' ought to be replaced with the expression 'the capacity to create natures.' Even this formulation is so grandiose that it leaves us hardly less baffled than Heidegger's oracle. For it to acquire a practicable sense, one would have to bring it down to this expression: the capacity to cooperate with natures. Cooperation requires foresight and relativizing oneself with respect to the other. In view of this task the word 'autodidacticism'—experimental self-instruction—takes on a fateful meaning for the species *Homo sapiens*. After modernity, in its unlimited experimenting, has blown open the system of Old European proportions, it will be the wisdom of the future to balance excess and foresight once more with each other. World society will be a society of foresight, or it will not be at all.

6

RULES FOR THE HUMAN PARK

A Response to Heidegger's "Letter on 'Humanism'"

Books, the poet Jean Paul once remarked, are long letters to friends.‐
With this statement, he appropriately characterized the essence and
function of humanism in a quintessential, graceful manner: it is
telecommunication that builds friendship in the medium of writing.
What from Cicero's time onward has been called *humanitas* belongs,
in the narrowest and broadest senses, to the consequences of literacy. Ever since philosophy has existed as a literary genre it has
recruited its members by writing in an infectious way about love
and friendship. Not only is it a discourse on the love of wisdom—it
also wants to move others to this love. The fact that written philosophy could at all remain contagious up to the present day, after its
beginnings more than 2,500 years ago, is something it owes to the
successful outcomes of its capacity to make friends by means of a
text. It has allowed its writing to continue like a chain letter across
generations. Despite all the copying errors, indeed perhaps because
of them, it has drawn copyists and interpreters under its befriending
spell.

The most important link in this chain of letters was undoubtedly
the Roman reception of the Greek message, since the Roman appro-
priation first opened up the Greek text for the empire and made it
accessible to later European cultures, at least indirectly, beyond the
fall of the Western Roman Empire. To be sure, the Greek authors
would have marveled at the sort of friends who would one day come
forward in response to their letters. The rules of the game for written
culture dictate that the senders cannot foresee their actual recipients. Nevertheless, the authors embark on the adventure of sending
their letters off to unidentified friends. Without the encoding of
Greek philosophy on transportable scrolls, those postal effects we

call tradition could never have been mailed; but without the Greek tutors who put themselves at the disposal of the Romans as assistants in deciphering the letters from Greece, these same Romans would not have been able to become friends with the senders of these texts. Friendship from afar thus needs both—the letters themselves and those who deliver or interpret them. Without the readiness of Roman readers, in turn, to become friends with the distant dispatches of the Greeks, recipients would have been lacking, and if the Romans had not entered the game with their distinguished receptivity, then the Greek messages would never have reached the Western European space that those interested in humanism today still inhabit. There would be neither the phenomenon of humanism nor any form of Latin philosophical discourse worth taking seriously, and just as little would there be later philosophical cultures with their national vernaculars. When today we talk in German of *humanen Dingen* [human matters], this possibility is owed not least to the readiness of the Romans to read the writings of their Greek teachers as though they were letters to friends in Italy.

If one takes the epochal consequences of the Greco-Roman mail into consideration, then it becomes evident that there is something special about the writing, sending, and reception of philosophical texts. Obviously, the sender of this genre of friendly letters sends his writings out into the world without knowing the recipients—or if he does know them, he is still conscious of the fact that sending a letter points beyond this particular transmission and can provoke a countless number of chances for friendship with nameless, often still unborn readers. From the erotological perspective, the hypothetical friendship of the author of books and letters with the recipients of his messages represents a case of long-distance romance—and it does so completely in Nietzsche's sense, who knew that writing is the power to transform love for those near and dear into love for the life of someone who is unknown to us, distant, and to come. Not only does writing create a telecommunicative bridge between proven friends who at the time the letter is mailed live separated from each other at a spatial remove; it also sets in motion an operation on unproven ground, it launches a temptation into the distance—put in terms of old European magic, it launches an *actio in distans*—with the aim of unmasking the unknown friend as such and moving him to enter into one's circle of friends. In fact, the reader who exposes himself to the long letter can understand the book as an invitation card, and if he lets himself warm up to the reading, then he will come forward in the circle of the addressed in order to acknowledge that he has received the message.

Thus one could trace the communitarian phantasm at the base of all humanisms back to the model of a literary society in which those involved discover through canonical readings their shared love for inspiring messages. Understood in this way, we discover at the core of humanism a fantasy of the sect or club—the dream of the fated solidarity of those who have been chosen to be able to read. For the Old World, indeed up to the eve of the modern nation-state, the ability to read actually meant something like membership in a secret society of the elite—grammatical knowledge once counted in many places as the epitome of sorcery: indeed, already in medieval English, the word *glamour*[1] developed out of the word *grammar*: whoever could read and write could easily manage other kinds of impossible things, too. Those who are humanized are initially no more than the sect of the alphabetized, and as in many other sects here too expansionist and universalist projects come to light. When alphabetism became fantastical and immodest, the grammatical or letter mysticism of the Kabbalah emerged, which raves of having insight into the world author's mode of writing.[2] In contrast, when humanism became pragmatic and programmatic, as in the *Gymnasium* ideologies of the bourgeois nation-states of the nineteenth and twentieth centuries, the paradigm of the literary society expanded into the norm for political society. From then on peoples were organized as forced, thoroughly literate associations of friendship that were sworn to mandatory reading canons established within each respective national space. Alongside ancient authors common to Europe, national and modern classics are hence mobilized as well—whose letters to the public are elevated by the book market and institutions of higher learning into effective motivating factors for the creation of nations. What are modern nations other than the quite effective fictions of reading publics, who through these very writings would become a congenial band of friends? The universal military conscription of male youth and the universal conscription of the youth of both sexes to read the classics characterize the classical bourgeois era, that is, the age of armed and literate humanity, on which new and old conservatives of today look back, nostalgically and helplessly at the same time, and completely unable to provide a media theoretical justification for the sense of a reading canon— whoever wishes to gain a current impression of this may check and see how pathetic the results of a national debate recently attempted in Germany over the supposed necessity of a new literary canon turned out.

In fact, it was from 1789 to 1945 that the reading-happy national humanisms had their moment of glory. Complacent and aware of their power, the caste of old and new philologists resided at the center; they knew they were entrusted with the task initiating their descendants into the circle of recipients of the definitive long letters. The power of teachers in this era and the key role of philologists were based on their privileged familiarity with authors who were qualified as senders of writings that establish communities. In substance, bourgeois humanism was nothing other than the authority to impose the classics on the youth and to assert the universal validity of national canons.[3] Thus bourgeois nations themselves would to a certain degree be literary and postal products—fictions of a fated friendship with peoples from distant lands and with sympathetically united readers of absolutely inspirational authors jointly owned.

If this epoch today appears to be irretrievably over and done with, then this is not because people would no longer be willing to fulfill their national literary task on account of some decadent mood. The epoch of national bourgeois humanism has reached an end because the art of writing love-inspiring letters to a nation of friends, however professionally it is still practiced, is no longer sufficient to form the telecommunicative bond between the inhabitants of a modern mass society. Through the media's establishment of mass culture in the developed world after 1918 (radio broadcasting) and after 1945 (television), and even more through current revolutions in how people are connected, human coexistence in societies today has been put on new foundations. These, as it is easy to show, are decidedly post-literary, post-epistolographic, and consequently post-humanist. Whoever takes the prefix 'post' in these formulations to be too dramatic can replace it with the adverb 'marginally'—so that our thesis runs as follows: Large modern societies can only still marginally produce their political and cultural synthesis via literary, epistolary, and humanistic media. By no means has literature therefore come at an end, though it has differentiated itself into a subculture *sui generis*, and the days of its being overrated as a bearer of national spirits are over. The social synthesis is no longer—nor does it even seem to be—mainly a matter of books and letters. Meanwhile, new media of political-cultural telecommunication have taken the lead and have reduced the schema of friendships born of writing to a modest level. The era of modern humanism as the model for schooling and formative education is over with, because the illusion can no longer be maintained that large political and economic structures could be organized on the amiable model of the literary society.

This disillusionment, of which those still receiving a humanistic education have been aware at least since the First World War, has a peculiarly warped history that is marked by twists and turns. For right at the lurid end of the national-humanist era, in the so very dim years after 1945, the humanistic model was supposed to flourish one more time. It was a matter of an organized and reflexive renaissance that has provided the paradigm for all subsequent minor reanimations of humanism. Were the background not so somber, one would have to speak of a contest in raving and self-deception. In the fundamentalist attitudes of the years after 1945, for understandable reasons it was not enough for many people to return from the horrors of war to a society that presented itself once more as a pacified public of reading friends—as though a Goethe Youth could make one forget about the Hitler Youth. To many people at that time it seemed agreeable to reopen, alongside the reissued Roman readings, the second basic reading for Europeans, that is, the biblical one, and to invoke the foundations in Christian humanism of what was again called the Occident. This late neo-humanism, desperately looking via Weimar to Rome, was a dream to save the European soul by means of a radicalized bibliophilia—a melancholy-hopeful raving about the civilizing, humanizing power of reading the classics—if we allow ourselves for a moment the liberty to put Cicero and Christ alongside one another and designate them as classics.

In these postwar humanisms, however born of illusions they may have been, a motif is revealed without which the humanistic tendency as a whole could never be comprehended—neither in the days of the Romans nor in the era of modern bourgeois nation-states: humanism as a word and as a subject matter always has something to which it is opposed, since it is essentially engaged in retrieving the human being from barbarism. It is easy to understand that precisely those ages of the world which have had their own experiences with the barbaric potential that is unleashed in violent interactions between states and factions are at the same time the eras in which the call for humanism usually becomes louder and more demanding. Whoever asks about the future of humanism and the media of humanization today wants at bottom to know whether there is hope of mastering the current tendencies toward bestialization among human beings. Here it becomes disturbingly important that bestializations, today as always, usually emerge alongside great displays of power, whether they are immediate martial and imperial brutality, or the everyday bestialization of human beings in the media of disinhibiting entertainment. The Romans provided Europe with the decisive models for both—on the one hand, with their omnipresent militarism, on the other hand, through their groundbreaking entertainment industry of bloody games. The latent theme of humanism is thus the de-bestialization of the human being, and its latent thesis runs: right reading tames.

The phenomenon of humanism deserves attention today above all because it recalls—in however veiled and timid a manner—the fact that human beings in high culture are continually engaged by two formative powers at the same time—we would like here, for the sake of simplicity, to designate them simply as inhibiting and disinhibiting influences. The conviction that human beings are 'impressionable animals' and that it is hence necessary to get them to come under the right kind of influences belongs to the credo of humanism. The label 'humanism' recalls—with false harmlessness—the constant battle for the human being, which is carried out as the struggle between bestializing and taming tendencies.

The two powers of influence can still easily be identified for Cicero's epoch, since each of the two possesses its characteristic medium. With regard to the bestializing influences, the Romans installed the most successful mass media network of the ancient world with their amphitheaters, their animal baiting, their fighting matches to the death, and their spectacles of execution. The disinhibited *homo inhumanus* got his money's worth in the clamoring stadiums around the Mediterranean as never before and as seldom afterward.[4] During the imperial era, supplying the Roman masses with brutalizing fascinations became an indispensable, routinely enlarged technique of domination, which has been retained in our memory up to the present day thanks to Juvenal's formulation of 'bread and circuses.' One can only understand Roman humanism if one conceives of it as taking sides in a media conflict—that is, as the resistance of the book against the amphitheater and as the opposition of the humanizing philosophical reading that makes one patient and promotes reflection against the dehumanizing, impatient, irascible maelstrom of sensation and intoxication in the stadiums. What the educated Romans called *humanitas* would be unthinkable without the demand for abstinence from mass culture in the theaters of cruelty. If the humanist himself should at some point stray into the roaring crowd then it is only to ascertain that he too is a human being and hence can be infected by bestializtion. He turns from the theater back home, ashamed of his involuntary participation in the infectious sensations, and is now inclined to admit that nothing human is alien to him. Thus it is implied that humanity consists in choosing taming media for the development of one's own nature and renouncing disinhibiting media. The meaning of this choice of media lies in weaning oneself from one's own possible bestiality and keeping a distance between oneself and the dehumanizing escalations of the theater's roaring mob.

These suggestive remarks make clear that with the question of humanism more is meant than the bucolic conjecture that reading is formative. In this, it is a matter of nothing less than an anthropodicy—that is, a determination of the human being as regards his biological openness and his moral ambivalence. Above all, however, the question of how the human being can become a true or real human being is from this point on inevitably posed as a media question, if we understand by media the communal and communicative means which human beings use to form themselves into what they can and will be.

In Autumn 1946—in the most miserable depths of the postwar European crisis—the philosopher Martin Heidegger wrote what was to become his famous essay on humanism—a text that on first glance can also be understood as a long letter to friends. But the procedure of befriending that this letter made use of to its own ends was no longer simply that of bourgeois communication among beautiful souls, and the concept of friendship that was drawn upon by this noteworthy philosophical epistle was no longer one of communion between a national public and its classicist. Heidegger knew when he formulated this letter that he had to speak with a broken voice or write with a reluctant hand and that the pre-established harmony between the author and his readers could in no way be taken for granted any longer. At that time he was not even certain as to whether he still had any friends; and if friends could still be found then the basis of this friendship would have to be determined anew, beyond everything that had counted in Europe and its nations as a reason for friendship between the educated. At least one thing is obvious: what the philosopher in the autumn of that year 1946 committed to paper was not a speech to his own nation and also not a speech to a future Europe; it was a polysemous, simultaneously cautious and daring attempt by the author to still imagine a sympathetic recipient of his message—and what thus emerged, oddly enough for a man of Heidegger's regionalist disposition—was a letter to a foreigner—a potential friend in the distance, a young thinker who had taken the liberty during the German occupation of France of becoming enthused by a German philosopher.

Thus a new technique of befriending? An alternative post? A new way of gathering those who are of one accord and sympathetic in thought around a piece of writing sent out into the great wide open? A new attempt at humanization? Another social contract between bearers of a homeless contemplativeness that was no longer humanistic in nationalist terms? Heidegger's opponents naturally did not fail to point out that the shrewd little man from Messkirch here instinctively seized the first opportunity that offered itself after the war to work toward his rehabilitation: he thus cunningly exploited the goodwill of one of his French admirers in order to abscond from political ambiguity to the highlands of mystical mindfulness.

These suspicions may sound suggestive and convincing, but they still miss the intellectual and communicatively strategic event which the essay on humanism represented, an essay that was first directed to Jean Beaufret in Paris and then later translated and published as a self-standing work. For by exposing and asking out beyond the conditions of European humanism in this writing, which formally aimed to be a letter, Heidegger entered a trans-humanist or post-humanist[5] realm of thought in which an essential part of philosophical reflection on the human being has moved ever since.

From Jean Beaufret's letter, Heidegger focused above all on one formulation: *Comment redonner un sens au mot 'Humanisme'*? The letter to the young Frenchman contains a mild rebuke of the questioner, which is revealed most clearly in the two direct replies:

> This question proceeds from your intention to retain the word 'humanism.' I wonder whether that is necessary. Or is the damage caused by all such terms still not sufficiently obvious?
>
> Your question not only presupposes a desire to retain the word 'humanism' but also contains an admission that this word has lost its meaning.[6]

A part of Heidegger's strategy thereby becomes manifest: the word 'humanism' must be given up if the actual task of thought, which in the humanist or metaphysical tradition wanted to appear as though it had already been accomplished, is to be experienced once more in its initial simplicity and inevitability. To put it sharply: why again tout the human being and his prevailing philosophical self-depiction in humanism as the solution when it has just been shown in the catastrophe of the present that it is the human being himself, along with his systems of metaphysical self-elevation and self-explanation, that is the problem? This revision of Beaufret's question is not without a certain magisterial malice, since, in Socratic fashion, it holds before the student the wrong answer already contained in the question. At the same time, this revision was given serious thought, since the three main remedies available in the European crisis of 1945—Christianity, Marxism, and Existentialism—are characterized side by side as varieties of humanism and only superficially distinguished from each other—put more sharply: as three ways and means of avoiding the ultimate radicality of the question concerning the essence of the human being.

Heidegger volunteers to bring the immense omission of European thought to an end—the omission of not posing the question concerning the essence of the human being in the only suitable way, which for him meant that of existential ontology. At the very least, the author

indicated his readiness to contribute turns of phrase—however
provisional they may be—to the advent of the question that was
finally to be posed correctly. With these seemingly modest phrases,
Heidegger brings disturbing consequences to light: humanism—
in its ancient, in its Christian, and in its Enlightenment forms—is
revealed to be the agent of a two-thousand-year failure to think. It
is accused of having obstructed the advent of the genuine question
concerning the human being's essence with its hastily offered, seemingly self-evident, and undeniable interpretations of what it means
to be human. Heidegger explains that in his work from *Being and
Time* onward he thought against humanism, not because humanism overestimates *humanitas*, but rather because it does not value it
highly enough.[7] But what does it mean to value the essence of the
human being highly enough? It means, in the first place, to renounce
a habitual false disparagement. The question of the human being's
essence does not get on the right track until one refrains from the
oldest, most intractable, and most pernicious practice of European
metaphysics: defining the human being as *animal rationale*. On this
interpretation of the human being's essence, the human being is
understood from the perspective of an *animalitas* enhanced by intellectual supplements. Heidegger's existential-ontological analysis
revolts against this, because for him the essence of the human being
can never be expressed from a zoological or biological perspective,
even when an intellectual or metabiological factor is added on.

Heidegger is relentless on this point; indeed, like an avenging
angel, swords crossed, he steps between the animal and the human
being, in order to deny any ontological commonality between the
two. He allows himself to be carried away by his anti-biological
and anti-vitalist fervor to almost hysterical utterances, for instance
when he explains that it appears "as though the essence of divinity
is closer to us than what is so alien in other living beings."[8] At the
core of this separative pathos is the recognition that the human
being is <u>ontologically different</u> from the animal, not of a different   *cf. Spinoza*
species or genus, for which reason under no circumstances may
he be conceived of as an animal with a cultural or metaphysical
addition. Rather, the human mode of Being is essentially and in
its basic ontology different from all other vegetative and animal
living beings, since the human being has world and is in the world,
while plants and animals are only tightly wound into their respective
environments.

If there is a philosophical reason for talking about the dignity
of the human being, then this is because it is precisely the human
being who is addressed by Being itself and, as Heidegger the pastoral philosopher liked to say, is assigned to tend it. For this reason

human beings have language—yet according to Heidegger they do not primarily possess it in order to come to an agreement through communication and thereby to mutually tame each other.

> Rather, language is the house of Being in which the human being ek-sists by dwelling, in that he belongs to the truth of Being, tending it.
>   So the point is that in the determination of the humanity of the human being as ek-sistence what is essential is not the human being but Being—as the dimension of the ecstasis of ek-sistence.[9]

In hearkening to these initially hermetic sounding formulations, a suspicion arises as to why Heidegger's critique of humanism imagines itself to be so certain that it does not lead to an inhumanism. In rejecting the claims of humanism to have already adequately interpreted the essence of the human being and opposing to it his own onto-anthropology, he still indirectly adheres to the most important function of classical humanism, namely the befriending of the human being by another's word—indeed, he radicalizes this motif of befriending and shifts it from the field of pedagogy to the center of ontological reflection.

That is the sense of the oft-cited and much derided manner of speaking of the human being as the shepherd of Being. Using images from the stock of motifs belonging to the pastoral and the idyll, Heidegger speaks of the human being's task, which is his essence, and of the human essence from which his task arises: namely, to tend Being and to correspond to Being. Of course, the human being does not tend Being like the sick person does his bed, rather he is more like a shepherd tending his herd in the clearing, with the important difference that here instead of a herd of livestock it is the world as an open circumstance that is to be watched over with serene releasement [gelassen]—and with the further difference that this tending does not represent a task of vigilance freely chosen in one's own interest, but rather the fact that human beings are appointed and employed by Being itself to be ones who tend it. The site at which this job is carried out is the clearing or the place where Being [Sein] arises as that which is there [da].

What assures Heidegger that he has surpassed and thought beyond humanism with such phrases is the fact that he involves the human being, conceived as the clearing of Being, in a sort of taming and befriending that runs deeper than any humanistic de-bestialization or any educated love for the text that speaks of love could reach. By defining human beings as shepherds and neighbors

of Being and characterizing language as the house of Being, he binds
the human being into a correspondence to Being that imposes a
radical restraint on him and relegates him—the shepherd—to the
vicinity or environs of the immense house. He exposes the human
being to a reflection that demands, more than the most comprehensive program of formative education ever could, that he keep
still and heed silence. The human being is subjected to an ecstatic
restraint that reaches further than the civilized pause of the pious
reader of texts before the words of a classic. Restrained dwelling in
the house of language à la Heidegger is determined to be an attentive listening to that which will be assigned by Being itself to be said.
It invokes a hearkening-into-the-vicinity for which the human being
must become quieter and more tamed than the humanist when he is
studying the classics. Heidegger wants a human being who would
be more of a hearkener than merely a good reader. He would like to
establish a process of befriending in which even he himself would no
longer be received only as one author among others. To begin with,
it would arguably be best if his audience, which can naturally consist
of but a small, perceptive number, paid heed to the fact that Being
itself has begun to speak once more through him, the mentor of the
question of Being.

Thus Heidegger elevates Being to the sole author of all essential
letters and appoints himself as its current amanuensis. Whoever
speaks from such a position may also record stammering and
publish silence. Being thus sends off the decisive letters, or, more
precisely, it gives hints to friends who have the presence of mind, to
receptive neighbors, to collected, quiet shepherds. But as far as we
can see no nations can be formed out of this circle of fellow shepherds and friends of Being, indeed not even alternative schools—not
least because there can be no official canon of Being's hints, unless,
for the time being, one lets Heidegger's *opera omnia* count as the
measure and the voice of the nameless über-author.

In view of these shadowy communions it must remain completely
unclear for the time being how a society of neighbors of Being could
be composed—until this becomes clearer, such a society must arguably be conceived of as an invisible church of dispersed individuals,
each of which in his own way listens to the immense and waits for
the words that will express what it is that language itself gives to the
speaker to say.[10] It is pointless to enter into more detail regarding
the crypto-Catholic character of these figures of speech that belong
to the Heideggerian meditation. What is decisive now is only the
fact that, through Heidegger's critique of humanism, a change of
attitude is propagated, one which refers the human being to a reflective *askēsis* that points beyond all humanistic educational goals.

Only by virtue of this *askēsis* would a society of the reflective beyond the humanistic literary society[11] be able to be formed. This would be a society of human beings who would have shifted the human being from center stage, because they would have grasped that they only exist as 'neighbors of Being'—and not as independent homeowners or as tenants living in furnished rooms with non-terminable leases. As long as it remains oriented to the model of the strong human being, humanism can contribute nothing to this *askēsis*.

The humanist friends of human authors are lacking the blessed frailty in which Being reveals itself to those who are touched or addressed by it. For Heidegger, no path leads from humanism to this intensified ontological practice of humility. Rather, he believes he sees in humanism a contribution to the history of the armament of subjectivity. In fact, Heidegger interprets the historical world of Europe as the theater of militant humanisms. It is the field on which human subjectivity carries out its seizure of power over all beings with fateful consistency. Seen from this perspective, humanism must present itself as a natural accomplice of any merely possible atrocity that could be committed in the name of human well-being. Even in the tragic gigantomachy of the mid-century among Bolshevism, Fascism, and Americanism it was only the case—in Heidegger's view—that three variations of the same anthropocentric violence[12] and three candidates dressed up in humanitarian fashion for world domination were in confrontation—in the course of which Fascism stepped out of line by flaunting its contempt for the inhibiting values of peace and formative education more openly than its rivals. In fact, Fascism is the metaphysics of disinhibition—perhaps even a disinhibiting form of metaphysics. On Heidegger's view, Fascism was the synthesis of humanism and bestialism—that is, the para-doxical coincidence of inhibition and disinhibition.

In view of such immense distortions and perversions it was natural to pose anew the question concerning the basis for human taming and human formative education. If Heidegger's ontological pastoral plays—which already sounded odd and objectionable in their time—appear today to be completely anachronistic, they still, regardless of their awkwardness and their clumsy outlier status, retain the merit of having articulated epochal questions: What tames or still educates the human being when humanism founders as a school of human formation? What tames or educates the human being when his efforts at self-taming to this point have led in the main to his seizure of power over all beings? What tames or educates the human being when, after all his experiments with the education of the human race, it is still unclear who or what educates the educators, and to what end? Or can the question concerning the

cultivation and formation of the human being no longer be compe-
tently posed within the framework of mere theories of taming and
education?

In what follows, we will not follow Heidegger's instructions to
stick only with the concluding figures of reflective thought. We
will instead attempt to characterize in a historically more precise
sense the ecstatic clearing in which the human being lets himself be
addressed by Being. It will become apparent that the human sojourn
in the clearing—put in Heideggerian terms, the human being's standing into or being held into the clearing of Being—is by no means a
primal ontological relationship that would be inaccessible to any
further interrogation. There is a history of the human being's stepping out into the clearing that is resolutely ignored by Heidegger—a
social history of the human being's ability to be affected by the question of Being and a historical movement in the gaping open of the
ontological difference.

On the one hand, we must speak here of a natural history of
releasement [*Gelassenheit*], by virtue of which the human being was
able to become the animal that is capable of the world. On the
other hand, we must speak of a social history of taming, by which
human beings experience themselves primordially as the beings
who pull themselves together [*zusammennehmen*][13] in order to correspond to the whole. The real story of the clearing—from which a
deeper reflection on the human being that goes beyond humanism
must take its point of departure—is thus composed of two larger
narratives that converge in a common perspective, namely in the
explanation as to how the sapiens-human came to be from out of
the sapiens-animal. The first of these two narratives provides an
account of the adventure of hominization. It relates how in the long
periods of prehuman-hominid prehistory a species of immaturely
born beings came into existence from the viviparous mammal that
is the human being. These beings—if we may speak paradoxically—
entered into their environments with an increasing surplus of animal
immaturity. Here the anthropogenetic revolution is carried out—
the bursting open and transformation of biological birth into the
act of coming-to-the-world. With his obstinate reserve in the face
of all anthropology and his zeal to keep his point of departure,
namely, Dasein and the Being-in-the-world of the human being,
ontologically pure, Heidegger did not pay nearly enough attention
to this explosion. The fact that the human being could become the
being that is 'in the world' has species-historical roots. These can
be indicated by the abyssal concepts of premature birth, neoteny,
and the chronic animal immaturity of the human being.[14] One could
go so far as to characterize the human being as the being that has

foundered in its being an animal and remaining an animal. Through
its foundering as an animal the indeterminate being plummets out
of its environment and thus attains the world in the ontological
sense. This ecstatic coming-to-the-world and this 'conveyance'
[*Übereignung*] to Being is something the human being starts out
with from his species-historical inheritance. If the human being is
in-the-world then this is because he belongs to a movement that
brings him forth and exposes him to the world. He is the product of
a hyper-birth that makes a worldling out of a nursling.

This exodus would only generate psychotic animals if, along with
the emergence into the world, an entrance into that which Heidegger
called the house of Being did not take place as well. The traditional
languages of the human race have rendered the ecstase of Being-in-
the-world livable, insofar as they have shown human beings how
their Being at home [*bei*] in the world can also be experienced as
Being-at-home-with-oneself [*Bei-sich-selbst-Sein*]. To this extent,
the clearing is an event at the limit of the history of nature and
culture, for the human coming-to-the-world incorporates from early
on the features of a coming-to-language.[15]

Yet the history of the clearing cannot be developed solely as the
tale of human beings' entrance into the houses of languages. As
soon as speaking beings live together in larger groups and attach
themselves not only to houses of language [*Sprachhäuser*], but also
to constructed enclosures [*Gehäuse*], they enter into the force field
of settled modes of Being. From then on, they no longer allow only
language to shelter them; they also allow themselves to be tamed
by their dwellings [*Behausungen*]. In the clearing arise—as its most
salient marks—the houses of human beings (along with the temples
of their gods and the palaces of their masters). Cultural historians
have made it clear that, with settlement, the relationship between
humans and animals came under new auspices. With the taming
of the human being by the house, the epic of domestic animals
[*Haustieren*] begins as well. Their attachment to human houses is,
however, not only a matter of acts of taming, but also one of training and breeding.

The human being and the domestic animal—the history of
this monstrous cohabitation has yet to be presented in a suitable
manner, not to mention the fact that philosophers up to the present
day are still in denial concerning what they themselves should look
for within this history.[16] In only a few places is the veil of the philosophers' silence concerning the house, the human being, and the
animal as a biopolitical complex lifted, and what was then to be
heard were dizzying references to problems that for the time being
are too difficult for human beings. The least of these problems is

the intimate connection between domesticity [*Häuslichkeit*] and the formation of theory. One could go so far as to define theory as a variety of housework, or rather as a kind of domestic leisure; for theory according to its ancient definitions resembles looking serenely out of a window—it is chiefly a matter of contemplation, while in modernity, ever since knowledge is supposed to be power, it clearly took on the character of work. In this sense, windows would be the clearings of walls, behind which human beings became beings capable of theory. Even strolls, in which movement and reflection are merged, are derivatives of domesticity. Even Heidegger's notorious thoughtful wandering along field paths and timber tracks [*Feld- und Holzwege*] are typical movements of one who has a home to which to return.

Yet this derivation of the clearing from secured domesticity concerns only the more innocuous aspect of becoming human in houses. The clearing is simultaneously a battleground and a site of decision and selection. In this regard, nothing more is to be ascertained from the turns of phrase of a philosophical pastoral. Where there are houses it must be decided what should become of the human beings who inhabit them. It is decided in the deed and by the deed which types of housing occupants will prevail. In the clearing it becomes manifest what the stakes are over which human beings are fighting, as soon as they emerge as beings who build cities and establish empires. What is really going on here has been described by the master of dangerous thinking, Nietzsche, with nightmarish overtones in the third part of *Thus Spoke Zarathustra*, under the heading "On Virtue That Makes Small":

For he [Zarathustra] wanted to learn what had transpired in the meantime *among human beings*; whether they had become bigger or smaller. And once he saw a row of new houses, and he was amazed then and he said:

"What do these houses mean? Truly, no great soul placed them here, as a parable of itself! . . .

And these parlors and chambers; can *men* go in and out here? . . ."

And Zarathustra stood still and reflected. At last he said sadly: "*Everything* has become smaller!

Everywhere I see lower gateways; whoever is like me can still pass through, but—he has to stoop! . . .

I walk among these people and keep my eyes open; they have become *smaller* and are becoming ever smaller: *but this is because of their teaching on happiness and virtue.* . . .

A few of them will, but most of them are merely willed. . . .

Round, righteous and kind they are to one another, like
grains of sand are round, righteous and kind to one another.
To modestly embrace a small happiness—that they call
'resignation.' . . .
At bottom these simple ones want one simple thing: that no
one harm them. . . .
To them virtue is whatever makes modest and tame; this is
how they made the wolf into a dog and mankind himself into
mankind's favorite pet."[17]

In this rhapsodic sequence of sayings there is concealed a theoretical
discourse on the human being as a taming and breeding force. From
Zarathustra's perspective, human beings of the present moment are
above all one thing: successful breeders who have made it possible
to draw the last man from the strong man. It is self-evident that this
could not have happened with humanist, taming-training-educative
means alone. With the reference to the human being as a breeder
of the human being the humanist horizon is burst open, insofar as
humanism can and may never think beyond the question of taming
and education: the humanist presupposes the human being and then
applies to the latter his means of taming, dressage, and formation—
convinced, as he is, of the necessary connection between reading,
sitting, and pacifying.

In contrast, Nietzsche—who read Darwin and St. Paul with equal
attention—thinks that he perceives a second, darker horizon behind
the bright horizon of the formation of the human being in schools.
He perceives a space in which inevitable battles over directions of
human breeding will begin—and it is this space in which the other,
veiled aspect of the clearing is revealed. When Zarathustra goes
through the city in which everything has become smaller, he perceives the outcome of a politics of breeding that to this point has
been successful and gone unnoticed: human beings—so it seems to
him—have, with the aid of an artful linking of ethics and genetics,
managed to breed themselves small. They have subjected themselves
to domestication and initiated a kind of selective breeding with the
aim of achieving an interpersonal companionableness suitable for
domestic animals. From this conjecture springs Zarathustra's peculiar critique of humanism as a rejection of the harmlessness with
which the modern good human being surrounds himself. In fact, it
would not be harmless if human beings bred human beings with the
aim of achieving harmlessness. Nietzsche's suspicion of all humanist culture insists on airing humanity's secret of domestication. He
wants to call the proprietors of the monopoly on taming up to this
point—the priests and teachers who present themselves as friends of

the human being—by their name and to designate their secret function; he wants to launch a world-historically new kind of contest between different breeders and different kinds of breeding programs.

This is the fundamental conflict of the future postulated by Nietzsche: the battle between the breeders of small human beings and big human beings—one could even say between humanists and superhumanists, friends of the human being and friends of the Übermensch. The emblem 'Übermensch,' in Nietzsche's reflections, does not stand for the dream of a hasty disinhibition or a flight into bestiality—as the jackbooted bad readers of Nietzsche from the 1930s imagined. The expression does not stand for the idea of breeding the human being back to the status of the time before domestic animals and church animals. When Nietzsche speaks of the Übermensch he is thinking of an age of the world that is far beyond the present.[18] He takes his measurement from previous millennia-long processes, in which the production of the human being up to that point was carried out by virtue of intimate entwinements of breeding, taming, and education—admittedly in an operation that knew how to make itself largely invisible and that, under the mask of schooling, had for its object the project of domestication.

With these adumbrations—and more than adumbration in this field is neither possible nor allowable—Nietzsche marks out a gigantic terrain on which the determination of the human being of the future will have to be accomplished, regardless of whether recourse to the concept of the Übermensch plays a role in this or not. It may very well be that Zarathustra was the spokesman of a philosophizing hysteria whose contagious effects have today and perhaps forever faded away. But the discourse concerning the difference and entwinement of taming and breeding, indeed even the reference to the dawning of an awareness about the productions of the human being and more generally about anthropotechnics— these are givens from which thinking today cannot avert its gaze unless it wants to devote itself anew to rendering things harmless. In all likelihood, Nietzsche went too far when he advanced the suggestion that making the human being into a domestic animal had been the deliberate work of a pastoral breeder's association, that is to say, a project of the clerical, Pauline instinct that senses everything which could turn out autonomous and sovereign in the human being and immediately deploys its methods of eradication and mutilation against this. This was certainly a hybrid thought, on the one hand because it fails to conceive the potential process of breeding over the long term—as though a few generations of priestly rule were all it took to make dogs out of wolves and Basel professors out of prehistoric humans.[19] But it is even more a hybrid thought because it inserts a conspiring perpetrator where a breeding without breeder, thus a biocultural drift without subjects, should be reckoned with instead. Yet even after we take away the overextended and suspicious-anticlerical layers, a sufficiently durable core of Nietzsche's idea remains to provoke a later reflection on humanity beyond humanist harmlessness.

2.   The domestication of the human being is the great unthought; it is that before which humanism from antiquity to the present day has averted its eyes. To appreciate this is sufficient to find oneself in deep water. Where we can no longer stand, the evidence rises over our heads that the educational taming and befriending of the human being could never have been accomplished with letters and words alone. To be sure, reading [*Lesen*] was a great formative power for human beings—and it still is, within more modest dimensions. Yet selection [*Auslesen*]—however it may have been carried out—was always in play as the power behind the power. Readings and selections [*Lektionen und Selektionen*] have more to do with each other than any cultural historian was willing and able to consider, and if it also appears to us for the time being to be impossible to reconstruct with sufficient precision the connection between reading and selection [*Lesen und Auslesen*], it is nevertheless more than a tentative hunch that there is something real about it.

Written culture itself, up to its recently implemented universal literacy, has had sharply selective effects. It has riven its host societies and formed a divide between literate and illiterate human beings, whose unbridgeability almost attained the firmness of a species differentiation. If one wished, despite Heidegger's dissuasions, to speak anthropologically again, then the human beings of historical times could be defined as the animals of whom some can read and write while the others cannot. From here it is only a single step, if a demanding one, to the thesis that human beings are the animals of whom some breed those like them, while the others are bred—a thought that belongs to the pastoral folklore of Europeans since the time of Plato's reflections on education and the state. Something of this is still heard in Nietzsche's statement that few of the human beings in the small houses will, but most are willed. But to be only willed means to exist merely as an object, not as a subject, of selection.

It is the signature of the technological and anthropotechnological era that human beings become increasingly involved in the active or subjective side of selection, without having to be voluntarily thrust into the role of the selector. Additionally, one may observe that there is an unease in the power of choice; soon it will become an instance of opting for innocence when human beings explicitly refuse to exercise the power of selection that they have in fact managed to achieve.[20] But as soon as powers of knowledge are positively developed in a field, human beings cut a poor figure if they—as in earlier times of incapacity—wish to allow a higher force, whether it be God or chance or something else, to act in their stead. Since mere refusals and dismissals generally fail in their sterility, in the future it will arguably be necessary to actively enter the game and formulate a code of anthropotechnics. Such a code would even retroactively transform the significance of classical humanism—since it would disclose and put in writing the fact that *humanitas* not only involves the friendship of human being with human being; it always implies as well—and with growing explicitness—that the human being represents the higher force for the human being.

Nietzsche had something of this in mind when he dared to characterize himself, in regard to his long-term effects, as a *force majeure*. One can ignore the offense that this statement provoked, since it is centuries too early for a judgment on such pretensions, if not a millennium. Who has enough esprit to imagine an age of the world in which Nietzsche will be as historical a figure as Plato was for Nietzsche? It suffices to make clear that the next long spans of time for humanity will be periods of species-political decision. In them it will be revealed whether humanity or its main cultural factions will succeed in at the very least initiating once again effective procedures of self-taming. Even in the present culture the gigantomachy between taming and bestializing impulses and their respective media is being waged. Even greater successes in taming would be surprising in view of a civilizing process in which an unparalleled and apparently unceasing surge of disinhibition rolls on.[21] But whether long-term development will also lead to a genetic reform of attributes of the species—whether a future anthropotechnology will advance to an explicit planning of traits; whether humanity will be able to carry out, on the level of the species as a whole, a switch from the fatalism of births to optional birth and prenatal selection[22]—these are questions with which the evolutionary horizon begins to clear before us, however indistinctly and frighteningly.

It is a characteristic feature of *humanitas* that human beings are confronted with problems that are too difficult for them and that nevertheless cannot be left unaddressed on account of their difficulty. This provocation of the human being by something that can be neither avoided nor mastered left an unforgettable trace behind already at the beginning of European philosophy—indeed, perhaps philosophy itself is this trace in the broadest sense. After what has been said, it is no longer all that surprising that this trace turns out specifically to be one of the first discourses on tending and breeding human beings. In his dialogue *Politikos*—often translated as *The Statesman*—Plato put forward the Magna Carta of a European pastoral politology. This text is significant not only because it shows more clearly than anywhere else what antiquity understood thinking to be—the attainment of truth through careful classification and division of groups of concepts and things. Its incommensurable position in the history of thinking about the human being above all consists in the fact that it is conducted as though breeders were having a conversation about work. It is not a coincidence that those who participate in the conversation are atypical for Plato, namely, a Stranger and a younger Socrates, as though ordinary Athenians are not for the time being to be allowed to participate in conversations of this kind; and how could they be, when it is a matter of selecting a statesman who does not exist in Athens and planning out a people for the state who cannot yet be found in any empirical city. Thus this Stranger and his counterpart, the Younger Socrates, devote themselves to the tricky endeavor of placing the politics of the future or the herdsmanship of the city under transparently rational rules.

With this project, Plato bears witness to an intellectual unrest in the human park, which could never again be entirely pacified. Ever since the *Politikos* and the *Politeia* [*The Republic*], there have been discourses in the world that speak of the human community as of a zoological park that is at the same time a theme park. Keeping human beings in parks or cities from now on appears to be a zoö-political task. Whatever purports to be a reflection on politics is in truth a fundamental reflection on rules for the operation of human parks. If there is a dignity of the human being that merits being expressed in philosophical reflection, then this is above all because human beings are not only kept in political theme parks, but keep themselves there. Human beings are self-nurturing, self-tending beings that—wherever they live—produce parks around themselves. Whether in city parks, national parks, state parks, or eco-parks—everywhere, human beings must form an opinion about how their self-maintenance is to be regulated.

Regarding the Platonic zoo and its new establishment, what is at issue is thus to learn for all the world whether between the population and the directorship there is merely a difference of degree or a difference in species. According to the first assumption, the distance between those who tend human beings and their fosterlings would obviously only be a contingent and pragmatic one—in this case, one could attribute to the herd the capacity to periodically rotate their herders. However, if a difference in species prevails between the managers of the zoo and its inhabitants, then they would be so fundamentally different from each other that an elected directorship would not be advisable, but rather only a directorship based on insight. Only the false zoo directors, the pseudo-statesmen, and political sophists would then tout themselves with the argument that they are just like their herds, while the one who truly tends the body politic would focus on difference and make it discreetly understood that, because he acts from insight, he stands closer to the gods than to the confused living beings whom he guides.

Plato's dangerous sense for dangerous themes runs into the blind spot of all high-cultural pedagogies and politics—the actual inequality of human beings vis-à-vis the knowledge that confers power. Under the logical form of a grotesque way of defining things, the dialogue of *The Statesman* develops the preambles of a political anthropotechnics. Here it is a matter not only of the taming guidance of the herds already tamed of their own accord, but also of a systematic new kind of breeding of human exemplars who approximate to the archetype. This approach begins so comically that even the not quite so comic ending could easily be passed over in the laughter. What is more grotesque than the definition of statesmanship as a discipline that has to do with the beings living in herds who go about on foot—since the leaders of human beings do not practice, god knows, a breeding of animals that swim, but rather of those going about on land? Among those going about on land, one must separate off the winged from those without wings that go about on foot, if one is after human populations, which, as is well known, lack feathers and wings. In Plato's dialogue, the Stranger now adds that precisely this pedestrian folk among the tame by nature is divided in turn into two clearly separate subsets—"one of which is assigned to the horned portion of the herd, the other to the hornless portion."[23] An interlocutor who is quick to learn does not need to be told that twice. These two subsets correspond once more to two kinds of herdsmanship, namely herding horned herds and herding non-horned ones—it should be obvious that one only finds the true leader of the human group when one excludes the herders of horned herds. For if one wished to allow herders of horned cattle to tend human beings—what else could one expect than encroachments by those who are not suited to the task? The good kings or *basileis*, the Stranger says, put a truncated herd without horns out to pasture (265d). This is not all: in addition, they are occupied with the task of tending living creatures that are purebred—that is, creatures that do not breed outside their own species, such as a horse and a donkey are accustomed to do; they must thus mount guard over endogamy and try to hinder bastardizations. Finally, if one also adds the feature of bipedalism—or put in modern terms, upright posture—to these wingless, hornless beings that mate only with their own kind, then the art of tending that pertains to the wingless, hornless, purebred bipeds would have already been well chosen as the true art and demarcated from all competencies that merely seem like it. This caretaking art of tending, for its part, must once more be divided into violent-tyrannical or voluntary. If the tyrannical form is excluded, in turn, as untrue and deceptive, then genuine statesmanship remains: it is defined as "the voluntary herd-keeping . . . of voluntary living beings" (276e). [24]

To this point, Plato knew to situate his doctrine of the statesman's art entirely in images of herdsmen and herds—from among dozens of illusions concerning this art, he selected the one true image, the valid idea for the matter in question. Yet now that the definition seems complete, the dialogue suddenly skips to another metaphorics—this occurs, however, as we will see, not in order to abandon what has been achieved, but rather in order to take up, all the more energetically from a changed perspective, the most difficult part of the art of human tending, namely, the breeder's guidance of reproduction. Here, the famous metaphor of the statesman as a weaver appears. The real and true justification for the royal art cannot, according to Plato, be found in the vote of fellow citizens, who give or take away their confidence in the politician at their whim. It also does not lie in inherited privileges or new arrogations. The Platonic master finds the justification for his mastery only in the royal knowledge of breeding, thus in an expert knowledge of the rarest and most prudent kind. Here the phantom of an expert kingship emerges whose rightful basis is the insight into how human beings would best be sorted and combined—without ever acting detrimentally to their free will. Royal anthropotechnics demands from the statesman in particular that he know how to most effectively interweave the properties of human beings who can be governed of their own free will that are most favorable to the body politic, so that by his hand the human park may achieve optimal homeostasis. This happens when the two relative optima of humankind, martial courage on the one hand and philosophical-human prudence on the other, are both woven with equal force into the fabric of the body politic.

· However, because both virtues in their one-sidedness can result in specific kinds of degeneration—the first, in the militarist lust for battle together with its disastrous consequences for the homelands, the second, in the privatism of the intelligent and quiet minds in the country, who can become so removed from the state and tepid that they can find themselves in bondage without noticing it. Hence the statesman must comb out the unsuitable natures, before he proceeds to weave the state with the suitable ones. The good state is only produced with the noble and free-willing natures that remain behind—whereby the courageous serve as the coarse warp, while the prudent serve as the "plumper, softer, weft," as Schleiermacher puts it.[25] One may say a bit anachronistically that the prudent enter into the business of culture.

> This, then, is the end, let us declare, of the web of the states-man's activity, the direct interweaving of the characters of prudent and courageous men, when the royal science has drawn them together by friendship and community of sentiment into a common life, and having perfected the most glorious and the best of all textures, clothes with it all the inhabitants of the state, both slaves and freemen, holds them together by this fabric. (311b-c)[26]

For the modern reader—who looks back on the humanist gymnasia of the bourgeois era and on fascist eugenics, and at the same time already looks ahead to the biotechnological era—the explosiveness of these reflections is impossible to miss. What Plato allows to be expressed through the mouth of his Stranger is the program of a humanist society that is embodied in a singular full-humanist, the master of royal herdsmanship. The task of this über-humanist would be nothing other than the planning of features in an elite that must be specially groomed for the sake of the whole.

A complication remains to be pondered: the Platonic herder can only be credible as someone who tends the human being because he embodies the terrestrial likeness of the sole and original true herder—the god who in the earlier age, under the rule of Cronus, tended human beings directly. One should not forget that even in Plato only the god is qualified to be the one who originally tends and breeds human beings. But now, after the great revolution (*metabolē*), since the gods have withdrawn under the rule of Zeus and have left human beings to tend to themselves, the wise one remains behind as the worthiest of those who tend, in whom the memory of the heavenly beholding of the best is most vivid. Without the paradigm of the wise the care of the human being by the human being remains a useless passion.

Two and a half thousand years after Plato was writing it appears as though not only the gods but also the wise had withdrawn and left us altogether alone with our ignorance and partial knowledge. What remains for us in place of the wise are their writings in their sheer radiance and their growing obscurity. They still exist in more or less accessible editions; they could still be read if one but knew why they should still be opened. It is their fate to stand on silent shelves, like letters for general delivery that are no longer picked up—likenesses or phantoms of a wisdom in which contemporaries are no longer able to believe—sent by authors of whom we no longer know whether they can still be our friends.

Letters that are no longer delivered cease to be messages sent to possible friends—they change into archived objects. Even this, that the representative books of old have increasingly ceased to be letters to friends and that they no longer lie on the coffee tables and nightstands of their readers, but rather are buried in the drab stillness of archives—even this has for the most part deprived the humanist movement of its former impact. Ever less frequently do the archivists descend into the textual antiquity in order to look up earlier commentary on modern catchwords. Perhaps it happens now and then that in such researches into the dead cellars of culture, pages that have not been read for a long time begin to glimmer, as though distant lightning flashes were streaking across them. Can even the archival cellars become the clearing? Everything indicates that archivists and record keepers have reported for the duty of succeeding the humanists. For the few who still have a look around in the archives, the view becomes compelling that our life is the confused answer to questions posed in places we have forgotten.

7

WOUNDED BY MACHINES

Toward the Epochal Significance of the Most Recent
Medical Technology

1. The Subjective Cost of Enlightenment

Recent biology has made us familiar with the thought that the physical life of the individual is synonymous with its fully developed
immune system. In this light, life appears to be the wondrous drama
of the successful delimitation of the organism from invasive environments. In extending this systemic approach it becomes apparent
that the principle of immunity is not only to be understood in terms
of biochemistry, but also psycho-dynamically and mentally. From
this angle, we should regard it as an accomplishment of organismic
vitality in the human being that, as an individual and as a communal
being, he is capable of a spontaneous and energetic privileging of
his own way of life, of his own valuations, of his own convictions,
and of his own stories that interpret the world. From the systemic
vantage point, powerful narcissisms are indications of a successful
affective and cognitive integration of the human being into himself,
into his moral collective and into his culture. Resilient narcissism
among individuals, as in the case of groups, would be the immediate indicator of a vital, successfully developed history that has
allowed its bearers to this point to move within a continuum of
self-affirmations and self-preferences. Where the narcissistic shield
is intact the individual lives convinced of the unparalleled advantage
of being itself. It can permanently celebrate its similarity with itself.
The habitual form of this celebration is pride. Whoever takes pride
in himself and his group endogenously produces a material-imma-
terial vitamin, as it were, that protects the organism from invasive
information.

Invasive information that breaks through the narcissistic shield of ‒

a psychical organism is called a 'wound' in everyday speech. When the individual's pride is attacked, it has the experience that information which initially could not be warded off has invaded and that it is thereby in a state of lost integrity. A wound is the pain of having something break through that for the moment or for a sustained period of time is stronger than the narcissistic homeostasis. If one understands primary narcissism as the psychical 'organism's' operative phantasm of integrity, then the concept of wounding describes a pathogenic attack on the individual's shield of elation. Not just any breach operates in a manner that wounds, but rather only that invasion of the organism that convinces one of the disadvantage of being oneself. Nevertheless, human intelligence appears to have at its disposal the capacity for getting over such experiences of disadvantage and for integrating them into more mature states. The paradigm for this dynamic of maturation is found on the somatic level: so-called childhood illnesses can be described as a curriculum of bodily crises, through which immune systems in specific environments train themselves for their microbial invaders. On analogy to this, the child psyche would have to pass through a sequence of well-controlled wounds; by working through them, it achieves the power of delimiting and asserting itself in its contact with what is like it and with what is alien to it. The result of this passage through a series of informative wounds would in a favorable course of events be a maturation of the narcissistic shield to the level at which the confrontations between the adult psychical organism and its environment typically take place in a given culture. The mature individual enjoys the advantage of being itself after overcoming episodes in which it had experience with the disadvantage of being itself. Goethe formulated the position of post-traumatic narcissism in a classic way: past suffering is dear to me.

With the speculative extension of the concept of immunity I have obtained a background against which to critically read the legend that Sigmund Freud introduced into the world concerning the three instances in which the sciences wounded modern humanity. As is well known, Freud and his colleagues during the founding years of the psychoanalytical movement were irritated over the supposedly grudging acceptance of their doctrines in professional circles as well as among the general public. While from a historical distance one is rather prone to observe the rapid spread of psychoanalysis as a successful and seductive phenomenon, which scarcely has its like in the history of science and culture, Freud himself and the first generation of his students were under the impression that they were encountering a massive wave of misunderstanding, rejection, and indifference. They pondered methods of presenting the supposed resistances to psychoanalysis as an additional argument for the truth of their publications. In the year 1917 Freud composed a momentous short essay under the title *Eine Schwierigkeit der Psychoanalyse* [A Difficulty in the Path of Psychoanalysis], in which he interpreted the supposed rejection of the public to accept his theory of neurosis as a phenomenon of "narcissistic resistance" to insights that are wounding. Without doubt, these defense statements would have been forgotten, like numerous other lesser quarrels amongst the educated, had they not been embedded in an ingenious little theory in which the history of modern sciences as a whole was interpreted as a process of progressive instances of wounding. Here the motif uncovered by Nietzsche of the disadvantage of analysis for life was translated into a short history of modernity. With a great talent for simplification Freud fabricated a model of an increasing disadvantage of the human sense of self on account of growing insight—a kind of three-stage theory of the progress of wounding. Copernicus first landed a knockout blow against the cosmological narcissism of humanity, when he brought forth proof for the heliocentric image of the world and thus displaced the human homeland, the earth, from the central position in the universe. Darwin afterward prepared an end for the elevation of humans over the animal world when he set the human being back into the animal kingdom through his theory of descent and imputed to the human being kinship with the great apes. Finally, psychoanalysis caused the third and most sensitive wound by mustering evidence for the thesis that our sexual drives are not to be fully subdued and that the decisive psychical processes chiefly proceed unconsciously—from which the compelling conclusion follows that the ego is no longer master of its own house.

This contrived mythos is not constructed without finesse, on the one hand because it shifts the unnamed name of Freud into the succession of authorities, Copernicus and Darwin, and on the other hand because it thus allows one to surmise something like a teleology in the process of wounding, insofar as the succession from the cosmological to the biological to the psychological purportedly provides an increasing subjectivization. The concept of wounding takes on an increasingly more intimate cognitive hue in this history. It points to an intellectual development in which the curious human being who is open to truth increasingly turns out to be the one who incurs a growing disadvantage of being himself. He expiates his enlightenment with severe harms to his cognitive immunity shield.[1] The cost of achieving enlightenment about the position and function of the human being in evolution is—so Freud seems to want to say following Nietzsche—the expulsion from the narcissistic-illusionary paradises. "The world—portal to a thousand deserts, empty and cold. . . ."[2]

It is noteworthy that such views do not bring the bold psychologist to the conclusion that he should give up his undertaking. Like his contemporary, Max Weber, Freud holds fast to the modestly heroic conception that human beings who are involved in the disenchantment of the world by means of science must prove equal to their unavoidable disillusionment. From his stoic will to sobriety he derives the right, indeed the duty, to a certain publicist sadism. He is obviously proud of his ability to expose earlier than others the wounds that are historically due, in order to pass these on to a public of those who are still to be wounded. This pride allows one to suppose that those who feel it expect to make a good business of this. Whoever anticipates and publicizes wounds can emerge from the general disillusioning as a relative winner—from the disadvantage of the knower's being who he is, the publicist of disenchantment draws the advantage of getting ahead of the others and of telling them outright what is unwelcome to them. In such a presentation enlightenment turns out to be a wicked game. To the extent that it must progress as a history of wounding, it would be the attempt to inoculate the retrovirus of knowledge into the narcissistic immune systems of a group still sheltered in illusions, in order to deconstruct this group from within. The enlightener is the friend who has not spared my illusion.

Regarding what I said about a latent sadism in the scientific journalism having to do with wounds, I would like to specify that this may only be understood within narrow limits as an *ad hominem* argument. The morality and character of individuals like Darwin and Freud play a subordinate role for understanding the process for which they are advocating. The grandmasters of research that disrupts narcissism are only participants in an epochal cognitive project that is carried out through them with the force of the unavoidable. That can be seen above all by the fact that the procedure stylized by Freud to his own benefit did not come to a stop with the psychoanalytical enlightenment. One can with good reason be of the opinion that the instances in which science wounded anthropological narcissism all the way up to Freud have ultimately been only of the rhetorical kind and that the hardcore[3] phase of the history of disillusioning only begins beyond the third wound.

In fact, in comparison with the representatives of foundational research, psychologists who are educated in the Freudian tradition today operate like a *schola* of beautiful souls. The cognitive biologist Gerhard Vollner has described the scientific history of the last fifty years as a storm surge of continually accelerating waves of wounding, whose force has carried away even the last remnant of the sweepstake human narcissism—whether religiously or metaphysically coded—of the species.[4] According to Vollmer, the fourth wound is to be attributed to human ethology, thus to that science which seeks to include not only human physis, but also beyond this human cultural relations in phylogenetic continuity with developments in the animal realm. According to him, evolutionary epistemology triggers a fifth wound. It gets at the heart of rationalist narcissism, which is compelled to the insight that the human cognitive apparatus is just adequate enough to illuminate the cognitive niche that *Homo sapiens* inhabits—that is, the mesocosmic world of appearance—in certain aspects as a space that has been opened up. In contrast, the human cognitive apparatus is only suited for sleepwalking when it comes to the immense expanses of micro- and macrocosmic realities. On this view, the human being still remains, to be sure, a logical exception among animals, but he is only the mole of the universe, who digs himself forward in a narrow cognitive tunnel. This epistemological wound assails the deepest layers of our immemorial cognitive optimism and deals a devastating blow to the primal intellectual trust in our cognitive apparatus' ontological power of adequation. Already in the next moment we must prepare ourselves to receive the assault of the sixth wave, which is advanced by controversial sociobiology. It shatters—at least, according to its originators' own understanding—the human being's flattering self-deception that he could base his behavior on holistic, altruistic, idealistic, and disinterested motives: sociobiology 'uncovers' at the basis of all behavior an egotism of genes that is indifferent to the interests of the individual and the species. Accordingly, neither species nor individuals would occupy the world theater's center stage; both would be only masks and means for a pre-human central power, which can be identified as the gene's will to power. From the perspective of moral philosophy, if these conjectures were true, a millennium of wolves would be heralded, and that egotism which was opposed in all high cultures as the epitome of evil would in one fell swoop receive a scientific sanction—genes would be reckless gods, as it were, who pursue their goals in sovereign blindness. In Vollmer's scenario, wounding by computers follows in the seventh place; it has in essence two faces, one anthropological, which regards the human being as its machine double and embarrasses him with its aping; the other a media-historical face, which downgrades the human being up to this point, to the extent that he was a cultured animal that could perceive, speak, and write, and forces on him the awareness of how antiquated and inadequate he is on these scores going forward.

But this only describes the series of wounds that have already been carried out, and it is certain that the scale of humiliations for anthropological narcissism is upwardly open. Already, two more

uncanny guests are announced, who promise to throw the host that
is the human being out of his own house for good. On the one hand,
there is the ecological wounding, which sets about to demonstrate
that human beings of hot cultures over the long term only mis-
construe and ruin complex environmental systems, but can neither
understand nor protect them. And finally, there is a neurobiological
wounding that will proceed from the alliance of genetics, bionics,
and robotics and that will bring about in short order a situation
in which the most intimate manifestations of the self in human
existence such as creativity, love, and free will sink into a mire of
reflexive technologies, therapies, and power plays that is dotted with
will-o'-the-wisps.

This macabre list signifies at least two things: on the one hand,
one can read off from it an impersonal megatrend, which is implac-
ably carried out beyond rejection and approval, and which one
would have characterized as fateful in earlier times. In this trend the
scientistic motif becomes prevalent in a sustained manner according
to a threefold manifestation as naturalism, mechanism, and constructivism with sudden propulsions across a constant current. On
the other hand, the list makes clear that in every wave of wounding
there comes to be a clear asymmetry between what is active and
what is passive. Because enlightenment proceeds from the avant-
garde to the rearguard—Rosenstock-Huessy says: "Humanity
marches in wedge formation"—there is a clear-cut gradient between
the despatchers and recipients of the respective wound. Obviously,
the one who produces the wound has a privileged opportunity to
compensate for the narcissistic disadvantage that he makes public
with a gain in the narcissism of publication, such that the publicist
regenerates himself *ipso facto*, while all risks accrue to the consumer of the wound. The latter lags behind with the imposition
to correspond to the new state of things as a mere patient, except
where it discovers a procedure that for its part resells the bitter pill.
Whoever cannot step up as an innovator or an intermediary of an
instance of wounding—i.e., as an enlightener—has every prospect
of landing at the wide base of the pyramid, where the end consumers
of narcissism-destroying information gather, left alone with the disadvantage of being themselves. The awareness of this disadvantage
is typically articulated in depression. Whoever only receives deconstructive enlightenment becomes a pure patient. The entire process
has the character of a nihilistic chain-letter campaign, in which—as
in all enterprises of this kind—the later recipients can only be losers.
In contrast, for those who become further mediators of wounds
at the right time, the enlightenment enterprise remains a sweepstake, on the narcissistic-economic view, so long as it finds ways

to exchange the contemplative illusion for an operative or at least a destructive/'critical' power. This exchange is the primary transaction of enlightenment in psychodynamic terms. It explains why such a precarious endeavor as the gradual degradation of anthropological narcissism together with its illusions of center, identity, and sovereignty recruit such great numbers of active teammates.

I would like to postulate the psycho-historical hypothesis that all cultural history is the history of the reformatting of narcissisms—in other words, the history of the injury and regeneration of mental immune systems. The concept of childhood illness obviously also has an intellectual-historical and psychical-historical sense. It is obvious that modern enlightenment journalism and journalism having to do with wounding would be an impossibility in psycho-economic terms if they could not use a suggestive analog-model of the maturation of consciousness for their own purposes. They tout further enlightenment with the promise that all wounds are only inoculations with the truth, which after the crisis of the primary reactions puts at our disposal regenerated powers of immunity and more mature feelings of elation. On such a view, humanity would form an inoculation-pyramid, which is composed of those who are thoroughly inoculated, those who are half-inoculated, and those who are not inoculated. At its apex there would be, to put it in terms of ideal types, those in whom the entire transformation of infantile and religious primary narcissism into an adult and technological narcissism of capability is carried out—let us say personal unions of the most Machiavellian politicians and the most sanguine chief physicians, with a supplement of systems theory for coping with the everyday crises of meaning and a supplement of joyful paranoia for coping with the more acute crises of meaning. At the bottom of the pyramid one would find indolent populations that are still dependent on pre-enlightenment and pre-technological immunizations, yet are continually in danger of sinking to the level of depressive proletariats. In the middle of the pyramid there would be a multiply tiered, cognitive propertied bourgeoisie comprising candidates for becoming adult, which at their respective levels work to replace the primary immunity of illusion with the more mature immunity of power—a process that is generally described with the concept of training. It is thus no wonder that one hardly anywhere encounters a public that so enjoys training as among the members of the wounding professions.

From this psycho-economic perspective high cultures and modern societies appear to be enormous narcissism-converters, which allocate to their members the advantages and disadvantages of belonging to groups. The binding powers operative in such systems only become comprehensible when one is attentive to the distribution of narcissistic energy in municipalities, churches, and corporations. Feudal societies, for instance, regulate their collective narcissisms with the dazzling presentation of regal majesty and the authorization of vassals and their retinue to participate in the radiance of the sovereign pole. Even modern institutions obey the law of binding their members by the distribution of narcissistic advantages. For example, one will never understand what a medical association is if one does not know what a corporative plastic art of narcissism is. Modern nation-states can only be conceived as political plastic arts of narcissism—they functionalize showing off with blood and culture (I refer in this context, incidentally, to the human tragedy of the medical specialist Radovan Karadzić, who imagined he could be a politician, although anyone could have easily recognized that he was predestined to become president of a Serbian medical association). Likewise, we can do justice to churches and religious groups on the systemic view only when we recognize them as plastic arts of participation and installations of illusions, which sustain their members with affective gratifications and mental powers of immunity. All of these collectives demand a price for membership from those who belong to them, but as long as they achieve their group success they are reimbursed by the privileged access to convictions and instruments of power, by virtue of which they experience the advantage of being themselves with sufficient evidence.

2. Mechanical Engineering—The Prosthetic Modernity

Our reflections to this point, as rhapsodic and impetuous as they are, allow us to diagnose the current unease in technological culture more precisely. One understands why any direct answer to the question of whether, for instance, the newest robotic and biotechnological medicine is 'still' human is not possible and that, in order to get at its meaning, one must divide it into at least three sub-questions that can be concretely treated. Thus I ask first: At which point in the process of scientific instances of wounding and the conversions of wounding does a specifically medical contribution emerge? Next: In what way does the current unease with robotic medicine articulate the typical descending gradient between the producers and the consumers of technological wounding? And finally: How does the disadvantage of being outclassed by robots turn into the advantage of a coexistence with intelligent machines? Although I have distinguished different ways of looking at the problem, I would nonetheless like to consolidate their respective discussions into a common train of thought.

As one recalls, there was talk of a psychological wounding in the Freudian sketch of the history of scientific instances of wounding. No genuine contribution to the destruction of the fantasies of an anthropological midpoint and sovereignty is allotted to medicine in general. On closer observation, this portrayal turns out to be factually implausible and historically false. If one would like to engage in a speculative form of psychodynamic intellectual history regarding this tendency in general, then one must acknowledge that the medical factor came powerfully into play right from the beginning of the whole process. It is not only the cosmological wounding associated with the name of Copernicus that gets the ball rolling for the critical process and that, in Goethe's words, imposes on the human being the necessity "to renounce the immense privilege" of representing the midpoint of the universe.[5] At the same time as the cosmological reversal, an anatomical wounding takes place through which the cadaver became the real lectrice of anthropology. In the wake of the wonders of early anatomists and their colleagues, woodcut artists and engravers, the living human body [*Leib*] first achieved the status of a 'physical body' [*Körpers*] in the sense of recent physics, a subject of the law of gravity, of the scalpel and of perspectival portrayal. Here one would have to speak of a Vesalian wounding. In its journalistic dissemination, anatomists practically asserted the right to abstract from the theological grandeur of their object; they cut through the human body as though it were a matter of indifference for their procedure that the same bodies went to Mass in their lifetimes, celebrated the Eucharist, and were designated by the fellows of the theological faculty as temples of the Holy Spirit. This anatomical onslaught was from the beginning much more than a contest among faculties. The anatomist and the theologian stood against each other as opponents in the epochal question of the relation between nature and the supernatural in regards to the human being. The role of the aggressor thereby fell *eo ipso* to the anatomist, that of the defender naturally to the theologian. This scenario has gone on with changing lineups up to the present day: for four hundred years the scene repeated itself of the naturalist aggressor compelling the defender of dimensions outside of the natural to a retreat into ever more modest enclaves. The victor takes everything this time, too. Once the question of the soul's localization can be posed in anatomical-biological concepts, then the defeat of religious, metaphysical, or even merely humanistic anthropology is only a matter of time.

With the anatomical paradigm there appears on the scene at the same time a communicative paradox that is characteristic for recent history as a whole: in fact, no peace is possible between the pride of the modern sciences and the narcissism of Christian-humanist practices of faith, without there being a loser or at least one who is more burdened. For how can one explain to the human being the anatomical discovery that one has cut him open and could not find an organ of the soul? How does one tell the human being who has been baptized and is hoping for the Resurrection that in the course of dissecting the external human being no inner human being emerges? To put this more sharply: how does one say to the soul which believes it has a chance at salvation that according to the latest findings there is no soul? From the side of the offender this problem of communication can be well endured for the time being, because here too the narcissism of the enlightener in transmitting deconstructive messages gets his money's worth. Much more difficult is the role of the one who has to receive the wound: if he tries to balk at the new insights he loses the connection to the state of the art; if he opens himself up to the new pieces of evidence, then he has resigned himself to incursions into his cognitive immune system. As long as the supernatural doctrine is as powerful in terms of political ideas as were the churches of the sixteenth and seventeenth centuries, a counter-insurgent strategy readily suggests itself: the naturalist enlightener is suddenly made diabolical. If the defender, in the course of time, becomes too weak to diabolize the offender, orderly retreat is all that remains. We know from history that this can drag on for centuries. While in retreat, those who have been offended defend their honor even with intellectually dubious means, and they refuse, ever anew, to become mere patients of the enlightenment—they reject the cognitive compulsory inoculation. But however far the maneuver of retreat belonging to religious pride may go, the vanishing point of all defensive movements must lie beyond narcissistic self-assertion. From out of the wounding of the soul, the proof of the soul ultimately imposes itself upon those who have been offended. The soul is now what can say: I am wounded, therefore I am—one could call it the traumatological cogito. This finding becomes conclusive for the human being only in the depths of depression: he apprehends himself when he savors the disadvantage of being himself to the bitter dregs. This leads him out of the constituted religious systems.

The mathematician and philosopher Blaise Pascal belonged to the first of those who reflected on the connection between the dignity and the frailty of the human being. According to him, the human being is the frailest creature—a reed that snaps all too soon, yet a reed that thinks. If one intensifies Pascal's reflection then the proposition must result: the human being is in extremis a wound,[6] yet one that knows itself. A concept of human dignity that is beyond successful narcissism with its cycles of damage and recovery is thereby indicated. From the philosophical point of view, human dignity is constituted not by the fact that the human being can feel well under the protection of illusions of integrity—whether primary or regenerated ones—but rather by the fact that he lives with the risk of seeing his vital illusions founder. Thus already in the seventeenth century a tragic anthropology was delineated, in which a pride without pride is articulated as the ultimate horizon of human dignity.

With the anatomical wounding in the sixteenth century the psychosomatic existence of the human being was drawn into a relentlessly ongoing process of objectification. The image of the human body was thus modeled on the cadaver and that of the cadaver on the machine. If two magnitudes are equal to a third, then they are equal to each other: through the mediation of the cadaver consequences become evident for the equation of the human being and the machine, which were conceptually formulated in the French materialism of the eighteenth century, particularly in La Mettrie, and were developed in the naturalism of the nineteenth and twentieth centuries. One may ask, for good epistemological reasons, whether what Freud called the second and third wounds, the biological and psychoanalytic ones, are not in fact machine-theoretical wounds: Darwinian theory portrays evolution as automatic animal machine engineering; the Freudian unconscious exhibits features of a biopsychical machine that functions as a transformer between energy flows and formations of signs. The supposed first one, the cosmological wounding, already has a latent machine-theoretical sense, because after it the earth no longer appears to be the stage for acts of grace upon which God has manifested himself to the human being, but rather as an eccentric magnitude in an astrophysical gravitational system that, as far as we can see, is not interested in the human being. Thus the earth would have been downgraded from a theatrical-narcissistic central authority to a subordinate component of one solar system among many.

Consequently, it seems as if the equation of the human being and the machine underlay all instances of wounding human narcissism, and it warrants further commentary because of its elementary dynamic. Whoever identifies human beings with simple machines actually attacks anthropological pride in three sensitive places at once: in the awareness of complexity, in the awareness of ends, and in the awareness of replaceability. Even the least sophisticated human being knows or has an inclination that he must be constructed in an infinitely more complicated manner than any tool or any machine that he uses. All machines that have been known until just recently were based on overly simple counter-natural geometries and extreme reductions, such that the equation of human beings and machines must always already include an affront to human dignity as a hyper-complex, indeterminate, and thus enigmatic reality. Furthermore, even the humblest human being, indeed even the trained slave, knows that he is not exhausted by his Being-for-the-other and is always existentielly more than a means for alien ends: hence he has compelling reasons, when he is identified with a trivial machine, to feel offended in his awareness that he can be his own end. And ultimately most human beings—if they are not dualist mystics or transcendental philosophers—include their entire innervated body in their living sense of self, for which reason they initially have to react with outrage to the machine-theoretical imposition of needing to take any and every part of the body to be fungible within the framework of the progress of the art of prosthetic engineering.

It is not very hard to show that, ever since, things have changed much in relation to these three unconditionally justified human vulnerabilities. The possibilities for the contemporary human being to feel affronted by his equation with machines is continually diminished with respect to recent technology. Advanced cybernetic machines today are not so far removed from organismic complexity as were the clockworks of the seventeenth century. Smart computers simulate signs of spontaneity, personality, even aesthetic playfulness. Prosthetics has reached a technical level that has taken away much of the fear of having to get used to organ transplants; the age of wooden legs and iron hands is long past. In this regard, one could go so far as to speak of a convergence between what is human and what is machinelike. To the extent that this development is corroborated, the humanistic accusation that the machine has affronted it would one day have to lead to acquittal because of the proven absence of any intention to wound the human being.

If there is actually a comprehensive machine-theoretical instance of wounding the modern human being—and everything seems to speak in favor of this finding—then we have reason to ask about the scientific and historical motives for the emergence of this wounding force. The answer that still leads the way is found in the Baconian formulation: knowledge is power. This over-cited statement loses its seeming triviality as soon as one understands what he effectively means: knowledge of machines confers power, operational knowledge produces sovereignty. Enlightenment is hence not only and not so much a modification of the collective mentality in the direction of a democratization of power. It mainly signifies competence in mechanical engineering—and subsequently a deployment of machines against mere nature, together with their implementation against unenlightened human beings, that is to say, human beings who are mechanically poor. Corresponding to this are modernity's typical attempts to achieve advantages in power from mechanistic knowledge: in the mechanical engineering of the state in Thomas Hobbes, in the mechanical engineering of labor in James Watt, in the mechanical engineering of truth in Leibniz, in the mechanical engineering of beauty in both baroque opera and courtly ritual, in the mechanical engineering of education by the Jesuit *Gymnasium*, in the mechanical engineering of the military with absolutism's standing armies, in the mechanical engineering of personal identification by absolutist police forces, in the mechanical engineering of health by modern hospitals, and in the mechanical engineering of knowledge by late-baroque academies. The cognitive economy of the seventeenth century is marked by the transition from the rhetorical model of power as the disposal over signs to the technical model of power as mechanical engineering.

But what is it that allows the idea of the machine to accrue such powerful constructive energies and have such soaring human hopes placed on it? It seems to me that this can only be explained by the effort of the modern intelligentsia to escape from the metaphysical imprisonment in which human beings must feel themselves to be God's creatures. In the will to mechanical engineering—to put it more generally, in the will to artificial constructions—a widespread revolt of modern human beings against constriction by natural and divine heteronomy manifests itself. At the basis of the modern constructivist impulse there is the refusal to stand before a prefabricated world as only a suffering and receptive part. In fact, under the regime of metaphysics, the whole of the world is organized into the realm of nature and the realm of grace. Because of his dual citizenship in both realms the human being is the dual subject: now as a creature in the whole of nature, insofar as he has to do with the God of regularity, on another occasion as a recipient of charisms or gifts of grace, insofar as he encounters the God who makes exceptions. In the one as in the other realm the human being experiences himself as something passive and as a power compelled to surrender itself. If he wants to demolish this heteronomous position and to become a candidate for sovereign activities himself then for all the world he must attempt to avoid the alternative of nature and grace. It turns out that there is a third dimension in the space of beings that escapes this ontological alternative: the machine, the artificial construction, that which is man-made. Between the realm of nature and the realm of grace there gapes an initially almost imperceptible fissure—the narrow domain of tools, works of art, and machines. As soon as one seriously makes the attempt, it becomes immediately evident that they were neither produced by God in the six days of creation nor were they allowed by the same God to later fall gracefully from heaven in wondrous breaches of orderly nature.

In European cities since the late fourteenth century a fantastic rumor was making the rounds among craftsmen, chancellors, merchants, and artists which must have electrified the wise and the strong: the rumor that the machine, the artificial construction, and calculation present a crucial opportunity for the human being. Around 1450 the great thinker of the late Middle Ages, Nicholas of Cusa, took up this rumor that had been spreading among laypersons and composed the most powerful text of early modernity concerning the creative power of the human intellect: *Idiota de mente, The Layman: About Mind*. In fact, at the beginning of modernity we observe an unrest among the educated Europeans that will lead to a twofold exodus from the old world. Among those who are in a state of unrest early on, one part immigrates over the Atlantic to the New World, to the two Americas, where nature itself seemed to stand open like an instance of grace, free of Old European subservience and original sin. They cross over into the transatlantic beyond, where former Europeans have ever after hoped to be able to begin again as though from scratch. Just as little do those who are not emigrants remain where they were; they emigrate from the old passivity into the third 'realm' ['*Reich*'] of machines and artifices. They immigrate to progress. In this, one can sidestep nature and grace and put something new, free, and one's own into the world from human ingenuity. Knowledge of machinery is power; power is the capacity to effect what is neither realized in old nature nor conferred by grace, but rather is to be unequivocally chalked up to the human being as art, as technique, as strategy, as machine. The realm of the skillful is the element of the modern human being. His age is replete with a single event: with an immediate immense emigration—a departure into the time of artificialities. With this departure, the European intelligentsia of artists, engineers, and doctors decamps into the play-space of freedom belonging to machines and means, to works and operations.

We thus encounter a reversal of our original supposition: prior to all instances of wounding by machines there is the unparalleled satisfaction occasioned by the capacity to be able to build machines. The affective kernels of modern forward progress are the I-can and the it's-a-go. The phenomenon of wounding immediately follows, since finding satisfaction in one's competence in mechanical engineering can only occur in modern populations in a manner that is characterized by stark asymmetrical distribution. For each one who can, there are initially and continually thousands, tens of thousands, later millions, who cannot. Inevitably, the intellectual history of modernity develops into a sadomasochistic drama between the mechanical engineering and non-mechanical engineering factions, between the few who first break through to having capability, and the many who voluntarily and involuntarily receive the capability of the ones who are capable. The rest are problems of transmission, transformations of narcissism, histories of reception. An embrace that is as exciting as it is adversarial is formed between engineers and non-engineers, artists and non-artists, entrepreneurs and non-entrepreneurs, surgeons and non-surgeons—in recent times, the relation between sponsors and non-sponsors has been added. On all these playing fields cooperation and *ressentiment* contend with each other; the striving for one's own share in the advantages of technology vies everywhere with the fear of being counted among the losers in the implementations of technology.

A coherent history can only be formed from such serious games so long as it succeeds in convincing each respective passive majority of the fact that it has a chance to appropriate the sadistic capacity of offensive minorities and thus to become a fellow winner in the wave of innovation. The modern idea of cultural formation [*Bildungsidee*] functions as a buffer between the parties; it transforms one's mistrust of those who are active into admiration and imitation. The cult of genius, as what forms a love-hate relationship between those who are creative and those who are receptive, has its systemic locus here. But even what emerges today as an advertisement for new technologies, as visionary marketing and idealistic politics, is in fact for the most part nothing other than a seductive performance at the sadomasochistic theater of escalating mechanical engineering. It guides its reception by a public that cannot know in advance whether or not it will get a fair share of enjoyment with the aid of the most recent recommendations. For the highly technologized zones of the First World the observation can be confirmed that populations of consumers and learners have followed, step by step, the advancing invitations of mechanical engineering that have come in waves after a typical hesitation at the beginning. From this perspective, modernity is above all the history of the reception of mechanical engineering competence and its popularization among users.

The unease in highly technologized culture can thus be deduced in terms of the history of machines; it has its main cause in the fact that the traditional world of Being as it has been encountered begins as a whole to become strange to us because of the twofold rejection of nature and grace. A culture that has sought its opportunity in mechanical engineering still may not wonder about the technological alienation of the world. To be sure, the Romantic return to nature and the neo-religious return to grace belong to modernity, too, but both reactions can change nothing for us of the alien character of the artificially developed world. Modernity arises from the will to artificiality, and this is nowhere more evident than in modern medicine. This has long since operated self-evidently and self-consciously in a space that is neither grace nor nature. Modern doctors and patients manage sicknesses and afflictions neither through graceful instances of miraculous healing nor through non-operational trust in the *natura sanat*. There certainly are recoveries that have the character of a miracle; nature also heals up of its own accord, and it would be presumptuous not to marvel at the fact that human beings generally possess the capacity to regain lost health. Yet the specific opportunity of the modern human being only opens up when we come across the third, that is, the technical field.

If quite numerous consumers of the most recent medical technologies, indeed not seldom even doctors themselves, nonetheless get the creeps, then this is because the instruments openly, perhaps all-too-openly, present the standpoint of the power of machines. Machines are essentially prostheses—and as such are intended to supplement and to supplant the first instance of mechanical engineering, which is claimed by nature, with a second one from out of the spirit of technology. One must guard against understanding by prostheses only primitive surrogates for perfect organs. It is rather the reverse: the essence of prosthetics is to substitute imperfect organs with machines that are more efficient. The offensive quality of these replacements comes into view when one disregards reparative prostheses and conceives of the expansive ones as what is decisive. Prosthetics may well have begun as an incorporation or addition of foreign bodies to one's own body, but it comes into its own only when it creates extended bodies that not only repair the old body, but enhance and transfigure it as well. From this perspective invalids are forerunners of the human being of tomorrow. Perhaps not for nothing did modernity's most intense genius of power, Napoleon, once erect a royal chapel for invalids. Afterward, one only needed a chapel dedicated to prostheses, and if one really thinks this over, such a chapel was long since erected in the form of the modern technological lifeworld. Do we not inhabit a global prostheses-park? Do we not increasingly experience the world as a great clinic and as a telematics commune? Prosthetological modernity labors in an ongoing manner on operative, sensory, and cognitive extensions of the body, which strike us as miracles without miracles and which will soon have become self-evident as natures alongside nature. They all belong to the alien space of technology and allow us to trace the chilling consequences of our immigration to the third realm.

All categories of foreignness arise within the clinical reality: foreign bodies as mechanical or electronic prosthetic limbs; foreign organs as transplanted natural machines or as fully synthetic allo-plastics; foreign movement as electro-mobile or robotic locomotion; foreign rhythm as a technological substitute for vital frequency dis-semination in active endoprostheses such as a pacemaker; foreign sleep with the aid of anesthetics; foreign moods with psychotropic drugs; foreign cognition by means of neuro-designing and neuro-linguistic manipulation; foreign eyes as invasive and non-invasive optic scopes for seeing into the old obscurity of the body; foreign pregnancies by means of placental prostheses and artificial uteri. Prosthetics to this point is surpassed only by the foray of genet-ics into the synthetic level, where human beings gain the power to provide alternative biological imperatives; here foreign technogenic living beings appear on the horizon. In their totality these practices now massively redound upon the inhabitants of the technological environment and necessitate an ontology of prosthetic realities. The time has come for reaching an agreement on the real status of all these ontological half-siblings of the human being. The current rush toward virtuality unmistakably contains the demand for an ontology of technological Being and appearance. The ontological privilege of our first and individual body is still, to be sure, vitally felt on all sides—as long as the first body remains irreplaceable. However, in fact and in tendency it has been abolished, insofar as we ever more cross over from the natural body to the technologically expanded body. Extended bodies provide us with the evidence that, as machines, we are at an advantage.

3. The Ages of the Psychological

We are not generally accustomed to relate the concept of an era to psychological circumstances. This is understandable, because our historical attention is above all directed to events and forces that have shaped the epoch in political, religious, and artistic terms, while we hardly ever contemplate the psychical factors of the human condition in an evolutionary light. But all human history is natu-rally always also the history of circumstances of ensoulment, and its reversals and transitions are invariably also meant when one speaks of what is 'human' and of its endangerment by powers of alienation. On analogy to the standard historical division of antiquity, Middle Ages, and modernity I would here like—without further argu-ments or explanations—to present a thesis that has been inspired by Gotthard Günther in particular. The thesis is that the phenomenal territory of the psychological also knows three ages or eras: an animistic antiquity, a subjectivist or personalist Middle Ages, and an a-subjectivist or cybernetic modernity.

One can interpret this three-stage sequence of the psychological as a history of progressive desubstantialization, or, if you will, the functionalization of the psychological. The movement of animism to subjectivism or personalism and from the latter to cybernetics provides the matrix for all episodes in the history of the narcissistic instances of wounding humanity. There are more than a few arguments supporting the supposition that in each contemporary individual the entire sequence of the ages of the world is portrayed in a peculiar abbreviated form. In every human being tailored in the modern fashion there are presumably two affronted ancestors: an affronted animist from the ancient time of the psyche, who at the beginning of the era of high cultures was repressed by a subjective and personalist reformation of the psychological; and an affronted personalist, who from the onset of the technological era has to register that he has been surpassed by a-subjective and cybernetic-machinist concepts of the psychological. In every modern individual one must thus reckon with a certain inclination to the return of the surpassed, even without a latent willingness to ally oneself with psychological antiquity or the Middle Ages against modernity (which is why there are two distinctly dated ways in which one evades modernity, a personalist-monotheistic one and an animist-polytheistic one).

Only against the background of the model of eras can one determine what the concept of 'human' means. What is human is primarily the regard for the new in contrast to the old after the victory. Humanity was initially nothing other than the historical compromise of personalism with animism after it had prevailed over the latter. We can still take up humanism today as our 'ancient heritage' to the degree that we ourselves sympathize with the necessity of repeating the transition from the age that belongs to univalent thought toward the one that belongs to bivalent thought. If the victorious, 'human' human being of the personalist Middle Ages was able to bring himself to confess that nothing human is alien to him, then what was thereby said is that even in the high-cultural personalist regime of the relations among God, soul, and world certain animistic motifs are to be integrated and accepted, motifs which it was nevertheless the evolutionary destiny of the ancient avant-garde to surpass.

Original humanity emerges as high-cultural humor in dealing with what in ourselves and in our neighbors is, after all, not so entirely high-cultural. Humanistic humor is the condescension of the present toward a past that has been overcome and has nevertheless not disappeared. It moderates dealing with our inner archaic. If some surgeons wear amulets, then it is a sign of humanity not to make fun of them for it. Metaphysical personalism, as a rule, only becomes humorless where it defends its substance: the unconditioned super-ordination of monotheistic ethics and ontology over polytheistic customs. It must speak of the latter, especially at the initial stage in which they are rejected, as though of unacceptable abominations and regressions. By studying the ancient history of religions, one can be convinced that for ancient humanity the transition to personalist-monotheistic images of the world and dispositions of faith signified a crisis with many victims, which left behind wounded animists everywhere. For the sake of inner peace the new formation had to keep formulations of reconciliation at the ready for the animistic need.

On the psycho-historical view, humanism is a semi-animism, which sees to the compromise between the psychological Middle Ages and psychological antiquity. The Catholic universe with its cult of saints, of the Mother of God and of the Sacred Heart and with its inclination toward radical mystics, is only to be understood if one keeps in view the fact that it was the religio-historical task of the Catholic millennium to compensate for and to integrate the animistic part that was not overcome. Still more impressive is the synthesis that has developed between magical ancient religion and more recent Brahmanist metaphysics in Hinduism.

It is plausible to consider an analogous occurrence of compromise in the latest transitional crisis between the personalist Middle Ages and modern technological civilization. Anti-technological *ressentiments* lead no further than to the formation of subcultures that are populated by those who have been rendered obsolete, with their typical mystifications; they are plagued by the double-morality, which therapy cannot treat, of thinking pre-technologically and living technologically. Whoever believes in intelligent potential cannot help but work on a renewed historical compromise between the formations of the psychological. This will be articulated in two stages, according to the state of things—on the one hand, as a balance between cybernetics and personalism, and on the other hand, as a compromise between machine culture and animism. In order to attain human plausibility the dominant machinist ontology must unleash a starkly new idea of cultural formation. Its thought is inevitably at a more complex psycho-historical level than its high-cultural predecessors. Jewish personalism, Christian Platonism, and Stoic humanism have been pressed into reactionary positions by the advent of a cybernetic and systemic intellectual culture.

'Reactionary' means a position from which only protest is possible, not further thought. Classical humanism, which had stepped into the world as a personalist management of humbled animism, is today practically exhausted; indeed, it is itself humbled and on the defensive. In vain does it seek refuge in the debate over 'values.' Superior mediation can only still be accomplished by machinist modernity: it must declare itself to be the greater human power. One must become a cyberneticist to be able to remain a humanist.

Of a techno-human culture that wants to be more than a successful barbarism, two things above all are required: psychological cultural formation and the cultural capacity for translation. Mathematicians must become poets, cyberneticists must become philosophers of religion, doctors must become composers, computer scientists must become shamans. Was humanity ever something other than the art of managing transitions? If the poles lie far apart, art becomes rare and neglect likely. Yet if human beings are machine-engineering animals then they are even more so beings that create metaphors. As soon as the intelligent machines of the future are successfully integrated into semi-personalist and semi-animist relationship games with human beings, there would be no need for people to fear becoming friends with their robot partners. It is the task of our times to develop a postmodern humor that allows cyberneticists to communicate in a collegial manner with Voodoo priests, mullahs, and cardinals. Why should human beings who build satellites, decipher the genome, and transplant cerebral tissue not be in a position to understand that in certain respects it still makes sense to conceive the human being as a likeness of God, as a bearer of inalienable rights and as a medium of influential ancestors? It could contribute to the historical compromise between cybernetics and personalism if the hanging of crucifixes in computer labs and operating rooms were legally prescribed in Bavaria—no matter what the dead souls of Karlsruhe say of it.

Even if robots will have convinced the soul in the technological era that it cannot exist for the purpose in which it once believed, there still remains for the desubstantialized soul the pride in discreetly suffering this wounding. Its misery is proof that it exists. At the apex of machinist modernity there is repeated in some individuals the birth of humanity from out of the knowledge of the vulnerability of life in the midst of the most advanced architectures of security. The advantage of being a technologist was never greater than it is now. The human compromise will continue to be in effect in advanced technological medicine for as long as there are doctors who share with their patients, on fair terms, the disadvantage of being a human being.

8

THE TIME OF THE CRIME OF THE MONSTROUS

On the Philosophical Justification of the Artificial

Translated by Wieland Hoban, with revisions by Ian Alexander
Moore and Christopher Turner

As we approach the bi-millennium, we begin to look upon the
Modern Age as a period in which monstrous things are achieved
by human perpetrators—entrepreneurs, technicians, artists, and
consumers. This monstrous is neither sent by the old gods nor represented by classical monsters; the Modern Age is the era of the
man-made monstrous. To be modern, one must be touched by the
awareness that, beside the inevitable fact of being a witness, one
has been drawn into a sort of complicity with the newer form of
the monstrous. If one asks a modern person, 'Where were you at
the time of the crime?' the answer is: 'I was at the scene of the
crime'—that is to say, within that totality of the monstrous which,
as a complex of modern criminal circumstances, encompasses its
accomplices and accessories. Modernity means dispensing with the
possibility of having an alibi.

The monstrous in a cross-section of modern deeds cannot be
summed up in any single term or restricted to a particular field—it
is a work of art, but far more than a work of art; it is great politics,
but far more than great politics; it is technology, but far more than
technology; it is illness, but far more than illness; it is crime, but far
more than crime. It is a project, but far more than a project. For
this reason, all juridical, aesthetic, politological, technological, and
pathological discourses are only of limited use in describing the
modern world, because these languages serve to check phenomena and document states, but cannot express the supra-phenomenal
monstrous of modernity. So the moderns, when they drop their
alibis, can be found where this is much more premeditated, committed, and attested. Modernity is something that can sooner be
expressed in confessions than described in programs. One is involved

in it like a fever that provokes its victims into a new mode of Being beyond healthy and sick. Complicity with and cognizance of the monstrous in our time is more likely to be confessed in works than recorded at symposia.

From this perspective, theory of modernity is always already, and only ever, possible as a reflection on the sublime in the man-made; it is itself an echo from the monstrous in the sum of the new actions carried out in the time of the crime; its object can be no other than the supra-objective man-made or man-mediated immeasurable. That is why theory, insofar as it explicates the new monstrous, becomes a sublime form. This reveals the decisive reason why thought in modernity can no longer be a metaphysics in the old style—but no mere academic research either. The former was committed to the mission—immemorial even for itself—of interpreting beings as a whole as the greatest of all possible domestic spaces; its passion was to carry out the equation of the cosmos and the home; classical metaphysics was sworn into the project of trivializing humans as the temporary inhabitants of a timeless world house. When it did mention the monstrous, it interpreted it directly as the God who makes us, the mortals, suffer whenever He shows Himself or takes action. In classical metaphysics, the monstrous is possible only for God, which is why, in the metaphysical age, sublime theory could only appear as theology. Modern theory, on the other hand, begins from the monstrous-ness of the humanly possible. It deals, in an anthropological form, with the supra-anthropological content of the newest history of power. For it, humans are the beings that have abandoned their houses—even if only under the pretext of settling into them better. Essentially, the Modern Age is the era of the exit from the house of Being. It is the time of the crime of the monstrous.

The man-made monstrousness of the Modern Age has three faces, three areas of appearance; these reveal themselves as the monstrous in man-made space, the monstrous in man-made time, and the monstrous in the man-made thing. Accordingly, I shall begin by speaking of the earth as the represented gathering place of the human species; then of the millennium as the represented duration of the Modern Age human; and finally of art and technology as the represented power of humans. The decisive representation of the earth in the Modern Age is the European-made and European-used globe as geodicy; the decisive interpretation of history as the realm of human actions is the post-historical millennium as end time without end; and the decisive projection of the coming human possibilities is the future as the advent of power in its threefold quality as the future of organization, the future of apparatus, and the future of art.

1. Geodicy

Today we can face the fact that Jacob Burckhardt's famous Renaissance formula in its principle concept contains an erroneous description, because the event of the fifteenth century that pushed open the door to the Modern Age was not 'the discovery of the world and of humans' but the connection of a human routine structure to the spatial and technological monstrous. What we call the Modern Age is the explosion of the Old European space of possibility through experimenting technologies and arts. That is why Europeans of the late fifteenth century were the model moderns of the Old World, less discoverers than experimenters; expansion routines were their profession; their world-space grew because they knew how to include new space in new routines of reaching out. So the essential quality of the Modern Age is not so much the discovery of unexplored spaces—as if unknown continents had wanted to be woken by Europeans from the slumber of their undiscovered state. The distinctive characteristic of the Modern Age is rather the opening of extended operational spaces by means of new procedures. The nautical routines of the Portuguese and the Spanish brought forth the two Americas as their concrete by-product;[1] the manufacturing routines of architects, doctors, and painters in the fifteenth century revealed new horizons of feasibilities as their material result. The world is not everything that is to be discovered; it is everything that can be incorporated into routines of action. In that sense, 'Modern Age' is a name for the execution of the operativistic revolution. It leads to a new state of the world in which mastering higher-degree artificialities will become the norm.

The most important testament to Modern Age routines in reaching out for the cosmic foundation of the species is the production of globes; from the late fifteenth century on, they spread among European earth-users as the primary medium of geological enlightenment. Originating from Greek and Arab prototypes, globes became the dominant signifiers of the operable earth idea from the start of the Modern Age onward. They not only represented the earth as a geological monad before the eyes of European expansionists with varying accuracy; in a sense, they were what produced the earth as a foil of action for Modern Age humanity in the first place. The earth and the globe form the paradigm of modern semiotics; representational geography marks the start of the 'age of the world-picture.'[2] Because the earth was depicted 'accurately enough' on the globe, the truth of meaning for modern users of iconic systems was established; whatever was no more inaccurate in its depictive power

240 The Time of the Crime of the Monstrous

than a globe in relation to the earth could be considered sufficiently true.

The oldest surviving globes from the early period of European representations of the complete earth, the Behaim Globe from Nuremberg and the Laon Globe—both from the final decade of the fifteenth century—still show the pre-Columbian outlines of the continents; in graphic terms, they are premodern and pre-American. Nonetheless, both offer a perfect demonstration of the new access to the earth's totality among scholars, merchants, and ministers in the early Modern Age. They made the earth ready-to-hand [*zuhanden*] for Europeans; with their left hands, the Nuremberg councilors could turn this globe, made in 1492 by the young merchant Martin Behaim, who had just returned from Lisbon with new geographical insights; with a diameter of 50.7 cm, the image of the earth had been reduced to a scale of 1:25,000,000. The metal Laon Globe—with a diameter of 17 cm—could even be held in one hand; at first glance, it might have been mistaken for an imperial orb from the Middle Ages. Nonetheless, the imperial orb and the globe belong to fundamentally different eras: if the imperial orb, as an image from the holy sphere, represents the ball of the existent [*des Seienden*] in the left hand of the German Caesars, this is a feudal symbol of the world that shows how the cosmos lies in a single human hand as a divine fief.[3] The globe, on the other hand, is the profane world-signifier of an age in which all points of the earth were imagined with the central assumption of equal accessibility and exploitability for Europeans—it was no longer a metaphysical symbol, but rather a medium of earthly traffic that had become routine. Even if semanticists felt obliged to remind people that the map is not the land, the majority of Modern Age Europeans did believe that the globe was the earth. This carefree equation expresses the fact that we represent and produce the earth and the globe in the same spirit. The globe is the earth insofar as it reveals the complete use of the earth for human history upon it. The total use of the earth is preceded by the globe lesson, which teaches that all points on the earth's surface can be described through the postulate of homogeneous accessibility and availability for Euro-American interventions.

Consistently with this, the result of the globe era is the acute globalization of human interventions on the earth. Here the man-made monstrous becomes visible. No one can still miss the fact that, in the half-millennium between Columbus's voyage and the first journey into space, the neo-European habit of practical earth-use established itself in the real earthly space. The use of the earth for history takes on—corresponding to the threefold basic definition of history—three different meanings. First, a dramatic one, insofar as history means a campaign or struggle for supremacy between economic and political empires; here the earth is used primarily as a stage for a play that absolutely must be enacted. Second, an economic-alchemical one, insofar as history primarily constitutes an undertaking to acquire wealth; here using the earth means interpreting it as a resource and framework for all fabrications. Third, a reading of history as exodus and emancipation; here everything narrow, local, and rooted is liberated into the boundless, into the Promised Land of the everywhere; here using the earth means applying it as a foil for world traffic—as a background for messages, a terrain for crossings, and a carrier for transports.

The monstrous in geodicy via the European globe manifests itself in two ways: as a shallow monster, to the extent that the globe provides the model uniform for our cosmic place—with the image of earth as a guide for everyday titanism; or as a deep monster, if we look through the globe to observe the geological monad. This latter—because it is a singularity—can by its nature not be understood, only meditated upon in its uniqueness. As the only encompassing and uncanny house of life, it is an unspeakable individual. Modernity is the time of the crime of the geological monstrous because it carries out the process of geological enlightenment in global operative routines. Thus the twentieth century plays a culminating part in the time of the crime of modernity because, in its course, historical and regional alibis were increasingly eliminated so that all contemporaries could potentially be acquired as witnesses and accomplices to the man-made monstrous. In the twentieth century, the pictorial world exploded primarily in the sense of shallow monstrousness: the image of the earth now provided the frame for the space through which all other images must be transported. The earth became the illustrated magazine on which all other illustrations circulate.

Certainly one also finds works appearing in the great art of modernity which reply to the deep monster that is the earth. Only rarely, however, do they reach the level of equal monstrousness alongside the geological monad. In great works of art, the monstrous of the Modern Age comes to itself as a time of the crime. In this sense, all significant works of thought and form in our age are indirect monuments to our geodicy. They show the state of what is possible on earth. They attest that the humanly possible now always means the monstrous, whether in routine or singular actions. It is of this earth, illuminated by its artistic outbursts, that Heidegger wrote in one of his greatest texts: "The earth appears as the un-world of errancy. In terms of the history of Beyng, it is the errant planet."[4] Two questions formulated by Deleuze and Guattari answer as if from a different planet: "Who does the earth think it is?" and "Who does man think he is?"[5]

2. Millennium

On the eve of the bi-millennium, six world languages have established themselves on what Heidegger, around 1945, termed the 'errant planet': English, the dollar, multinational brands, popular music, the news, and abstract art. Their functional commonality is the synchronization of intra-species traffic. Through the effects of the Eurocentric age from 1492 to 1945, there developed on the earth a system of interactions that is realized in economic, diplomatic, and informatic routines. The necessity of bringing the 'partners' scattered across the earth into a shared world time takes effect on the basis of all globalization routines. The purpose of all cultural revolutions is synchronization—meaning the initiation of humans into the simultaneity of the earthly present. Hence the Modern Age is always also the age of mankind *en marche*. By annulling the original scattered mode of Being among the human species that had prevailed for millions of years and throughout the old regional empires, globalization forced the un-united together in the hazardous form of the current world traffic commune. European expansions and the world market bring the age-old anthropological diaspora to an end. From 1492 onward, the monstrous in time is the 'world society' squeezed together into a new, simultaneously existing unity. The mental trauma of the Modern Age is not the loss of the middle, but rather the loss of distance from the many others. As a result, modernization takes place as an establishment of temporal communism for the species as a whole. Where humans interpret their position in space and time according to modern standards, they must view themselves as members of a forced commune that no longer permits any escape—whoever has seen globes and the news can scarcely have any illusions about belonging together with the rest of the species; we have now become chrono-communists and bio-communists against our will, as it were, dismayed members of a genetic universal church that surrounds us with relatives on all sides. The modern ones are those who must wonder what the Chinese and the Icelanders are up to today. Robert Walser already found a formula for this at the start of the twentieth century: "Running around with the problem of nations in one's head—doesn't this mean falling prey to disproportion? Dragging in millions of people willy-nilly, what a burden on the brain! . . . In the jumble comprised of the sentences above, I think I hear in the distance the Minotaur, who represents, it seems to me, nothing more than the shaggy difficulty of making sense of the problem of nations."[6]

The problems of nations are the small change of the question of mankind, where we view the monstrous as the norm. The depiction of earth actionism in the 'world-picture' is necessarily followed by a world clock system and a world news system. The use of both is as far from being harmless as the observing of globes was in former times; its ultimate consequence is to separate people from their local histories, their ethnic rhythms, and their national calendars to incorporate them in the homogeneous, synchronous world time. This makes them active players in the game of the disproportionate. What we call modernity is complicity with the synchronous world-form; modernization is the adaptation of forms of life to synchronous world-routines; and modernism is the ethos of this adaptation as the existentialism of synchronization. It implies the ultimate form of egalitarianism as the equality of all before the homogeneous earthly present, which realizes itself as the equality of humans before the news. For news is not simply a world-language genre in the aforementioned sense among others, but simultaneously the adjustment from historicism to actualism. The news systems of today only become possible in a globalized world form where a homogeneous event space is probed for differences from previous states. The result of such probings is fed into the pipelines of the synchronous world media; these are, as it were, the performative of the eternal present of homogenized humanity with itself. Their only task is to inform the synchronized world of its synchronization.

There are always some heads of state meeting somewhere for some world summit on some subject; there are always some troops advancing, under some pretext and in some numbers, on some enemy who is accused of some crime; there are always some currencies falling below some previously unthinkable minimum levels; there are always some major firms merging with some others in some joint ventures. There are always some commemorations of some events in some past time taking place on some day with the sympathy of the general public; something is always so-and-so many years ago and can act as material for some generally consumed memory. There are always some works by some artists being somehow honoured in some retrospectives.

The staging of simultaneity takes place in two ways in the synchronous world: as a culture of currentness, the synchronous culture combs daily through the threads of events in global events to find those knots and differences that stand out sufficiently to attract attention; as an anniversary culture, it ensures that we maintain the same distance from all regionally powerful events from the past. It asserts the rule that all things which once advanced history as potencies and events are now transformed into homogeneous anniversary material. In this sense, the information system of the synchronous world guarantees our incipient post-historicity. We are living in a constant state of transition into it.

Whenever we have reason to think that this transition is irreversible, we also have reason to confirm modernization. Then we count each one of our steps into modernity. It is not implausible that we today, at a very conservative estimate, are located in the fifth modernity, because the Modern Age, as a modernization process, has progressed through at least four crises or major reactions: Counter-Reformation, Romanticism, vitalism, and fascism; consequently we are presently in transition to the sixth modernity, as the triumph of constructivism over regionalism and anti-globalism is becoming apparent before our eyes as the—for now—last anti-modernisms.

The persistent final event in the historical world is the current globalization as the production of the constant earthly present. For the current generations, this major man-made event runs through the middle of their lives. It is the monstrous in time. We can tell from it that Modern Age humans are—contrary to the claims of philosophies of history—essentially uninterested in making history, but more concerned with concluding history and bringing about post-historical conditions. The continuous movement toward the eternal present, in which the sum of all events would be zero, was the true project of modernity. In this sense, the idea of the Third Reich was not simply a fascistoid parody of Christian millenarism as it had developed from Joachim from Fiore to Lessing, Schelling, and Saint-Simon; at the same time, it remains the latent matrix for all demanding modernisms, because it was the first to grasp the logical form of a potentially final age with sufficiently formal standards. In order to be modern, perhaps even final, an age must be a third—at least structurally. An age is final if its constitution is such that no matter how much might happen in it, nothing during or after it could be epoch-making. Because of the temporal logic of its design, modernity is actually a constant dawning of a third or millenary age, an incessant crossing-over from history into post-history, a continuous transition into an end time without end. This cannot be any other way, because modernity's ambition to be an age of penetrating self-reflexivity is formally unsurpassable.

The soundness of this claim can be verified by means of a thought experiment in which we ask how, from the perspective of modernity, one might imagine a subsequent epoch. There are two kinds of answer to this: the catastrophic and the continuous. With catastrophic answers, one has to assume that modernization as a whole would be broken off through a completely incommensurable event and diverted in an unpredictable direction—either through a biosystemic disaster or a theological epiphany, or through an extraterrestrial intervention. If we exclude the catastrophic variants from the discourse of modernity and post-modernity on account of their excessive and irrational implications, that leaves only the continuous form of response. According to this, the only thing that could possibly succeed modernity would be a further, later, heightened aggregate state of modernity. Located within its own continuum, modernity is an enduringly accumulative process, and only keeps moving through continuous self-upgrade. That is why the 'project of modernity' futurizes itself. A world process that produces its own futures, however, corresponds to the concept of the millennium or of end time without end. In that sense, the non-excessive version of a theory of modernity is forced at least to admit to the millenarist aspect of the current world form. That is already far more than a conventional theory, one that is committed to a balanced middle ground and proclaims itself as critical, could grant. This concession would bring the monstrous character of modernity's temporal structure alarmingly into view. The conventional forms of modernism, pragmatism and populism resolutely turn a blind eye to the monstrous to which they belong; they are fanaticisms of normality.

Nonetheless, time has shown that in its temporal structure too, the nature of the Modern Age as the time of a crime is so disproportionate that it cannot be fully formulated in conventional theoretical or programmatic texts. There is no theory of the monstrous, only hyperbolic projections. One can utter them, just as the feeling of going insane can be articulated; one can confess to them as one confesses to sensing that one has committed a crime of an indeterminable nature in a dream. Like a radical suspicion towards oneself, participation in modernity can only be confessed to.

3. Art History and Nothingness History

Having discussed the monstrous as a spatial and temporal form of modernity, we should now speak of the monstrous in the object-forms of modernity. Any contemporary can easily convince themselves of the increasing presence of the artificial in Modern Age lifeworlds. Modernity as a campaign for the increase of comfort and routines of competence implies furnishing 'subjects' with ever more effective equipment for self-enhancement: we have long existed in technologized lifeworlds where classical and cybernetic machines are the leading factor in our shaping of existence. In the light of these evident phenomena, it is easy to assert the interpretation of modernization as artificialization. The law of modernity is the increasing employment of artificiality in all essential dimensions of existence. What is more difficult is defending this finding against the widespread and growing unease in modernness.[7] For the grammars of advanced civilizations are, for the time being, no help to us in the attempt to state the place of the artificial in the real.[8]

All traditional thought forms agree that they stir up a certain suspicion of nihilism toward artifacts; since Plato, the private parts of technology and the world of images have been considered deficient forms of Being; at least the self-assured monisms of the Indians let Samsara and Nirvana converge. Within the tradition of the thinking of Being, as embodied in the high forms of Western meta-physics, unease about the artificial is a solid constant. It expresses the fact that a language of Being is inadequate for articulating what machines, sign systems, and works of art are 'according to their nature.' It seems to be their nature to break with what nature typically is. For everything that is a work claims to negate substantial Being through representation and to augment it with invented additions. If anything in the Western tradition is exempt from the suspicion of being mere illusion and nothingness, it is the 'great works' of art, to which even classical thought—reluctantly, as it were—grants a preferred participation in substance and the soul, despite their extreme artificiality.

It is not without significance that some have attempted in recent art history to show that images are based more fundamentally on cult than artifice. Cult too is a derivative of Being; it cloaks the images in a gestural, religious, indeed physiological meaning; it wants the foam of signs to begin from the flesh of things, from ritually harnessed life itself. This is easy to understand: if one presupposes the primacy of Being, artificialities can only be viewed as ontological bastards in which part of Being's wealth had unrightfully been seized by nothingness. Aesthetics and technology theory under the sign of Being always and inevitably lead to more or less explicit denunciations of the 'illusory world' as a sphere comprising unnecessary additions to an older stock. Works of art, like those of technology, are really the children of nothingness—at best, half-siblings of the truly existent [*des wahren Seienden*]; they are constructs of ontological injustice, devoid of archetypes and only comprehensible as dilutions of opulence, uncovered in their origins and insubstantial in the strong sense of the word. In them, a supplementary nothing tricks its way into the dense world of natural and essential orders.

One can understand how, with the fundamental growth of the artificial factor in modernity, this line of thought would have to result in a totalizing criticism of the artificial worlds' abandonment by Being [*Seinsverlassenheit*]. The last thinkers of Being inevitably view themselves as the last ones alive in an environment of colorful death—that is, machines, simulacra, and streams of signifiers. For them, the most recent phase of art history is a *danse macabre* illuminated by lost leftovers of souls. The artificial world, viewed with the eyes of the faithful ancients, putrefies as nihilistic voluntarism. At the center, the curator sits enthroned as the pope of abandonment by reason (or alternatively the director, features editor, cultural consultant, or festival director). Heidegger countered this artificial and ontologically secondary world with a first nature still backed by the opulence of origin:

> The birch never exceeds its possibilities. The colony of bees dwells within its possibilities. It is only the will, which established itself in technology with universal validity, that drags the earth into the exhaustion, exploitation, and alteration of the artificial. It forces the earth beyond the developed circle of its possibilities into something that is no longer the possible, and is therefore the impossible.[9]

Anyone who wants to read the history of art and technology as a history of Being—as Heidegger's case illustrates—will find nothing but terminations everywhere: forgetfulness of Being, the end of art history as an interpretation of substance, the plunge of humanity into the impossible and multimedial for dead souls. One cannot escape the necessity of admitting to oneself that the history of the artificial can no longer be developed in the style of the history of Being. The artificial thing—if conceived from the perspective of Being—will never shake off the suspicion of a betrayal of an initial wealth of sense and the soul. The thinking of Being is not sufficient for an understanding of what constitutes modernity: de-animism in action and redistribution of subjectivity among humans and things. While the advanced civilizations were founded on the discovery and development of the difference between subject and object or soul and thing, modernity destabilized these time-honored distinctions along with their oversimplifying power. This sets in motion a progressive redistribution in which what were things of the soul are shifted to the sphere of things and the previously subjective into the scope of the objective. Gotthard Günther, to whom we owe the most advanced theory of technology in the twentieth century, points to the world-historical purpose of these shifts: "In the history of technology until now, the relationship between subject and object has been mistakenly described, insofar as traditional thought assigns to the realm of the soul an overflowing wealth of qualities that actually belong on the side of things, where they can be understood as mechanisms of a higher order."[10] This leads to an unlimitedly far-reaching program of corrections to the image of themselves that humans fashioned in the period of advanced civilizations. "The process of this correction is to be the central issue in the next major period of world history."[11] Modernity as the millennium of progressive artificialization then has its substance in the technical as the 'progressive conquest of nothingness.' The depth of the future can only be thought today as a complex of growth dimensions of the artificial. Such an increase, however, can no longer be viewed as a phase in the history of Being; if one is to deal with it conceptually, it must be treated as the unfolding history of nothingness. Nothingness is increasingly transpiring as the true element of progressive capacity. If thought must correspond to Being, then correspondences with nothing are daring leaps into the operation: wanting, acting, and composing are then adequate responses to the realization that in nothingness, although nothing can be identified, anything can be achieved. In this sense, one can say that nothingness is the element of modernity; its beginning was, and shall ever remain, the deed—or, in modern parlance, the undertaking. Through the operatively capable will, enormous steps can be taken in nothingness to increase artificialization; these will provide later thought with the blueprints for reflection on beings.

If, almost three thousand years ago, classical thought developed under the overwhelming impression of a supposedly ever-complete nature with a seemingly insurmountable head start on all human action (which provides the logical basis for religious feeling), this thought, already precise, also articulates—despite feeling overwhelmed by the Being before it—a mental deed with its own ontological weight whose most distant consequences would only reveal themselves in modernity. By seeking to contemplate the nature of natures, classical reason produced the characteristically metaphysical semblance of sublime calm. Its elements were spirit or stone, both understood as the extreme substantialities that were above all action and made the respective other seem meaningless beside them.[12] Modern thought, on the other hand, is dazed from its own might; it notices itself as power, consummation, and capability; increasingly disconcerted, activated and attentive to its own acts, it follows man-made history, which must finally be carried out systematically. It interferes to a constantly growing extent in 'that which is.' In the course of its elevation, it had to approach a point from which the human will would become sufficiently powerful to become a rival of classical substance. Now nature and Being lost their ontological monopoly: they found themselves provoked and replaced by successions of artificial creations out of nothingness and the rise of a post-natural world of the will.

It is hardly surprising that the strongholds of Being in the age of advanced civilizations always saw a dark shadow creeping around them—it was that same nothingness which could initially (under the predominance of a monovalent concept of Being in which only Being is, and nothingness is not) only be imagined as that which goes against Being, as the void that fools humans with illusions and phantoms. With modern nihilism, however, the power of humans to commit unprecedented and fathomless acts and invent new things, a prime characteristic of the Modern Age, was officially recognized and presented generally under a striking, albeit still defamatory, name: nothing now became something—the ontological field presented itself as multivalent. Since then, the malignant appearance of the nothingness of nihilism has peeled away. As we now know, the nothingness of nihilism represents the reverse of creativity—and what modernity would allow itself to be deprived of its birthright to creative life and projections of the will? For the entire world time of coming states of modernity, no doubts are possible about the primacy of the will to artificiality over the willingness to submit to a defined nature or a normative antiquity. No neo-Catholic trends can change that. At the core of modernity, once its conception has been taken further, only inventors, artists, and entrepreneurs can play a key role in shaping themselves—and no longer thinkers, in the strict sense of the philosophical tradition. It is obvious that 'thought' per se, as a correlate to beings, is becoming a merely partial function of the culture of will and projects. The shepherds of Being—trapped in the beautiful dream of pure extra-technological existentiality and a purely obedient reflection—move toward the sidelines; in fact, Being itself, as the realm of past freedom, now seems like a narrow ontological province—it has been pushed to the periphery of the nothing-'based' empire of will, creations and projects.

One can now observe a flight from Being [*Seins-Flucht*], just as there was a rural flight to the cities; the new entrepreneurs in the project space, the artists, the organizers, the writers of programs and also the entrepreneurs in the traditional sense are constantly emigrating from the old world of contemplatively sheltered Being to settle dynamically in the new world of the nothingness that is open for projects. The typical gesture of these escapees of Being is the assumption of leadership by a constructivity reaching for a power that is based on capably continuing. Entrepreneurs and artists do not guard or conserve what 'there is'; they unleash and create works from what has never existed in that form, constantly repulsing the given. Old Being and its beings find themselves overgrown with an increasingly powerful supplement of new realizations whose results spread as acts of artificialization in cultures of apparatus and images.

What was once called Being already resembles a chapel standing amidst skyscrapers—or a proof of God's existence on a computer printout. Out of glass and steel, new working materials and new writing systems, grows an unclosable in-between world that cannot be controlled by any synthesis, and is neither nature nor a will to novelty still incubating unrealized, but rather a crystallized world of apparatus as past will, along with technical refuse as waste from the mass of devalued artifacts; giant cities, museums, and rubbish heaps are typical contemporary products of the monstrous as an industry.

Since the seventeenth century, the activation revolution has developed into a self-motivating escalation system. Its consistent success ensures that an end of art history is no more the case than an end of technological history or an end of state history. There is no reason not to believe that the best is being created at this moment or is yet to come. Anyone who thinks they are seeing the imminent end of whatever lies ahead is drawing mistaken conclusions about world events on the basis of fatigue. What genuinely ends is the possibility of thinking over the histories of art, technology, and the will from the perspective of a history of Being. Modernity as a world process escalates further, reaching the time of the crime of the openly monstrous; for it remains the form of consummation for an unreconsiderable history of nothingness that primarily has power over reality. The realization that the old natures still require nurturing within it leads, in our time, to the growth of an idea—a historically unprecedented type of conservatism as a space of green concern. Configuring the latter productively with the freedom-historical results of modern forms of society and life: such a task now marks the foremost frontline of the thought that was once called philosophical.

Mankind, therefore, where it extends its horizons of will in constantly expanded routines, can look out into a broadly arranged depth of temporal layers. In this era, whoever relies purely on Being will experience wear on all fronts. The power of continuous modernity is the impossibility of exhausting nothingness.

9

THE SELFLESS REVANCHIST

A Note on Cioran

One can gauge the significance, or at least the independence, of a thinker not least by how long and by what means he eludes his emulators, even those who purport to be faithful commentators or to have been called upon to develop his impulses. In this respect, Cioran might without further inquiry have to be reckoned among the most significant philosophical writers of the twentieth century, since in a manner other than the star philosophers of existentialism, Critical Theory, or poststructuralism, who achieved their goals in protest of imitation, Cioran invested his intellectual suffering entirely in his inimitability. Yet the concept of significance does not do justice to the phenomenon that is Cioran, since the fundamental impetus of his thought is not that of seeing his name registered in a history of ideas or in an account of great authors. Rather, he wants to see that his pride in defending his inimitability against students and copycats is satisfied. While the great masters of the modern culture of dissidence, that is to say, Heidegger, Sartre, Adorno, and Derrida, could reckon their successes in multitudes of emulators, Cioran, more proud, more demonic, more despairing than they were, recognizes his success in discouraging potential emulators already when they are on the brink of making the attempt. He knew that all emulation ends up in parody and that whoever takes his ideas more seriously than their success shields them from the parodies that follow their impact.

The question is thus how one manages to transition from emulative negativity, which as revolutionary engagement, radical critique, aesthetic anarchism, or deconstructivist subversion forms a school, to an inimitable, completely idiosyncratic negativity that nonetheless shines light on the whole. In this context, we might recall the relevant difference in late ancient Egyptian and Syrian monasticism between friars living in cloisters and anchorites, of which the first, according to an observation by Hugo Ball, existed as athletes of mourning, while the second existed as athletes of despair. It cannot be doubted that Cioran's place in this alternative must be sought among the anchorites, those who have withdrawn and cut themselves off from the terrestrial realm. In this position, it is no longer a matter of struggling with and reworking beings according to critical methods, but rather of putting God and the world on trial by holding one's own shattered existence against them as proof of their failure and waywardness. While critical or subversive negativity has the effect of forming schools to the degree that its standpoint can be charted, established, copied, and simulated in beings, despairing negativity withdraws into an exile that cannot be taught, is fathomless, and cannot be emulated. In the elaboration of this position of exile lie Cioran's singular strengths. After Kierkegaard, he is the only thinker of distinction who had the irrevocable insight that no one can despair according to sure methods.

Whoever intends to obtain his *doctorat* should not take the trouble to first ask Cioran whether he would like to supervise the work. The distance from the world that is characteristic of critical theorists, aesthetic anarchists, and deconstructivists is always based on a reserve from which the respective schools claim, not unjustly, that within limits they can be learned by means of a method. What Husserl called the *epochē*, the break with the natural attitude, means nothing other than the perfectible practice of opting out of the stream of gesticulating, intending, involved life. To this belongs the methodical cheerfulness of theory's spectating disposition, even for mournful miens. In contrast, Cioran works with a pathological *epochē*, of which it cannot be ascertained how one should copy or convey it. His uprootedness is not grounded in a theoretical distancing from a normal and naive life; it arises from the curse of finding oneself to be a really existing anomaly. His reserve is anything but methodological, it is demonic. In his case, critique was preceded by torture. While ordinary critical theory, to say nothing of ordinary positive theory, distances itself from merely living out one's life, in order to emancipate the thinker from his conditions and provide him with the resources to resist and rework the real, desperate theory is only interested in bearing witness to the failure of the construct of reality as such. Its distance is not taken up arbitrarily, but rather can be found already before all theory as an effect of a suffering in the thinker.

Cioran's Archimedean point, from which he unhinges the normative view of the world and its philosophical and ethical superstructure, is the discovery of the privilege of sleeping, from which all other minds, not least such as take themselves to be relentlessly critical, profit as though from something self-evident. His unparalleled clear-sightedness in the disenchantment of all positive and utopian constructs has its basis in the pervasive stigma of his existence—in a sleeplessness that was undoubtedly of a psychogenic character and which marked him for years in his formative phase. This is what lends an envenomed *epochē* to the thinker, Cioran. The insomniac knows, in contradistinction to the critic, that he is not the master of his premises. Insomnia is not an assumption that is made, not a disposition of the practicing subject, not a provisional vacation from one's own life in support of a pure attentiveness, and certainly not a theoretical preparatory exercise for practical revolution. A putting into question of existence and its fictions imposes itself on the insomniac, which reaches deeper than any reflective, subversive, or aggressive deconstruction. For the subject of insomnia the evidence is produced, in a way that is not sought, that all acts of both the naive and the critical life are descendants of the privilege of sleep, which again and again makes possible for its possessors the return to a minimal vital illusion. Sleep fulfills the tired human being's demand for relief by means of discreet downfalls of the world; it is the small change of the redemption from evil; its coming to pass answers the natural prayer of fatigue. Cioran's insomnia-apriori, in contrast, opens up for thought the possibility that the subject's plea for a temporary cancellation of the world's compulsion of life is not answered. It is in this sense the meditation of the unanswered, which must be endured as continual wakefulness. Such an existence is a kind of torture in which the torturer is not identified and his questions not precisely posed. Already the early Cioran thinks from the position of a permanent ontological crucifixion that never reaches the point at which the victim may say *consummatum est*. Because sleeplessness is not a work, neither one that redeems nor one that is enlightening, it can never be declared to be finished. The insomniac is not nailed to the cross of reality, but rather is included in the gelatinous mass of the half-real. He finds out that what is gelatinous is more implacable than what is hard. While one is shattered by the latter and meets his end, one is wrecked by the former and remains spared for endless continuations. Sleeplessness is deconstruction without deconstructivists.

Cioran often noted that the characteristic impulse of his thought and writing was the reversal of a curse into a distinction. But how can the crippling effect of lost sleep be reversed into an active disposition? In a twofold way: insofar as the author, as he says himself, changes his being worn down into something chosen, and insofar as he gains an intense desire for vengeance from his forced vigilance.

With both turnings, Cioran proves himself to be a Judeo-Christian theologian in the Nietzschean sense of the term. The analyses from *Beyond Good and Evil* and *On the Genealogy of Morality* on the origin of the spirit of the theologian from out of *ressentiment* are initially fully accurate when applied to him. Cioran is in fact a theologian of reactive wrath, who imputes to the creator God his failure and to the created world its inability to take him in. In the mode of his reaction, Cioran reveals himself to be a dark doppelganger of Heidegger. Where the latter elaborated the crypto-Catholic thesis that thinking means thanking, Cioran unfolds the black-Gnostic counter-thesis that thinking means avenging oneself. In both cases thinking is a corresponding: a logical gathering and giving back of that which was sent to the thinker as a gift of Being. But while Heidegger's thoughtful giving back—after its heroic beginnings— subsides into a mild, positive wanting-to-be-an-answer, in Cioran the instinct for an immense restitution remains acute. It is always clear to him that where there is a gift there is always a giver who remains to be exposed. While the spirit of the fundamental ontologist, relieved by sleep, continually and gratefully meditates anew on Being as giver and gift [*Gabe*], the consciousness which revolts, continually sharpened by the deprivation of sleep, devotes itself to the task of transforming the poison of Being [*Seinsgift*] in its own existence into precise powers of immunity and of denouncing the poisoner. *Nihil contra venenum nisi venenum ispe.*[1]

Cioran's singularity can be recognized in the fact that he developed a systematically revanchist praxis of thinking. He did not declaim against the temptations of Being and invitations to faith as an avenger in some private affair, nor as someone debased and aggrieved in the sociological sense, but rather as a medium of a transcendental wrath and as an agent of an offensive skepticism. He is a wrathful Job, who displays his defects as striking arguments against the sadistic creator. As the guardian of a chosen wrath he is as selfless as only the founder of an ascetic order could be. As guardian of his pride in this wrath he is as egomaniacal as only a Satanist could be. His philosophical revanchism is the negative of thoughtful thankfulness. Like no one else in this or any century he made it clear that thinking is a thankless occupation—especially when the intelligible future today belongs less than ever before to thinking, which is not able to move beyond meditating and stewing in its wrath, than it does to the will that formulates projects and sets operations in motion. Cioran is only lucid in not-willing, while willing for him— as for his distant kinsman Heidegger—remains an alien mode. He never sets foot in the world of willing; his whole life long he will hear nothing of what is pragmatic. He is suspicious of those who are able to believe. His hatred applies to those who are able to will.

His thankless thought lapsed into absurdity, because in him the impulse for vengeance against God extends further than does the belief in God. Under the auspices of the absurd, Cioran, the son of a priest, reaped an anachronistic aftercrop of the era of religious metaphysics, by contriving for himself the role of the reactionary blasphemer. He toppled the idols that were no longer up to date; he holed up in his garret like an anchorite, whose ascetic practice consists in piling up disappointments. By virtue of his revanchism, Cioran held onto a juvenile, vicious negativity his whole life long. It was his early and never revised pride in not lowering himself to maturity. This is what makes his writings so uniquely dense, insistent, and monotonous. He knew that his malaise was his strength and that he as an author should only treat a single theme so as not to sink into arbitrariness. He grasped it early enough: his only chance consisted in repeating himself. Sartre's critical words, that vice is on principle the love of failure,[2] registers what Cioran should have chosen as his motto. In contrast to Nietzsche, another son of a clergyman of whom there is continual talk, Cioran marked an important point through his insistence on revenge. If the former was committed to the attempt to bank his thought completely on aristocratic, affirmative, and non-reactive drives, Cioran abandoned himself to a descent into the hell of a non-aristocratism and reaction. On the basis of his degradation he also bore within himself the discovery that there is a magnanimity of vengeance which rivals all-affirming thought. His work is vengeance without an avenger and payback that knows no loss.

For this reason, his writings have therapeutic effects. Their clarity in forlornness immunizes against the temptation to amorphously surrender. In a manner different than Nietzsche, Cioran did not behave like someone who has overcome his own decadence, perhaps because he even saw through Nietzsche's ultimate illusion, the sick dream of a great health. He accepted his decadence, his morbidity, his foreordained condemnation to skepticism as poisons of Being and distilled his writings as antidotes. The knowers and the needy may make use of this as it seems wise to them. Yet the emulators will not find in Cioran's apothecary what their ambition seeks.

I recall a conversation with the old Cioran in the German House of the Cité Universitaire in Paris in the mid-1980s, in the course of which I brought the conversation around to his suspicious and disparaging statements about Epicurus. He immediately seemed to understand what I had in mind with my query. He candidly explained that he recanted his claims and now felt Epicurus to be very close, that he saw in him today one of the real benefactors of humanity. The word 'benefactor,' quietly uttered aloud, sounded oddly significant on his tongue. For on this occasion he dispensed with any sarcasm. Perhaps the recognition had ripened in the garden of his sleeplessness that there is need of a special kind of generosity that allows the human being a retreat from the fronts of the real, and that this world can less than ever do without teachers of retreat. Our century has known none more decisive than him.

10

"AN ESSENTIAL TENDENCY TOWARD NEARNESS LIES IN DASEIN"[1]

Marginalia to Heidegger's Doctrine of Existential Place

It seems to have been clear to only a few Heidegger interpreters that under the sensational programmatic title of *Being and Time* there is also an embryonically revolutionary treatise on Being and space. Under the spell of Heidegger's existential analytic of time, it has for the most part been overlooked that the latter is anchored in a corresponding analytic of space, just as both are in turn grounded in an existential analytic of movement. Hence it comes about that one can read a whole library on Heidegger's doctrine of temporalization and historicity—ontochronology—a few treatises on his doctrine of movedness [*Bewegtheit*] or ontokinetics, yet nothing on his attempts at a theory of the primordial making room [*Einräumung*] for space [*Raum*] or ontotopology—except for pietistic paraphrases unfit to be cited.

Heidegger's inquiry achieves a positive portrayal of the spatiality of Dasein as *bringing near* and *orientation* over the course of two destructive steps. It is in fact the concepts of space in 'vulgar' physics as well as in metaphysics that must be cleared away before the existential analytic of Being-in can be addressed.

What does *Being-in* mean? Initially, we supplement the expression Being-in with the phrase "in the world," and are inclined to understand this Being-in as "Being-in something." With this term, the kind of Being of a being is named which is "in" something else, as water is "in" the glass, the dress is "in" the closet. . . . Water and glass, dress and closet, are both "in" space "at" a location in the same way. This relation of Being can be expanded; that is, the bench in the lecture hall, the lecture hall in the university, the university in the city, and so on until: the bench in "world space." These beings whose being "in" one another can be determined in this way all have the same kind of Being—that of being objectively present—as things occurring "within" the world. . . .

In contrast, Being-in designates a constitution of Being of Dasein, and is an *existential*. But we cannot understand by this the objective presence of a material thing (the human body) "in" a being objectively present. . . . "In" stems from *innan-*, to reside, *habitare*, to dwell. "*An*" means I am used to, familiar with, I take care of something. It has the meaning of *colo* in the sense of *habito* and *diligo*. Being as the infinitive of "I am": that is, understood as an existential, means to dwell near, to be familiar with.[2]

With the reference to the old German verb *innan*, inhabiting, Heidegger already early on in his inquiry reveals the point of the existential analysis of spatiality. What he calls Being-in-the-world means nothing other than "to in" the world in a transitively verbal sense: residing in it while enjoying its disclosure in attunements and instances of reaching out accomplished in advance. Because Dasein is always already an accomplished act of residing—a result of a primal leap into inhabiting—spatiality inseparably belongs to existence. The talk of inhabiting the world does not amount to simply imputing domesticity on a colossal scale to those who exist: for it is precisely being-able-to-be-at-home in the world that is in question, and to proceed from it as though it were a given would already be a regression to the container model of physics that is supposed to be overcome here; this is, incidentally, the error in reasoning that is committed in all holistic world-pictures and doctrines of uterine immanence and can be found rigidified in pious half-thoughts. The house [*Haus*] of Being, however, is also not an enclosure [*Gehäuse*] in which those existing enter and exit. Its structure is more comparable to an orb of care in which Dasein has spread itself out in a primordial being-outside-itself. Heidegger's radical phenomenological attentiveness cuts the ground from under the multi-millennial reigns of the container model of physics and metaphysics: the human being is neither a living being in its environing world nor a rational being in the heavenly vault nor a perceiving being within the interior of God. Consequently, even idle chatter about the environment [*Umwelt*], which has been in the ascendant since the 1920s, is also subject to the phenomenological critique: biology does not think, just as little as does any other standard science. "The saying used so often today 'Human beings have their environment' does not say anything ontologically as long as 'having' is undetermined."[3] But what is meant by the "aroundness of the environment"?

> According to what we have said, Being-in is not a 'quality' which Dasein sometimes has and sometimes does not have, *without* which it could *be* just as well as it could with it. It is not the case that human being 'is,' and then on top of that has a relation of being to the 'world' which it sometimes takes upon itself. Dasein is never 'initially' a sort of a being which is free from Being-in, but which at times is in the mood to take up a 'relation' to the world. This taking up of relations to the world is possible only *because*, as Being-in-the-world, Dasein is as it is. This constitution of Being is not first derived from the fact that besides the being which has the character of Dasein there are other beings which are objectively present and meet up with it. These other beings can only 'meet up' 'with' Dasein because they are able to show themselves of their own accord within a *world*.[4]

Traditional thought's existential blindness to space manifests itself in the ancient world-pictures, insofar as they integrate the human being, more or less without further ado, into an enclosing nature as cosmos.[5] In modern thought, Descartes's division of substances into thinking substances and extended substances provides the severest example of the unwillingness to consider the place of 'meeting up' as still particularly worthy of question. Because everything that Descartes has to say on the theme of spatiality remains based on the complex of body and thing as the sole bearers of extension, the question of where thinking and extension meet up cannot occur to him. The thinking thing remains an authority without a world, which, oddly enough, seems to be able to entertain the fanciful notion that it sometimes takes up a relation to extended things and sometimes does not. The *res cogitans* bears features of a spectral hunter who braces himself for excursions into what is recognizably extended, only to withdraw afterward into his worldless stronghold in that which is without extension. Heidegger responds to this with the primordial Being-in of Dasein in the sense of Being-in-the-world. Even knowledge is only a derivative mode of dwelling in the spaciousness of the world that is disclosed by circumspective concern:

> In directing itself toward ... and in grasping something, Dasein does not first go outside of the inner sphere in which it is initially encapsulated, but, rather, in its primary kind of Being, it is always already 'outside' together with some being

encountered in the world already discovered. Nor is any inner sphere abandoned when Dasein dwells together with a being to be known and determines its character. Rather, even in this 'being outside' together with its object, Dasein is 'inside,' correctly understood; that is, it itself exists as the Being-in-the-world which knows. Again, the perception of what is known does not take place as a return with one's booty to the 'cabinet' [*Gehäuse*] of consciousness after one has gone out and grasped it. Rather, in perceiving, preserving, and retaining, the Dasein that knows *remains outside as Dasein.*[6]

In his positive statements concerning the spatiality of Dasein, Heidegger emphasizes above all two characteristics: de-distancing and directionality.

De-distancing means making distance disappear, making the being at a distance of something disappear, bringing it near. Dasein is essentially de-distancing. . . . Initially and for the most part, de-distancing is a circumspect approaching, a bringing near as supplying, preparing, having at hand. . . . *An essential tendency toward nearness lies in Dasein.*[7]
. . . In accordance with its spatiality, Dasein is initially never here, but over there. From this over there it comes back to its here. . . .[8]
As Being-in which de-distances, Dasein has at the same time the character of *directionality.* Every bringing near has always taken a direction in a region beforehand from which what is de-distanced approaches. . . . Circumspect heedfulness is a directional de-distancing.[9]
Letting innerworldly beings be encountered, which is constitutive for Being-in-the-world, is 'giving space.' This 'giving space,' which we call *making room*, frees things at hand for their spatiality. . . . As circumspect taking care of things in the world, Dasein can change things around, remove them or 'make room' for them only because making room—understood as an existential—belongs to its Being-in-the-world. . . . The 'subject,' correctly understood ontologically, Dasein, is spatial.[10]

Whoever would have believed that the big show was about to begin after these powerfully worded opening acts would have seen his expectation disappointed. The existential where-analysis transitions in one fell swoop to a who-analysis, with no mention whatsoever of the fact that only the beginning of a thread had been drawn out, a thread that for the most part remained on the spool. Had one

unfurled it further the polysemous universes of existential spaciousness would have inevitably opened up, which are expressed anew by
the key term 'spheres.' Inhabiting spheres, however, cannot be expli-
cated in detail, as long as Dasein is conceived above all by means
of a supposedly essential tendency toward solitude.[11] The analytic
of the existential 'where' demands that one bracket all suggestions
and moods of essential solitude, in order to be assured of the deep
structures of accompanied and supplemented Dasein. In view of
this task, the early Heidegger remained an existentialist in the problematic sense of the term. His swift turn to the who-question leaves
behind a solitary, weak, hysterical-heroic existential subject that
intends to be first when it comes to dying, and which lives wretch-
edly in suspense over the concealed features of its embeddedness in
intimacies and solidarities. An inflated 'who' in a confused 'where'
may be in store for very bad surprises when, given the occasion, it
wants to anchor itself in the next best people [Volk].

When, during the 'national revolution,' Heidegger was carried
away by imperial delirium and wanted to enjoy being a bigshot, it
became apparent that existentiell authenticity without a radical clarification of its situation leads to blindness. From 1934, Heidegger
knew, even if only implicitly, that his enthusiasm [Bewegtheit] for
the National Socialist uprising had been a Being-in-the-slipstream:
here time had become space. Whoever is pulled into the slipstream
appears to be here while he lives in another sphere, on a distant stage,
in an opaque inner There. Heidegger's late work discreetly draws
the consequences of the lapse. The deceived nationalist [völkische]
revolutionary expects only little from the history that is taking place
around him; he has retired from the work of power. In the future,
he will seek his salvation in still more intimate nearness exercises.
He tenaciously sticks to his anarchic province and arranges guided
tours through the house of Being, i.e., language—an entirely magical
concierge, equipped with heavy keys, always ready to meaningfully
beckon. In animated moments he evokes the sacred Parmenidean
sphere of Being, as though he had returned to the Eleatic, tired
of historicity as of an unholy specter. Heidegger's late work plays
out, ever anew, the resigned figures of a revolutionary deepening of
thought, without ever again reaching the point from which the question of the primordial and always already universal making room
for the world could have been fruitfully taken up.

The project of Spheres can also be understood as an attempt
to salvage—at least in one essential aspect—the project Being and
Space, which was tucked into Heidegger's early work as a sub-
theme, from its entombment. We are of the opinion that as much of
Heidegger's interest in rootedness as can be saved comes into its own

through a theory of pairs, of geniuses, and of supplemented existence. To have grasped hold of a ground in the existing duality: this
much autochthony or anchoring in the real must also be retained,
even if philosophy continues to vigilantly pursue its indispensable
escape from the empirical commune. For thought, it is now a matter
of working through the tension between autochthony (*ab ovo* and in
regard to the community) and liberation (in regard to death or the
infinite) anew.

Notes

Preface

1 See the first section of chapter 3.
2 For the critique of emergency reasoning, cf. Bazon Brock, *Die Re-Dekade: Kunst und Kultur der 8oer Jahre* (Munich: Klinkhardt and Biermann, 1990); as well as Heiner Mühlmann, *The Nature of Cultures: A Blueprint for a Theory of Culture Genetics*, trans. Robert Payne (Vienna: Springer, 1996); Heiner Mühlmann, *Kunst und Krieg: Heiner Mühlmann über Bazon Brock; Das säuische Behagen in der Kultur* (Cologne: Salon, 1998).
3 Peter Sloterdijk, *L'heure du crime et le temps de l'œuvre d'art*, trans. Olivier Mannoni (Paris: Calmann-Lévy, 2000).
4 Cf. Peter Sloterdijk, *La domestication de l'être: Pour un éclaircissement de la clairière*, trans. Olivier Mannoni (Paris: Éditions Milles et une nuits, 2000).
5 [*Schickliche Übertreibung des Wahren.* Quintilian's phrase is rendered as *eine schickliche Übersteigerung des Wahren,* or "a proper straining of the truth," in the third section of chapter 4.]

1 The Plunge and the Turn

1 The expression refers to a lecture series held by *Südwestfunk Baden-Baden* [Southwest Radio, Baden-Baden] and the *Städtische Bühnen Freiburg* [Urban Stages of Freiburg] in collaboration with the *Institut für soziale Gegenwartsfragen* [Institute for Contemporary Social Questions], Freiburg, at the *Großen Haus* [Main Stage] of the City Theater from 1995 on.
2 The audiobook, Peter Sloterdijk, *Ödipus oder Das zweite Orakel* (Cologne: supposé, 1999), on two CDs, offers an excerpt from my Karlsruhe lectures on Greek drama.
3 Paul Virilio's Platonizing thesis takes aim at the critical moment when

the theater becomes the political mass medium from out of the medium of the cultic community: "What we have on the ancient theater stage is already actual *plagiarism of the visible world*. The first mass media, designed to crack open the secret and educate public opinion, are just a trick effect of reality." Paul Virilio, *The Art of the Motor*, trans. Julie Rose (Minneapolis: University of Minnesota Press, 1995), 29.

4 Cf. Klaus Schneider, *Die schweigenden Götter. Eine Studie zur Gottesvorstellung des religiösen Platonismus* (Hildesheim: Olms, 1966).

5 Julian Jaynes contests this, by pointing to an even more ancient epiphanic formation: the hallucinatory system of what he calls the "bicameral psyche"; cf. Julian Jaynes, *The Origin of Consciousness in the Breakdown of the Bicameral Mind* (Boston: Houghton Mifflin, 1977).

6 Cf. my *Thinker on Stage: Nietzsche's Materialism*, trans. Jamie Owen Daniel, foreword by Jochen Schulte-Sasse (Minneapolis: University of Minnesota Press, 1989); and also my *Nietzsche Apostle*, trans. Steve Corcoran (Los Angeles: Semiotext(e), 2013).

7 We leave aside the question to what extent the logo-kinetics of the Neoplatonist Proclus, especially his doctrine of the circular structure of intellect and the soul's circular courses, can be regarded as a precursor to Heidegger's onto-kinetics.

8 [The German word *Fall* can also mean 'case,' which itself comes from the Latin *casus*, meaning 'fall,' and *Ernstfall* can mean 'emergency.']

9 Cf. Elias Canetti, *The Numbered*, trans. Carol Stewart (London: Martin Boyars, 1984).

10 Hans Jonas already presented ancient Gnosticism in its fundamental ontological expressions along these lines in his dissertation, *Der Begriff der Gnosis* (Göttingen: Hubert, 1930), written under Heidegger. [An abridged English version is available under Hans Jonas, *The Gnostic Religion: The Message of the Alien God and the Beginnings of Christianity*, 3rd ed. (Boston: Beacon, 2001).] Barbara Merker pointed out analogies between the Gnostic mythos and Heidegger's 'conversion to authenticity' in her book *Selbsttäuschung und Selbsterkenntnis. Zu Heideggers Transformation der Phänomenologie Husserls* (Frankfurt: Suhrkamp, 1988), 176–193.

11 Martin Heidegger, *Being and Time*, trans. John Macquarrie and Edward Robinson (New York: Harper & Row, 1962), 178–180 [translation modified; here and in what follows, page references to *Being and Time* are to those of the German edition indicated in the margins of the translation].

12 Cf. my "Was heißt: sich übernehmen? Versuch über die Bejahung," in Peter Sloterdijk, *Weltfremdheit*, 6th ed. (Frankfurt: Suhrkamp, 1999), 267–293.

13 Heidegger, *Being and Time*, 299.

14 Ibid., 297.

15 Heidegger's choice in 1933 gives occasion to emphasize this. For the "fitting in with and adapting to the entire prevailing and fate of the world in general" of which Heidegger already speaks in the great metaphysics lecture course from Winter 1929–1930 is not to be thought without ambiguity, choice and decision [Martin Heidegger,

The Fundamental Concepts of Metaphysics: World, Finitude, Solitude,
trans. William McNeill and Nicholas Walker (Bloomington: Indiana
University Press, 1995), 28]. Even the 'prevailing' [*das 'Waltende'*] can
only be conceived as a kind of play that is operative in multiple ways
and does not seize hold of things in a univocal fashion.

16 [Literally, *Urteil* means 'primal division.']
17 References to this idea can be found in the contributions to the volume
edited by Michael Eldred, entitled *Twisting Heidegger: Drehversuche
parodistischen Denkens* (Cuxhaven: Junghans, 1993), especially in those
of Raffael Capurro, John Sallis, and John D. Caputo. The last-men-
tioned author concretizes the demand, raised not for the first time, to
think with Heidegger against Heidegger in his book *Demythologizing
Heidegger* (Bloomington: Indiana University Press, 1993).
18 Heidegger, *Being and Time*, 179.
19 Ibid., 180.
20 Ibid., 177 [translation modified].
21 Martin Heidegger, "What Is Metaphysics?," trans. David Farrell Krell,
in *Pathmarks*, ed. William McNeill (Cambridge: Cambridge University
Press, 1998), 87.
22 Johann Gottlieb Fichte, *Science of Knowledge; with the First and Second
Introductions*, ed. and trans. Peter Heath and John Lachs (Cambridge:
Cambridge University Press, 1982), 162n.2.
23 [In English in the original.]
24 Concerning the interlocking natural and technological historicity of
the human position, cf. below the essay "The Domestication of Being:
The Clarification of the Clearing." The motif "foundered as animals" is
taken up below in the speech "Rules for the Human Park."
25 Cf. Werner Jaeger, *Paideia: The Ideals of Greek Culture*, 3 vols., 2nd
ed., trans. Gilbert Highet (Oxford: Oxford University Press, 1986).
26 Plutarch, *Moralia*, vol. 4, trans. Frank Cole Babbitt (Cambridge, MA:
Harvard University Press, 1927–2004), 383–421.
27 Cited in Hugo Ott, *Martin Heidegger: A Political Life*, trans. Allan
Blunden (London: Basic Books, 1993), 202.
28 Martin Heidegger, "The Point of Reference," in *Bremen and Freiburg
Lectures: Insight into That Which Is and Basic Principles of Thinking*,
trans. Andrew J. Mitchell (Bloomington: Indiana University Press,
2012), 4.
29 Cf. Bruno Latour, *We Have Never Been Modern*, trans. Catherine
Porter (Cambridge, MA: Harvard University Press, 1993), 126.
30 Cf. John C. Caputo, "Heidegger's Essentialism," in *Demythologizing
Heidegger*, 118–130.
31 [Friedrich Hölderlin, "Memnosyne (Third Version)," in Hölderlin,
Poems and Fragments, trans. Michael Hamburger (London: Anvil Press
Poetry, 2004), 587.]
32 Cf. Gilles Deleuze, "Plato, the Greeks," in *Essays Critical and Clinical*,
trans. Daniel W. Smith and Michael A. Greco (Minneapolis: University
of Minnesota Press, 1997), 136.
33 [This word resembles the German *notwendig*, which ordinarily translates as 'necessary,' but literally means 'need-turning' or
'emergency-turning.']

34 Philippe Lacoue-Labarthe, in *Heidegger, Art and Politics: The Fiction of the Political* (Oxford: Blackwell, 1990), characterized Heidegger's "politics" as "National Aestheticism." His aim here is right, but since it is never a matter in Heidegger of aestheticism in the ordinary sense of the word, the expression "National Ergology" might be even more fitting. For Heidegger it is a matter of the obliging power of the work (*ergon*) that is given to us as an assignment by truth, whatever that might mean here. The work is the good side of en-framing [*Ge-stells*], which one could call 'en-housing' [*Ge-Häuse*] and which is later clothed in concepts such as 'dwelling' or 'sojourn.'

35 [Where Lenin is, there is my fatherland.]

36 Martin Heidegger, *Contributions to Philosophy (Of the Event)*, trans. Richard Rojcewicz and Daniela Vallega-Neu (Bloomington: Indiana University Press, 2012), 256.

37 Heidegger, *Being and Time*, 179.

38 Ibid., 260 [translation modified].

39 A more distant variation on Augustine's deduction of evil can be found below in "Luhmann, Devil's Advocate: Of Original Sin, the Egotism of Systems, and the New Ironies."

40 [For an explanation of the term *Be-wëgung*, see Martin Heidegger, "The Way to Language," trans. Peter Hertz, in Heidegger, *On the Way to Language* (New York: Harper & Row, 1971), 129–30.]

41 Heidegger, *Contributions to Philosophy*, 185 [translation modified; Sloterdijk's citation does not italicize *dislodging*, even though he refers to the page of the German in which it is italicized; the same phrase can be found, unitalicized, on 22 of the English and 26 of the German: Martin Heidegger, *Beiträge zur Philosophie (Vom Ereignis)*, *Gesamtausgabe*, vol. 65, ed. Friedrich-Wilhelm von Herrmann (Frankfurt am Main: Vittorio Klostermann, 1989)].

42 Martin Heidegger, "Language in the Poem," in Heidegger, *On the Way to Language*, trans. Peter D. Hertz (New York: Harper & Row, 1971), 167.

43 Martin Heidegger, "The Nature of Language," in Heidegger, *On the Way to Language*, 102.

44 Martin Heidegger, "The Thinker as Poet (*Aus der Erfahrung des Denkens*)," in Heidegger, *Poetry, Language, Thought*, trans. Albert Hofstadter (New York: Perennial Classics, 1971), 6. Let us hold fast to the idea that even letting and finding/being-found are to be thought in a multivalent way, because, among what is found, there can be authentic occasions for intervention; among what is to be accepted "with releasement [*gelassen*]," unavoidable provocations to speech and action announce themselves. Even those who do not bring along a will to act can be "conscripted" into willing. In this sense, the figure of an "engaged releasement" forms the horizon that a contemporary ethics cannot surpass.

45 Cf. my "Ist der Zivilisationsprozeß steuerbar? Versuch über die Lenkung von Nicht-Fahrzeugen" in *auf, und, davon: Eine Nomadologie der Neunziger*, ed. Steirischen Herbst (Graz: Droschl, 1990), 41–63.

46 Heidegger, *Being and Time*, 179.

47 See J. H. Parry, *The Discovery of the Sea* (Berkeley: University of

California Press, 1981); and also Alfred W. Crosby, "Winds," in Crosby, *Ecological Imperialism: The Biological Expansion of Europe, 900–1900*, 2nd ed. (Cambridge: Cambridge University Press, 2004), 104–131.

48 [This term can also mean 'convalescing' or 'twisting free' in Heidegger. Unlike an *Überwindung* (overcoming), a *Verwindung* does not leave behind that from which it attempts to twist free; rather, it incorporates it. See Martin Heidegger, *The End of Philosophy*, trans. Joan Stambaugh (Chicago: University of Chicago Press, 2003), 84.]

49 Heidegger, "The Thinker as Poet," 4.

2 Luhmann, Devil's Advocate

1 Cf. Gary M. Simpson, "The Linguistification (and Liquefaction?) of the Sacred. A Theological Consideration of Jürgen Habermas's Theory of Religion," *Exploration* 7 (1989): 21–35.

2 Cf. Niklas Luhmann, "Ich sehe was, was du nicht siehst," in Luhmann, *Soziologische Aufklärung* 5, *Konstruktivistische Perspektiven*, 2nd ed. (Opladen: VS Verlag für Sozialwissenschaften, 1993), 228–234. Luhmann traces the structural intolerance of Critical Theory to its adherence to old European ontological premises; it is fixated on an obsolete concept of truth that requires convergence in the objective, because it proceeds from ontological univalence (being is) and reserves the second valence (negation) for the sphere of reflection and intersubjective agreement concerning the one truth. The unavoidable consequence of this is compulsory consensualism; this does not directly impose one's own opinion on others but rather a procedure from which one hopes for the same result. The hopelessness of this position was already clearly indicated by Gotthard Günther in 1968 in a review of Habermas's *On the Logic of the Social Sciences*. Cf. Günther, *Beiträge zur Grundlegung einer operationsfähigen Dialektik*, vol. 2 (Hamburg: Meiner, 1979), 169: "*Habermas* stands in an honorable tradition that has nevertheless irrevocably fallen into decline, which only scrapes by where it can work with outdated modes of thinking."

3 Cf. Odo Marquard, "Indicted and Unburdened Man in Eighteenth-Century Philosophy," in Marquard, *Farewell to Matters of Principle*, trans. Robert M. Wallace, with the assistance of Susan Bernstein and James I. Porter (New York: Oxford University Press, 1989), 38–63.

4 Cf., inter alia, *Thus Spoke Zarathustra: A Book for Everyone and No One*, trans. R. J. Hollingdale (London: Penguin, 1969), part 4, "Among the Daughters of the Desert," 314: "There I was farthest away from cloudy, damp, melancholy Old Europe!"

5 [Where does evil come from?]

6 [The principle that every being is good.]

7 Luhmann was able to read this birth of evil from out of difference in the plain words of the treatise of the Renaissance author Virgilio Malvezzi, Bologna, 1553: "In my opinion, Lucifer did not intend to make himself great and elevate himself in order to surpass God, for then he would have not broken unity open but rather would have wished to improve

it, which with the merely natural endowment of reason he was able to see to be impossible. Consequently, the idea occurred to him to elevate himself and to break away on one side, and thus by separating himself from the One to create the Second. Around the latter he then drew his own circle, which was different than the circle of God. He would not have been able to separate himself from the One had he not become evil, since everything that is good is one." Cited in Niklas Luhmann, *Die Wirtschaft der Gesellschaft* (Frankfurt am Main: Suhrkamp, 1988), 266n. [The original Italian can be found in Luhmann's footnote as well as in the following source cited by him: Benedetto Croce and Santino Carmella, eds., *Politici e moralisti del Seicento* (Bari: G. Laterza & figli, 1930), 270f.] Luhmann here remarks that removing the privilege of the One suffices for achieving the fundamental moral evidence of modernity: that the observer of a unity does not have to count per se as a devilish dissident from it.

 8 For what follows see *De Civitate Dei*, Liber XI.15–17, XII.1–9, XIV.11–14.
 9 [More literally, *Eigensinn* means 'own or proper sense.']
10 Cf. Malvezzi's description of the Devil's activity in note 7, above.
11 Karl Marx, "A Contribution to the Critique of Hegel's 'Philosophy of Right: Introduction,'" in Marx, *Critique of Hegel's 'Philosophy of Right,'* trans. Annette Jolin and Joseph O'Malley, ed. with an introduction and notes by Joseph O'Malley (Cambridge: Cambridge University Press, 1970), 133.
12 Niklas Luhmann, *Archimedes und wir. Interviews* (Berlin: Merve Verlag, 1987), 104.
13 In essence, the crudity of the opposition between the lifeworld and the system is to be traced back to the relationship, which has only been pushed aside and never clarified, between Habermas and Heidegger, who for his part had already distinguished between the sphere of poetic dwelling and that of devastation by en-framing. Whoever takes up this difference unwittingly thereby inherits not only neo-mythic figures but also the moral dilemma of dualism between the regions of Being of authentic and inauthentic Dasein.
14 Arnold Gehlen, "Über die Geburt der Freiheit aus der Entfremdung," *Archiv für Rechts- und Sozialphilosophie* 40, no. 3 (1952): 338–353.
15 Whether this suffices as an adequate appreciation of the subsystem-encompassing dynamic of *Wirtschaft der Gesellschaft* will be left aside here.
16 Edmund Husserl, *Cartesian Meditations: An Introduction to Phenomenology*, trans. Dorion Cairns (Dordrecht: Kluwer, 1999), 149.
17 *The Way Towards the Blessed Life or The Doctrine of Religion*, in *The Popular Works of Johann Gottlieb Fichte*, trans. William Smith, LL.D., 4th ed. in two vols., vol. 2 (London: Trübner & Co., Ludgate Hill, 1889), Lecture 10, p. 474.
18 Ernst Behler, *Ironie und literarische Moderne* (Paderborn: Ferdinand Schöningh, 1997), 115–149.
19 A synoptic study of the motifs of anti-egotism in high cultures is still lacking. In any case, it ought to be noted that this form of critique of human self-regard and self-preference is also extensive in cultures

outside of Europe. It could be a formal implication of high-cultural constructions of the world-picture. One of the sharpest peaks of the Christian anti-narcissism tradition is found in Martin Luther's religious anthropology: "prudentia carnis est ... se in omnibus querit et sua. Hec facit hominem esse sibi ipsi obiectum finale et ultimum et idolum." *Die Vorlesung über den Römerbrief*, in *Martin Luthers Werke, Kritische Gesamtausgabe*, vol. 56 (Weimar: H. Böhlaus Nachfolger, 1936), 361. ["The 'prudence of the flesh' ... in all matters ... looks out for itself and its own interests. The prudence makes man feel that he himself is the final and ultimate object in life, an idol." *Luther's Works*, vol. 25: *Lectures on Romans; Glosses and Scholia*, ed. Hilton C. Oswald (St. Louis: Concordia, 1972), 350.] *Die Vorlesung über den Römerbrief*, 237: "quia homo non potest nisi que qua sua sunt, querere et se super omnia diligere, que est summa omnium vitiorum." ["For man cannot but seek his own advantages and love himself above all things. And this is the sum of all his iniquities." *Lectures on Romans*, 222.] In addition, it ought to be noted that the strategic practical value of scolding egotism is not limited to moral, cultural, and ethically critical discourses, but is also deployed in political contexts. Thus the dictator-messiah of Ghana, Kwame Nkrumah, enjoyed castigating the 'self-seeking' and 'career-ism' of his political rivals. Cf. Daniel Yergin and Joseph Stanislaw, *The Commanding Heights: The Battle for the World Economy* (New York: Touchstone, 2002), 68.

20 Spinoza, *The Ethics*, in *The Chief Works of Benedict de Spinoza*, vol. 2, trans. R. H. M. Elwes (New York: Dover 1951), part 3, preface.

21 ["Moral sense" is in English in the original.]

22 Niklas Luhmann, *Theory of Society*, vol. 2, trans. Rhodes Barrett (Stanford, CA: Stanford University Press, 2013), 173.

23 [W. A. Mozart, Emanuel Schikaneder, *The Magic Flute*, trans. Michael Freyhan, in Michael Freyhan, *The Authentic* Magic Flute *Libretto: Mozart's Autograph or the First Full-Score Edition?* (Lanham, MD: Scarecrow Press, 2009), 239.]

24 Cf. Florian Rötzer, "Reflexionsschleifen über Zumutungen oder: Was heißt es, sich in komplexen Systemen zu orientieren?" in *Das Böse: Jenseits von Absichten und Tätern oder: Ist der Teufel ins System aus-gewandert?* ed. die Kunst- und Ausstellungshalle der Bundesrepublik Deutschland (Göttingen: Steidl Gerhard, 1995), 32. Luhmann's intuitions that are critical of moralism converge in a noteworthy manner with Michel Serres's considerations regarding the im- and hyper-personal character of evil and the tragic constant in the human condition; Serres recommends conjugating active evil as an impersonal verb: "It's raining, it's freezing, it's thundering." "From a permanent, fluctuating cloud, precipitations fall indifferently upon the heads of each and all." Cf. *Conversations on Science, Culture, and Time: Michel Serres with Bruno Latour* (Ann Arbor: University of Michigan Press, 1995), 192–193. [Sloterdijk's quotation does not appear to be a direct translation of any of the French material he cites, so we have rendered his German into English directly.] These observations are directed against the "philosophies of suspicion," whose presence in French intellectual cultures is hardly less massive than it is in Germany.

25 [Sloterdijk writes these two terms in English, misspelling the latter as "local looser."]

26 The necessity of guarding against undesired hypermoral effects of binary moral judgments, was, as Luhmann emphasizes, already perceived by Enlightenment authors: "The 18th century invented humour for this purpose, a breakwater as it were for unexpected moral storms." In "Paradigm Lost: On the Ethical Reflection of Morality. Speech on the Occasion of the Award of the Hegel Prize 1988," *Thesis Eleven* 29, no. 1 (1991): 90. For further observations on the connection between thinking in metaphysical alternatives and emergency thinking [*Ernstfalldenken*] cf. also my *Neither Sun nor Death*, with Hans-Jürgen Heinrichs, trans. Steve Corcoran (Los Angeles: Semiotext(e), 2011), 303ff.

27 Peter Sloterdijk, *Globes: Spheres*, vol. 2: *Macrospherology*, trans. Wieland Hoban (Los Angeles: Semiotext(e), 2014), 528ff.

28 I have explained that one nevertheless ought to reckon with alternatives to the total embrace of 'Being-in-the-world': see Peter Sloterdijk, *Weltfremdheit* (Frankfurt: Surhkamp, 1993).

29 [In English in the original.]

30 [Robert Musil, *The Man without Qualities*, vol. 1: *A Sort of Introduction* and *Pseudoreality Prevails*, trans. Sophie Wilkins, editorial consultant Burton Pike (New York: Vintage International, 1996), 77.]

31 [Ibid., 260.]

32 Niklas Luhmann, "The Modern Sciences and Phenomenology," trans. Joseph O'Neil and Elliott Schreiber, in Luhmann, *Theories of Distinction: Redescribing the Descriptions of Modernity*, ed. William Rasch (Stanford, CA: Stanford University Press, 2002), 52–53.

33 Cf. Hinderk M. Emrich, "Die interpersonale Struktur des Bösen als Verweigerung des 'Zwischen,'" in *Das Böse* (cf. note 24, above), 280f.

34 Niklas Luhmann, *Observations on Modernity*, trans. William Whobrey (Stanford, CA: Stanford University Press, 1998), 39.

35 Niklas Luhmann, "Geld als Kommunikationsmedium: Über symbolische und diabolische Generalisierung," in Luhmann, *Die Wirtschaft der Gesellschaft* (Frankfurt: Suhrkamp, 1988), 253.

36 *Der Mensch—das Medium der Gesellschaft?*, ed. Peter Fuchs and Andreas Göbel (Frankfurt: Suhrkamp, 1994), 36.

37 Cf. Jan Künzlcr, *Medien und Gesellschaft: Die Medienkonzepte von Talcott Parsons, Jürgen Habermas und Niklas Luhmann* (Stuttgart 1989).

38 [Libido of belonging.]

39 Cf. Niklas Luhmann, "Die Soziologie und der Mensch," in Niklas Luhmann, *Soziologische Aufklärung 6: Die Soziologie und der Mensch* (Opladen: VS Verlag für Sozialwissenschaften, 1995), 274.

3 The Domestication of Being

1 Martin Heidegger, *Fundamental Concepts of Metaphysics: World, Finitude, Solitude*, trans. William McNeill and Nicholas Walker (Bloomington: Indiana University Press, 1995), 347.

2 The motif that metaphysics and errancy belong together is taken up again in the fourth section of this speech, below.
3 Cf. Stephen Matuschek, *Über das Staunen: Eine ideengeschichtliche Analyse* (Tübingen: De Gruyter, 1991).
4 Jean-Paul Sartre, *"What Is Literature?" and Other Essays* (Cambridge, MA: Philosophical Library, 1949), 178.
5 Ibid., 182; my emphasis. The original speaks of a *littérature des grandes circonstances*. I would like to note that the clearest opposition to this terror-mimetic position (which was also Adorno's in a certain respect) has been formulated by Michel Serres: according to him, all thought after the terror must be a sort of philosophical peace research, even more, a peace praxis. Cf. Michel Serres with Bruno Latour, *Conversations on Science, Culture, and Time*, trans. Roxanne Lapidus (Ann Arbor: University of Michigan Press, 1995), 1–42.
6 György Lukács, *Soul and Form*, trans. Anna Bostock, ed. John T. Sanders and Katie Terezakis, with an introduction by Judith Butler (New York: Columbia University Press, 2010), 31.
7 "Declaration of Support for Adolf Hitler and the National Socialist State (November 11, 1933)," in *The Heidegger Controversy: A Critical Reader*, ed. Richard Wolin (Cambridge, MA: MIT Press, 1993), 51.
8 Friedrich Nietzsche, *The Will to Power*, trans. Walter Kaufmann and R. J. Hollingdale, ed. Walter Kaufmann (New York: Vintage, 1968), §749, 396.
9 Rüdiger Safranski, *Martin Heidegger: Between Good and Evil* (Cambridge, MA: Harvard University Press, 1999); Bernard-Henri Lévy, *Sartre: The Philosopher of the Twentieth Century* (Cambridge: Polity Press, 2003).
10 For the prehistory of the century of radicalism the following are instructive: Bernard Yack, *The Longing for Total Revolution: Philosophic Sources of Social Discontent from Rousseau to Marx and Nietzsche* (Berkeley: University of California Press, 1992); Maxime Rodinson, *De Pythagore à Lénine: Des activismes idéologiques* (Paris: Fayard, 1993); and, regarding the era itself, Modris Eksteins, *Rites of Spring: The Great War and the Birth of the Modern Age* (New York: Houghton Mifflin, 1989); Ernst Nolte, *Der europäische Bürgerkrieg, 1917–1945. Nationalsozialismus und Bolschewismus* (Frankfurt: Propyläen, 1988); and Eric Hobsbawm, *The Age of Extremes: A History of the World, 1914–1991* (New York: Vintage, 1994).
11 For the connection between the twentieth-century complex of extremism and Critical Theory cf. the essay below: "What Is Solidarity with Metaphysics at the Moment of Its Fall?," in particular the section "Hyberbolic Theory."
12 Rev. 3:16; cf. Philippe Garnier, *La tiédeur* (Paris: Presses Universitaires de France, 2000).
13 Cf. Norbert Bolz, *Auszug aus der entzauberten Welt: Philosophischer Extremismus zwischen den Weltkriegen* (Munich: Fink, 1989), 11.
14 For a critique of the trivial monstrous in the twentieth century, see Friedrich Georg Jünger, *Die Titanen* (Frankfurt: Klostermann, 1944); see also Helmut Willke, *Atopia: Studien zur atopischen Gesellschaft* (Frankfurt: Suhrkamp, 2001), 192f.

15 *Regeln für den Menschenpark: Ein Antwortschreiben zu Heideggers Brief über den Humanismus* (Frankfurt: Suhrkamp, 1999), chapter 6 in this volume.
16 [As If the Human Being Did Not Exist.]
17 Where this error is self-aware it presents itself under the title 'anthropic principle.'
18 In this regard our undertaking is connected with that of Bruno Latour, who, with the necessary clarity, breaks away from the pietism of the remembrance of Being, lacking as it is in empiricism: "Has someone, however, actually forgotten Being? Yes: anyone who really thinks that Being has really been forgotten. . . . But what is missing is you your-self, not the world! . . . On the contrary: we have everything, since we have Being, and beings, and we have never lost track of the difference between Being and beings. We are carrying out the impossible project undertaken by Heidegger." In Bruno Latour, *We Have Never Been Modern*, trans. Catherine Porter (Cambridge, MA: Harvard University Press, 1993), 66–67.
19 Martin Heidegger, "Letter on 'Humanism,'" trans. Frank A. Capuzzi, in Heidegger, *Pathmarks*, ed. William McNeill (Cambridge: Cambridge University Press, 1998), 248 [translation modified].
20 Rudolf Bilz, *Die unbewältigte Vergangenheit des Menschengeschlechts. Beiträge zu einer Paläoanthropologie* (Frankfurt: Suhrkamp, 1967), 56.
21 Konrad Lorenz, who emphasized the special place of the human being less than the continuity of biological regularities, drew attention to the discovery that the so-called world-openness of *Homo sapiens* developed along the lines of the great mammals' behavior of curiosity. It merely continued an evolutionary trend that led from stenoecious (fixed in the orbit of their own structure) animals to the 'cosmopolitan' steppe wan-derers. It hardly needs to be said that the philosophically understood difference between the world and the environment is not at all touched on by this argument.
22 Friedrich Nietzsche, *Beyond Good and Evil: Prelude to a Philosophy of the Future*, ed. Rolf-Peter Horstmann and Judith Norman, trans. Judith Norman (Cambridge: Cambridge University Press, 2002), apho-rism 150, p. 70.
23 On the problem of modern philosophy as a hermeneutics of the mon-strous cf. my "Chancen im Ungeheueren. Notiz zum Gestaltwandel des Religiösen in der modernen Welt im Anschluß an einige Motive bei William James"; foreword to the German edition of William James's *The Varieties of Religious Experience* under the title *Die Vielfalt religiöser Erfahrung: Eine Studie über die menschliche Natur* (Frankfurt: Suhrkamp, 1997), 11–34.
24 We must adhere to this thesis in opposition to claims recently to be heard that 'the human being' may be in the position to become 'master of his own evolution for the first time' by means of genetic technol-ogy. We will suggest further arguments below for why the positions of 'master' and 'producer,' which are based on an antiquated grammar, are no longer meaningful in regards to hyper-complex processes.
25 Heidegger, "Letter on 'Humanism,'" 248–249, 252, 253, 254, 258, 261 [translation modified; square brackets are those of the translator

of Heidegger; curly brackets Ian Alexander Moore and Christopher Turner]; we note that Heidegger takes his most famous metaphor from Nietzsche, *Thus Spoke Zarathustra: A Book for All and None*, ed. Adrian Del Caro and Robert Pippin, trans. Adrian Del Caro (Cambridge: Cambridge University Press, 2006), part 3, "The Convalescent," 175: "Everything breaks, everything is joined anew; the same house of Being builds itself eternally. Everything parts, everything greets itself again; the ring of Being remains loyal to itself eternally" [translation modified].

26 [Also 'holds sway' or, more literally, 'essences,' where 'essence' is to be heard verbally as 'to essence.']

27 Jacques Derrida, "Khōra," in *On the Name*, ed. Thomas Dutoit (Stanford, CA: Stanford University Press, 1995), 89–130.

28 Cf. my *Bubbles: Spheres,* vol. 1: *Microspherology*, trans. Wieland Hoban (Los Angeles: Semiotext(e), 2011), chapter 2, "Between Faces: On the Appearance of the Interfacial Intimate Sphere," 139–206.

29 [As will become apparent below, Sloterdijk intends this term as a play on Heidegger's *Gestell* or *Ge-Stell*, typically translated as 'enframing' or 'en-framing.']

30 The founder of the theory of the *Umwelt* ['environment'], Jakob von Uexküll, supports this spatial-theoretical conjecture when, without critical concerns about metaphors, he speaks of "animals' houses" and of their "dwelling-shells." Cf. Jakob von Uexküll, *A Foray into the Worlds of Animals and Humans:* with *A Theory of Meaning*, trans. Joseph D. O'Neill (Minneapolis: University of Minnesota Press, 2010), 146f.

31 The concept of neoteny was coined in 1885 by the evolutionary biologist Julius Kollmann to characterize the prolongation and stabilization of juvenile forms into adult or sexually mature states. In 1922, the British zoologist Walter Garstang further generalized these observations in his concept of paedomorphism: this expresses the fact that many animal groups derive their distinctive features not from adult exemplars but rather from the larvae of distant ancestors. Thus the Haeckelian recapitulation theory is refuted or at least qualified. According to the theory of paedomorphism, the earlier stages of an evolutionary sequence are not repeated embryonically; on the contrary, the mature parent forms are neutralized in the course of evolution, while the larval forms achieve autonomy. We might note that the neoteny hypothesis and related theories were for this reason put on ice in the current paleobiological discussion not so much because they were refuted or persuasively replaced, but rather because by and large one forgot to raise the questions to which neoteny is the answer.

32 The reference to Miller's theorem, presented in *Progress and Decline: The Group in Evolution* (Los Angeles: W. Ritchie Press, 1963)—as to a large number of the motifs indicated in the sketch that follows—I owe to Dieter Claessens, to whose groundbreaking study *Das Konkrete und das Abstrakte. Soziologische Skizzen zur Anthropologie* (Frankfurt: Suhrkamp, 1980) one cannot pay enough attention.

33 Jonathan Kingdon, *Self-Made Man: Human Evolution from Eden to Extinction?* (New York: John Wiley & Sons, 1993), 41.

34 Jean-Jacques Rousseau, *Discourse on the Origins of Inequality.*

35 [Originally published as *Das Menschheitsrätsel: Versuch einer prinzipiellen Lösung* (Dresden: Sibyllen, 1922). Translated into English and revised by Alsberg himself as Paul Alsberg, *In Quest of Man: A Biological Approach to the Problem of Man's Place in Nature* (Oxford: Pergamon, 1970).]

36 Cf. the title of the new [German] edition of *Das Menscheitsrätsel: Der Ausbruch aus dem Gefängnis—Zu den Entstehungsbedingungen des Menschen*, foreword by Dieter Claessens (Gießen: Focus, 1975).

37 Cf. Frédéric Joulian, "Peut-on parler d'un système technique chimpanzé? Primatologie et archéologie comparée," in *De la préhistoire aux missiles balistiques: L'intelligence sociale des techniques,* ed. Bruno Latour and Pierre Lemonnier (Paris: Cairn, 1994), 60.

38 [Literally, 'primal division.']

39 Cf. my "Pariser Aphorismen über Rationalität," in *Eurotaoism: Zur Kritik der politischen Kinetik* (Frankfurt: Suhrkamp, 1989), 243–265.

40 The theological sense of the unattainability or difficult attainability of this substance can be recognized in typical stories in advanced cultures of those who search for God. Stories of those who flee from God serve as an inverted image of this. Cf. Franz Reitinger, *Schüsse, die Ihn nicht erreichten: Eine Motivgeschichte des Gottesattentats* (Paderborn: F. Schöningh, 1997).

41 Cf. Jacques Poulain, *De l'homme. Elements d'anthropobiologie du langage* (Paris: CERF, 2001).

42 ['Gene flow' is in English in the original.]

43 ['Natural history' is in English in the original.]

44 The authors of such 'natural histories' generate buzz by leaping from animal interaction to conclusions about human behavior, while undervaluing the autonomy of cultural processes. Thus do natural histories of rape, promiscuity, sexual perversions, greed, xenophobia, and so on, emerge, in which such things are deduced biologically. As a rule, it does not occur to such authors that there could be just as much a natural history of distancing from instinctual programming. In contrast, the defenders of culturalism are damned to more or less helpless idealisms when they neglect the natural history of distancing from nature as well as the emergence of metabiological spaces of leeway. When it comes to their explanations of the possibility of freedom, they are condemned to change course as cluelessly as Richard Dawkins does when, with respect to morality, nothing better occurs to him against his own theorem of egoistic genes than the most hackneyed of all idealist excuses, namely, that the human being has the capacity—from where exactly?—of rebelling against the 'dictatorship of genes.'

45 ['Tool making' is in English in the original.]

46 Cf. Eduard Kirschmann, *Das Zeitalter der Werfer: Das Schimpansen-Werfer-Aasfresser-Krieger-Modell der menschlichen Evolution* (SWAK) (Hannover: Eduard Kirschmann, 1999). [*The Age of Throwers: A New View of Humanity; The Chimpanzee-Thrower-Scavenger-Warrior Model of Human Evolution*, trans. Susan E. Way (Amazon Digital Services, 2013). Available at http://armedapetheory.de/blog/wp-content/uploads/2010/09/age-of-throwers.pdf.] Also see William H. Calvin, *The Cerebral Symphony: Seashore Reflections on the Structure of*

Consciousness (New York: Bantam Books, 1990), especially chap. 11, 233–51, "A Whole New Ballgame: Bootstrapping Thought through Throwing." Kirschmann distinguishes three stages in the evolution of throwers: 1. throwing to ward off predators (since about 5 million years ago), 2. throwing to acquire carrion by driving rivals away (since 2.5 million years ago), and 3. throwing in intraspecific confrontations (since 2 million years ago).

47 Anthropologists have often referred to the spectacular steatopygia among Khoisan women ('The Hottentot Venus'), which should be interpreted above all as effects of local sexual selective breeding.

48 Cf. Christopher Wills, *The Runaway Brain: The Evolution of Human Uniqueness* (New York: Basic Books, 1993). The formulation 'runaway brain' points to the fact that in evolutionary terms the human brain is a 'sprinter' that, in a genetic feedback which was effective long-term and rewarded intelligence, was formed with the help of primary cultural technologies—in our terminology: by the human greenhouse effect.

49 In substance, Heidegger comes closest to the concept of en-housing during the time of the artwork-essay, 1935, when he worked on the concept of a good en-framing ("the artwork installs a world").

50 Louis Bolk, *Das Problem der Menschwerdung: Vortrag, gehalten am 15. April 1926 auf der XXV. Versammlung der anatomischen Gesellschaft zu Freiburg* (Jena: Fischer 1926). Bolk speaks more often of fetalization than of neoteny, but means the same complex of observations: the phenotypic retention of juvenile or even fetal developmental traits. Portmann places more emphasis on the temporal and mental aspects of human premature birth than on the morphological manifestations of neoteny.

51 Heidegger has expressed this abstractly by having the dimension of the future [*Zukunft*] depend on provenance [*Herkunft*] without leveling the difference between future and provenance. Critics occasionally called Heidegger's approach a 'temporalization of the philosophy of origin' in order to accuse him of archaicism or anachronism, yet they did not notice that the so-called philosophy of origin itself already rests on the discovery of the temporality of the essence, that is to say, on the insight into the difference between that which has arisen [*Entsprungenen*] and the origin [*Ursprung*].

52 This drawing of nudes corresponds to the demand raised by Bruno Latour for a 'symmetrical anthropology' (that is to say, one that mediates between human beings and their things), because 'nudity' is understood here as the effect and counterpart of the cultural clothing of the human being with things. It has nothing to do with the ideological nudity of *homo sociologicus* or the hypostasized indigence of the human being in philosophies of dialogue and interaction.

53 Desmond Morris has the merit of, if not solving, then at least emphasizing the evolutionary riddle of the nakedness of *Homo sapiens*. Cf. his *The Naked Ape* (New York: Delta, 1967), 32ff. Among the cited attempts at explanation, in Morris, too, neoteny is assigned a privileged role; nevertheless, the author makes no secret of his fascination with the aquatic ape hypothesis (cf. Elaine Morgan, *The Descent of Women* [London: Souvenir, 1972]). In most Darwinian explanations of the loss

of fur in the case of *Homo sapiens*, category mistakes and teleological overinterpretations appear, which on the whole follow the schema: if the phenomenon is present then one must look for the adaptive advantage that it embodies. In truth, one ought to proceed from the basic feature of the sapiens life form as Being-in-en-housing and then ask how this becomes somatically consequential. Then it becomes manifest that countless phenomena specific to the human being do not embody any evolutionary *advantage*, but rather express the *tolerance* of the human way of life for variation; think of traits like having light eyes and the astounding diversity of nasal formations and sizes, for which, according to biologists, there is 'still' 'no satisfactory explanation.' The most impressive support for the hypothesis of the luxuriating and selectively neutral character of most variations emerges from the observation that these differences, describable in terms of molecular biology, between individuals constitute approximately 84 percent of the anthropological variance, while a mere 16 percent of it is allocated to racial and ethnic differences that are adaptively conditioned or co-conditioned.

54 The biologist Christopher Wills speaks in this context of breaking out of stupid-world.

55 Thus it can be understood why modern intellectuals divide into those who remain with Kant and those who do not. Kant's philosophical strategy consists in metaphysicalizing language: with his transcendental philosophy he has developed the most extreme possibilities of a world-view from the standpoint of the speaking subject. To be a 'subject' means to assert the priority of the *a priori* (the program) before the *a posteriori* (the text): the environment must comply with the standards (the *a priori* conditions) of the system in which it is known. Old and new idealists, including critical theorists and linguistic pragmatists, all stop here. Non-Kantians or hardware theoreticians take notice of the fact that even the *a priori* (system, brain) is a mechanism in the world that has emerged (and is probably able to be modified). "The brain is part of the material world; the material world is not part of the brain." Henri Bergson, *Matter and Memory*, trans. Nancy Margaret Paul and W. Scott Palmer (London: George Allen and Unwin, 1911), 4.

56 Cf. Heiner Mühlmann, *The Nature of Cultures: A Blueprint for a Theory of Culture Genetics*, trans. Robert Payne (Vienna/New York: Springer Verlag, 1996).

57 Maurice Merleau-Ponty, *Phenomenology of Perception*, trans. Colin Smith (London: Routledge, 2002), 161.

58 [In English in the original.]

59 In the European tradition, since the Spartan and Roman eras, there has been a concern about 'impending decadence,' which proceeds from the observation that after long periods of peace societies lose their orientation to preparedness for violence and war, in terms of being always ready to mobilize, as well as the willingness of individuals to sacrifice themselves for the sake of their own cultural group. Such concerns place 'healthy' battle at the beginning and battle-less decadence at the end. Modern nation-states are still linked to the ideology of Rome and Sparta—war as an educator and a program of anti-effeminization. In contrast, radical historical anthropology places 'decadence,' that is to

say, the psychosomatic luxuriating of the human being, at the beginning and has training for battle in cultures of war (which have not yet been superseded but whose supersession is imminent) following only very late. Bolk, *Das Problem der Menschwerdung*, 8: "If I wanted to express the principle of my conception in a somewhat sharply formulated statement, then I would characterize the human being in regards to corporeality as a primate fetus that has achieved sexual maturity." This theory, as shocking as it is plausible, took the ground from under all political primitive Darwinisms and biologies of conflict. One must keep in mind that the decisive labors of Kollmann (neoteny) already took place in the nineteenth century, and those of Garstang (paedomorphosis), Bolk (fetalization), and Schindewolf (proterogenesis) in the 1920s, in order to measure the extent of the theoretical regression in biology, which gained the upper hand after 1933, due to the ideology of National Socialism. The results of this regression can be detected in the current feuilleton-phantasms over the risks of genetic technology.

60 Mühlmann, *The Nature of Cultures*.

61 Cf. Dirk Baecker, *Wozu Kultur?* (Berlin: Kadmos, 2000), 46f.

62 ['Enhancing the human' is in English in the original.]

63 ['In the long run' is in English in the original.]

64 Cavalli-Sforza is of the opinion that human genetics, aside from medical goals, will above all be used for the suppression of unwelcome variation: an additional reason for the standstill of human biological evolution. Cf. Luigi Luca Cavalli-Sforza, *Genes, Peoples, and Languages*, trans. Mark Seielstad (New York: North Point, 2000), 205–206.

65 Boris Groys has demonstrated this in his study *Under Suspicion: A Phenomenology of Media*, trans. Carsten Strathausen (New York: Columbia University Press, 2012). In connection with this work it can be understood that the guiding epistemological phantasm of philosophy, that thinking can be set at rest in evidence, was never anything other than the postulate that what is disquietingly covered up may for once coincide entirely with that which is comfortingly opened up, in connection with the insinuation that it is not possible for a god for whom everything is always already manifest to be a *genius malignus*.

66 "When philosophy attends to its essence it does not make forward strides at all. It remains where it is in order constantly to think the Same. Progression, that is, progression forward from this place, is a mistake." Martin Heidegger, "Letter on 'Humanism,'" 255.

67 For this term see Sloterdijk, *Bubbles: Spheres*, vol. 1: *Microspherology*, 9–13. The *Spheres*-project works out a cultural, media, and spatial-philosophical concept of transference. Cf. Marshall McLuhan, *Understanding Media: The Extensions of Man* (Berkeley, CA: Gingko, 2013), 160: "Each form of transport not only carries, but translates and transforms the sender, the receiver, and the message."

68 Biologists have emphasized that in the case of *Homo sapiens* a drama conditioned both by genetic dispositions and by early influences is played out between neophilic and neophobic tendencies. The best theoretical interpretation of the human march into situations of the extended world with increasing complexity and of the techniques for

reconnecting the abstract to the concrete is given by Dieter Claessens in *Das Konkrete und das Abstrakte*, 145–306.

69 Cf. Peter Sloterdijk, "'In Dasein There Lies an Essential Tendency towards Closeness': Heidegger's Doctrine of Existential Place," in *Bubbles: Spheres,* vol. 1: *Microspherology*, 333ff. Also in this volume [under the title "'An Essential Tendency toward Nearness Lies in Dasein': Marginalia to Heidegger's Doctrine of Existential Place"]. We note that Hans Blumenberg's elaborately arranged metaphorology can be understood as a hostile takeover of Heidegger's fundamental linguistic-philosophical insight.

70 Georg Wilhelm Friedrich Hegel, *Lectures on the History of Philosophy*, trans. E. S. Haldane, vol. 1 (London: Kegan Paul, Trench, Trübner, 1892), 150, 152.

71 Second Corinthians 5, 1–2.

72 Heidegger, "Letter on 'Humanism,'" 258–259 [translation modified]. In his *Minima Moralia* (London: Verso, 2005), which appeared at the same time, Adorno notes: "Dwelling in the proper sense is now impossible. . . . The house is past. The bombings of European cities, as well as the labour and concentration camps, merely proceed as executors, with what the immanent development of technology has long decided was to be the fate of houses. . . . It is part of morality not to be at home in one's home. . . . Wrong life cannot be lived rightly" (38–39, §18).

73 Michel Houellebecq, *The Elementary Particles* (New York: Alfred A. Knopf, 2000), 253.

74 Cf. Peter Sloterdijk, "*Alētheia* or the Fuse of Truth: Toward the Concept of a History of Unconcealment," in this volume.

75 In any case this solution is waiting halfway up to be defended once again—is it possible?—at full height. Cf. Alain Badiou, "The Philosophical Recourse to the Poem," in *Conditions*, trans. Steven Corcoran (London/New York: Continuum, 2008), 35–48.

76 Corresponding to this on the critical side are the ontological theses of Nietzsche, Heidegger, and Derrida: 'the desert grows,' 'en-framing runs rampant,' 'deconstruction happens.'

77 The first case (biologism) can be found when, for example, Jürgen Habermas believes he has to rebel against what he calls the 'slavery to genes'; the second case (helpless humanism), when Ernst Tugendhat takes it to be necessary to say there exist 'no genes for morality' (which incidentally is not only naive, but also substantively false, because there undoubtedly are genetically determined behavioral dispositions—without it being the case that one would misunderstand the difference between dispositions and norms). Both can be found at the same time when Robert Spaemann, from the viewpoint of Catholic personalism, wants to advocate 'human dignity' in contrast to 'anthropotechnics' reduced to genetic technology.

78 Heidegger, "Letter on 'Humanism,'" 268.

79 On the redefinition of the human as a historical compromise between cybernetics and personalism, cf. the essay "Wounded by Machines" below.

80 Vilém Flusser above all has contributed this motif to the discussion.

81 [We are in a situation (or on a level) where principally there is technology.]

82 Karl Rahner, "Experiment Mensch. Theologisches über die Selbstmanipulation des Menschen," in *Die Frage nach dem Menschen. Aufriß einer philosophischen Anthropologie, Festschrift für Max Müller zum 60. Geburtstag* (Freiburg/Munich: Alber, 1966), 53. I would like to thank Rafael Capurro for the reference to this text.

83 *Tractatus Politicus*, IV.4. *A Political Treatise*, in Benedict de Spinoza, *A Theologico-Political Treatise* and *A Political Treatise*, trans. R. H. M. Elwes (New York: Dover, 1951), 310.

84 [More commonly and less literally, 'stubbornness' or 'obstinacy.']

85 The US strategist Edward N. Luttwak describes the 'geo-economic arms race' between the economic blocs (USA, Japan, Europe) as the most dangerous and the most likely development of the twenty-first century.

86 Joined with them are names such as Yuri Ovchinnikov, vice president of the Soviet Academy of Sciences, who convinced Brezhnev of the usefulness of extensive production of biological weapons. In distinction to nuclear weapons, biological weapons have never been employed in war against human beings. One may consider whether this does not indicate the declining marginal utility of allotechnological perversion.

87 ['Biotech century' is in English in the original.]

88 Thus Jeremy Rifkin in his book of the same name, in which he warns of genetic technology and at the same time touts it, as though it contained opportunities for a 'new Renaissance.'

89 Deuteronomy 30:19, KJV.

4 What Is Solidarity with Metaphysics at the Moment of Its Fall?

1 [We live under the reign of hyperbole.]

2 Theodor Adorno, *Minima Moralia*, trans. E. F. N. Jephcott (London: Verso, 2005), §153, 247.

3 Clemens Albrecht, Günther C. Behrmann, et al. have recently informed us about the set of problems that surrounds the school's name. *Die Intellektuelle Gründung der Bundesrepublik. Eine Wirkungsgeschichte der Frankfurter Schule* (Frankfurt/New York: Campus, 1999). The invention of the label 'Critical Theory' would, according to them, be an effect of the media that made its presence felt only after the student unrest in the summer of 1967, whereby conceptual figures from the thirties were again engaged and were used as brands. From here on a critical theory became Critical Theory.

4 Theodore W. Adorno, *Negative Dialectics*, trans. E. B. Ashton (New York: Continuum, 1973), 408 [translation modified].

5 Ibid.

6 Cf. Norbert Bolz, "Erlösung als ob. Über einige gnostische Motive der Kritischen Theorie," in *Gnosis und Politik*, ed. Jacob Taubes (Munich: Ferdinand Schöningh/Wilhelm Fink, 1984), 264–289.

7 According to a Valentinian baptismal formulation, cited by Clement of Alexandria in *Excerpta ex Theodoto*, 78. [Translation found at http://gnosis.org/library/excr.htm.]

8 Regarding the œuvre of Samuel Beckett; cf. Theodor Adorno, *Aesthetic*

Theory, trans. Robert Hullot-Kentor (Minneapolis: University of Minnesota Press, 1997), 81.

9 This point, which was almost invariably muted through the texts of late antiquity, is one that especially Barbara Aland has corroborated, with a discreet polemical sting against the tendentious misinterpretations of Gnosticism that are oriented to modern existentialist nihilism. The latter can be found in the Jonas school and have been carried further by Blumenberg and Marquard. Cf. Barbara Aland, "Was ist Gnosis? Wie wurde sie überwunden? Versuch einer Kurzdefinition," in Taubes, *Gnosis und Politik,* 54f.

10 [The only meaning of the word 'beyond': you're in poetry.]

11 "Notes on Surrealism," in Jacob Taubes, *From Cult to Culture: Fragments toward a Critique of Historical Reason* (Stanford, CA: Stanford University Press, 2010), 104. Preisendanz, in his discussion with Taubes, recalls that the Surrealist concept of transcending into the work of art was prefigured by certain Romantic ironists, particularly Solger and E. T. A. Hoffmann.

12 Max Horkheimer, *Critical Theory: Selected Essays* (New York: Continuum, 2002), 204 [translation modified].

13 Adorno, *Minima Moralia,* §18, "Refuge for the Homeless" (38–39). This much-cited thesis is the hyperbolic concluding sentence of a series of remarks on modern, in particular American, designer furniture, in which to be 'at home' is impossible, in the author's view.

14 Adorno, *Negative Dialectics,* 406 [translation modified].

15 For the derivation of the thought of alienation from Gnosticism cf. Peter Sloterdijk and Thomas H. Macho, *Weltrevolution der Seele. Ein Lese- und Arbeitsbuch der Gnosis von der Spätantike bis zur Gegenwart* (Zürich: Artemis & Winkler, 1993).

16 Max Horkheimer, *Gesammlte Schriften,* vol. 18 (Frankfurt: Fischer, 1996), 445.

17 Adorno, *Minima Moralia,* §143, 222.

18 The *Institutio Oratoria* of Quintillian, with an English translation by H. E. Butler, M.A., 4 vols. (Cambridge, MA: Harvard University Press, 1969), VIII.VI.67 [translation modified: Butler has 'elegant' rather than 'proper,' which we have chosen because it better fits the context and the German translation of *decens* as *schicklich*].

19 Ibid., VIII.VI.73.

20 Ibid., VIII.VI.76 [Sloterdijk's interpolations of the Latin].

21 *Quintilian as Educator: Selections from the* Institutio Oratoria *of Marcus Fabius Quintilianus,* trans. H. E. Butler, ed. with an introduction and notes by Frederic M. Wheelock (New York: Twayne, 1974), I.Preface.15.

22 Nietzsche, *Human, All Too Human,* trans. R. J. Hollingdale (Cambridge: Cambridge University Press, 1986), no. 137, 74.

23 Martin Heidegger, "Declaration of Support for Adolf Hitler and the National Socialist State (November 11, 1933)," in *The Heidegger Controversy: A Critical Reader,* ed. Richard Wolin (Cambridge, MA: MIT Press, 1993), 51.

24 Cf. Martin Heidegger, *Nietzsche, Volume Four: Nihilism,* trans. Frank A. Capuzzi, ed. David Farrell Krell, in Heidegger, *Nietzsche, Volume*

Three: The Will to Power as Knowledge and as Metaphysics; Volume Four: Nihilism, ed. David Farrell Krell (New York: HarperCollins, 1991), 78–79. Also cf. Friedrich Nietzsche, *Writings from the Late Notebooks* (Cambridge: Cambridge University Press, 2003), 219 (11[99]).

25 Cf. Norbert Bolz, *Auszug aus der entzauberten Welt. Philosophischer Extremismus zwischen den Weltkriegen* (Munich: Fink, 1989).

26 Adorno, *Minima Moralia*, §29, 50.

27 Ibid., §18, 39.

28 This is the point at which Adorno's negativism and Derrida's ultra-skepticism meet. That one can cut both authors down to size with a single sentence was discovered by Habermas from his own partisan position, when he wrote regarding Derrida and Adorno: "The critique of origins, of anything original, of first principles, goes together with a certain fanaticism about showing what is merely produced, imitated, and secondary in everything." Jürgen Habermas, *The Philosophical Discourse of Modernity: Twelve Lectures*, trans. Frederick G. Lawrence (Cambridge, MA: MIT Press, 1987), 187. It is characteristic of the realizer of critical theory that he also already recognizes in the hyperbolist the fanatic, even the fundamentalist (in any case, the negative fundamentalist). A less tendentious view of this constellation is developed in the contributions in Sigrid Weigel, ed., *Flaschenpost und Postkarte. Korrespondenzen zwischen Kritischer Theorie und Poststrukturalismus* (Cologne/Weimar/Vienna: Böhlau,1995).

29 Adorno, *Aesthetic Theory*, 35.

30 Ibid., 190.

31 Friedrich Nietzsche, *The Will to Power*, trans. Walter Kaufmann and R. J. Hollingdale, ed. Walter Kaufmann (New York: Vintage, 1968), §749, 396.

32 Cf. Monika Plessner, *Die Argonauten auf Long Island. Begegnungen mit Hannah Arendt, Theodor W. Adorno, Gershom Scholem und anderen* (Berlin: Rowohlt, 1995), 61.

33 Adorno, *Minima Moralia*, §29, p. 49.

34 Cf. Martin Heidegger, "The Origin of the Work of Art," 1936/1937, in *Basic Writings*, rev. and exp. ed., ed. David Farrell Krell (New York: Harper & Row, 1993), 188: "The dawning world brings out what is as yet undecided and measureless." That Heidegger still thinks purely hyperbolically, and not critically of hyperbole, is shown in the very next sentence: "and thus discloses the hidden necessity of measure and decisiveness." Otherwise it would have been necessary to say: 'and thus provokes a discourse suitable to the undecided and measureless.'

35 How one can attempt both at the same time, the tending of fire and participation in enlightenment extinguishing, is shown in the remarkable book of Andreas Pangritz, *Vom Kleiner- und Unsichtbarwerden der Theologie. Ein Versuch über das Projekt einer 'impliziten Theologie' bei Barth, Tillich, Bonhoeffer, Benjamin, Horkheimer und Adorno* (Tübingen: Theologischer Verlag, 1996).

36 In this context, the position of the American philosopher Stanley Rosen, who has developed a kind of Young Platonism, is particularly informative: According to him contemporary academic philosophy

should take its 'next step' as a step '*downward*, back into the rich air of everyday life' [in English in the original]. This would precisely be the genuine meaning of the Platonic doctrine. Rosen's position—he calls himself an 'ordinary-language metaphysician' [in English in the original]—not only is implemented with technical brilliance, but also is authentically philosophically 'wise,' insofar as it is presented both (classically) hyperbolically and at the same time (in modern terms) anti-hyperbolically. Cf. Stanley Rosen, *The Question of Being: A Reversal of Heidegger* (New Haven, CT: Yale University Press, 1993).

37 William Shakespeare, *Othello*, act II, scene 1. [In English in the original.]

38 Cf. Peter Sloterdijk, *Nietzsche Apostle* (Los Angeles: Semiotext(e), 2013).

39 Friedrich Nietzsche, *Thus Spoke Zarathustra*, ed. Adrian Del Caro and Robert B. Pippin, trans. Adrian Del Caro (Cambridge: Cambridge University Press, 2006), part 3, "Before Sunrise," 132.

40 Ibid.

5 *Alētheia* or the Fuse of Truth

1 Cf. Harold A. Innis, *A Plea for Time* (New Brunswick, NJ: Rutgers University Press, 1950), and Thomas Macho, "Die erste Jahrtausendwende?" in *Tausend Jahre Abendland. Die großen Umbrüche 1000, 1500, 2000* (Frankfurt: Suhrkamp, 1999), 20–35.

2 Cf. Hesiod, *Works and Days*, V.109–201; Ovid, *Metamorphoses*, Book I, V.89–150.

3 Cf. Hans Maier, *Die christliche Zeitrechnung* (Freiburg/Basel/Vienna: Herder, 1991).

4 We here use this expression without comment, without failing to recognize the legitimacy of the critique of this concept by diverse cultural studies and philologies. Jan Assmann in particular, in his book, *Cultural Memory and Early Civilization: Writing, Remembrance, and Political Imagination* (Cambridge: Cambridge University Press, 2011), 265, convincingly pointed out that Echnaton (fourteenth century BC) and Mohammed (seventh century AD) also in fact belong in the sequence of so-called axial-age reformations, such that the phenomenon of supposed synchronicity loses its plausibility and its mysterious aura. The core of the axial age's effect would in truth be the reorganization of cultures of ritual coherence into ones of textual coherence. It reflects the transition from oral cultures to literacy.

5 *Metamorphoses*, Book XV, V.63–64, trans. Brookes More.

6 Ibid., V.143–147.

7 Xenophanes, *Fragments and Commentary*, trans. Arthur Fairbanks (London: K. Paul, Trench, Trubner, 1898), Fragment 16 [translation modified].

8 Martin Heidegger, *The Fundamental Concepts of Metaphysics: World, Finitude, Solitude*, trans. William McNeill and Nicholas Walker (Bloomington: Indiana University Press, 1995), 29.

9 That there is alongside this history of the theft of concealment also a

history of the self-opening-up of what is veiled: this would need to be shown through a historical critique of epiphanic reason.

10 [Master and owner of nature.]

11 [Transference of philosophy to the Germans.]

12 Gotthard Günther has expressed this in his foundational writings on the philosophy of technology: "One goes all the way back to the ultimate conditions of material existence itself and seeks to identify whether there is not another way to create Being that is capable of reflection from out of the basic forms of objective existence. We are already familiar with the first way. It is the one that 'nature' itself followed when it produced organisms. "But it is a still entirely open question as to whether that is the only ontologically possible way or whether there perhaps exist still other, non-organic possibilities. Hence also the intimate kinship of cybernetics with the problems of crystallography, and in general the physics of solid bodies and the perspectives of quantum theory." Gotthard Günther, *Das Bewußtsein der Maschinen. Eine Metaphysik der Kybernetik* (Baden-Baden und Krefeld: Agis, 1963), 68.

13 ['After the birth of Christ,' 'after imitated nature.']

14 For the ontological difference between "The Homunculus and the Robot," cf. the essay of the same name by Gotthard Günther in *Das Bewußtsein der Maschinen*, 166–173. While alchemists only sought an accelerated arrangement of the effective powers that belonged to *natura naturans*, robotics engineers construct the entire cybernetic operational system from elements specifically constructed to this end. In the laboratory scene of Goethe's *Faust, the Second Part of the Tragedy*, these circumstances are unmistakably laid bare. Wagner and Mephistopheles gaze in fascination at the glass flask in which the reaction takes place, while Wagner remarks: "It will be! The mass is clearer!" "It rises: flashes, there's expansion..." "It darkens, clears: it must have being!" The impersonal turns of phrase make evident that the laboratory process is entirely constructed on nature's own achievements. In this sense alchemy thinks in preconstructivist terms. Yet Wagner's affirmation that the traditional begetting of the artful mode of production should be surpassed is modern: "God Forbid! How unfashionable! / We're free of all that idle foolery" (trans. A. S. Kline).

6 Rules for the Human Park

1 The English expression for *Zauber* [i.e., 'glamour,' though this is archaic and *Zauber* is generally rendered in English today as magic, sorcery, charm, or enchantment] comes directly from the word for grammar.

2 That the secret of life is closely connected to the phenomenon of writing is likewise the great intuition of the legend of the golem. Cf. Moshe Idel, *Golem: Jewish Magical and Mystical Traditions on the Artificial Anthropoid* (Albany: State University of New York Press, 1989). In his foreword to [the French edition of] this book [Moshe Idel, *Le Golem*, traduit de l'anglais par Cyrille Aslanoff, préfacé par Henri Atlan {Paris:

Les Éd. du Cerf, 1992}], Henri Atlan refers to a report from a commission appointed by the U.S. president [President's Commission for
the Study of Ethical Problems in Medicine and Biomedical Research]
under the title *Splicing Life: A Report on the Social and Ethical Issues of
Genetic Engineering with Human Beings* (1982), whose authors refer to
the legend of the golem.

3 Obviously also the national validity of the universal canon.

4 Modern mass culture reaches the level of the ancient consumption of
bestiality only with the genre of the Chainsaw Massacre movies. Cf.
Marc Edmundson, *Nightmare on Main Street: Angels, Sadomasochism
and the Culture of the American Gothic* (Cambridge, MA: Harvard
University Press, 1997).

5 This move is missed by those who would like to see in Heidegger's onto-
anthropology something like an 'anti-humanism,' a foolish formulation
that suggests a metaphysical form of misanthropy.

6 Martin Heidegger, "Letter on 'Humanism,'" trans. Frank A. Capuzzi,
in Martin Heidegger, *Pathmarks*, ed. William McNeill (Cambridge:
Cambridge University Press, 1998), 241, 262.

7 Ibid., 251.

8 Ibid., 248 [translation modified].

9 Ibid., 254 [translation modified].

10 Incidentally, it is just as unclear what a society comprising nothing but
deconstructivists would look like, or a society comprised of nothing but
students of Levinas, who would always give precedence to the suffering
Other.

11 [Sloterdijk uses the Latinate word *Sozietät* for 'literary society' here,
whereas every other instance of 'society' in this text is a translation of
the Germanic *Gesellschaft*. *Gemeinschaft* has been rendered as 'community,' *Gemeinwesen* as 'body politic.']

12 Cf. Silvio Vietta, *Heideggers Kritik am Nationalsozialismus und der
Technik* (Tübingen: Niemeyer, 1989).

13 On the motif of 'gathering' [*Sammlung*], cf. Manfred Schneider,
"Kollekten des Geistes," in *Neue Rundschau* 2 (1999): 44ff.

14 Regarding this, cf. the above essay, "The Domestication of Being:
The Clarification of the Clearing," especially section 3, "Thinking the
Clearing."

15 I have described elsewhere in what way one also and even more so has
to reckon with the human being's coming-into-the-picture [*Ins-Bild-
Kommen*]: Peter Sloterdijk, *Bubbles: Spheres*, vol. 1: *Microspherology*,
trans. Wieland Hoban (Los Angeles: Semiotext(e), 2011); and *Globes:
Spheres*, vol. 2: *Macrospherology*, trans. Wieland Hoban (Los Angeles:
Semiotext(e), 2014).

16 A few exceptions to this are found in the philosopher Elisabeth de
Fontenay, with her book *Le silence des bêtes. La philosophie face
à l'épreuve de l'animalité* (Paris: Fayard, 1999), as well as the phi-
losopher and historian of civilization Thomas Macho, "Tier," in *Vom
Menschen: Handbuch Historische Anthropologie*, ed. Christoph Wulf
(Weinheim and Basel: Beltz, 1997), 62–85, and the same author's
"Der Aufstand der Haustiere," in Marina Fischer-Kowalski et al.,
Gesellschaftlicher Stoffwechsel und Kolonisierung von Natur: Ein

Versuch in sozialer Ökologie (Amsterdam: GIB Verlag Fakultas, 1997), 177–200.

17 Friedrich Nietzsche, *Thus Spoke Zarathustra: A Book for All and for None*, ed. Adrian Del Caro and Robert B. Pippin, trans. Adrian Del Caro (Cambridge: Cambridge University Press, 2006), part 3, "On Virtue that Makes Small," 133–135.

18 The fascist readers of Nietzsche intractably misunderstood that in regards to them it was only a matter of the difference between the all-too-human and the human.

19 On the genesis of the dog, neoteny, etc., cf. Dany-Robert Dufour, *Lettres sur la nature humaine à l'usage des survivants* (Paris: Calmann-Lévy, 1999).

20 Cf. Peter Sloterdijk, *Eurotaoismus: Zur Kritik der politischen Kinetik* (Frankfurt: Suhrkamp, 1989); especially the remarks on an ethics of forbearance and on 'slowing down' as a progressive function.

21 I here refer to the upsurge in violence that is currently overwhelming schools throughout the Western world, particularly in the United States, where teachers are beginning to build security systems to protect against students. Just as in antiquity the book lost the battle against the theater, so today the school could lose the battle against indirect formative forces, such as television, violent films, and other disinhibiting media, if a new cultivating structure that tempers violence does not emerge.

22 To put it generally: to manipulation of biological risks.

23 [Plato, *The Statesman*, trans. Harold N. Fowler (Cambridge, MA: Harvard University Press, 1925), 265C.]

24 [We have translated Sloterdijk's citation of Schleiermacher's German translation directly here. There should be another ellipsis between the second instance of 'voluntary' and 'living,' where Schleiermacher has *zweibeinige* or 'bipedal.' Fowler has "the voluntary care of voluntary bipeds."] Interpreters of Plato such as Popper are happy to overlook this double occurrence of 'voluntary.'

25 [Schleiermacher, in his German translation of *The Statesman. Platons Werke* von F. Schleiermacher. Zweiten Theiles Zweiter Band (Berlin 1807 in der Realschulbuchhandlung), 350 (Stephanus page number 309C). Fowler has "thick and soft like the threads of the woof."]

26 [Trans. Fowler with modifications.]

7 Wounded by Machines

1 Hence there is no free admission to the process of enlightenment—it is always paid at a psycho-traumatic cost. Only such individuals as always already bring along much more injury than could be caused by mere cognitive attacks on their narcissistic system have an apparently free backstage pass to it. Such candidates, like the highly talented of a special type, obtain their degree in wound studies free of charge. For them psychical sacrifices that only affect the cognitive immunity-shield appear to be forms of relief—for which reason they move about in the region of obscure theory like fish in water.

2 [This line comes from Nietzsche's poem "Vereinsamt," which has *stumm* ('mute') instead of *leer* ('empty').]

3 ['Hardcore' is in English in the original.]

4 Gerhard Vollmer, "Die vierte bis siebte [sic] Kränkung des Menschen—Gehirn, Evolution und Menschenbild," *Philosophia naturalis* 29 (1992): 118ff. [Sloterdijk's interpolation].

5 Goethe and Freud similarly disregard the fact that the central position of the earth in the Ptolemaic-Aristotelian model of the world in no way implied a preferential position. Rather, the entire sublunary zone represented the weak point of the cosmos, where death and finite, linear, and warped movements are at home. Cf. Peter Sloterdijk, *Globes: Spheres*, vol. 2: *Macrospherology*, trans. Wieland Hoban (Los Angeles: Semiotext(e), 2014), 391–403.

6 [Here the German is *Wunde*, whereas 'wounding' and its cognates elsewhere translates *Kränkung* and its cognates. The latter is rendered as 'blow' in Freud's "A Difficulty in the Path of Psychoanalysis."]

8 The Time of the Crime of the Monstrous

1 See Peter Sloterdijk, *Globes: Spheres*, vol. 2: *Mascrospherology*, trans. Wieland Hoban (Los Angeles: Semiotext(e), 2014), chapter 8: "The Last Orb: On a Philosophical History of Terrestrial Globalization," 765–959.

2 See Martin Heidegger, "The Age of the World Picture," in Martin Heidegger, *Off the Beaten Track*, ed. and trans. Julian Young and Kenneth Haynes (Cambridge: Cambridge University Press, 2002), 57–85.

3 See Percy Ernst Schramm, *Sphaira. Globus. Reichsapfel: Wanderung und Wandlung eines Herrschaftszeichens von Caesar bis Elisabeth II; ein 'Beitrag' zum 'Nachleben' der Antike* (Stuttgart: Hiersemann, 1958).

4 Martin Heidegger, "Overcoming Metaphysics," in Heidegger, *The End of Philosophy*, trans. Joan Stambaugh (New York: Harper and Row, 1973), 108–109 [trans. Hoban].

5 Gilles Deleuze and Félix Guattari, *A Thousand Plateaus: Capitalism and Schizophrenia*, trans. Brian Massumi (New York: Continuum, 2004), 44 and 71.

6 Robert Walser, *Masquerade and Other Stories*, trans. Susan Bernofsky (Baltimore: Johns Hopkins University Press, 1990), 180.

7 [Wieland Hoban's translator's note: "The phrase *Unbehagen in der Modernität* is almost certainly meant to recall Freud's *Das Unbehagen in der Kultur*, which, though published in English as *Civilization and Its Discontents*, would be more accurately translated as 'Unease in Culture.'"]

8 See Hans Blumenberg's essay "Nachahmung der Natur: Zur Vorgeschichte der Idee des schöpferischen Menschen," in Hans Blumenberg, *Wirklichkeiten, in denen wir leben* (Stuttgart: Reclam, 1981), 55–103.

9 Heidegger, "Overcoming Metaphysics," 109 [trans. Hoban].

10 Gotthard Günther, *Beiträge zur Grundlegung einer operationsfähigen Dialektik*, vol. 3 (Hamburg: Felix Meiner, 1980), 224f.
11 Ibid.
12 The old ontology of things makes reflection unreal; the old ontology of spirit makes material unreal. Both reductions (conditioned by ontological monovalence) are in effect to this day, massively guided by the former (positivistic) mode.

9 The Selfless Revanchist

1 Nothing works against poison except poison itself.
2 Jean-Paul Sartre, *Being and Nothingness: A Phenomenological Essay on Ontology*, trans. Hazel E. Barnes (New York: Washington Square Press, 1984), 493.

10 "An Essential Tendency toward Nearness Lies in Dasein"

1 Martin Heidegger, *Being and Time*, trans. Joan Stambaugh (Albany: State University of New York Press, 1996), 105 [translation modified, italicized in the original; here and in what follows, page references to *Being and Time* are to those of the German edition indicated in the margins of the translation].
2 Ibid., 53–54 [translation modified].
3 Ibid., 57.
4 Ibid. [translation modified].
5 In his analytic of place Aristotle, at any rate, already attained a wonderfully explicit approach to the problem of an 'existential' topology, even if for him the Being of 'something in something' could not yet be interesting in an existential regard. In the fourth book of the *Physics* the following explanation of the eightfold sense of 'in' is found: "The next step we must take is to see in how many senses one thing is said to be 'in' another. (1) As the finger is 'in' the hand and generally the part 'in' the whole. (2) As the whole is 'in' the parts: for there is no whole over and above the parts. (3) As man is 'in' animal and generally species 'in' genus. (4) As the genus is 'in' the species and generally the part of the specific form 'in' the definition of the specific form. (5) As health is 'in' the hot and the cold and generally the form 'in' the matter. (6) As the affairs of Greece centre 'in' the king, and generally events centre 'in' their primary motive agent. (7) As the existence of a thing centres 'in' its good and generally 'in' its end, i.e., in 'that for the sake of which' it exists. (8) In the strictest sense of all, as a thing is 'in' a vessel, and generally 'in' place. One might raise the question whether a thing can be in itself, or whether nothing can be in itself—everything being either nowhere or in something else" [trans. R. P. Hardie and R. K. Gaye].
6 Ibid., 62 [translation modified].
7 Ibid., 105 [translation modified].
8 Ibid., 107–108 [translation modified].
9 Ibid., 108 [translation modified].

10 Ibid., 111 [translation modified].
11 Thus in Heidegger's most significant lecture course in Freiburg, held in
    Winter Semester 1929–1930: *The Fundamental Concepts of Metaphysics:*
    World, Finitude, Solitude, trans. William McNeill and Nicholas Walker
    (Bloomington: Indiana University Press, 1995). In the announce-
    ments on the bulletin board of the Freiburg institute 'individuation'
    [*Vereinzelung*] was found instead of 'solitude' [*Einsamkeit*].